The Doctrine of the British Army

The Conception & Implementation of Field Service Regulations 1900–1918

David Keable-Elliott

Helion & Company

Helion & Company Limited
Unit 8 Amherst Business Centre
Budbrooke Road
Warwick
CV34 5WE
England
Tel. 01926 499619
Email: info@helion.co.uk
Website: www.helion.co.uk
X (formerly Twitter): @Helionbooks
Facebook: @HelionBooks
Visit our blog at http://blog.helion.co.uk/

Published by Helion & Company 2025
Designed and typeset by Mach 3 Solutions (www.mach3solutions.co.uk)
Cover designed by Paul Hewitt, Battlefield Design (www.battlefield-design.co.uk)

Cover: Officer cadets, postcard, author's collection.

ISBN 978-1-804517-68-0

British Library Cataloguing-in-Publication Data.
A catalogue record for this book is available from the British Library.

Contents

Part I

Preface to Part I

Professor John Bourne wrote, in 1999, that 'in future, there seems little doubt that Haig's reputation [and that of any other senior officer] will be finally determined not by studies of the man himself, but the man in the context of the armies he commanded, and especially by detailed operational analyses at the army, corps, divisional, brigade and even battalion level. That time is not yet.'[1] Twenty-five years on, that time is now.

For historians in the last century, there was no perception of a doctrinal baseline against which the performance of generals, or units, could be judged. Analysis of performance had to rely on collating comments from various sources, some of them tainted, and then reaching a conclusion. There was undue reliance on texts such as Brigadier General James Edmonds' *Official History of the Great War*, or Sir Douglas Haig's *Diaries*, both of which have their own agendas and fail to consider doctrinal issues. This approach has its place, but reputations should not rest on subjective anecdotalism. It was not appreciated in 1999 that from 1900, the British Army was transforming itself from a poorly administered, haphazardly led police force for a sprawling Empire into a tightly knit professional army that was fit to compete in a continental war; that it was doing so by consensus, first agreeing, and then firmly adopting, a set of regulations which defined a new doctrine for the British Army. This doctrine was laid down in a document entitled *Field Service Regulations* (*FSR*), which was published in 1909, adopted wholeheartedly by the pre-war army, and remained in force for the duration of the First World War. This doctrine constitutes a gold standard against which tactical narratives and command styles on the Western Front can be objectively measured. *FSR* lays down principles which define how an expeditionary force should be commanded, and how it should deploy and fight. Operational analysis assesses how a part of that expeditionary force was commanded, and how it deployed and fought on any one day of battle. Assessing outcomes while simultaneously recording the degree of compliance with *FSR* provides an objective measure of any officer's thinking and the impact of that thinking on the performance of his unit.

The classic texts on the British army prior to 1914, such as John Dunlop's *Development of the British Army*, published in 1938; Brian Bond's *Victorian Army and the Staff College, 1854-1914* (1972), and John Gooch's *Plans of War* (1974), all fail to give the evolution of this doctrine the attention it deserves. All contain serious errors of fact. It is the privileged inheritance of modern historians that they can easily access important archives and enable these errors to be corrected.

1 John Bourne, 'Haig and the Historians', in Brian Bond and Nigel Cave (eds), *Haig, a Re-Appraisal 80 Years On* (Barnsley: Pen & Sword, 2009 [reprint, 1999]), p.5.

'Trench warfare at Ypres in 1914' (Author's collection)

It may surprise some to learn the extent to which Sir John French, Sir Archibald Murray, Sir Henry Wilson, and Sir Henry Rawlinson participated in the genesis of the doctrinal principles that in 1909 were published as *FSR*. The careers of, for instance, Edmund Allenby, William Robertson, Herbert Plumer, and Horace Smith-Dorrien were shaped by their pre-war acceptance of these principles. Those of Douglas Haig and Hubert Gough, again amongst others, were defined by their selective rejection of some of its principles. Between 1904 and 1909, all army tactical publications were 'for guidance' and, even before 1904, all such were targeted at specific parts of the army. In contrast, *FSR* was mandated on the whole army, and compliance with its principles was required in all parts of it. This was a new departure, part evolution, part revolution. But for the first time in history, the British Army had a doctrine.

The principal message of this book is that an in-depth knowledge of *FSR* is an essential tool for the academic historian to use in the analysis of all aspects of war on the Western Front from 1914 to 1918. To use that tool, one needs to understand how doctrine developed, who developed it, and most importantly, what it did or did not say when it was mandated on the army in 1909. Immediately, there is a problem. It is almost beyond belief, but *FSR*, vaguely referenced by historians for over 50 years, has never been academically analysed.

I am not from a military background. I offer an analysis in mild trepidation. Doubtless, others will see principles where I have not, particularly those from a background which gives them a detailed understanding of current military doctrines. But I have had authoritative guidance. My grandfather was an artillery subaltern, educated at Woolwich in 1912. He went with the 3rd Division to France in 1914, and by 1918, he had been mentioned in dispatches five times, won the MC and bar, DSO and bar, and was in temporary command of an artillery brigade. His mother kept his letters, nearly a thousand of them with associated diaries and papers, as he wrote home from the front line of almost every major battle on the Western Front from Mons in 1914 to the Armistice in 1918. His letters record not only his adherence to *FSR*, but that of his peers: their horror when it was ignored, their contentment when it was being followed. Not once does he make explicit reference to *FSR*, but once one is aware of the regulations, it is implicit in every page of his correspondence.[2] Why, I asked myself, having edited the letters, are the *FSR* principles he thought so important, ignored in so many war narratives? It has taken seven years to reach this point, and I still do not know the answer.

There can be no preconception that compliance with *FSR* correlated with success in war. Even in 1914, no such assumption could be made. Maybe ignoring its principles would be the key to success. This book will argue that the opposite was true, but if one accepts that *FSR* doctrine defined the army's ethos and practice in 1914, then tracing the influence of the doctrine into the war becomes a necessary exercise. This is particularly true for biographical works which describe the modus operandi of the various generals who shaped tactics and strategy. An understanding of *FSR* is an essential tool in the armoury of the serious biographer, especially once the war is underway. Every officer can be categorised by the relative rigidity of his adherence to the principles described so clearly in *FSR*; on a spectrum from strict unthinking adherence to the letter of it, through a more relaxed interpretation, to outright rejection of its principles. Many biographical works rely much too heavily on personal diaries, subjective reports, and anecdotes, highlighting social standing and character traits as the reason for animosities or sackings. They fail to understand that every military decision, every controversy, from 1909 on, had a doctrinal backdrop.

There are virtually no useful books on *FSR* and operations which can be recommended, except the documents themselves, which will repay the several months that officer cadets between 1910 and 1914 took to study and understand them. Some historians, who should have taken the time to make this study, have either ignored *FSR* in their entirety, or so misinterpreted what is said in them, that their theses with respect to it are valueless. *FSR* and administration is far better served. Ian Malcolm Brown's book on *British Logistics* is the most comprehensive.[3] All that most amateur historians will know about *FSR* is that Douglas Haig is widely credited with developing it for use in 1909. A close study of the origins and content of *FSR* does not confirm this 'fact'. There were many officers who contributed to its content and participated with zeal in ensuring the implementation of the doctrine, but Haig was not one of them. The first part of this book lays out, in perhaps excessive detail, the narrative of the genesis, consensus publication, and robust implementation of its teaching in the British Army. Haig is conspicuous for his lack of involvement in all stages of this process. However, since historians of the stature of

2 David Hutchison, *The Young Gunner: The Royal Field Artillery in the Great War* (Kibworth Beauchamp: Matador Press, 2016). The author's given name is David Keable-Elliott.

3 Ian Malcolm Brown, *British Logistics on the Western Front 1914–1919* (Westport: Praeger, 1998).

Hew Strachan and Michael Howard have authoritatively ruled that Haig defined *FSR*; and since many academic historians have based their theses on the fundamental premise that he was intrinsic to their publication, any rebuttal must be forensic. It should be noted that this book was written before the publication of the December 2024 edition of *Records*, the proceedings of the Douglas Haig Fellowship, in which Major General Mungo Melvin, quoting my work, states that Haig's biographers are 'pretty much agreed' that 'Douglas Haig had either little or nothing to do with the writing of [*FSR*] *Part I*.'[4] If true, this constitutes a major change in the historiography which this book will reflect.

The second part of the book addresses those principles which can most rewardingly be used in operational analysis or assessment of administrative procedures; on a year-by-year basis as the war progresses. In 1914, every regular British Army officer was required to observe *FSR*, and most did. A study of the Mons campaign finds almost universal compliance with it. By 1915, some officers believed that not all its principles were applicable to trench warfare, and an increasing percentage of officers were not familiar with it. As Peter Simkins says in his book on Kitchener's Army. 'Many retired officers [returning to command] found they could not adapt to the changes wrought by the introduction of the new Field Service Regulations'.[5] But this does not invalidate *FSR* as an assessment tool. There are many operations in 1915, or at the Somme in 1916, at which its principles were followed closely. Other times, they were not. These are objective facts, allowing actions to be classified, commanders to be compared, and evolving tactics to be followed. Inevitably, there is frequent mention of Sir John French and Sir Douglas Haig as Commanders-in-Chief of the British Army on the Western Front, but their views are presented in the context of an ongoing conflict. Doctrine, not personalities, is the subject of this book.

FSR does not just deal with operations. It has as much to say on organisation and administration. An understanding of *FSR* will inform those who are studying the history of units and the development of all the services which supported and cared for the British Army at war. As Haig acknowledged so clearly in his valedictory dispatches at the end of the war, *FSR*, as a doctrine, was all-pervasive in guiding and determining its course and its result. Always in the back of the minds of all regulars and all senior generals – not always observed, occasionally problematic, usually constructive – *FSR* served as one constant in a complex and evolving industrial war.

4 Major General (Retd) Mungo Melvin, 'Field Service Regulations 1909, Douglas Haig and the "Man on the Spot"', *Records, the Douglas Haig Fellowship's Journal*, Number 27, December 2024, p.12.

5 Peter Simkins, *Kitchener's Army: The Raising of the New Armies, 1914–1916* (Barnsley: Pen & Sword, 2007), p.217.

1

Combined Training and a Staff Manual 1900–1904

The ideas behind what would become *FSR* were first conceived in 1900, having their origins in the soul-searching that occurred in the British Army in the middle stages of the South African War at the turn of the century.[1] It was not proving a glorious episode in the history of the army, and it was obvious that many officers, and many units, arriving in South Africa were dangerously unprepared for war. This was true even of regular army units, and as Venter and colleagues have recently explained, it was even more true of the 100,000 yeomanry and volunteer recruits from Great Britain and Ireland, and the 80,000 colonial volunteers, many of whom served in 'irregular' units.[2] It was also widely perceived that the army lacked a consistent organisational structure.

It is not difficult to understand how this situation had arisen. In the late Victorian era, the British Army was almost continuously at war, but there was no consistency in the type of war that this was. Generals learnt their craft by experience, first in junior roles, the more competent progressing through administrative postings to operational command of expeditions, using the regular and locally raised troops available to them. An excellent example of this career progression is that of Lord Roberts of Kandahar. Born Frederick Sleigh Roberts in India in 1832, he was educated at Eton and Sandhurst and then returned to India in 1851 to join the Bengal Artillery. He distinguished himself in the Indian Rebellion of 1857, being lightly wounded at the Siege of Delhi and was subsequently attached to the staff as a Deputy Assistant Quartermaster General during the relief of Lucknow. He won the Victoria Cross in the dying stages of the campaign and was mentioned in dispatches. He transferred to the British Army in 1861 and, between 1863 and 1872, participated in campaigns on the Indian North-West frontier, in Africa, and in North-East India. Being rapidly promoted, he served as Quartermaster General of the Bengal Army from 1875, then commanded a Field Force in Afghanistan in 1878. By 1881, he was commanding the Madras Army and in 1885, he took command of the Indian Army.

1 The National Archives (TNA): WO 279/18: 'Conference of General Staff Officers, January 1908', Colonel Walter Adye on the history of FSR, p.26.

2 Louis Venter, Dr Marietjie Oelofse and Dr Johan Van Zÿl, 'The Composition of the Imperial British Forces in the Anglo-Boer War, 1899–1902: A Military and Socio-Historical Overview', *Scientia Militaria 2024,* vol.52, no.2, pp.53–69.

In each of the campaigns that Roberts served, unique logistical and operational challenges presented themselves. Commanders and administrators had to be very flexible in their thinking, managing quite small, non-uniform, armies. It was almost impossible to train officers except on the job. And if that job was based at Chelsea Barracks in London, performing ceremonial duties, very different types of officers emerged. The army hierarchy was aware of the problem to the extent that a Staff College, with rudimentary origins as far back as 1802, had evolved sufficiently by 1870 to have its own commandant and offer formal two-year courses. The first commandant was Sir Edward Hamley, who had written a book called *The Operations of War*. Updated versions of this book became the main textbook for the entry exam to the Staff College during the 1880s and 1890s.[3]

Hamley's experience was very different from that of other officers of a slightly later vintage, like Roberts and Sir Horace Smith-Dorrien, who were constantly at war. He had served on the staff of the artillery in the Crimean War between 1853 and 1856, but was mainly an academic soldier thereafter. He became a professor of Military History at Sandhurst in 1859 and published the first edition of his book in 1867, updating it regularly. After serving as Staff College commandant, he was appointed the British representative on a body responsible for determining the frontiers around Turkey, both in Europe and Asia, in 1879. He did, however, command a division on Lord Wolseley's expedition to Egypt in 1882.[4]

Strachan describes his book as being both 'mired in the tactical past and limited in conception', which is a fair comment. 'Hamley believed that … operations were a matter of planning and logistics, of choosing one's own line of operations, and mastering those of the enemy.'[5] Adam Dighton, more recently, says that the book is derivative, presenting 'strategy as essentially unchanging as campaigns fought decades apart [are] invoked to illustrate the same strategic principle.' The book avoids 'reference to changing technology or psychological factors,' he says, an almost insuperable difficulty, one would think.[6] In the 1886 edition, Hamley grapples with the impact of railways, but using Prussian or Napoleonic examples of battle does not inspire confidence in the military solutions he proposes. It is difficult to imagine Lord Roberts reading the book with any enthusiasm.

That is not to say that the Staff College in the 1890s was moribund. The main star was Colonel G.F.R. Henderson. Born in 1854, the son of a clergyman, he was educated at Leeds Grammar School and won a scholarship to Oxford. He entered the army at the age of 24, serving in India and then joining the Egyptian Campaign of 1882, where he participated in four battles and was mentioned in dispatches. When his regiment was sent to the West Indies in 1884, he used his leisure time to study the American Civil War, publishing *The Campaign of Fredericksburg, A Tactical Study for Officers*, in 1886, and *Stonewall Jackson and the Science of War* in 1889. That year, at the age of 35, 'he became Instructor in Tactics, Military Law and Administration at Sandhurst. From this post he proceeded as Professor of Military Art and History to the Staff

3 Sir Edward Bruce Hamley, *The Operations of War, Explained and Illustrated, Fourth Edition* (Oxford: Blackwood and Sons, 1886), pp.8–51.

4 *Encyclopædia Britannica* (Cambridge: Cambridge University Press, 1910), vol.12, p.896.

5 Hew Strachan, 'Operational Art and Britain, 1909–2009', in John Andreas Olsen and Martin van Creveld (eds), *The Evolution of Operational Art: From Napoleon to the Present* (Oxford: Oxford University Press, 2010), pp.100–101; Hamley, *The Operations of War*, pp.8–51.

6 Adam Dighton, 'Jomini versus Clausewitz: Hamley's Operations of War and Military Thought in the British Army, 1866–1933', *War in History*, 2020, vol.27 (2), pp.184–185.

College (1892–1899)', at Camberley.[7] By this time, his was a household name since books on military matters were best-sellers of the time. He has been credited with being 'perhaps the leading military thinker of his generation.'[8]

Colonel G.F.R. Henderson, as portrayed in the front plate of *The Science of War* by G.F.R. Henderson, published in 1905.

Strachan gives him pride of place in sketching out his influence on British military thinking, though he fails to emphasise that he died in 1903, which detracts slightly from his otherwise excellent account.[9] 'Many military memoirs testify to his standing', says Jeffries, and his influence on Henry Wilson was clearly profound, since he consciously copied his old tutor's style of working on tactical problems, even years later.[10] The American historian Jay Luvaas in his *Military Legacy of the Civil War*, written in 1959, describes the major impact Henderson had on military thinking on both sides of the Atlantic.[11] Henderson's views are summarised in *The Science of War*, a posthumous compendium of essays and lectures. Dating from both before and after the South African War, they muse on the role of the cavalry in a modern war, and on the necessity for young officers to take responsibility for the local tactics of their units during a battle. He did not reject the advantages of studying historical campaigns to glean insights into how current campaigns should be fought, far from it. But he did challenge the rigid thinking that such study was all that was required to create a successful general.[12]

Rigid thinking is, however, reflected in *Infantry Drill* 1896, the principal training manual used for basic training by British infantry before the South African War. Its introduction sets the tone:

7 *Annual Register for 1903* (London: Longmans, Green, and Co. 1904), Obituary. Lieutenant Colonel George Francis Robert Henderson, pp.125–126.
8 Douglas Scott, *The Preparatory Prologue, Douglas Haig Diaries and Letters, 1861 to 1914* (Barnsley: Pen & Sword, 2006), p.61.
9 Strachan, *Operational Art*, pp.101–105.
10 Keith Jeffery, *Field Marshal Sir Henry Wilson, a Political Soldier* (Oxford: Oxford University Press, 2006), p.17.
11 Jay Luvaas, *The Military Legacy of the Civil War, The European Inheritance* (Lawrence: University Press of Kansas, 1988 [1959]), pp.170–202.
12 Lord Roberts, 'Memoir' in G. F. R. Henderson (ed.), N. Malcolm, *The Science of War: A Collection of Essays and Lectures 1891–1903* (London: Longmans, Green and Co., 1912 [1905], Alpha Editions, 2019).

> Generals and other officers commanding are enjoined to devote their utmost attention to carrying out the system of training, drill, and manoeuvre laid down in this book, the aim of which is to obtain, at the decisive moment, the greatest development of infantry fire under the most careful supervision and control. To secure this, a thorough training is essential – great precision being inculcated in the early stages of the soldier's instruction.[13]

Early training concentrated on ceremonial and large-scale manoeuvres. *Infantry Drill* encourages instruction by rote, transferable to the battlefield, and firm direction by senior officers. It is true that *Infantry Drill* did recommend some delegation to more junior officers, as training progressed, but it is difficult to see how this delegation is compatible with being 'under the most careful supervision and control.'[14] Using these principles, the first few weeks of the South African War proved humiliating for the British army, with three serious defeats during 'Black Week' in December 1899. Marching into battle in serried ranks at Stormberg and Magersfontein had proved disastrous. Using the artillery as a forward strike force had been an even less successful tactic at Colenso. Nearly 3,000 men had been lost in three battles, and nothing gained. As Nick Evans points out in his 2008 paper on British Army tactics from 1897, Roberts had challenged current training methods when organising a pre-war tactical exercise in Ireland, which incorporated lessons learnt in the Tirah Campaign of 1897.[15] But these lessons had not been adopted by the wider army.

Field-Marshal Lord Roberts was still in England at the time of the disasters of 'Black Week,' having just been appointed Commander-in-Chief in South Africa. Aware of Henderson's strong views on tactical deployment, Roberts recruited him as his Director of Intelligence. Henderson, in turn, recruited William Robertson, who had passed out of the staff college with distinction the year before, as staff captain. Robertson, as an ex-ranker, stood out as an oddity in the British army of the time, 39 years old and with a strong regional accent. He never forgot Henderson's patronage of him and was fiercely loyal to his memory. Roberts and his team arrived in Cape Town on 10 January 1900. On 26 January, Roberts issued *Circular Memorandum, number 5*, almost certainly after consultation with Henderson.

This memorandum can be cited as the army directive, which kick-started the doctrinal reform of the British Army in the early twentieth century. 'The enemy', it said, 'thoroughly understand how to take advantage of the ground, are adept in improvising cover and most skilful in the use of their weapons.' 'Battalion and Company Commanders should take every opportunity' to utilise 'cover', 'look out for and occupy' strong positions and 'further the general scheme of attack.' In other words, frontal attack in rigid formations was forbidden, and junior officers were authorised to use initiative in the pursuit of victory over Boer forces, thus contradicting the ethos of *Infantry Drill*, which demanded close supervision and control by senior officers. The memorandum goes on to assert the importance of keeping artillery out of range of snipers and of cooperating with the infantry in attack; cavalry commanders are advised to reconnoitre intelligently and ensure their findings are reported back.[16] These were not new concepts, having been

13 *Infantry Drill 1896* (London, War Office, 1896) p.III.
14 *Infantry Drill 1896* (London, War Office, 1896).
15 Nick Evans, 'From Drill to Doctrine: Forging the British Army's Tactics, 1897 – 1909' (Kings College, London, 2008), pp.61–65.
16 TNA: WO 105/40: Field Marshal Lord Roberts, *South Africa 1900*, 'Circular Memorandum Number 5 – Notes for Guidance in South African Warfare' (London: Harrison & Sons, 1900), pp.49–50.

learnt and adopted by all competent officers engaged in the many small wars of the Victorian era, but though echoes of them feature in *Infantry Drill* and other manuals, they were not considered relevant to basic training. This time, with Roberts in command, the ideas did not die once the action was over.

Henderson was never robust, and he was invalided home in February 1900, dangerously ill, only a few weeks after arriving in South Africa.[17] When he recovered, in the following August, Roberts, most unusually, took him back onto his personal staff in London, into 'special employment … graded as Assistant Adjutant General.'[18] He instructed him to update *Infantry Drill, 1896* into a new edition incorporating his pre-war ideas, and the philosophy of the 1900 *Circular Memorandum*. This was high-handed, since it was Lieutenant General Sir Evelyn Wood, the Adjutant General, who had responsibility for commissioning and updating training manuals.[19] However, there was little he could do about it, and he accepted this appropriation of his responsibilities with reasonable grace.

Roberts returned to London at the end of December 1900 and was impatient to publish Henderson's work. But it was still in draft form and had divided naturally into two parts – a drill and training component that pertained only to the infantry, and a supplement, which was of wider application. Even the former was radically rewritten, incorporating a new section on musketry, which demanded that recruits adapt their firing positions to terrain; and not fire, even if ordered to do so, unless they had a target. It introduced, throughout, an emphasis on the need for junior officers to take responsibility for the training and tactics of their own units.[20] In the light of experience in South Africa, it was not controversial, but even this part needed significant further editing, and even then it could not be published without the authorisation of the Adjutant General. Henderson needed help, and Roberts set about recruiting Gerald F. Ellison, again disconcerting Wood, in whose department he worked.

Lieutenant Colonel Ellison was the son of a clergyman and had passed through Sandhurst, aged 20, in 1882. He was commissioned into the Royal North Lancashire Regiment and immediately showed an aptitude for staff work. He graduated from the Staff College in 1889 and served as Staff Captain at army headquarters from 1894 to 1897. In 1889, 1890 and 1895, he visited Germany and was greatly impressed by the efficiency of the German Imperial Staff at their manoeuvres.[21] He published a book, *Home Defence,* in 1898 and was at the War Office when the British army mobilised in 1899. He subsequently served as a Deputy Assistant Adjutant General with the 2nd Division in South Africa, being mentioned in dispatches.[22] Unimpressed

17 Lord Roberts, 'Memoir', in Henderson, *The Science of War*, p.xxxv.

18 Lieutenant General H.G. Hart, *Hart's Annual Army List, Militia List, And Yeomanry Cavalry List, 1902* (London: John Murray, 1902), pp.3, 50.

19 J.S. Ross, *The War Office List and Administrative Directory for the British Army* (London: War Office, 1903), p.3.

20 *Infantry Training, (provisional), 1902* (London: War Office, 1902), pp.81–158.

21 National Army Museum (NAM): 8704/35/818/19: Ellison papers, Lieutenant General Sir Gerald Ellison, 'From Here and There, Reminiscences' *The Lancashire Lad; Journal of the Loyal Regiment*, July 1933, Section VIII, pp.7–8. Ellison's autobiographical 'Reminiscences' were published as monthly instalments in this journal from 1931 to 1938. There is no reason to doubt their general truth, but the detail needs to be interpreted with caution. He did not wish to stir up old controversies.

22 Robert Simpson, *Major General Sir Gerald Francis Ellison KCB KCMG MiD*, <https//:www.anzac-biographies.com/2017/05/29/ellison-major-general-sir-gerald-francis-kcb-kcmg-mid/>, accessed February 2020.

by the structure of British staff arrangements on campaign, he wrote, in 1899, a very basic manual for staff officers of the South Natal Field Force, which was printed locally.[23] He was promoted, but then he too was invalided home, seriously ill, in early 1901.[24] While he was recovering, Roberts became aware of his talents, his long experience in the Adjutant General's department, and his editorial experience.

Gerald Ellison in 1914. (Courtesy, Maryborough Museum, Victoria, Australia)

In August 1901, Roberts arranged for Ellison to meet Henderson, who was just about to depart for South Africa, having, in June, accepted a lucrative contract to write an official history of the South African War.[25] Ellison says, in his '*Reminiscences*', published long after the events described in them, that Henderson needed help with two projects. The first was to guide to publication his revision, in two volumes, of *Infantry Drill 1896*. The second was to write for him 'a simple little manual' dealing with staff organisation and staff work in the field.'[26]

Lord Roberts, now Commander-in-Chief of the Forces, based in London, was determined to tackle the roots of the problems he had found in South Africa.[27] As well as the training issues affecting the fighting troops, the arrangements for the care and supply of the Army in South Africa had been shambolic. There had been no uniformity in administration and supply procedures. In the absence of any authoritative leadership, local arrangements had been made at every depot. As Douglas Haig later observed, 'three entirely different systems were adopted concurrently by three different headquarters.' So, 'before the end of the South African War, the then Commander-in-Chief decided that the army should be provided with two important manuals – one dealing with training, the other with the organization and administration of an army in the field.'[28] Roberts had Henderson

23 NAM: 8704/35/15: Ellison papers 'South Natal Field Force – Standing Orders with notes on Supply, Transport, etc.' November 1899.
24 Hart, *Annual Army List, 1902*, pp.53, 211.
25 Peter Donaldson, *Remembering the South African War: Britain and the Memory of the Anglo-Boer War, from 1899 to the Present* (Liverpool: Liverpool University Press, 2013), pp.144–145.
26 NAM: 8704/35/818/56–57: *The Lancashire Lad*, Feb 1937, XXI, pp.12–13.
27 John Gooch, *The Plans of War, the General Staff and British Military Strategy c. 1900–1916* (London: Routledge & Kegan Paul, 1974), pp.27–28.
28 TNA: WO 279/18: 'Conference of General Staff Officers, January 1908', comment by Haig during presentation by Colonel Walter Adye, pp.26–27.

working on training. Now, he wanted Ellison to start work on defining the administration of an expeditionary force. Henderson left for South Africa almost immediately, and Ellison took over his work.[29]

Roberts found a suitable niche for Ellison at the War Office, working half time as Assistant Adjutant General under Wood, and half time in his own office, where he assumed responsibility for Henderson's 'draft proof's' on his departure, and started work on the 'little manual'. He soon realised that his 'little manual' would be anything but little, but he cannot have thought that he would still be working on it eight years later. An easy first step so far as Henderson's work was concerned was to arrange for the drill and training component of the revised 1896 infantry manual to be sent, with Wood's approval, to Chelsea Barracks, which housed the Guards on ceremonial duties, for testing and appraisal.[30]

The next problem that Ellison and Roberts faced was how to progress the second volume of Henderson's work. This was much more problematic since his draft contained 'a great deal of military doctrine which was common to all arms.'[31] Nothing quite like it had ever been produced for the British army before. Ellison waited until 1 October 1901, when Sir Thomas Kelly-Kenny replaced Sir Evelyn Wood as Adjutant General. On Kelly-Kenny's desk, on his first day at work, was a letter from Ellison, dated 29 September 1901, quite explicitly proposing two 'general service manuals', one dealing with combined tactics and the other with war administration.[32] Kelly-Kenny asked for details, and Ellison supplied them. It appears 'that the C-C [Roberts] wishes both administration [his little manual] and tactical subjects to be dealt with in' a new Field Service manual. But Ellison went on to argue against such an approach on the grounds that it would unreasonably delay the project. Far better, he said, to keep the two parts separate, preparing the administration manual from scratch, and expanding the 'general tactical manual' for all arms, with the advantage that future manuals specific to infantry, cavalry or artillery could be slimmed down.[33]

Ellison was a masterly politician. Sir Evelyn Wood might well have turned down the whole concept of a new and different manual, as proposed by Ellison and Roberts, as an unacceptable abrogation of the responsibilities of his department. But Ellison gambled, correctly, that Kelly-Kenny, on his first day in his new job, would not wish to upset his Commander-in-Chief by turning down his request to approve the commissioning of this new document. Ellison offered Kelly-Kenny an olive branch. He could refuse to approve the administration component, thus asserting his independence, but let the concept of an all-arms tactical manual be further considered. Kelly-Kenny accepted this compromise.

Only a month later, after further pressure from Roberts, Kelly-Kenny wrote on 31 October, without any enthusiasm at all, to the new commander at Aldershot, Major General Sir Henry

29 NAM: 8704/35/35: Ellison papers, draft letter, Ellison to Kelly-Kenny, Oct 1901; NAM: 8704/35/818/56–57: *The Lancashire Lad*, Feb 1937, XXI, p.12.

30 NAM: 8704/35/34&35: Ellison papers, draft letters, Ellison to Kelly-Kenny, Aug and Oct 1901; NAM: 8704/35/818/56–57: *The Lancashire Lad*, Feb 1937, XXI, pp.12–13.

31 John Dunlop, *The Development of the British Army 1899–1914* (London: Methuen, 1938) p.225.

32 NAM: 8704/35/818/56–57: *The Lancashire Lad*, Feb 1937, Section XXI, pp.12–13. See also NAM: 8704/35/34: Ellison papers, draft letter, Ellison to Kelly-Kenny, Sep 1901. There were three main draft documents in Ellison's possession, and the inconsistent nomenclature used in correspondence to describe them has been clarified in this account.

33 NAM: 8704/35/35: Ellison papers, draft letter, Ellison to Kelly-Kenny, October 1901.

Hildyard, to say that he had been 'directed' by Roberts to request that a committee be convened there, with Major General Charles Douglas, Commander of the 1st Infantry Brigade at Aldershot, and later Chief of the Imperial General Staff in 1914, as President. This committee was to 'test, revise if necessary and edit Volume I' of Henderson's work, the drill component of which had by then been checked over at Chelsea Barracks. In addition, Hildyard, as an ex-commandant of the Staff College, was to consider the idea of setting up a second committee, 'composed of representatives of all arms', with Major G.F. Ellison as secretary, to consider Volume II of Henderson's work, and evaluate whether it can 'with some alterations and additions, be made applicable to the army as a whole.'[34]

The Douglas Committee tackled the job of editing what would soon be published as *Infantry Training (Provisional) 1902* swiftly and decisively. By 3 December, they were on to their third draft. The Hildyard Committee also convened promptly and started work. On 2 January 1902, Kelly-Kenny wrote again to Hildyard, again under heavy pressure from Roberts, to request that his committee expand its brief, and 'also consider and report on a Field Service Manual which is being drafted by Lieutenant Colonel Ellison, the Secretary of your Committee.' This should describe, 'briefly and clearly, for the information of the army as a whole, and of Staff Officers in particular, what our system and accepted staff arrangements are in war.'[35]

Kelly-Kenny soon came to regret this letter. He had been forced by Roberts to officially endorse Ellison's work, so far as that was necessary, on a possible reorganisation of his, and the Quartermaster General's, responsibilities on campaign. In the short term, he could use this to deflect some of the heavy criticism that the army was enduring in newspaper reports and editorials as the full extent of its inefficiencies in South Africa was revealed, but in the longer term, it threatened to upset the status quo at the War Office. That time was some way off since Ellison had no draft to present to Hildyard's committee, and in practice, the committee membership, as recruited by Hildyard, had no expertise in administration or organisation. Hildyard had been a reforming commandant at the Staff College when Henderson was teaching and had an infantry background. He had commanded a division in South Africa before taking over at Aldershot. On his committee, the infantry was additionally represented by Douglas and the cavalry by Colonel Richard Lawrence, who had been a professor at the Staff College under Hildyard. This was a somewhat unfortunate choice since he was based in a remount facility in Kent and was not involved in the considerable controversies that were developing on the role of the cavalry at war.[36] The artillery representative was Colonel Neil Findlay, who later commanded the 1st Division artillery in 1914. There was also a representative from the Royal Engineers. The committee concentrated on Henderson's work, with Ellison doing most of the editorial work as secretary. Within a few months, both Henderson's drafts had been amended and were ready for publication. *Infantry Training (Provisional) 1902* was issued in April, and *Combined Training (Provisional) 1902* in May of that year.[37] Henderson himself had little opportunity to get involved in the deliberations of either committee, returning to England in early

34 NAM: 8704/35/37: Ellison papers, letter, Kelly-Kenny to O/C Aldershot, 31 October 1901.

35 Hart, *Annual Army List, 1902*, p.97; NAM: 8704/35/37: Kelly-Kenny to O/C Aldershot, 2 January 1902.

36 The Marquess of Anglesey, *A History of the British Cavalry 1816–1919, Volume 4, 1899–1913* (London: Leo Cooper, 1986), p.284.

37 *Combined Training, (Provisional) 1902* (London: War Office, 1902); *Infantry Training, (provisional), 1902* (London: War Office, 1902).

1902, quite unwell. He spent several months convalescing before leaving England for the last time in January 1903, dying in Egypt two months later.[38]

But these handbooks articulated a revolutionary training philosophy which influenced the professional British army for many years to come. Both are pocketbooks, and all the key features of *FSR, 1909* are there, albeit advice on the duties of officers is less directive, the re-definition of the relationship between junior and senior officers less clear-cut, the difficulty of requiring all arms cooperation, whilst allowing the cavalry operational independence, not so firmly addressed, and the command structure of units on active service less clearly defined. These were all somewhat problematic. Evans documents the strength of feeling amongst those demanding training reform and a new army doctrine incorporating initiative.[39] The level of initiative allowable to junior officers in the documents is comparable to that allowed in *Circular Memorandum 5*, but that had been issued in wartime. Senior officers were prone to championing the desirability of initiative in theory but were not so keen on it in practice. The exercise of initiative in peacetime often came perilously close to insubordination. To allow limited operational independence to subordinates in the interpretation of their orders was one thing, but to allow them to ignore orders was quite another, especially if there was not a formally accepted and defined command structure which allocated operational responsibilities, an issue not settled till 1908. Roberts directed that both manuals be adopted as additional guidance for army training.[40] This meant that *Combined Training (Provisional) 1902* was now essential reading for all line officers. Following its general advice was required, but the handbooks of individual arms, especially in the cavalry, usually took precedence. Officers who wished to stay up to date, and please their Commander-in-Chief, needed to read it.

As well as arranging the publication of *Infantry Training* and *Combined Training*, in 1902, Ellison continued work on what he was now calling '*A Staff Manual for War*.' By this time, it was becoming clear to Ellison that framing regulations defining the duties of staff officers of the Adjutant General's and Quartermaster General's Departments on campaign was dependent on the responsibilities and duties of these War Office departments in peacetime.[41] With almost continuous reorganisations taking place in the army as a result of the fall-out from reports on the South African War, it was hard enough for him to find a niche from which to continue his own work, let alone produce an authoritative draft to reflect this reality. Half of his time was employed in the Mobilization Division of the Adjutant General's Department from June 1902.[42]

Meanwhile, the army had to respond to the Akers-Douglas Report of 1902, tasked 'to Consider the Education and Training of Officers of the Army.' This recommended an immediate and independent review of current training establishments, further suggesting that 'the supervision and control of Military Education throughout the Army should be entrusted to a General Officer.'[43] It also suggested, probably with awareness of the work of Henderson and

38 NAM: 7101/23/46/68: Roberts papers, Henderson to Roberts, 30 December 1902.

39 Evans, 'From drill to doctrine', pp.206–220.

40 TNA: WO 279/516: *Military Manoeuvres and Field Training 1903–1905*, vol.2, 'Preliminary Training of the IInd Army Corps and the Preparations for the Army Manoeuvres 1903', p.12.

41 NAM: 8704/35/818/59: *The Lancashire Lad*, May 1937, XXII, p.56.

42 G.K. King, *The War Office List and Administrative Directory for the British Army, 1905* (London: H.M.S.O., 1905), pp.99, 237.

43 The Rt Hon. A. Akers-Douglas (Chairman), *The Report of the Committee approved to consider the Education and Training of the Officers of the Army* (London: HMSO, 1902), p.38.

Ellison, that a new basic training handbook was desirable, binding on all officers in the army. Hildyard was moved from his post as commander at Aldershot and, on 15 January 1903, became the Director of a new Department of Military Education and Planning.[44] This department assumed control of those parts of the Adjutant General's Directorate, which covered drill and military instruction (A.G.4.) and the army schools (A.G.5.). Hildyard was given two assistants, graded as Assistant Adjutant Generals, Colonel Sir Henry Rawlinson, and Lieutenant Colonel Henry Wilson, both appointed on 1 April 1903. Both had been pupils of Henderson at the Staff College.[45] Roberts had, in South Africa, identified 'a coterie of talent', and amongst those protégés were both Wilson and Rawlinson.[46] They were appointed at the instigation of Roberts, who was determined that the 1902 *Combined Training* document should be competently updated.[47]

Wilson records this appointment under Hildyard in his diary for 1903. He seldom mentions his day job, but he does describe his partnership with 'Rawlie.' Wilson and Rawlinson were to work with the head of A.G.4, a Major Walter Adye, who had been at the War Office since 1900 and who had already inherited Ellison's role in drafting desirable amendments that would feature in any update of *Combined Training 1902 (Provisional).* Walter Adye had had a very undistinguished South African War, having been captured and then released in a prisoner exchange. He was a poor speaker but a meticulous editor who conscientiously attended training conferences and kept army handbooks up to date at the War Office for 10 years. An unsung hero of this narrative, he was destined to quietly guide both *Combined Training* and Ellison's fledgling *Field Manual* to eventual publication as *FSR, Parts I and II.*

Neither John Dunlop, in his *Development of the British Army*, nor John Gooch, in his *Plans of War*, both authoritative and extensively quoted by contemporary historians, are entirely correct in their paraphrasing of the early genesis of *FSR*. Dunlop suggests, without citing any evidence, that 'General Stopford' became chair of the Hildyard Committee at some stage.[48] Gooch says, wrongly, that Hildyard, Rawlinson, Wilson and Ellison formed a small committee which 'duly produced a *Manual of Combined Training* and a *Staff Manual*.'[49] The Hildyard Committee at Aldershot had dispersed by October 1902, although Ellison had told both Roberts and Kelly-Kenny that *Combined Training* was still a work in progress. The 'Manual will occupy one officer's whole attention for some months to come', he wrote, while refusing to take on the task himself, being fully occupied with his own work.[50] He was not posted into Hildyard's new directorate in 1903. Thus, the main workload of revising *Combined Training* fell, within Hildyard's new Directorate, on Rawlinson, who would command a corps in 1914, and Wilson, who would be on the staff at Mons. As early as 27 April 1903, Wilson records in his diary that the 'Chief

44 Gooch, *Plans of War*, p.27.
45 Ross, *The War Office List, 1903*, p.43, 49, 51.
46 Jeffery, *Field Marshal Sir Henry Wilson,* p.39.
47 NAM: 7101/23/88/6: Roberts papers, Wilson to Roberts, thank you letter, 27 June 1903.
48 Dunlop, *The Development of the British Army* pp.291–292. Referenced in the index as Colonel Sir Lionel Stopford, who became deputy assistant Quartermaster General, Staff College, in 1904. Major General Frederick Stopford was not at the War Office until 1904.
49 Gooch, *Plans of War*, p.28.
50 NAM: 8704/35/35: Ellison papers, draft letter, Ellison to Kelly-Kenny, 3 October 1902; NAM: 8704/35/818/59: *The Lancashire Lad*, May 1937, XXII, p.56.

[Roberts], Hildy, and Rawley and I had our first Committee Meeting about the manoeuvres.'[51] This is a reference to the upcoming combined manoeuvres, planned for September, which Roberts was determined should demonstrate adherence to the training advice in *Combined Training*. Uniquely, he required Wood, who was now commandant at Aldershot, to produce a report on the preliminary training of the army corps, even before its participation in these manoeuvres.[52] But most of Rawlinson and Wilson's work in mid-1903 addressed educational reforms at the staff and cadet colleges.

Ellison, meanwhile, was working hard on his *Staff Manual* under the auspices of Kelly-Kenny, to whom he was now reporting. Ellison sent Kelly-Kenny a series of updates, retaining copies in his files. In the first, probably in August 1902, he reports that the document was progressing 'under Colonel G.F.R. Henderson's supervision', though this supervision must have been purely nominal since Henderson spent most of his time in South Africa and was in very poor health. Ellison asks for general instructions.[53] The second, in October 1902, acknowledges these instructions and reports on progress, attaching a preliminary draft of the manual.[54] The third, in April 1903, accepts that he has not done enough consultation on the first draft, and attaches an update.

> I have, in conjunction with the branches of the War Office concerned, been drafting chapters on various administrative subjects, e.g. the supply of an Army in the field; medical arrangements; bivouac cantonments and camps; office work, returns and diaries in war; the function of Staff and Departments; transport; railway, telegraph, postal and signaling arrangements; prisoners of war and prizes, etc. Naturally these matters will require a great deal of discussion in the War Office before they can be referred to General Hildyard's Committee.[55]

Some of these chapters had already gone out for consultation. For instance, that on 'camps, cantonments and bivouacs' was already on the agenda of a committee chaired by 'Colonel Heath of the Q.M.G.'s department.'[56] In this work, Ellison had the help of a single assistant, Captain MacEwan. Both Ellison and MacEwan had been notified that they should return to regimental duties at the end of July 1903, and Ellison vigorously protested this decision.[57] Kelly-Kenny deferred his return to regimental duties, doubtless mindful of the watchful eye that Roberts was keeping on Ellison's progress. Roberts was impatient to see his vision of a new staff system in place and kept up the pressure for Ellison's document to be published.[58]

51 Imperial War Museum (IWM): 73/1/2: Diaries of Field Marshal Sir Henry Wilson, entry 27 April, 1903.
52 TNA: WO 279/516: *Military Manoeuvres*, vol.2, Preparations for the Army Manoeuvres 1903.
53 NAM: 8704/35/38: *Ellison papers*, draft letter, Ellison to Adjutant General, Sir Thomas Kelly-Kenny, August 1902, date, semi-legible, deduced from context.
54 NAM: 8704/35/35: *Ellison papers*, draft letter, Ellison to Adjutant General, Sir Thomas Kelly-Kenny, October 1902, date deduced from context.
55 NAM: 8704/35/38: Ellison papers, draft letter, Ellison to Kelly-Kenny, mid-1902.
56 Colonel H.N.C. Heath was at almost every relevant conference for the next six years, and on the Mulcahy Committee of 1907–1908 which drafted the final version of *FSR, Part II*. It is likely that he had considerable influence on the development of *Part II*, though his input is difficult to pin down.
57 NAM: 8704/35/38: *Ellison papers*, draft letter, Ellison to Kelly-Kenny, April 1903, pp.4–5.
58 NAM: 8704/35/35: *Ellison papers*, draft letter, Ellison to Kelly-Kenny, October 1902, date from context.

Before further addressing the development of the two halves of what would eventually become *FSR*, it is worth considering the political background which influenced their development. Penning manuals was a favourite army pastime, and by this time, the drafts of both documents contained contributions from a widening array of sources. Hugh Arnold Foster, on becoming Secretary of State for War in 1903, complained that, 'at present, as in the past, every officer… has his own opinion on every conceivable military subject.'[59] Any senior officer with an opinion made sure it was written down. Evans lists 69 different training manuals issued between 1900 and 1906, and over a hundred more between 1906 and 1913, all published by the War Office. These publications ranged from technical handbooks on new or existing weaponry to routine updates. For example, *Garrison Artillery Training* went to seven editions between 1902 and 1905. In addition, between 1900 and 1902, multiple reports were commissioned (Evans lists 53 such), or committees set up, to consider every aspect of the army's generally unimpressive performance in South Africa.[60] Many committees produced paragraphs, or sections, which found their way into an updated *Combined Training* or the *Staff Manual*. 'Precise authorship of these manuals can be hard to determine' is something of an understatement.[61]

There was an international dimension as well. Ellison says that he asked an old friend, Lieutenant Colonel William Balck, a past professor of tactics at the German Imperial Staff College, for his thoughts on *Combined Training* in 1902. Balck was critical, saying that in advising the avoidance of frontal assault, the British were in danger of training a generation of officers lacking aggression. Ellison also discussed staff arrangements in South Africa, to which Balck's response was 'then you had no general staff at all.'[62] Balck was back in England the next year, and Ellison introduced him to Wilson, who was spellbound. He 'is the Henderson of the German War Office', he wrote in his diary in April 1903.[63] Ellison reports that *Combined Training* was amended in light of his comments. Balck published an influential book on tactics in Berlin that year, and was the father of Hermann Balck, a formidable panzer general in the Second World War.

As previously described, Roberts was determined that the army manoeuvres in mid-September 1903, which followed the summer training season, should incorporate the lessons learnt in the South African War, as laid down in *Combined Training*. He directed 'Combined Manoeuvres' himself, with Rawlinson as an assistant. 'Combined Training, 1902, has been studied and applied to the training of the troops', Sir Evelyn Wood, now Field Marshal Commanding IInd Army Corps at Aldershot, reported to Roberts, before the manoeuvres started. Roberts, in his final report after them, suggested some modifications to *Combined Training*, but he congratulated both Wood and Sir John French, his opposing commander, on the army's general compliance with it. French, of course, would go on to command the British Expeditionary Force in 1914. In his own report on the manoeuvres, Wood also addresses specific regulations in *Combined Training*, suggesting modifications to the provisional document. 'I was impressed by the advance in tactical efficiency made by all Arms', he concludes. This was not a small

59 Evans, *From drill to doctrine*, presented as a quote, p.290. But referenced impenetrably.

60 Evans, *From drill to doctrine*, pp. 401–405, 469–471.

61 Timothy Bowman and Mark Connelly, *The Edwardian Army, Recruiting, Training and Deploying the British Army, 1902–1914* ([2012] Oxford Scholarship Online, 2012), p.66.

62 NAM: 8704/35/818/57: *Ellison papers*, The Lancashire Lad; *Journal of the Loyal Regiment*, February 1937, Section XXI, p.13.

63 IWM: 73/1/2: Diaries of Henry Wilson, entry 22 April, 1903.

exercise: 9,850 infantrymen took part, along with artillery, cavalry, and even a balloon contingent. Charles Douglas and Herbert Plumer, an army commander by mid-1915, commanded brigades; James Grierson and Archibald Murray, respectively corps commander and chief-of-staff in 1914, had lesser commands.[64] All would have been familiar, from this early date, with the ethos of *Combined Training*. Wilson observed the manoeuvres, and in mid-January 1904, he attended a meeting with Roberts, Wood, French, Kelly-Kenny and Hildyard to discuss the various reports. Two days later, Wilson records in his diary that he was working on the 'new Training Regulations.'[65] This cycle of summer training for autumn manoeuvres continued, year-on-year, up to 1913. All military exercises were intended to assess the relevance and effectiveness of basic training, and reports on them invariably suggest amendments which could be incorporated in training and procedural updates.

During 1903, Ellison was still answerable to Kelly-Kenny, who was becoming increasingly anxious at the direction that Ellison seemed to be following as his *Field Manual* developed. He was right to be suspicious. By Ellison's own account, he had not briefed his superior fully on the reforms he had in mind. What is more, Ellison had form in this regard. In 1895, he was working in the War Office on mobilisation arrangements. According to Ellison, these were somewhat shambolic and he worked up a plan that would, in its initial stages, cause disruption, closing some small depots and enlarging others, but which, once fully implemented, would enable mobilisation to take place much more smoothly. He presented his proposals directly to Lord Wolsey, the Commander-in-Chief, disguising the degree of initial disruption and by-passing his immediate superior, the then Adjutant General, Sir Redvers Buller. Lord Wolsey approved the scheme, and it went through, though not without causing Ellison some sleepless nights when the Jameson Raid of December 1895 temporarily destabilised the balance of power in South Africa and threatened to trigger mobilisation in Great Britain and Ireland – at a time when all the necessary stores were in the wrong places.[66] Kelly-Kenny may or may not have known of this episode, but, in mid-1903, he ordered Ellison to prepare an explanatory memorandum outlining the implications of his *Field Manual* proposals.

Ellison was forced to reveal that he 'proposed a system on Wellingtonian lines, whereby the Quartermaster General was head of an operation staff and the Adjutant General the "organizer" of the army.'[67] 'Intelligence and operations were to be the concern of the Q.M.G, the A.G. stood for discipline, interior economy and the health and well-being of the troops, while maintenance and transportation were to be the responsibility of the Commissary General.'[68] Ellison lightly describes what was a huge row in the upper echelons of the War Office, as Kelly-Kenny realised the extent to which his department was going to be trimmed of influence. The memorandum was submitted to Roberts, who endorsed it and instructed Kelly-Kenny to allow Ellison to carry on with his work. Then, in November 1903, Ellison was invited to serve as Secretary to Lord Esher's War Office Reconstitution Committee, a position of enormous influence.

Reginald Baliol Brett, 2nd Viscount Esher, was an impeccably connected socialite and intellectual who dabbled in politics and religious affairs for many years. He served briefly as a Liberal

64 TNA: WO 279/7: 'Report on Combined Manoeuvres 1903', pp.1–5, 21, 25, 30–31; TNA: WO 279/516: *Military Manoeuvres*, vol.2, Preparations for the Army Manoeuvres 1903, p.12.
65 IWM: 73/1/2: Diaries of Henry Wilson, entries 11&13 January 1904.
66 NAM: 8704/35/818/31: *The Lancashire Lad*, October 1934, XII, p.7.
67 Gooch, *Plans of War*, p.28.
68 NAM: 8704/35/818/61: *The Lancashire Lad*, May 1937, XXII, p.58.

Member of Parliament until 1885, but by the early 1900s was using his charm and close friendship with King Edward VII, before and after his accession in 1902, to meddle, with the best of motives, in many of the political controversies of the day, the most pressing, after the South African War, being the projected reform of the army. He served on the Elgin Commission, which took evidence from a very wide range of witnesses to establish the problems which had prevented the rapid and successful conclusion of the South African War of 1899 to 1902. He was a shadowy but influential presence in the corridors of power.

Ellison, in his account of his recruitment, says, somewhat disingenuously, that he had no idea who Esher was when he dropped into his office and offered him the job. It is likely that Ellison was still maintaining confidentiality on the political machinations that manoeuvred him into the post against the wishes of Kelly-Kenny and other War Office traditionalists – even though much time had passed between the events and his writing of them.[69] The War Office, and especially the Adjutant General's department, was a febrile workplace at the time. Ellison and Wilson had a close working relationship, both working in the Adjutant General's branch. They were friends, too. While Ellison was having a difficult time with Kelly-Kenny, Wilson, according to his diaries, did his best to keep Kelly-Kenny happy by exercising his horse on cold mornings. On Friday, 13 November, Wilson records 'KK sent for Gerald Ellison and gave him a real dressing down … he was very angry … and he is now trying to prevent him from becoming Secretary of the Esher, Fisher, Clarke Committee, which is a real shame.' The following Monday, 'Ellison tells me he has really been given the Secretaryship … I am very pleased as he and I have talked over [the organisation of the War Office] a hundred times.'[70] Kelly-Kenny had asserted his right to refuse to allow Ellison's appointment, and it took the intervention of the King to authorise his release from the Adjutant General's department to take up the post, even though Ellison had already been endorsed by Arnold-Foster, Secretary of State for War.[71]

Within a matter of weeks, in early 1904, the Committee reported, proposing sweeping reforms of the army. The first action of the Esher Committee was to recommend that the King and Prime Minister set up an Army Council. This new body was to be headed by the Secretary of State for War, with two other civilians, a Parliamentary Under-Secretary, and a Financial Secretary, and four military members: the Chief of the General Staff, the Adjutant General, the Quartermaster General and the Master General of Ordnance. A Secretary to the Committee was also appointed. Once this was done, this council had the authority to implement further Esher Report recommendations, which it proceeded to do at breathtaking speed.

Amongst many more significant recommendations, the Esher Report formally made a proposal that must have been influenced by Ellison, though they were endorsing a specific recommendation of the Akers-Douglas Report. 'A general work setting forth the accepted principles as regards the training of the Forces for, and their administration in, war' should be published. This work, to be known as 'Field Service Regulations', should be in two parts. *Combined Training* should be further developed, and the portion dealing with 'War Administration, at present, in proof form' should be completed. All other training and administrative manuals, applicable only

69 NAM: 8704/35/818/62–63: *The Lancashire Lad*, Aug 1937, XXIII, pp.113–114.

70 IWM: 73/1/2: Diaries of Henry Wilson, entries 13 & 16 November 1903.

71 NAM: 8704/35/52: Ellison papers, letter, War Office to Ellison, 18 Nov 1903; Gooch, *Plans of War*, p.42; see NAM: 8704/35/818/63: *The Lancashire Lad*, Aug 1937, XXIII, p.114.

to sub-sections of the army, should be conceptually compliant with these two documents. This recommendation is phrased with great clarity and, as protection to what had become during 1903 an increasingly vulnerable project, the committee recommended that a new Directorate of Staff Duties be created, partly to take responsibility for it.[72]

In March 1904, therefore, oversight of the development of the *Staff Manual* was taken away from Roberts and Sir Charles Douglas, who had replaced Kelly-Kenny as Adjutant General, and given to Major General Henry D. Hutchinson, the new Director of Staff Duties. Hildyard's Department of Military Education and Planning was abolished, and its staff was redeployed into Staff Duties, along with all responsibility for officer training. As Wilson recorded in his diaries, this transition was not entirely smooth, and Wilson took over as Acting Director of Staff Duties until Hutchinson arrived.[73] Hildyard was posted to South Africa, and Rawlinson became the new commandant of the Staff College.

Thus, the stage was set. It was no longer a question of if both parts of *Field Service Regulations* would be implemented to define the British Army, but when. Recommendations of the 1904 Reconstitution Committee, chaired by Esher, were binding policy on the army.

72 Viscount Esher, J.A. Fisher, G.S. Clarke, *Report of the War Office (Reconstitution Committee) 1904, Presented to both Houses of Parliament by command of His Majesty* (London: H.M.S.O., 1904), Part II, Section IV, paras 20 and 21, pp.23–24.

73 IWM: 73/1/2: Diaries of Henry Wilson, from 1 February 1904.

2

Field Service Regulations, Part I, 1904–1909

The new Directorate of Staff Duties was set up at the instigation of Esher's Reconstitution Committee, and Major General Hutchinson was chosen as its first director. Henry Hutchinson, aged 57 in 1904, was an Indian Army veteran. He had served in the Sikkim Expedition of 1887 and was at the relief of Chitral in 1895. He had a particular affinity with the Gurkhas, but more relevantly, he had served as Director of Military Education in India from 1896 to 1901 and then became Assistant Military Secretary for Indian Affairs in 1902. He was the author of several military manuals and histories. His book on the Tirah Campaign of 1897, written in 1898, discusses both operational and administrative aspects of it.[1] In short, as a newcomer to the War Office, he was ideally suited by career trajectory and temperament to take on his new role. His primary task, as defined by the Esher Committee, was to guide to publication the two halves of what was now called *Field Service Regulations, Parts I and II.*

He was also required to direct military education at the Royal Military College at Sandhurst, the Royal Military Academy at Woolwich, and the Staff College at Camberley. This last was important because Henry Rawlinson, who had worked on *Combined Training* under Hildyard, had just taken over as commandant there. A new Directorate of Military Training, under Major General Frederick Stopford, took on the training of other ranks.[2]

Colonel Wilson and Major Adye became Hutchinson's assistants at Staff Duties, and continued their work updating *Combined Training (provisional) 1902*.[3] Before Hutchinson arrived in England, a committee had been appointed to consider the mechanism by which *Combined Training*, now formally entitled *Field Service Regulations*, should be updated. The origins of this committee are not clear, but Hutchinson took over the chairmanship of it on 28 June 1904. 'It was decided that the writing of the Field Service Regulations could not be satisfactorily undertaken by one Committee, but that each chapter should be written by a Sub-Committee of the branch concerned, with Colonel Adye as an additional member in each case.'[4]

1 Colonel H.D. Hutchinson, *The Campaign in Tirah, 1897–1898* (London: Macmillan & Co., 1898).
2 Dunlop, *Development of the British Army*, pp.225–226. Dunlop says 'General Stopford' had been chairman of the Hildyard Committee in 1902. Brigadier General Frederick Stopford was at Aldershot in 1902.
3 Hart, *Annual Army List, 1905*, pp.3, 120.
4 TNA: WO 237/13: *Recommendations of Committees on Army Matters, 1900–1920* (War Office, London, 1920) number 569, p.136.

Troops in Great Britain and Ireland were still using the 1902 edition in training during 1904; and Hutchinson, Wilson, and Adye were on the staff of that year's autumn manoeuvres directed by Lieutenant General Sir Neville Lyttelton, the new Chief of the General Staff. The scenario set was that an invading force, 1st Corps from Aldershot commanded by Sir John French, was landing in Essex with the cooperation of the Royal Navy and was met by an opposing army, commanded by Major General Wynne, from Eastern Command with instructions to repulse it. French commanded two infantry divisions, each of two infantry brigades. Wynn commanded one division of two infantry brigades. Both had attached artillery, cavalry, and cyclists.

Lyttelton's report points out that 'the broad principles of attack and defence as laid down in *Combined Training* are based on experiences gained in fairly open country' and goes on to question its applicability in the 'close' country with woods and valleys in which the manoeuvres took place. Field Marshal HRH, the Duke of Connaught, Inspector General of the Forces and Umpire-in-Chief disagreed. 'Manoeuvring in such a county, I think, made it clear to all ranks the great value of the principles laid down in Combined Training … and the results of neglecting them. The principles laid down for the conduct of night operations… did not to me appear to have been fully mastered.' He goes on to suggest specific amendments to the umpire's regulations in *Combined Training*. General Lord Methuen, one of his two senior umpires, 'followed, as His Royal Highness desired, the order of the table of contents of the Manual of Combined Training.' He goes on to say that he considered 'that the principles of Combined Training, 1902, have been thoroughly and intelligently studied and applied by the Officers of the Army, both staff and regimental, and have now gone over into the flesh and blood of the Army.' He then, as directed, goes through the manual, section by section, making recommendations for review of specific regulations. The other senior umpire filed a similar report, though with less specificity in following the manual. In view of the size of the exercise, many who went on to serve in the First World War were there, including Sir John French, Walter Congreve, Archibald Murray, and John Du Cane.[5]

If he had not realised it before, Hutchinson appreciated then that the development of *Combined Training* had to be by consensus. According to Gooch, when Hutchinson pointed out to French that his operation orders did not comply with the manual, French took it as a personal insult and spoke his mind.[6] Even at this early date, it was close to alleging military incompetence if one suggested that another officer was not following regulations as laid down. Hutchinson could not just appoint and supervise little committees to draft changes to the document and expect them to be followed by the army. He needed a larger forum, building on the manoeuvres, by which consensus could be seen to be being achieved. He quickly found a solution. Colonel Rawlinson, previously Hildyard's senior assistant working on *Combined Training*, had taken command of the Staff College, and in January 1905, he and Hutchinson jointly hosted a week-long tactical conference under the auspices of Lyttelton, the Chief of the General Staff. Its primary purpose was to address key sections of *Combined Training* in the light of lessons learnt at the manoeuvres and elsewhere, and to stimulate debate. Richard Haking, a future corps commander, lectured on 'Principles of Strategy and Tactics', and on Hutchinson's favourite subject, 'Operation Orders in the Field'. Thompson Capper, who was killed at Loos in 1915, contributed on 'Concentration of Movements by Troops', and 'Expeditions across the Seas', specifically referencing the 1904

5 TNA: WO 279/8: 'Report on Army Manoeuvres, 1904,' pp.8–11, 76–90.
6 Gooch, *Plans of War*, p.67.

manoeuvres. Both were on the staff at the College. Hutchinson himself spoke on the 'General and Administrative Staff', demonstrating his ownership of an updated draft of *FSR, Part II,* though this was still mainly Ellison's project. Rawlinson and James Grierson, now Director of Military Operations, finished the conference with lectures on the colonies, India, and lessons to be learnt from the Russo-Japanese War.

Attending this 1905 conference were representatives from Aldershot, from four regional commands, and from six divisions. Netheravon Cavalry School and Sandhurst were represented by their commanders, Julian Byng and Gerald Kitson, respectively. There were at least six attendees, including Archibald Murray, who went on to reach general rank by 1914 and commanded in France and Belgium.[7] Rawlinson's input into the conference was likely to have been considerable. Prior and Wilson briefly summarise his years at the Staff College. 'All the time, Rawlinson was seeking to divine the lessons to be learned from recent wars and current changes. With the aid of his travels, he pondered on the Russo-Japanese War and the military establishments of Germany and Japan. He continued to keep abreast of developments in artillery and to stress the importance' of machine guns. They do not even mention *FSR* in their book, or Rawlinson's contribution to it.[8] Nor incidentally does Brian Bond mention it in his book on the Staff College.[9] But, according to Christopher Pugsley, Rawlinson's views, those of other military thinkers, and 'lessons from field training and annual manoeuvres were incorporated into written doctrine.'[10]

Henry Wilson observed and took notes at the conference and recorded that he was 'appreciating and manualising', in his diary on the third day. Summing up the conference at the end of the week, he writes that 'it was entirely my idea, carried out entirely on my lines', though the final report is not kind enough to acknowledge it.[11] Over the next few weeks, he, Adye and Hutchinson completed updating *Combined Training 1902,* and *Combined Training, Field Service Regulations, Part I, 1905* was published almost immediately.[12] Roberts, who had been Commander-in-Chief of the Forces until February 1904, had written an effusive foreword to the 1902 edition:

> Success in war cannot be expected unless all ranks have been trained in peace to use their wits. General and Commanding Officers are, therefore, not only to encourage their subordinates in so doing by affording them constant opportunities of acting on their own responsibility, but they will also check all practices which interfere with the free exercise of the judgement, and will break down, by every means in their power, the paralysing habit of an unreasoning and mechanical adherence to the letter of orders and to routine when

7 TNA: WO 33/2747: 'Report of a Conference and Staff Ride as carried out at the Staff College by Senior Officers of the General Staff, January 1905,' pp.3–7.

8 Robin Prior and Trevor Wilson, *Command on the Western Front: The Military Career of Sir Henry Rawlinson 1914 – 1918* (Barnsley: Pen & Sword, 2004 [1992]), p.9.

9 Brian Bond, *The Victorian Army and the Staff College, 1854–1914* (London: Eyre Methuen, 1972), pp.232–252.

10 Christopher Pugsley, 'We have been here before: the Evolution of the Doctrine of Decentralised Command in the British Army 1905–1989', *Occasional Paper No. 9* (Sandhurst: Royal Military Academy, 2011), p.8.

11 IWM: 73/1/2: Diaries of Henry Wilson, entries 5 and 11 January 1905.

12 TNA: WO 123/47: *Army Orders 1905* (London: Harrison & Sons, 1906), January, AO10, p.10.

> serving under active conditions. All works and regulations which have hitherto dealt with the subject contained in this manual have been, or shortly will be, revised. Meanwhile this manual is to be regarded as authoritative on every subject with which it deals.[13]

But there was no longer a Commander-in-Chief who was empowered to order its use by the army in Great Britain and Ireland, or anywhere else. To 'be regarded as authoritative', this new manual needed to be endorsed by the new Army Council, and that endorsement was limited: 'This Manual is issued by order of the Army Council for the guidance of all concerned.'[14] *Field Service Regulations, Part I, Combined Training, 1905* was just another training manual, equal in status to older manuals specific to individual arms. The issue of contradictory advice was not addressed.

Hutchinson was not entirely happy with it anyway. Many of the same criticisms that could be made of the 1902 version still applied. He focused on two specific issues. Henderson had drafted *Combined Training* in 1901, using *Infantry Training 1896* as a template, and then adding paragraphs pertaining to the artillery and cavalry to broaden its scope. For the artillery, this had worked very well. They were being integrated into infantry divisions, and their role in battle was becoming increasingly tightly defined.

But *Combined Training* did not work well for the cavalry. If the role of the cavalry on campaign was to constitute a completely independent advance guard, combination with other arms was not possible. This independence in the advance to a battle is categorically asserted in cavalry training handbooks and accepted in *Combined Training 1905*. In adopting this approach, the cavalry required a commander in total control of his own force, reacting quickly to events without reference to the Commander-in-Chief of the army. The cavalry commander would be giving verbal orders, not necessarily just to immediate subordinates, from the back of his horse. Traditionally, the cavalry commander had minimal staff. This is not the philosophy of *Combined Training*, which mandates both combination with other arms, and a strictly hierarchical operational command structure with the establishment of robust communications down to companies or batteries and back up to the Commander-in-Chief. Part of this problem had arisen because the cavalry hierarchy was not adequately consulted in 1902. Roberts himself had recognised this, and when, in the second half of 1903, the new *Cavalry Training (Provisional)* handbook, published in 1904, was nearing completion, he had, justifiably, complained that 'there is not one word about Artillery or Dismounted Fire' in an early draft.[15] He had asked Wilson to involve himself in its compilation, and although Callwell, in his biography of Wilson, says that he did get involved, it is difficult to find corroborating evidence.[16] The views of Roberts and his allies, and Haig and his, on the role of cavalry, had polarised to such an extent that there was very little middle ground. At least one meeting dissolved into a shouting match. On 25 September 1903, Haig attended a 'meeting of Officers under Presidency of Lord Roberts at War Office re Cavalry Questions. I strongly maintain that the chief method of action is the mounted role. He

13 *Combined Training, (Provisional) 1902* (London: War Office, 1902), p.4.

14 *Combined Training, Field service Regulations, Part I, 1905* (London: War Office, 1905), p.2.

15 Roberts to Kitchener, 24 September 1903, Roberts Papers, 7101/23/122/6, as quoted by Gerard De Groot, *Douglas Haig, 1861-1928* (London: Unwin Hyman, 1988), p.241.

16 Major General Sir C.E. Callwell, *Field-Marshal Sir Henry Wilson Bart., GCB, DSO, His Life and Diaries, Volume 1* Kindle edition (Ontario: Legacy Books, 2021 [London: Cassel and Company, 1927]), p.56.

hotly opposes me.'[17] The whole issue of the role of the cavalry needed addressing in a somewhat calmer atmosphere.

As Spencer Jones points out in his paper on the tactics of the pre-war British Army, the views of Sir Douglas Haig and Sir John French were 'not as divergent from Roberts and his supporters as it initially appeared' in the immediate aftermath of the South African War.[18] French participated in Robert's combined manoeuvres of 1903, and the manoeuvres of 1904, and had the opportunity to discuss the content of *Combined Training* both personally and in his reports. Spencer Jones goes on to suggest that Robert Baden-Powell's views on the importance of cavalry as a reconnaissance force prevailed, at least in Britain, while he was Inspector General of Cavalry from 1903 to 1907.[19]

Hutchinson made a determined effort to involve the cavalry at the 1906 Conference, again under Lyttelton. He asked Byng, who had just finished as commandant of Netheravon Cavalry School, to serve as an assistant. Edmund Allenby, who commanded a cavalry brigade at Aldershot, attended. Brigadier General Michael Rimington, who had commanded an irregular cavalry force in South Africa and now commanded a brigade in Ireland, gave a key address. His paper was on 'Cavalry, its Role in War, and its Training in Peace'. He reveals himself as a strong supporter of the concepts put forward in *Combined Training*, and he made a plea for funding to be allocated to allow greater integration of training with other arms, proposed limitations on its independent deployment, and identified, with scorn, archaic tactics as described in *Cavalry Training*. 'The old system of a cavalry screen, or what General Douglas Haig describes as the pepper box system, is out of date', he boldly declared.[20] Despite this very public criticism of the views of a much senior officer, his suggestions were approved by the conference, without dissent from Byng or Allenby. When *Amendments to Combined Training, Field Service Regulations Part I, 1905*, was published in 1907, the word 'independent', describing the role of the cavalry, is replaced by the word 'protective' in many regulations, and a long section is added to define, and limit, the role of the cavalry on a modern battlefield.[21] This was in defiance of the views of traditional cavalry opinion. Haig also published in 1907. His *Cavalry Studies* bases its tactical advice on nineteenth-century military campaigns. He assumes that the cavalry will act independently as it always had, without formal staffing arrangements. There is no mention of small patrols reporting to a Commander-in-Chief or of cavalry combining with other arms.[22] Haig's views were not the consensus view, or at least not the consensus view of the progressive wing of cavalry opinion in the United Kingdom.

There was a great deal of competition to attend Lyttelton and Hutchinson's second staff conference, which ran from 2 January 1906 for nine days, incorporating a staff ride. But

17 National Library of Scotland (NLS): Haig papers, diary, 25 September 1903, as quoted by De Groot, *Douglas Haig*, p.242.

18 Spencer Jones, 'The Influence of the Boer War (1899–1902) on the Tactical Development of the Regular British Army 1902 – 1914', Thesis, June 2009, University of Wolverhampton, p.147.

19 Spencer Jones, 'Scouting for Soldiers: Reconnaissance and the British Cavalry, 1899–1914', *War in History*, vol.18, no.4 (November 2011), pp.504–508.

20 TNA: WO 279/9: 'Report of a Conference and Staff Ride as carried out at the Staff College by Senior Officers of the General Staff, January 1906', p.35 in pp.31–50.

21 *Amendments to Combined Training, Field Service Regulations Part I, 1905* (London: War Office, 1907), pp.9–12.

22 Maj-Gen Douglas Haig, *Cavalry Studies, Strategical and Tactical* (London: Hugh Rees Ltd, 1907).

Hutchinson limited the numbers, selecting key participants and emphasising the focus of it by issuing every attendee with a copy of *Combined Training 1905* in advance. Charles Monro, commandant of the Musketry School at Hythe, spoke on 'Tactics in Relation to Rifle Fire', generating by far the most spirited debate of the week. Again, some regulations were fine-tuned in *Amendments 1907* as a result. No regulation in *Combined Training* was set in stone. With the Chief of the General Staff as the ultimate arbitrator, amendments could be agreed upon and forwarded to the Army Council for ratification and publication. This process became more formalised as the years passed, but it was at this 1906 conference that Hutchinson settled on the format to ensure that the regulations in *Combined Training*, now *FSR, Part I, 1905*, could be annually re-evaluated and updated with at least a degree of consensus.

Two other lectures at the 1906 conference are significant, given by older men. Hutchinson invited Lieutenant General Edwin Collen and Sir Thomas Holdich, both veterans of the Indian Army, to speak on supply and transport in India, and on the defence of its borders, respectively. *Combined Training* dealt only with war against an organised enemy. There was a gap in its advice, which had been partially filled by Charles Callwell's book, *Small Wars, their Principles and Practices*, which had first been published in 1896, revised in 1899, and was then updated for publication by the War Office as a useful reference in 1906. Callwell was not an easy man, though he was a brilliant one, well-known for his many publications. An artilleryman, he was solitary, dismissive of committees, and he never married. He was commissioned in 1878 and saw action in both India and South Africa before attending the Staff College in 1885. A staff officer thereafter, he served with distinction in the South African War and then, as a colonel, at the War Office in the Adjutant General's department.[23] He certainly knew Ellison since both worked in the mobilisation department in 1903, and they served together on a Battle Honours Committee in 1908, although, slightly bizarrely, he makes almost no reference to him in his biography of Wilson.[24] He knew Hutchinson as well, assisting him on a staff ride in May 1907. He was passed over for promotion that year and left the army in 1909. In *FSR, Part I, Operations*, 1909, a new chapter, 'Warfare against an Uncivilised Enemy' is included, which has no antecedents in either *Combined Training 1905*, or in *Amendments to*, of 1907. All that can be said is that Hutchinson planned his conferences with purpose.

Small Wars was not the only 'officially sanctioned textbook', as Jim Beach describes such publications. *Field Intelligence, Its Principles and Practice* was written by 'Lieutenant Colonel David Henderson, the Director of Military Intelligence [in South Africa] from 1900', and published in 1904. As Beach explains, this describes a permanent intelligence capability, administered centrally, but with regular staff attached to 'the headquarters of every independent formation', and an organised local hierarchy in the field. Beach suggests that Robert Baden-Powell's *Scouting for NCOs and Men* (1899) also influenced the development of intelligence collation by prioritising reconnaissance findings in *FSR, Part I*'s summary in its chapter on information.[25] In an operations handbook, this prioritisation seems logical, but it was far from the final word on the development of intelligence services, the head of which was a director within the War Office.

23 Daniel Whittingham, *Charles E Callwell and the British Way in Warfare* (Cambridge: Cambridge University Press, 2020).

24 Callwell, *Henry Wilson Diaries,* vol.1, p.62; NAM: 8704/35/818/31: *The Lancashire Lad*, February 1938, XXV, p.191.

25 Jim Beach, *Haig's Intelligence: GHQ and the German Army, 1916–1918* (Cambridge: Cambridge University Press, 2015 [2013]) pp.14–17.

Just after the 1906 Conference, there had been a general election, and following this, Richard Haldane was appointed Secretary of State for War. Although a significant event, it had little or no immediate impact on the work on *Combined Training* that Hutchinson and Adye were overseeing. In August 1906, Douglas Haig took up the post of Director of Military Training and, after a few weeks of familiarisation, he recorded in his diaries that he had started working, at Haldane's instigation, on the creation of a Territorial Force.

Before this, Hutchinson directed a supplementary staff ride in May 1906 that further explored cavalry deployment. Wilson and William Robertson, Quartermaster General in 1914, were on the staff, as was Samuel Lomax, who commanded the 1st Division in 1914. In his report on the exercise, Hutchinson again expresses irritation that *Combined Training* was not being followed with respect to operation orders.[26] As Bowman and Connelly put it, 'the General Staff, as created in 1906, did not take a lead in the creation of doctrine, as might have been expected.'[27]

Wilson remained as assistant to Hutchinson until January 1907, when he succeeded Rawlinson at the Staff College. Dunlop says that *Combined Training* continued to be updated annually within the Directorate of Staff Duties as the *Field Service Pocket Book* in 1906 and 1907, and as the *Field Service Book* in 1908, but this is not strictly accurate.[28] These handbooks were a useful precis of a number of manuals, including *Combined Training*, but they were not updatings of it.[29] During these years, Wilson did, however, continue to suggest minor alterations to *Combined Training* (and *FSR, Part II*), in his capacity as commandant at Camberley. He wrote regularly to the Directorate of Staff Duties, and he arranged staff tours, conferences and rides, which addressed tactical issues, leading him to advise on amendments to the draft *FSR* documents held in the directorate, particularly with reference to combined operations with the Royal Navy.[30] Certainly, *FSR, Part I, 1909* is a much-amended version of *Combined Training*, and much longer, with 193 pages of relevant text, against 155, disregarding the indexes in both.[31]

It had been Adye's responsibility since 1904 to collate any amendments to *Combined Training*. Adye headed S.D.2, a sub-section of Hutchinson's directorate, and was responsible for 'writing, revising, and publishing all works and regulations, relating to the Education of Officers.'[32] When Hutchinson retired as Director of Staff Duties (DSD) on 9 November 1907, Haig succeeded him.[33] Adye was promoted to colonel and his brief expanded, though he still had only two assistants. He became responsible for 'strategical and tactical principles of the employment of all

26 TNA: WO 279/512: 'Report on a Staff Ride held in Scotland under the direction of the Director of Staff Duties in May 1906', p.14.
27 Ian Beckett, Timothy Bowman and Mark Connelly, *The British Army and the First World War* (Cambridge: Cambridge University Press, 2017), p.40.
28 Dunlop, *The Development of the British Army*, p.292.
29 *Field Service Pocket Book, 1907* (London: War Office, 1907). An excellent guide to the duties and knowledge base of serving officers.
30 Jeffery, *Field Marshal Sir Henry Wilson*, p.58; See, for instance, TNA: WO 33/2982: 'Naval and Military Tour, carried out in April-May, 1907, Joint Report of the Commandant, Staff College, Camberley, and the Captain, Royal Naval War College, Portsmouth', p.12.
31 *Field Service Regulations, Part I, 1909* (London: War Office, 1909) and *Combined Training, 1905*. The latter has 195 pages, but 33 relate to peacetime training, which is not in *FSR, Part I, 1909*, and six pages of index. *FSR, Part I, 1909,* has 61 pages of index.
32 King, *War Office List, 1905*, p.68.
33 Dunlop, *Development of the British Army*, p.291, states that Haig became Director of Staff Duties in November 1906, an obvious misprint.

arms and services … revision of training books and manuals … works dealing with the education of cadets and officers; [and] co-ordination of all peace and war publications.' According to Evans, 15 routine handbooks were updated that year, which gives some idea of his workload. In addition, he was charged with overseeing the 'war organization of the Empire' and 'comparison with other military powers', which sounds like a job in itself.[34] Recognising this huge workload, Haig discussed with Haldane, and presumably Lyttelton, his immediate superior at the War Office, the responsibilities that he was prepared to offload. Gooch says that 'early in November, Haig discussed with Haldane and Lord Roberts proposals to alter the functions of the Director of Staff Duties (DSD) and Director of Military Training (DMT). The vital meeting took place on 8 November', and as Haig reported in his diary, we agreed 'proposals for rearranging duties in D.S.D. and D.M.T. on the lines that all education (except Staff Coll.) should pass to D.M.T. – and War Organization to go to D.S.D. By this means, D.S.D. will have sufficient officers to work out 'Principles of Employment of Troops' and other fundamental questions which have been hitherto ignored.'[35] As Gerard De Groot points out in his biography, Haig does not elaborate on what the fundamental questions that had been ignored were, and it is difficult to see what he meant.[36] Certainly, Duff Cooper, an earlier biographer, makes little of it. 'Except for office routine, his real work remained the same,' he says.[37] This decision to transfer 'education' to DMT under Brigadier General Murray as its new director had one important consequence. M.T.2, a sub-section of Murray's directorate, took responsibility for 'training and instruction of all arms, arranging manoeuvres', and for 'action on all manoeuvre reports'.[38] Action on manoeuvre reports meant drafting amendments to specific *Combined Training* regulations. Colonel John Du Cane, who had been at the Staff College and was later Artillery Adviser to French in 1914, was appointed to head M.T.2, and, therefore, took on the editorial management of *Combined Training*, under Murray.

The conference of general staff officers in January 1908 was attended by Haig as the new DSD, but, as had been the case with Hutchinson's conferences, it was directed by the Chief of the General Staff, Sir Neville Lyttelton. At this event, Lyttelton is unexpectedly decisive in laying down the agenda, which does not, like previous conferences, have a formal timetable at the beginning. He set aside the first morning to discuss arrangements for training. Given that this was the first session of the conference, and brigadier generals were being asked to justify the use of their training budgets to the titular head of the army, a degree of opacity is only to be expected, but some officers were remarkably candid. Brigadier General William Robertson, representing GHQ at Aldershot, the only corps command, spoke first. 'Commanders of units were left free to employ their own methods, so long as training manuals were followed', he said. 'They were judged entirely on results', and 'the carrying out of Tours, Staff Rides, &c., was left entirely to the Divisional General Staff.' Colonel Henderson then spoke on behalf of the divisions at Aldershot. 'Annual Training is left very much to the units', he says, and 'lack of time prevented … the instruction of individual officers.' Brigadier General Bethune, from Southern Command, had two large fortresses in his sector. 'Headquarters interfered as little as

34 H. Moggridge, *The War Office List and Administrative Directory for the British Army 1908* (London: War Office, 1908), p.48; Evans, 'From Drill to Doctrine', pp.403–405.

35 Gooch, *Plans of War*, pp.112–113.

36 Gerard De Groot, *Douglas Haig*, p.127.

37 Duff Cooper, *Haig* (London: Faber and Faber, 1935), p.116.

38 Moggridge, *The War Office List, 1908*, p.49.

possible', he said, and 'the keynote of their training was decentralization', meaning, presumably, that they did not interfere at all. In contrast, Colonel Haking, representing the 3rd Division in Southern Command, presented an impressively integrated training regime involving all arms, and feedback. This was the only presentation, that morning, which described training that was fit for purpose. Colonel Johnstone, for Eastern Command and the 4th Division, made much of administrative problems and said, amongst other things, that regimental 'officers had not always a clear idea of what they wanted to teach.' Northern and Western Commands, with coastal defence as their main priority, relied almost completely on the initiative and enterprise of their local commanders, the culture in Northern being more proactive than that of Western Command. No specific training document is mentioned at any stage of the proceedings.

To summarise a long and detailed series of reports, the training that any small unit received, anywhere in the country, depended almost entirely on its immediate commander, who was in turn dependent on the resources of time and financial help that more senior officers could, or more often could not, supply.[39] There were additional problems. 'Training in the British Army was complicated by the fact that recruits could be accepted at any time of year', and the constant 'need to find drafts to reinforce unit overseas also eroded training efficiency.'[40] Basic training was a soul-destroying job. All the best-trained men were posted almost immediately to India or elsewhere.

Lyttelton persisted in declaring the agenda for each session over the four days of the conference, and the discussion was very wide-ranging. Gone were formal lectures with little time for discussion. Now, the discussion was the session, and debate was actively encouraged. Manoeuvres was the main topic on day two, staff reorganisation on day three, and the education and training of officers on day four. So far as *Combined Training 1905* and its evolution into *FSR, Part I, 1909* is concerned, there are two significant entries. The first is that Adye's senior administrative assistant, Captain Duncan, confirmed, during the proceedings, that Murray was now responsible for the 'present revise of *Combined Training*', and 'would take up the points raised', confirming that the DMT was now in charge of updating it.[41]

The second point needs to be put into context. The conference occurred just after Haig, apparently without reference to Lyttelton, who nominally directed him, had negotiated with Haldane to reorganise his Staff Duties Directorate. In addition, Haig and Lyttelton had recent history. In October 1907, Haig, as Director of Military Training, organised a staff ride with Lyttelton as overall director. It was a high-profile event with 94 officers present, four of them, not including Lyttelton and Haig, being major generals or above. For whatever reason, Haig had not worked up his own scenario but instead instructed the participating officers to take up the dispositions of opposing forces at the conclusion of Hutchinson's successful ride, also under Lyttelton, in May 1907.[42] With inadequate preparation time, the new participants failed to divine any decisive tactical options in their daily reports and what is more, neither Haig nor Lyttelton in their daily summaries could suggest a way of breaking the deadlock. It was a stalemate. Nor did Haig follow convention in analysing the tactical choices available to commanders with reference to *Combined*

39 TNA: WO 279/18: 'Conference of General Staff Officers at the Staff College, 7th to 10th January 1908 under the direction of the Chief of the General Staff', pp.5–10.
40 Becket, Bowman and Connelly, *The British Army and the First World War,* p.41.
41 TNA: WO 279/18: 'Conference of General Staff Officers, January 1908,' p.43.
42 TNA: WO 279/14: 'Report of a Staff Ride held by Director of Staff Duties under Instructions from the Chief of the General Staff, 27th to 31st May 1907.'

Training, as all directors and umpires had done in military exercises in Britain since 1902. He started off by saying that 'a deep study of military history is the best guide' to the problems raised and peppers his subsequent commentary with learned historical references.[43] Lyttelton tried manfully to keep up, but the effort shows. Feedback at the end of the exercise was blunt. 'The work done … [was not] instructive,' it says. This is not a sentiment expressed in any other staff ride report of the era. To make matters worse, the staff involved had to work 'with only ¼ inch maps', so that it was impossible to define contours, and the assistant directors were not given sufficient clerical help to enable them to get 'the clerical work through.' *Combined Training* lays down detailed guidelines on how rides and manoeuvres should be conducted, including the provision of large-scale maps and adequate clerical help, and these had not been followed. In short, it had been a very public fiasco, exposing even Lyttelton to ridicule.[44] For two reasons then, Lyttelton had reason to want to reassert his authority over his subordinate. So, Lyttelton asking Haig to speak on manoeuvres at this conference, which he manages to do almost without reference to *Combined Training*, and then allowing Haig's views on this, and other subjects, to be robustly challenged at this major conference feels like revenge. There is more.

At the conclusion of the conference, 'the following paper was then read by Major General Haig at the request of [Lyttelton] the Chief of the General Staff.' The content of this prepared statement is surprising, as articulated by Haig: 'Our textbooks and regulations contain the principles of the Art of War which have been authoritatively laid down for the British Army', he somewhat surprisingly asserts, given obvious discrepancies between, for instance, *Combined Training* and *Cavalry Training*. He goes on to say that uniformity of interpretation of the regulations was mandatory and that the only way that the existing regulations could be altered was by consensus at this, or similar, conferences, which would be held annually or by a petition sent up the hierarchy to senior officers. Any officer could propose a change, but if the change was not agreed, he must accept that decision and comply with it. No officer would be allowed to act divisively, and the Chief of the General Staff would ultimately make the decisions. There was presumably a slightly stunned silence after this statement before Lyttelton concluded the conference by congratulating Haig for the clarity of his presentation and saying that this was a way forward with which he completely concurred.[45]

It is difficult to know what to make of this piece of theatre. Haig is saying that neither he nor any other officer had the right to make any change to the regulations as they currently stood. There was a procedure to be followed, and Lyttelton would be the ultimate arbiter. This was at a time when major amendments were being prepared for both parts of *FSR*. If, as seems likely, Lyttelton ordered Haig to read a statement that emanated from the Army Council, he was being sidelined with a vengeance. It seems that Lyttelton was determined to retain the ultimate say in the wording of regulations. The unity presented in this closing drama does not sit happily with the confusion of the current training practice laid bare on the first day of the conference. But Murray is clearly identified as Lyttelton's subordinate as he prepares amendments for approval by the Army Council in his 'revise' of *Combined Training*. Hutchinson retired in November 1907, and it is possible that he submitted his final draft of *FSR, Part I*, to the Army Council

43 TNA: WO 279/17: 'Report of a Staff Ride held by The Chief of the General Staff, 7th to 12th October 1907,' p.13. Also pp.10, 19, 46, 48, 49.
44 TNA: WO 279/17: 'Report of a Staff Ride October 1907,' pp.3, 5, 42, 45, 50.
45 TNA: WO 279/18: 'Conference of General Staff Officers, January 1908,' pp.43, 46–48.

in September 1907, at the same time as he submitted that of *FSR, Part II*, as will be described in the next chapter. The Army Council gave outline approval to *Part II* in December, while accepting that much more work needed to be done on it. It is possible that *Part I* was passed on the nod, with a similar proviso, at the same time. This would explain why Haig (or Lyttelton) was asserting that the 'regulations' were now fixed. The progress of *FSR, Part II*, was also discussed at this conference. How Lyttelton acknowledged Haig's ignorance of its contents is a story that must wait for the next chapter.

What is clear is that neither Haig, in Staff Duties, nor any other officer was allowed to personally influence the still evolving content of *FSR, Part I*. Murray and Du Cane's role in overseeing the final revision of *Combined Training* is confirmed by the proceedings of the January 1909 staff conference which was under the direction of Sir William Nicholson, the new Chief of the General Staff. As in previous years, this conference was not billed as being under the auspices of Staff Duties, and Haig is paired with Major General John Ewart, Director of Military Operations, in the list of attendees. On the first day of this conference, Murray, as Director of Military Training, and his assistant, Du Cane presented a series of major *Part I* regulations or sections for debate. The main agenda items were as follows:

1. Best methods of maintaining communication between attacking infantry and supporting artillery, especially as regards telephonic connection.
2. Tactical methods of handling partially trained troops. What modifications are necessary in the principles applicable to regular troops?
3. Conduct of the infantry fire fight.
4. The framing of operation orders.
5. Should parallel columns be covered by one advanced guard, or should each furnish its own?
6. The size and employment of a general reserve in battle.
7. The frontage of a division; (i) in attack, (ii) in defence.

Fifty-five officers attended. All the army commands in Great Britain and Ireland were represented, as were five regular divisions and 11 of the Territorial Force. There were officers from army headquarters, the Staff College, and a brigadier general representing the Inspector General of the Forces. The Commandant of the Royal Military College was there. Wilson and Rawlinson made significant contributions, as did Robertson (by proxy) and section heads of the Directorate of Military Operations. Not surprisingly, a wide range of views were offered, but this was not, as some authorities have suggested, evidence of a group of amateur officers agreeing to disagree, but rather evidence of a maturing professional army obtaining consensus on how their regulations should be worded. Haig made no personal contribution to the debate, but his assistant at Staff Duties, Colonel Lionel Kiggell, intervened in the discussion of item 5, on advanced guards, and this may well have been at Haig's instigation. He argued that advanced guards should be from one unit, presumably cavalry. But if he was trying to argue, on Haig's behalf, that the principle of an independent cavalry advanced guard be reinstated, his point got lost when other officers went on to discuss brigade advanced guards rather than corps or divisional ones.

Nicholson, Murray, and Du Cane were coordinating a final consensus edit of those sections of *FSR, Part I, Operations*, which were felt to be contentious. *FSR, Part III, Training and Manoeuvre*

Regulations had by this time been split off from *Combined Training* and was to be published as a separate document.[46] After the conference, Murray and Du Cane swiftly incorporated any final amendments approved by Nicholson. The final draft was approved by the Army Council and notice of the formal acceptance and implementation of *Parts I and III* appeared in *Army Orders* in March and May 1909 respectively.[47] The introduction in both these handbooks differs from that in previous versions. 'This Manual is issued by command of the Army Council. It deals with the general principles which govern the leading in war of the Army. The training manuals of the various arms are based on these regulations, which in case of any doubt arising, are the ruling authority.' Compliance with *FSR* was now mandated on all officers. The manual was issued 'by command', in contrast to all training handbooks since 1904, which had been issued for 'guidance'.

Of course, in early 1909, the 'training manuals of the various arms' were by no means compliant in many details. It would be some years before they were all re-written, and arguably, *Cavalry Training*, even in 1914, was not totally compliant. *FSR, Part I*, was not completely prescriptive. Sometimes, it offered choices, and the principle that circumstances might make certain regulations inapplicable was freely accepted. Du Cane, when trying to sum up on item 7, the frontage of a division, opined that 'it will probably be best to give no definite answer and to say that the matter must remain a matter of judgement which must be exercised by the responsible officer.' This pragmatism comes through in the final wording of many regulations.

M.T.2, headed by Du Cane, collated a *Memorandum on Army Training* that was issued to all officers by the Army Council in January 1909 prior to the formal publication of *FSR, Part I*, and its associated *Training and Manoeuvre Regulations*. These 'definitely lay down the system of organization and training for the army, in order to fit it for the task it will be called upon to perform in war.'[48] Again, the pragmatic nature of the training regulations in *Part I* is emphasised. They laid down a 'system' for training. Individual training regulations were not rules for war.

According to Dunlop, *FSR, Part I*, was 'accepted, and ratified, without much discussion', as a routine update of *Combined Training*. 'It was conceived by Colonel Henderson and approved by Lord Esher's Committee. There had been little difficulty … and a general agreement upon Strategical and Tactical principles had grown up.'[49] To summarise in a bit more detail, *FSR, Part I* was sponsored by Lord Roberts, conceived in an early draft by Henderson in 1901, worked on by Ellison, Hildyard, Douglas and others, with later input from Wilson and Rawlinson, and then guided to its final format by Hutchinson, Murray, and Nicholson, supported, at a distance, by Esher and Haldane, through Ellison. Administrative responsibility for its development after 1904 lay with Major General Hutchinson until his retirement in November 1907 and Brigadier General Murray thereafter. Other military thinkers certainly had an input, and there was a great deal of discussion in small committees as arranged by Hutchinson, but their contributions would have been specific, pertaining to individual sections of the final document. It was the above-named officers who developed and guided the military philosophy, which is the core of *FSR, Part I*.

Before proceeding to an analysis of what *Part I* lays down, it is necessary to go back a few years and follow the development of *Part II* because the content of each is inextricably interlinked.

46 TNA: WO 279/25: 'Report of a Conference of General Staff Officers at the Staff College, 18th to 21st January 1909, held under the direction of The Chief of the General Staff,' pp.2–20,41.

47 TNA: WO 123/51: *Army Orders 1909* (March), AO86, p. 29; *Army Orders 1909* (May), AO136, p.12.

48 TNA: WO 231/403: 'Memorandum on Army Training 1908', January 1909.

49 Dunlop, *The Development of the British Army 1899–1914*, p.292.

3

Field Service Regulations, Part II, 1904–1909

The evolution of *Part II* follows a simple path which could be described in perfectly adequate detail in a few pages. However, since the narrative presented in a string of authoritative publications is so inaccurate, it is necessary to address every step in the process in detail. As previously described, a new Army Council was set up in 1904 at the instigation of Esher's Reconstitution Committee, and they vested in Major General H.D. Hutchinson, the new Director of Staff Duties, the responsibility of ensuring that *Field Service Regulations* be published in its entirety. Colonel Walter Adye, in 1908, described how *Part II* was expected to evolve in the light of the Esher recommendations. Given that the new Army Council was to be headed by a new Chief of the General Staff – the post of Commander-in-Chief of the Forces being abolished – and that the Army Council would preside over all branches of the army, including those of the Adjutant General and Quartermaster General, the roles of each of these major offices would need to be redefined. Since *FSR, Part II* was intended to define the responsibilities of staff hierarchies in the field, it would need to recognise these new definitions, respond to them, and then be submitted for ratification and publication by the Army Council. That, in theory, was the plan in 1904. Like many of the recommendations of the Esher committee, the structure to effect reform was set up, but the reforms themselves failed to follow immediately. The first step, setting up a new Directorate of Staff Duties, was achieved, but there was no appetite within the major offices at the War Office to engage with a radical rethink of the army's structure, principally proposed by relatively junior officers. This remained the position all through 1905 and into 1906.[1] It was possibly somewhat naïve of Esher to expect a small administrative directorate in the War Office to publish a document that reformed the 'Organization, Formation and Instruction of the General Staff', even though that was its allocated role in 1905.[2] Hutchinson was a mere major general.

Kelly-Kenny, as Adjutant General in 1903, had recognised that if Ellison's 'Staff Manual', now *Part II*, was to be used on campaign, then the General Staff, at home, in peacetime, had to be reorganised to support it. It is worth repeating how Ellison envisaged his new staff structure being set up because it was this structure that Lord Esher and the other members of the Reconstitution Committee had recommended to the army. For an expeditionary force, Ellison

1 TNA: WO 279/18: *Conference at the Staff College,1908*, Adye on FSR, p.26.
2 King, *The War Office List, 1905*, p.67.

'proposed a system on Wellingtonian lines, whereby the Quartermaster General was head of an operation staff and the Adjutant General was the "organizer" of the army.'[3] 'Intelligence and operations were to be the concern of the Q.M.G, the A.G. stood for discipline, interior economy and the health and well-being of the troops, while maintenance and transportation were to be the responsibility of the Commissary General.'[4] In short, instead of allocating logistical and administrative responsibilities on campaign on an ad hoc basis, *Part II* suggested that responsibilities should be pre-ordained and follow the same basic structure wherever an expeditionary force should be sent.

But it would take more than a recommendation to get the newly appointed Army Council to agree to such a radical concept. The Army Council that Esher and his colleagues had set up in early 1904 was headed by the Secretary of State for War, Hugh Arnold-Forster, on the civilian side, and a new Chief of General Staff, Sir Neville Lyttelton, on the military side. The allocation of jobs in this new structure had been a brutal process and had destabilised the upper echelons of the army. Many senior posts went to men new to their jobs. Herbert Plumer became Quartermaster General, and Sir Charles Douglas became Adjutant General. Many new directors were appointed within what was now the Office of the Chief of the General Staff. As Esher wrote, somewhat ruefully, in April 1906, 'there is not one man on the Army Council, and very few among the Directors at the War Office, who have ever attempted to think about the work they now have to do before they were appointed to their present posts.'[5] 'The truth of the matter', Gooch writes, 'was that the recommendations of Esher's triumvirate were about to suffer the fate of many other reports and commissions, and become submerged in the welter of administrative cross-currents and personality conflicts to which the new War Office was as much prey as the old one had been.'[6] A relatively small, very hierarchical army, where senior officers shouted at junior officers and adopted favourites for patronage, had a febrile atmosphere more in common with a school playground than a debating society. Hutchinson's assistant, Wilson, thrived in this atmosphere, and his diaries record an endless round of meetings, little conspiracies, and optimistic meddling, which created friends and enemies in equal measure but unsurprisingly achieved very little.

Hutchinson, as a relative outsider, found himself involved in the detail of these squabbles, but he also retained perspective. He kept a focus on the development of *FSR, Part II*, which laid out the organisation of staff duties on campaign, the province of the Quartermaster General and Adjutant General, as much as the administration of training, intelligence, and planning, which was directed by the Chief of the General Staff. The main responsibility, within Hutchinson's Directorate, for curating the draft of the '*Staff Manual*', now known as *FSR, Part II*, was vested in Adye. 'From soon after the end of the Boer War, a colonel in the Staff Duties Directorate had been intermittently compiling material for a manual designed to produce a unified staff system', says Anglesey.[7] Or as Duff Cooper put it, 'Colonel Walter Adye in the Staff Duties Directorate had been working on it for years, but the Q.M.G., or someone, always baulked at it coming out.'[8] There is no evidence that Adye was anything more than a diligent secretary,

3 Gooch, *Plans of War,* p.28.
4 NAM: 8704/35/818/61: *The Lancashire Lad*, May 1937, XXII, p.58.
5 Esher Papers, Esher to Lord Knollys, 27 April 1906; quoted in Gooch, *Plans of War*, p.102.
6 Gooch, *Plans of War,* p.65.
7 Anglesey, *History of the British Cavalry*, vol.4, p.386.
8 Cooper, *Haig,* p.106.

but the task of recording drafts and amendments was, as for *Part I*, a very important one, and he deserves the references that are made to him. Even into 1905, Ellison was essentially the only individual contributing to the draft of *Part II*. From July 1904, he headed a department of 'man-power organization', from which he made relevant contributions. He also chaired a 'mobilisation committee' until December 1905.[9] He continued redrafting clauses in *Part II*, right up until publication.

Hutchinson recognised that if *Part II* was to be adopted, he needed to generate a consensus such as he was doing for *Part I*, but he received little political support. Anglesey observes that 'Lyttelton, Chief of the General Staff from 1904 to 1908, gave the project only tepid support.'[10] Arnold-Forster, Secretary of State for War until late 1905, 'presided over an indecisive period during which the definitive responsibilities of senior members of the General Staff were not finalized.' Hutchinson took the opportunity of his first staff conference, under Lyttelton, in January 1905 to present an early draft of *Part II*. He started his lecture by summarising Esher's recommendations:

> The Staff of the Army is now broadly divided into the General Staff and the Administrative Staff, the Administrative Staff being subdivided into two great branches, the Adjutant General's, and the Quartermaster General's… The ruling idea in making this distinction is to set one class of officers free from all cares of routine, so as to devote all their energy to such tasks as collating intelligence, preparing operations and improving training, while other officers do the routine work.[11]

A brief digression. The word staff 'is often used with different meanings.'[12] It is a virtually useless term, unless it is strictly defined every time it is used. At the 1904 manoeuvres, there were directing staff, headquarters staff, umpiring staff, staff to the two competing generals, and miscellaneous staff officers for specific functions such as medical services.[13] Hutchinson, here, distinguishes between General Staff, under Lyttelton, and administrative staff, under the QMG and AG. Other staff were not 'Staff'. Subsequent definitions were issued in Army Orders over the years, but most were widely ignored in general usage.

To return to Hutchinson's presentation – 'This seems like common sense, and continental armies have conducted their wars this way with success', he concludes. The presentation did not go down well. There is no record that Lyttelton even listened to it. Usually, he would be quoted in the discussion, but Hutchinson's last remark, in linking common sense and continental armies, merely confirmed to his audience that the changes were not for them. It was the British Army who were exercising pragmatic common sense, not foreign armies with their complicated structures. Staffing arrangements had always been left to the men on the spot in the British Army, especially on campaign, given the shortage of adequately trained staff officers. There was no appetite in his audience for changing a traditional system that had worked reasonably well in the small wars of the Victorian era.

9 NAM: 8704/35/818/70: *The Lancashire Lad;* February 1938, XXV, 190.
10 Anglesey, *British Cavalry*, vol.4, p.386.
11 TNA: WO 033/2747: 'Report of a Conference and Staff Ride 1905', pp.8–9.
12 TNA: WO106/51: *Staff Manual (Provisional) 1911* (London: War Office 1912), p.15.
13 TNA: WO 279/8: 'Report on Army Manoeuvres, 1904,' pp.8–13.

Hutchinson had to find a stick, not a carrot, if he was to get the army to admit to the necessity for change along the lines of *Part II*, even though Esher had mandated it. Members of the Army Council were the only officers with the power to effect this change, and they were much senior to Hutchinson, an outsider from the Indian Army. Opposition built to Hutchinson's stance. As Dunlop puts it, 'An irritated perception developed that change was being forced on the Quartermaster General and Adjutant General, amongst others, by the Directorate of Staff Duties', an unrelated part of the army. 'The branches of the Adjutant General and Quartermaster General could not see the necessity for a detailed organization of this nature.'[14]

Then, in January 1906, the political landscape changed dramatically. Arthur Balfour's conservative government, which had been in power since 1902, fell, and Henry Campbell-Bannerman became the new liberal Prime Minister. Richard Haldane was one of his most able colleagues and a clear candidate for high office. Haldane was a remarkable man. He was born in Edinburgh in 1856 into a family of high achievers in multiple disciplines: the civil service, medicine, and the arts. He was educated at the Edinburgh Academy and subsequently attended the University of Göttingen, in Germany, to study philosophy. Disdaining Cambridge, he got a first-class degree and multiple prizes at Edinburgh University. He studied law in London, joined chambers at Lincoln's Inn in 1879, and became an MP in 1885. He was a towering intellect, co-translating a philosophical work from German to English at an early age and writing several of his own books on the subject thereafter. He had a spectacular legal career, which made him very rich, and then devoted his life to politics, joining the Privy Council in 1902, primarily advocating educational reforms. It was, therefore, something of a departure when, in late 1905, he accepted the post of Secretary of State for War in the new liberal administration under Campbell-Bannerman, with the brief of curtailing army spending, which was widely felt to be out of control. Almost his first significant act was to appoint Ellison as his personal secretary.

From the start of his tenure, he issued monthly memoranda to the Army Council that brought clarity to the role of the army within the Empire. What was 'obviously required', he wrote in his first memorandum, dated January 1906, was 'a highly organized and well-equipped striking force which can be transported, with the least possible delay, to any part of the world … Behind it, there must be a sufficient supply of troops to maintain it' and to provide for 'home defence.'[15] Over the next few months, Haldane developed his thoughts on the composition of the staff that would organise this force. He also turned his attention to the hotch-potch of Volunteer Forces, Yeomanry and Militia units, which made up the Reserves and Home Defence reinforcements that might be available to the army in times of crisis, proposing a new Territorial Force to replace them. He studied the long reports of Lord Esher's War Office Reconstitution Committee, doubtless with the help of Ellison and Sir Edward Ward, who had been Secretary to the Army Council since its inception. Both had a clear grasp of the details of the recommendations that had been made.

Sir Edward Ward is an important figure. Born in 1853, he was commissioned into the Militia in 1873, but within two years, he was serving with the newly formed Commissariat and Transport Department, which went through a series of reincarnations, becoming the Army Service Corps in 1888. By this time, he held the rank of major and had served in Lord Wolsey's

14 Dunlop, *Development of the British Army*, p.293.

15 TNA: WO 33/3369: Richard Haldane, 'A preliminary memorandum on the present situation, being a rough note for consideration by the Members of the Army Council', 1 January 1906, p.2.

expedition to Khartoum in 1885. As a lieutenant colonel, he was on the Ashanti Expedition of 1895. He sailed to South Africa in 1899, and Lord Roberts rapidly promoted him, in 1900, to Director of Supplies for the South African Field Force, where he enhanced his reputation for efficiency and was knighted. Leaving the army, the next year, he was head-hunted to become a civil servant, being appointed a Permanent Under Secretary at the War Office. He became the Secretary to the Army Council when it was set up in 1904.

As such, he helped Haldane identify the main Esher recommendations that remained outstanding. The first was the failure to establish a General Staff that was capable of taking an expeditionary force to war, and servicing it. The basis of a new structure designed to ensure this was in Hutchinson's, and Ellison's, *FSR Part II*, but this was still a draft directed only at the lower echelons of the army in an expeditionary setting. The second was the failure to address financial, and political, accountability within the army. It was Haldane's genius that he realised that he did not need to address these issues piecemeal. He could incorporate all of them into *FSR*, and then ensure that this was ratified by the Army Council. *FSR, Part II*, could direct and define all the major reforms he envisaged in one document. Hutchinson was suddenly a key figure in Haldane's plans.

It was not long before Haldane had decided on his campaign and launched his first attack. In March 1906, he directed the Army Council to consider a paper, based on recommendations of the Esher committee and written by its own secretary, Sir Edward Ward, on allocating responsibility for army spending on campaign.[16] The council was hardly capable of generating a response, but this did not matter.[17] Haldane landed a second blow by following this up with a request that they decide on the general composition of an administrative staff on campaign. There was much prevarication as the council concentrated on the difficulties of finding competent staff officers, and even whether they should wear distinctive uniforms, but chivvied by Haldane through the summer, they agreed on its general composition in October.[18] Haldane immediately asked which specific responsibilities in the field would be held by the Adjutant General, which by the Quartermaster General, and which by the Commander-in-Chief or others in his General Staff. He received this information, almost on the back of an envelope, in November and attached it to his December memorandum.[19]

Also in November, Haldane issued a memorandum entitled 'The Incidence of Administrative Responsibility in the Field', marked secret, following it up with a 'Further Note on the Administrative System in War', in December. Now, all Haldane's demands were on the table. The memorandum, drafted by Ellison, states that 'the General Officer Commanding-in-Chief [in the field] will be the supreme authority in his command.' It goes on to summarise the proposals for financial oversight of an expeditionary force, as suggested in Ward's paper.[20] The further note states that:

16 NAM: 8704/35/130: Ellison Papers, Sir Edward Ward, 'The Division of Financial Responsibility for Army Expenditure', 31 March 1906.

17 'Minutes of Proceedings and Précis prepared for the Army Council for the Year 1906' records only decisions made in formal monthly meetings where publication was desirable. Council members were asked to respond individually, a tactic Ward used to keep subjects off the formal agenda.

18 TNA: WO 123/48: *Army Orders 1906*, Organization of General Staff, AO233, October 1906, pp.17–21.

19 TNA: WO 33/3379: Richard Haldane, 'Further Note on the Military System, Administrative System in War,' December 1906, p.5.

20 NAM: 8704/35/136: Ellison Papers, Richard Haldane, 'The Incidence of Administrative Responsibility in the Field,' November 1906.

> ...under our Constitution ... Command of the Army has always been, and remains one of the prerogatives of the Crown. The business administration of the Army, in so far as it depends on financial considerations, is vested in the House of Commons. The Commander of troops derives his authority from one of these authorities; the military administrator looks to the other.

The point is not made explicit, but the 'General Officer Commanding,' as supreme commander, was therefore subject to both. Haldane, and doubtless Ellison and Ward, understood that if the Army accepted financial oversight by Parliament, as was required by Esher, that meant political oversight as well.

Haldane also clearly articulated in his December memorandum a concept implicit in the combined *FSR*s: that the mindsets required for operational and administrative command were quite different. 'No one, I think, will dispute the proposition that, in war, two distinct types of men are needed for widely different purposes. At the one extreme stands the fighting man, pure and simple ... At the other is the man charged with administrative duties of a civilian nature, who needs only just so much military knowledge as will enable him to make his work conform to military requirements. These types ... represent, if not different temperaments, at least different circumstance of existence and [need] wholly distinct methods in training and education.'[21]

The military members of the Army Council had long rejected this concept. They considered themselves both fighting men and able administrators. All senior generals enjoyed operational roles, where risk-taking and success resulted in wider responsibility. Traditionally, the most successful administrators won similar rewards by extending the reach of their departments. The administrators on the Army Council had no wish to be tied down to a 'civilian' model. As for detailed financial controls, the concept was foreign to their experience. They repeatedly sent Haldane's documents back, requesting that they be amended.

Ellison and Ward were party to these developments. Haig, who became Director of Military Training in August, describes in his diaries how he was immediately immersed in the detail of reforming the Militia and setting up a new Territorial Force, in compliance with Haldane's thoughts on the subject.[22] He did discuss army finance, according to his diary, in September 1906, but his correspondence with Ellison that year deals exclusively with the composition of the Territorial Force, and there is no mention in his diaries of Haldane's debate with the Army Council.[23] Once Haig started work, it was not until 23 November 1906 that Haldane issued a memorandum documenting the very considerable progress that had been made in defining the 'organization and training of the Territorial Army [sic]' on which he, Haig, and Ellison, were working together.[24] As a confidant of Haldane and Ellison, Haig may well have been briefed on *FSR, Part II*, even though he had no remit over it, and its draft was in limbo during 1906. He

21 TNA: WO 33/3379: Richard Haldane, 'Further Note,' December 1906, p.1 of 4.

22 TNA: WO 33/3369: Memoranda of Haldane, January to May 1906: TNA: WO 33/3373: Richard Haldane, 'Notes on the Organization and Administration of the Military Forces of the United Kingdom,' 14 June 1906.

23 NAM: 8704/35/460: Ellison Papers, Haig to Ellison, 11 September 1906; NAM: 8704/35/461: Ellison Papers, Haig to Ellison 20 September 1906; Cooper, *Haig*, p.109.

24 TNA: CAB 37/85: 'Confidential Memorandum embodying a General Statement on the subject of the Organization and Training of the Territorial Army' 23 November 1906.

almost certainly, even then, appreciated the political importance Ellison and Haldane attached to it. But in 1906, Haig was battling the conservative wing of army opinion in his efforts to reform the Militia. He had nothing to gain by getting involved, and there is no evidence that he did. Meanwhile, the Army Council prevaricated into 1907.

In 1907, Haldane lost patience with the inertia of the military members of the Army Council. He prepared a further detailed memorandum for their April meeting and simultaneously instructed Hutchinson to set up a committee to 'consider the amendment of the draft *Field Services Regulations, Part II (War Administration)*, in accordance with the principles in the memorandum [on administrative responsibility].'[25] Hutchinson immediately forwarded this to the Army Council, with a request as to how to proceed. At their May meeting, the Army Council finally bowed to the pressure. They insisted on a few minor amendments to the memorandum, but, at the same time, set up a subcommittee, under their own auspices, to incorporate the contents of Haldane's memorandum into *FSR, Part II*. Its first meeting would be on 4 June 1907.[26]

Hutchinson surrendered the draft of *Part II* from his Directorate of Staff Duties to the chairman of this subcommittee, Major General F. E. Mulcahy, Director of Ordnance Stores, an Army Council member. Mulcahy immediately coopted Hutchinson and other senior staff officers onto it and appointed a 'working group' that included Adye, Ellison, Brigadier General Clayton of the Quartermaster General's Department, and Colonel Henry Heath, an Assistant Adjutant General, to incorporate Haldane's proposals on command and finance into the first five chapters of the existing draft. The remainder would be edited in line with these changes, once they had been endorsed by the Army Council.[27] The editorial group worked fast, and a new draft of the first five chapters of *FSR, Part II* was submitted to Mulcahy's Committee and approved by it on 30 September 1907.[28]

On 16 October, a meeting of directors, with Haig present as Director of Military Training, reviewed the documentation. Since the new draft 'had been drawn up under the direction of the Army Council', they agreed not to offer an opinion on it.[29] Neither Staff Duties nor any other directorate was responsible for it, and it had nothing to say of relevance to them since it pertained to the organisation and administration of an expeditionary force. It is not clear whether the documentation they reviewed included a major summary, in two parts, of the reforms to be addressed in *Part II* on 'War Systems' and 'Peace Systems.' Written in October 1907, these papers were presented by Adye at the Staff Conference of January 1908.[30]

Hutchinson retired as Director of Staff Duties on 9 November. Haig succeeded him but was not co-opted onto Mulcahy's subcommittee to replace him. The draft of the first five chapters of *Part II* was circulated to Army Council members on 21 November 1907. They approved these

25 TNA: WO 32/4735: 'Field Service Regulations, Amendment of, Committee,' Haldane to Hutchinson, 27 April 1907.
26 TNA: WO 32/4735: Edward Ward, 'Revised Précis no. 334 of Decision Reached at the 90th Army Council Meeting,' May 1907, Francis Mulcahy to Ward, entry in committee notes, 20/2711, p.6.
27 TNA: WO 32/4735: 'Committee notes,' as at April 1908, 20/2711. Mulcahy initially expected Hutchinson to supervise this working group, until it became a sub-committee. Mulcahy to Ward, entry in committee note 8, 10 September 1907.
28 TNA: WO 32/4735: *Field Service Regulations, Part II*, draft, 30 September 1907, chapters I–V.
29 TNA: WO 242/2: *Directors' Meetings 1907* (London: War Office, London, 1908), entry for 16 October 1907, 20/2711.
30 TNA: WO 33/3386: *1907 War System-Peace System Notes*; TNA: WO 279/18: *Conference at the Staff College, 1908*, pp.26-27.

and authorised work to begin on the rest of the document. Adye, Heath, and Ellisons' subcommittee remained under Mulcahy and the Army Council as they continued editing the remainder of *Part II* into 1908.[31] Both the Adjutant General, Sir Charles Douglas, and the Quartermaster General, Sir William Nicholson, members of the Army Council, liaised closely with Mulcahy as the manuscript developed. They studied the drafts and suggested a great number of 'minor' amendments in correspondence with Mulcahy in the first four months of 1908. There are a few submissions by other interested parties, particularly on finance, but none from Haig in the folder pertaining to this time frame.[32]

Neither Haig's diaries nor Ellison's correspondence with him makes any reference to the subcommittee's deliberations during 1907. The first documented association of Haig with *FSR, Part II*, occurs at the January 1908 staff conference, hosted by Lyttelton at the Staff College, and referred to in the last chapter. Duff Cooper and others have made much of an anecdote apparently told after the war by Major General De Pree, who was Haig's nephew. De Pree was at the conference, and he describes how Haig vigorously rebuffed a member of the Army Council who ridiculed the document, though, apart from Lyttelton, there were none present.[33] The anecdote is about the only evidence offered that Haig was involved with *Part II* by early 1908, and is one that grew in the telling if the formal records of the conference are anything to go by. These record that Colonel Adye delivered an update on papers pertaining to *Part II*, but he was a poor speaker and did not explain the proposed new structure with any clarity. Discussion ensued, but nobody in the hall, up to and including Lyttelton, understood the documents being discussed sufficiently well to be authoritative on the detail. Lyttelton regretted that the author of the papers, presumably Ellison, was not present to clarify matters. Haig said, at the end of the discussion, that he thought that the army 'must start with these regulations and give them a trial. If they were found not to work, they could be modified as experience dictated.'[34] This is the guarded opinion of a political supporter, not the knowledgeable enthusiasm of a principal author. This narrative does not support the assertion that Haig was key to the development of *Part II* from this early date, since this was already in the hands of the Army Council at the instigation of Haldane. Dunlop, writing in 1938, says that Haig was 'convinced of the [political] necessity' for *Part II*, and that is surely true.[35] Haig had great respect for both Ellison and Haldane, but just because he worked closely with them on the great project that was the launching of the Territorial Force, there can be no assumption that he played a major role during 1907 in the final editing of either part of *FSR*, as Gooch asserted in 1974, and many others since.[36]

In April 1908, there was a major reshuffle at the War Office. Lyttelton retired as Chief of the General Staff, and Sir William Nicholson took his place. Major General H. Miles became the new Quartermaster General, and Mulcahy left the Army Council.[37] At this point, Adye's

31 TNA: WO 32/4735: Edward Ward, 'Memorandum for Members of Army Council' 3 February 1908.
32 TNA: WO 32/4736: 'Coordination of Expenditure in the Field, 1908–1911'; TNA: WO 32/4735: 'Remarks by the Adjutant general and Quartermaster General on the Draft Field Service Regulations,' 28 January 1908.
33 Cooper, *Haig*, p.107.
34 TNA: WO 279/18: *Conference at the Staff College, 1908*, p.27.
35 Dunlop, *Development of the British Army*, p.292.
36 Gooch, *Plans of War*, pp.113–117.
37 Hart, *Annual Army List, 1907,* pp.3, 3a.

subcommittee became directly answerable to the Army Council, continuing to receive submissions on amendments directly from Douglas, Miles, and others.[38] Ellison resigned as Haldane's secretary and became Director of Organization, under Douglas, as an Assistant Adjutant General. Colonel Heath moved from the Quartermaster General's Department to join the Directorate of Military Training, alongside Du Cane, under Murray. Of the two other major editors of *Part II*, Adye remained based at Staff Duties and Clayton with the Quartermaster General.

In the early months of 1908, Haig was devoting his energy to the Territorial Force, which was launched, with the enthusiastic participation of the King, on 1 April. It was an astonishing achievement to have got the force up and running in well under two years, and, unsurprisingly, he then took a break for several months, pleading sickness, but more likely, he was just exhausted. Meanwhile, Haldane was watching the progress of *Part II*, satisfied that it now incorporated his political objectives but aware that it could still fail if it was not fit for purpose in defining the structure of the staff for the task of mobilising the army and administering an expeditionary force. A pre-publication dress rehearsal was required. When this idea first surfaced is not recorded, but Haldane authorised Sir William Nicholson, Chief of the General Staff, to direct a major exercise in the autumn of 1908. The introduction to its report sets out its terms of reference:

> The Staff Tour was arranged with a special view of affording an exercise in staff duties in the field, particularly with reference to the organization and working of the principal services of maintenance. The staffs were organized in accordance with the draft of the 'Field Service Regulations, Part II,' under consideration at the time; and the staff duties were carried out as laid down in the draft regulations.

It was a big exercise, involving 56 senior officers, all of whom had to familiarise themselves with the detail of the draft *Part II* regulations. Nicholson was one of the few officers who was thoroughly invested in *Part II*. He had been working on its drafting as Quartermaster General on the Army Council since December 1907. Nicholson's principal assistants, Major General Haig, Director of Staff Duties, and Major General C. Heath, Director of Transport, had the task of ensuring that all the participants were familiar with them.[39]

One of Haig's junior assistants at this exercise was a Major F. Maurice. After Haig's death in 1928, Major General Sir Frederick Maurice wrote an appreciation of him in the *British Legion Memorial* edition:

> I first came under the orders of Lord Haig twenty years ago. He was then Director of Staff Duties in the War Office, and one of his chief tasks on which he was engaged was the preparation of the first edition of the Field Service Regulations which defined the principles on which our armies should fight, and how they should be organized. I had been brought in to edit the new regulations … in those days I had almost daily talks with Sir Douglas Haig, as he was then, on the principles which should guide the British Army in a great war.[40]

38 TNA: WO 32/4736: *Army Organization, Draft Field Service regulations, 1908–1909*.

39 TNA: WO 279/22: 'Report on a Staff Tour held by the Chief of the General Staff, 26–30 October 1908,' list of participants and pp.5–11. Note that Major General C. Heath is not the Colonel H. Heath who participated in drafting *Part II*.

40 Major General Sir Frederick Maurice, 'Haig's principles', in *British Legion Memorial Number*, March 1928, pp.244–245.

This statement is unequivocal in stating that Haig worked on 'the preparation' of *FSR* while DSD. However, Maurice only joined Haig at Staff Duties in June 1908, so this is only evidence of Haig's participation after this date. Maurice joined Staff Duties just as the working draft of *Part II* was circulated to all those involved in the upcoming exercise.[41] Haig, as one of 12 'directing staff' headed by Nicholson, would certainly have had to study it hard to prepare himself for briefing the participants. Since Maurice was his assistant for the exercise, it is unsurprising that they discussed it in detail, but it is unlikely that there were any significant changes to the draft in the run-up to this exercise.

John Gooch, in his book, *Plans of War*, describes the exercise as he saw it.

> During the summer Haig and his assistant, Colonel L. E. Kiggell, worked on plans to test FSR (II) on a Staff Ride …The organization and conduct of the Staff Ride reveals the painstaking care that Haig took over his branch and its work. Preliminary war games were held at the War Office on 16 and 21 October to familiarise officers with the problems, and the tour met on 26 October for five days. It was attended by sixty-nine officers from the War Office and the various Commands … The scenario was war between Scotland and Holland on neutral ground … A wide range of problems confronted the players including disembarkation, entraining, accommodation, detraining and concentration and each branch was tested minutely … Questions which arose touched on the relative positions and powers in the field of the Quartermaster General and Inspector General of Communications and Railways and the degree of communication of intentions and information in orders. Lack of coordination was revealed as a major problem and resulted in the congestion of the army for several days.[42]

In short, the exercise degenerated into chaos. Gooch wrongly conflates the testing of 'staff duties in the field' with the remit of the Staff Duties Directorate. He fails to mention Nicholson, who was Director-in-Chief, and does not address his closing the conference by setting out the reasons for the 'lack of coordination'. To go back to the beginning, the report states that Nicholson, as Director-in-Chief, chaired the preliminary briefing conferences, the first on 16 October and the second from 21 to 24 October. No specific officer is named as being allocated the responsibility of ensuring that all participants completely understood the new rules they had to follow. Gooch suggests without any evidence that it was Haig, but it is quite possible that it was his fellow director, Major General C. Heath, Director of Transport and Remounts at the War Office, who was primarily responsible since transport was a major part of the exercise.

The 'lack of coordination' that ensued from early in the exercise suggests that either the regulations were flawed or that the participants had not complied with them. Nicholson wrote the definitive report. In it, there is no reference to his directing staff, and he does not thank them for the efficiency of their work. His first comment on 'Lack of Coordination of Staff Duties' sets the tone for the other major problems he identifies: 'This would not have occurred if the principles laid down in Field Service Regulations had been followed.' Nicholson's report is precise and meticulous, running to 20 main headings. In eight of these, he finds the problem to have been caused by non-compliance with specific regulations. In most of the remainder,

41 Hart, *Annual Army List, 1908*, p.3a.
42 Gooch, *The Plans of War*, pp.113–114.

he acknowledges that the relevant regulations needed some clarification, or tighter definition. Under only one heading did he consider the regulations, as proposed, inadequate, and that was 'instructions for requisitioning in the field', which he required to be rewritten.[43] It is likely that this was quite a traumatic two weeks for the participants, including Murray, who acted, for the purposes of the exercise, as Chief-of-staff of the Army, and Wilson, who acted as Inspector General of Communications and Railways. Other significant participants were Brigadier General Frederick Clayton as QMG, Ellison as AG, and Brigadier General Richard Haking, representing the commanders of the fighting troops.

It was Nicholson, then, who passed judgement, requiring Adye, who had also been on his staff, and his independent committee answerable to the Army Council, to refine the final draft of *Part II* in line with his personal recommendations. In the last months of 1908 and into 1909, Adye's 'Committee on Staff Duties in the Field', was also kept busy adding last minute additions which required wide consultation. For instance, Ellison asked the advice of Haig, as DSD, amongst others, on the issue of 'the enlistment of civilians in war', a query to which Haig responded. The folder is a big one, with many formal proposals and responses pertaining mainly to financial issues. The contributors to the debates are almost exclusively Army Council members, coordinated by Ellison.[44] It certainly cannot be said that Haig had no influence on the final draft of *Part II.* He was close to Haldane, who would have monitored the debate. Adye was employed in his directorate and had the task of amending the draft in line with the comments he received. It was presumably during this period that Maurice found himself 'editing the new regulations', and discussing them with Haig.[45] However, there is no evidence in the available records that Haig was a prime mover in formulating or amending its major principles. His forte was the appreciation of detail.

The military members of the Army Council committed to the publication of *Part II* on 23 December 1908, though revision was still ongoing. 'It has been over five years in the writing!' says Haig in his diary that day. Actually, it was nearer 10. Prior to publication, an Army Training Memorandum was collated within the Directorate of Military Training and issued by the Army Council on 18 January 1909. This required that all participants in staff tours 'make a careful study of [FSR, Part II]', when it came out, 'Only in this way can commanders, staffs and departments of the army be trained to carry out their duties in war.'[46]

FSR, Part II, was published a few months later, being announced in Army Orders of April 1909.[47] There is no doubt that its publication was a significant landmark in the development of the British army. Ian Malcolm Brown, in his masterly *Logistics on the Western Front*, published in 1998, acknowledges its fundamental importance, saying that 'the greatest strength of the British system of organization and administration lay in its inherent simplicity ... Administrative officers [now] knew exactly where they stood in the chain of command and how it had been laid out.'[48]

43 TNA: WO 279/22: 'Report on a Staff Tour, October 1908', pp.6–11.
44 TNA: WO 32/4736: 'Coordination of Expenditure in the Field 1908–1911', correspondence, November 1908 to March 1909.
45 See Major General (Retd) Mungo Melvin, 'Field Service Regulations 1909, Douglas Haig and the "Man on the Spot"', *Records, the Douglas Haig Fellowship's Journal*, Number 27, December 2024, pp.12–15.
46 TNA: WO 231/403: 'Memorandum on Army Training 1908', January 1909, p.8.
47 TNA: WO 123/51: *Army Orders 1909* (April), AO107, p.21.
48 Brown, *British Logistics,* p.44.

The credit for conceiving and subsequently ensuring that there was a political will to develop *FSR, Part II*, goes to Lord Roberts, Ellison, and the Esher Committee. Much of it was drafted by Ellison, but it was modified over many years by Hutchinson and the admirable Colonel Adye before becoming in 1907, as might be expected in view of its importance, the responsibility of the Army Council, at the instigation of Haldane. The final draft was refined by the Army Council and its sub-committees under Haldane's watchful eye and guiding hand. As to Haig, he was a strong political supporter of Ellison and Haldane's vision, and this was significant in smoothing its passage through the wider army. There is no evidence that he participated in defining its major concepts. Once these were agreed, his directorate almost certainly helped edit some sections of the final draft for publication. As Dunlop says, it was 'the powerful backing of the Secretary of State which carried along [its] preparation and final issue.'[49]

49 Dunlop, *Development of the British Army*, p.292.

4

The Principles of Field Service Regulations

FSR laid down, in 1909, for the first time in the history of the British Army, a doctrine which was to be taught to all new officer recruits. All serving officers, up to and including the most senior, were required to observe its provisions. The *FSR* handbooks are long and complex documents, with a combined 29 chapters, not including appendices, indices and *Part III, Training and Manoeuvre Regulations*. All parts are divided into a succession of regulations, none of which stand alone. *FSR, Parts I and II* overlap, so that one part cannot be fully understood without reference to the other. This analysis is with reference to the 1912 edition of *Part I* and the 1913 edition of *Part II* because these are freely available online, and applicable to the British Expeditionary Force that went to war in 1914.[1]

Chapter I of *Part I* is entitled 'The Fighting Troops and their Characteristics'. It is not an introduction in the modern sense of the word, though it has two introductory paragraphs, which are important:

> The principles given in this manual have been evolved by experience as generally applicable to the leading of troops. They are to be regarded by all ranks as authoritative, for their violation, in the post, has often been followed by mishap, if not by disaster. They should be so thoroughly impressed on the mind of every commander that, whenever he has to come to a decision in the field, he instinctively gives them their full weight.[2]

This is repeating what serving officers had already been told in the Army Memorandum issued to all officers a few weeks before publication. *FSR* would 'definitely lay down the system of organization and training for the army, in order to fit it for the task it will be called upon to perform in war.'[3] This first paragraph is intended for all who read the book. It goes on to a second paragraph:

1 *Field Service Regulations, Part I, Operations, 1909, Reprinted with Amendments 1912* (London: General Staff War Office, 1912); *Field Service Regulations, Part II, Organization and Administration, 1909, Reprinted with Amendments 1913* (London: General Staff War Office, 1913).

2 *Field Service Regulations, Part I*, p.13.

3 TNA: WO 231/403: 'Memorandum on Army Training 1908', January 1909.

> Success in war depends more on moral than on physical qualities. Skill cannot compensate for want of courage, energy, and determination; but even high moral qualities may not avail without careful preparation and skilful direction. The development of the necessary moral qualities is therefore the first of the objects to be attained; the next are organization and discipline, which enable those qualities to be controlled and used when required. A further essential is skill in applying the power which the attainment of these objects confers on the troops. The fundamental principles of war are neither very numerous nor in themselves very abstruse, but the application of them is difficult.[4]

This paragraph is an introduction to the rest of the first chapter, which explains, in the simplest possible terms, the difference between troops of the infantry, cavalry, and artillery, their separate tasks in war, and the weapons they use. These paragraphs are very basic and not intended for serving soldiers. This chapter is an introductory lecture on the ethos and structure of the army, intended for officer recruits. It could have been read out on their first day of training – and probably was.

It is sometimes asserted that the first two sentences of this second paragraph were inserted by Haig, or others, as a Clausewitzian clarion call to emphasise the greater importance of moral qualities over methodical preparations in offensive operations. Tim Travers was amongst the first to suggest this, and it is still being repeated.[5] A more prosaic interpretation of this paragraph is that it is instructing young officer cadets that they need verve and dash, which can then be sculpted into military competence by the application of the necessary book learning they are about to undergo.

FSR was adopted to professionalise the Army, and how it did so can be described under five headings, albeit there is much overlap.

The first agenda is to standardise procedures and define entities – basic education. The second agenda is to lay down command structures – to impose a command doctrine. The third agenda is to describe the duties and responsibilities of all officers. The fourth agenda is to lay down fundamental premises (principles) applicable to any force. The fifth agenda is to define principles arising from tactical training for war.

The First Agenda – Basic Education.

FSR lays down procedures and definitions to be used by every officer, imposing uniformity of process and understanding on a diverse army. In 1900, basic training was vague. There was a plethora of official, and unofficial, guidance. Regiments, of all arms, had their own traditions or training methods, and almost their own language in some cases. There was little uniformity in basic training, even at the cadet colleges. *FSR* sought to change this. Every officer in the British Army had to understand definitions, adhere to rules, and perform routine tasks in a standard way. For instance, in Chapter II

4 *Field Service Regulations, Part I*, p.13.

5 Tim Travers, *The Killing Ground, The British Army, the Western Front & Emergence of Modern War, 1900–1918* (Barnsley: Pen & Sword Military Classics, 2009 [reprint: New York: Harper Collins, 1987]), p.92; Tim Travers, 'The Offensive and the Problem of Innovation in British Military Thought 1870–1915', *Journal of Contemporary History*, vol.13 (1978), p.539.

of *Part I*, the different types of order that could be issued are defined, and the correct procedure to be followed in drafting each type of order is laid down. Similar detail applies to how orders should be issued, messages passed, reports framed, and communications set up.[6]

Chapter III goes on to lay down rules for marches, including the pace to be set, and how many men should walk abreast on a road.[7] Chapter IV deals with billets, bivouacs, and camps in equal detail, describing, for instance, the organisation of latrines and how far apart tents should be pitched, or horses picketed. These rules are variously applicable to life in base camp, on the march, in billets and in battle. *FSR, Parts I and II*, between them run to over 400 pages, so many such rules can be identified. The intention was to educate officers in consistent practice. This was a first step towards the professionalisation of the army. An intended consequence was that officers of every rank and speciality could move between units and find the same procedures and training methods being followed wherever they went, enabling speedy integration and a united army. The existence of these rules was designed to create a homogeneous professional officer corps.

The Second Agenda – Command Structures

In 1900, junior officers obeyed orders from any more senior officer. There was no uniformity in the administration of supply and support services. *FSR* defines three quite different command structures in an expeditionary force. The relevance of individual regulations to individual officers is dependent on which command structure they are serving under. The first command structure pertains to administration; the second to operations, that is, the army in the field; and the third to the staff attached to a general's headquarters. All officers required a clear understanding of how the army at war was organised, so that they could fulfil their allocated roles, as defined in the regulations, within this pre-ordained hierarchy.

The Commander-in-Chief (C-in-C) of an expeditionary force was the strategic manager of the force. He was the supreme authority: 'Unity of control is essential to unity of effort. This condition can be ensured only by vesting the supreme authority in one man, the C-in-C of the forces in the field,' though even he is 'subject to such orders as he may from time to time receive from the Government.'[8] The C-in-C's authority is channelled. He only 'exerts his authority over a limited number of subordinates.'[9] Thus he issues significant orders only to his immediate subordinates at the top of his chains of command. These orders must be obeyed.

Administrative Command Structure

FSR lays out a framework allocating administrative responsibility within, and for, an expeditionary force. This command structure is quite consciously modelled on bureaucracies such as existed in government departments or industrial enterprises in civilian life.[10] It defines direc-

6 *Field Service Regulations, Part I*, pp.21–43.
7 *Field Service Regulations, Part I*, pp.47–51.
8 *Field Service Regulations, Part II*, pp.22, 23, 28.
9 *Field Service Regulations, Part II*, p.25.
10 See *Field Service Regulations, Part II*, p.53.

torships and sub-directorships branching out from the very highest level.[11] The very top of this hierarchy is within the General Headquarters (GHQ) of an expeditionary force, with, amongst other senior staff posts, the Quartermaster General directing the transport, quartering, supplies and ordnance of the army, and the Adjutant General, managing the detail of its military organisation, including medical services. Both have responsibilities forward into the fighting force, but much of their work is directed back down the army supply and communication lines to the United Kingdom. This summary is necessarily simplistic, complicated by an intermediate Inspector General of Communications, based outside GHQ, and whose responsibilities were modified in late 1914.[12]

The heads of administrative directorates issue detailed orders direct to the level of implementation. Officers might receive orders from more than one source: 'The officers charged with administrative duties in connection with supplies are responsible both to their respective commanders and to heads of administrative services and departments for the collection and distribution of supplies.'[13] The rank of the officers is immaterial – it is the directorate hierarchy which determines who gives the orders and who actions these orders. The talents required of these officers are firm compliance with defined administrative procedures and meticulous attention to detailed paperwork. No feedback is required, except paper returns, and no debate on the content of orders is encouraged. It is the responsibility of the senior manager, not his sub-directorate commander, to ensure that the content of any order is distributed to those who need to know it. Policy decisions come from the top but may be influenced by *Part I*. For instance, the head of the medical directorate is responsible for allocating sectors for hospitals. This determines where and how the services are to be organised, as laid down in administrative regulations in *Part II*, but the exact location of medical facilities is also addressed in *Part I* in the regulations pertaining to quarters and the maintenance of health and hygiene.[14]

Of necessity, the basic hierarchy laid out in *Part II* evolved with the exponential growth of the complexity and size of the bureaucracy required to sustain the British Expeditionary Force (BEF) in the field. It proved relatively easy to staff this bureaucracy as it expanded, since many jobs in civilian life had similar hierarchies of responsibility. There is little difference between running a civilian factory and running a military repair depot in terms of the management skills required. *FSR* was the document which exactly defined the general responsibilities of the administrative staff and the organisation of the infrastructure. It, and staff manuals based on it, remained the definitive guide for the allocation of administrative responsibility for almost the entire war. There were anomalies, and as will be described, some of its detail proved unworkable in practice and had to be modified when the army went to war in 1914. But the command structure, based on detailed orders directed to the point of implementation, delivered practicality and flexibility. Flexibility within the C-in-C's headquarters is a principle of *FSR*. Discussing war establishments:

> …when a force is to be mobilized for a campaign to be fought under special conditions, certain modifications of organization will become necessary … Should the C-in-C during

11 *Field Service Regulations, Part II*, pp.44–48.
12 See *Field Service Regulations, Part II*, p.32.
13 *Field Service Regulations, Part II*, p.75.
14 *Field Service Regulations, Part II*, pp.117, 122, 124; Field *Service Regulations, Part I*, p.69.

> the course of a campaign consider it necessary to modify the organization of any unit, the amended war establishment of the unit, revised in accordance with his wishes, will be notified to all concerned.[15]

These are amongst the most important clauses in *FSR*. Their activation allowed the expeditionary army to develop and expand.

Operational Command Structure

When at war, in simple terms, the C-in-C puts his divisions, or corps, into position and tells them what to do. He has no further responsibility except to react to events that require a change in a division's position or intent. He, and all senior officers, issue only 'brief and very general instructions' to their immediate subordinates to this effect.[16] The C-in-C issues operation orders to his corps commanders, who issue orders to divisional commanders. 'The basis of the field army organization is the division', every division containing all the military elements that enabled it to fight as a free-standing force.[17] The artillery and engineers were divisional troops. The divisional commander issued orders to brigade commanders, and thence down the command hierarchy. Missing out a level is forbidden. Senior officers may not, in normal circumstances, interfere in the measures a subordinate takes to carry out his orders. 'A subordinate commander issues orders on all matters connected with the efficiency and maintenance of his command for the execution of the duties allotted to him.'[18] Subordinate officers carry out their 'brief' orders, with reference to the regulations.[19]

Every officer in this hierarchy knows the one, and only, immediate superior from whom he accepts operation orders. Senior officers wishing to direct junior officers in a different hierarchy can only request compliance, which should be refused unless the junior is convinced of its necessity and good sense. This structure eliminates the possibility of confusion caused by contradictory orders and ensures 'unity of control' filters down directly from the C-in-C to subordinate units. It is suitable for a well-trained professional army.

Operational Staff Command Structure

Every senior officer from the C-in-C down to brigadier general has an operational staff if he is commanding a fighting unit. *FSR* defines the role of these operational staff succinctly, though under multiple headings. 'An officer of the staff, [even a chief-of-staff] is vested with no military command … He assists a commander … and transmits his orders.'[20] A chief-of-staff signs orders, but these are deemed to have come directly from the general. He has many other responsibilities,

15 *Field Service Regulations, Part II*, pp.26–27.
16 *Field Service Regulations, Part I*, p.27.
17 *Field Service Regulations, Part II*, p.25; see also pp.14–19.
18 *Field Service Regulations, Part II*, p.29.
19 *Field Service Regulations, Part I*, p.28.
20 *Field Service Regulations, Part II*, p.25.

but the most important is that he set up an efficient office.[21] 'Central control … for the attainment of the common objective must be assured.'[22] The 'common objective', described here, is to support the general. 'The commander should rely upon reports which have been … prepared for him by his general staff.'[23] A great deal of information came into a senior headquarters, and the chief-of-staff was ultimately responsible for its receipt, collation, and appropriate dissemination. Reconnaissance information 'should be forwarded without delay to the nearest general staff officer.' 'The means of communication [must be] so organized as to ensure rapid transmission' of information.[24] Such information must be 'communicated with the least possible delay to the commanders for whose benefit it is intended.'[25] This includes reports which monitor the effectiveness of the wider command. Once any information arrives at headquarters, 'systematic arrangements must be made to ensure that every possible source of information is fully utilised, that all information received is immediately transmitted to the proper quarter, and that it is carefully sifted before any conclusions are formed. These are duties of the general staff.'[26] Once the general reaches a decision, 'orders must be issued in sufficient time to enable subordinate commanders to issue and distribute their own orders.'[27] 'If a commander intends to leave the main body of his command for any length of time, he should detail an officer, who should be provided with the necessary staff, to act for him in his absence.'[28] This, for a short absence, would generally be the chief-of-staff, but for longer absences it would be an immediate subordinate. In both cases, the stand-in assumes the authority of the absent general and must act decisively if necessary. The regulations quoted above are not drawn from one chapter, or even one part of *FSR*, but to sum up, an operational headquarters staff is directed rather than commanded. The staff should function in a 'cooperative' way, with intelligent 'delegation of duties.'[29] The desired atmosphere is collegiate, where officers of all ranks cooperate to ensure that the various tasks to support, inform and communicate the intentions of their general are addressed speedily and efficiently.[30]

Summary

There are very clear differences between these three command structures. The administrative command structure is designed to manage, with meticulous efficiency, the provision of services, with detailed orders to the point of implementation. The operational command structure, strictly hierarchical, is designed to provide unity of intent and flexibility in dealing with the uncertainties of war, with brief orders from immediate superiors only. The operational staff command structure is set up to support individual generals. Any officer moving between each of these three distinct hierarchies had to adapt to a new way of working with their colleagues. *FSR* lays down a command doctrine for the army.

21 See *Field Service Regulations, Part II*, pp.38–40 for the duties of the chief-of-staff to the C-in-C.
22 *Field Service Regulations, Part II*, p.24.
23 *Field Service Regulations, Part I*, p.117.
24 *Field Service Regulations, Part I*, p.32.
25 *Field Service Regulations, Part I*, p.124.
26 *Field Service Regulations, Part I*, p.112.
27 *Field Service Regulations, Part I*, p.124.
28 *Field Service Regulations, Part I*, p.21.
29 *Field Service Regulations, Part II*, p.38.
30 See Paul Harris, 'The men who planned the war: A study of the Staff of the British Army on the Western Front 1914–1918', PhD Thesis, King's College London, September 2013, pp.66–73.

The Third Agenda – The Duties and Responsibilities of Officers

To understand his duties and responsibilities on campaign, any officer had to have had a basic education, and he had to know the command arrangements applicable to his post within the wider army. *FSR* defines the duties and responsibilities of every officer of every rank. To refer but briefly to the duties and responsibilities of officers in the administration branches, meticulous adherence to detail is needed, relating to others within management teams, perhaps best summed up by a regulation already partially quoted.

> The essence of all efficient organizations lies in due sub-division of labour and decentralisation of responsibility among subordinates, each individual being given duties which he can perform adequately. At the same time, central control and coordination of subordinate parts for the attainment of the common objective must be assured ... The system must be sufficiently elastic to meet all the varying conditions which may arise, and which are impossible to foresee.[31]

This definition, quite deliberately, could equally apply to any responsive civilian bureaucracy. Administrative officers needed business management skills, financial awareness, and a detailed understanding of their area of expertise, be it, for example, logistics or personnel allocation.

For officers on campaign with the expeditionary force, *FSR* can be described as demanding intelligent soldiering, laying down guidance for the interpretation of the intent of orders and defining the circumstances in which limited variation is allowable. In 1900, junior officers were generally not expected to think. They obeyed orders. Displays of initiative in training were discouraged. 'In the aftermath of the conflict [in South Africa], evidence presented before the Elgin Commission was virtually unanimous in calling for officers and men to be trained to accept greater responsibility and demonstrate more individual initiative.'[32]

Many regulations are therefore directive in requiring an officer to perform various tasks automatically, without specific orders. The key feature is that a cluster of regulations, from different pages or chapters of *FSR*, becomes activated at the point that a junior officer receives a 'brief' operation order from his immediate superior. An officer of any rank receiving an order in the field must, conforming to regulations, know where he is and must already know the location of his immediate commander's headquarters.[33] He must make a swift appreciation of possible enemy threats, ensuring the protection of his unit as he obeys his order.[34] He must decide on the exact details of his deployment, which will be dependent not only on the intent transmitted in his brief order but on his own reconnaissance assessment.[35] He must ensure the concealment of his force.[36] Once he has moved in compliance with his order, he must ensure robust communications back to his commander and forward to any subsidiary units.[37] He must liaise, both with neighbouring units of his own arm and with neighbouring units of other arms,

31 *Field Service Regulations, Part II*, pp.23–24.
32 Jones, 'Tactical Development of the Regular British Army,' p.35.
33 *Field Service Regulations, Part I*, p.21. Specimen reference. Others repeat the requirement.
34 *Field Service Regulations, Part I*, p.87.
35 *Field Service Regulations, Part I*, p.104.
36 *Field Service Regulations, Part I*, p.98.
37 *Field Service Regulations, Part I*, p.109.

to establish boundaries and ensure mutual support. This requires the establishment of lateral communications in varying degrees of formality.[38] The principle that officers accept operation orders only from their immediate superior, and give them only to immediate subordinates, is no barrier to cooperative flexibility at all levels of command, even when there is a disparity in rank between the commanders of two adjoining units. His reconnaissance will also enable him to write 'orders for a possible retreat' which 'should always be thought out beforehand.'[39] He must report or send back any findings or reconnaissance information that may be of interest to his superior. 'Information in war may be obtained … by reconnaissance, from statements of inhabitants, from newspapers'.[40] All this is required while he is establishing an outpost, or preparing a defensive line, in conformity with the intent of his order. No chapter in *FSR* draws together these diverse duties, which would have been 'thoroughly impressed on the mind of every commander' during their training.[41] The well-trained officer needed no orders, after the first, to deploy his men and ensure their concealment, protection and well-being.

This paragraph encapsulates *FSR*. Officers either understood it and adhered to it, or they did not. Looking for adherence to these regulations in war diaries or personal journals informs operational analyses, pertaining to senior generals and junior subalterns alike. Whether one regards these sets of regulations as requiring officers to demonstrate initiative or merely show professionalism, they are completely different from strict control of subordinate officers by way of detailed orders and close supervision. This system of command allowed local tactics to be used to achieve the superior officer's intent at an appropriate level of implementation. The problem of poorly trained or inexperienced officers failing to achieve this level of professionalism is for a future chapter.

There is one set of *FSR* regulations in *Part I*, which is both integral and problematic. It pertains to orders given to units 'at a distance'. It is recognised that significant time might elapse between the issue of a brief order by a senior officer and its receipt by a junior subordinate, and that circumstances might change in that time. All subordinate commanders who are 'at a distance', should, therefore, 'take on themselves, whenever it be necessary, the responsibility of departing from, or of varying the orders they may have received.' Very clear guidelines are given as to how and when varying an order might be desirable. So, if a subordinate officer is out of touch, and obeying old orders, or receiving new orders that do not acknowledge changed circumstances, he is not only allowed but required to modify his orders and to act as he thought his senior officer would want him to. He is held accountable if he does not, and disaster occurs. The regulations recognise the danger of divided intent. 'Should a subordinate find it necessary to depart from an order, he should at once inform the issuer of it, and the commanders of any neighbouring units likely to be affected.'[42]

This was not optional. Again and again in the regulations, the importance of two-way communication, laterally and vertically, in retaining control of an army in the field is reiterated. In practice, modification of orders, on personal initiative, was tightly policed. An enquiry frequently followed the activation of this regulation. The importance of this set of regulations

38 *Field Service Regulations, Part I*, p.109.
39 *Field Service Regulations, Part I*, p.32.
40 *Field Service Regulations, Part I*, p.112.
41 *Field Service Regulations, Part I*, p.13.
42 *Field Service Regulations, Part I*, pp.31–32.

can be overemphasised. By 1909, communications had improved to such an extent that brigade, or even battalion, commanders were seldom out of touch with their immediate superior for long enough to undertake unilateral action without recourse to obtaining updated orders.

The Fourth Agenda – Fundamental Principles Applicable to any Force

FSR makes no attempt to define a doctrine based on the academic study of any one military strategist, be it Henderson, Hamley, Clausewitz, Jomini or Moltke. It is unsurprising that within *FSR* one can find clauses that resonate with one or other of these strategists since the problems of war are eternal, with the possible solutions ever evolving. But *FSR* is a twentieth-century creation. The principle that modern business management methods should be applied to the supply and administration of an army does not bow its head to the past, nor do the principles governing the deployment of a modern army by rail and under aerial observation.

FSR is not traditional. It does not follow the path of defining military or tactical doctrines. Most European armies defined their military doctrine. To train their large armies, senior commanders needed to know in advance the specific manoeuvres their formations would need to undertake. The huge German army, made up mainly of conscripts, trained for a war of manoeuvre, incorporating encirclement. The equally large French army, also mainly conscript, trained for a more defensive war, using a strong advance guard to probe the enemy positions and to identify points of weakness which the main body could attack. They had quite different and clearly defined military doctrines. The small professional British Army did not adopt a specific military doctrine. *FSR* was much more nuanced, incorporating elements of both, giving commanders a choice, based on circumstances.[43] The British Army had to be trained to fight anywhere in the Empire. The war in South Africa had taught them that the strategy needed for success varied according to climate, terrain, and their enemy's strength and dispositions. Hard and fast rules on strategic (and tactical) deployment were seen to be dangerous. *FSR* was as much of an exercise in avoiding disaster as in achieving success. *FSR* laid down principles, the violation of which, 'in the past, has often been followed by mishap, if not by disaster.'[44]

Some major principles are defined with precision within *FSR*, and others are implied by repetition. Many of its principles have already been addressed. The first agenda demanded rigorous basic training for all officers. The second agenda defined appropriate command structures to be followed. The third agenda established an intelligent professional approach by individual officers to the unique problem of every action in war. There are further principles which define the ethos of *FSR*. For such a long and complex document, it is surprisingly easy to itemise these fundamental principles.

By far the most important concept is 'All Arms Combination': 'The full power of an army can be exerted only when all its parts act in close combination.'[45] This statement is emphatically promoted as early as the second page of *Part I*. If all arms combination is not happening, *FSR* is not being followed. The concept of 'all parts' acting 'in close combination' is repeated again and

43 Anon. [L.H.R. Pope-Hennessy], 'The British Army and Modern Conceptions of War', *Edinburgh Review*, vol.213, no.436 (April 1911).
44 *Field Service Regulations, Part I*, p.13.
45 *Field Service Regulations, Part I*, p.14.

again, referring to ever smaller sections of the army. The need for artillery or mounted support should always be considered when posting even the smallest outpost or advance guard.[46] If infantry or cavalry advance, they should never be allowed to outrun their artillery support.[47]

Combination is much more than cooperation. This may appear to be a subtle point, but it is one that it is necessary to consider if one is assessing compliance or otherwise with *FSR*. An artillery barrage that intelligently supports an infantry attack in real time is combination. A fixed-timed barrage that is prolonged beyond the initial assault, and which fails to respond to the needs of the infantry in easing hold-ups and repelling counterattacks, is mere cooperation and not compliant with *FSR*.

All arms combination is fundamental to *FSR*. However, the concept of a cavalry 'advanced guard', sometimes disdaining even artillery support, was deeply ingrained in the psyche of some senior cavalry generals. The idea of a 'break-through' with unsupported infantry or cavalry exploiting a break in enemy lines was powerful and had been a feature of many notable victories from ancient times. Its impossibility, in the light of the damage that even a single machine gun, let alone a single field battery, could inflict on such a force, was not accepted by all pre-war generals who went on to command on the Western Front. But any battle plan that pitched infantry into attack with insufficient artillery support, or any plan which envisaged a break-through by unsupported infantry or cavalry, was not compliant with *FSR*.

Weaponry development imposed increasing complexity on the interpretation of this concept during the war. Machine guns could, in certain circumstances, replace massed infantry or be used as part of an artillery barrage. Trench mortars and the like might be defined as light artillery. Tanks, when they arrived, were analogous to mobile artillery or slow armoured cavalry. However, the basic concept of all arms combination remained central to the debate on how they should be used.

Another fundamental principle was that an army should retain an offensive spirit, even in defensive operations. The need for this is repeatedly emphasised. 'Every commander who offers battle must be determined to assume the offensive sooner or later.'[48] In the context of the small wars of the late Victorian era, this was an unchanged message. It can be regarded as a historical imperative, but it was not accepted that other core concepts could be ignored in its name, particularly in a great continental war against overwhelming odds. *FSR* demanded that risks be assessed before actions are taken. *FSR* was specifically written with the aim of avoiding 'mishap' or 'disaster.' In an early stage of development, *Part I* was accused of being overcautious.[49] The duties laid down on senior officers to analyse intelligence and carefully consider orders before issuing them, the responsibility laid on all officers to ensure the protection of their men, and the principles to be described in the fifth agenda all served, in theory, to prevent excessive impetuosity.

46 *Field Service Regulations, Part I*, pp.94, 101–102.
47 *Field Service Regulations, Part I*, pp.51, 137–140.
48 *Field Service Regulations, Part I*, p.126.
49 NAM: 8704/35/818/57: *Ellison papers*, The Lancashire Lad; *Journal of the Loyal Regiment*, February 1937, Section XXI, p.13. Ellison in conversation with Lt Col William Balck, of the German Imperial Staff College.

The Fifth Agenda – Principles Arising from Tactical Training for War

It is hard to avoid the use of the word principles in analysing *FSR*. It is a word used very freely both in the documents and in discussions about them. Adhering to principles, rather than the detail of some regulations, was intended to enable lateral thinking and intelligence to be used in solving the problems of war. But the word is very imprecise. The 'General principles of…', which introduces many chapters or sections in both parts of *FSR*, are not 'the fundamental principles' referred to in the first paragraph of *Part I*. 'General principles' usually define terms and can be classified as basic education. Many historians have examined single regulations and asserted that the text of that regulation constitutes a tactical principle. That is missing the point of the whole document. *FSR* accepts that war is a very uncertain science, with no one successful way of prosecuting it. Given the almost infinite variations that might present themselves in even the smallest skirmish, laying down rules was a recipe for disaster. It was far better to suggest principles for the avoidance of disaster than to prescribe rules to obtain success.

In 1900, the tactics derived from drill manuals were demonstrably archaic. Many units learnt appropriate tactics for the small wars of the Victorian era, including the South African War, on campaign, but their learning was not uniform. *FSR* changed that, but it presented tactical training ideas, not a tactical doctrine. The principles arising from tactical training were dependent on all the principles so far described. The training regulations were to be followed in training exercises, staff rides and manoeuvres, but two units could perform the same tactical exercise quite differently, both in compliance with *FSR*. There are concepts which were forcefully presented as best practice, albeit remarkably few of them. The regulations were pragmatic, accepting that training exercises could never fully simulate war conditions. Many of its detailed training ideas were outdated almost before they were printed, serving their purpose by stimulating debate. Little is achieved by focusing on the detail of contentious regulations, relating to subjects like firepower, citing contemporary differences of opinion at the annual amendment conference. It is the core concepts, or principles, which matter, particularly those which were found applicable to war on the Western Front.

One such is deployment in depth, which is addressed repeatedly in different contexts. In times of war, every unit at rest is required to set up outposts to protect against surprise. If there is no expectation that the enemy will be encountered, these outposts will be defensive, meaning they will be small and often not of all arms. Their positions are not to be held in the face of a sustained attack. They are there to give warning and to hold up the enemy, if necessary, giving time for the main body behind them to deploy appropriately. Hopeless defensive positions should not be held without very good reason.[50] If the unit is participating in an advance towards the enemy, its outposts in that direction will be offensive. These are larger than defensive outposts and will invariably be of all arms since they will constitute the vanguard for the next day's advance. Every force planning concerted action, be it offensive or defensive, is required to maintain a reserve close at hand. That reserve should generally be larger in attack than in defence. There is no one section which draws together this set of regulations. *FSR* recommends the principles of defence in depth, and close coordination of advance guard, main body and reserves in attack.[51] This can

50 *Field Service Regulations, Part I*, pp.98–111, 142.
51 *Field Service Regulations, Part I*, pp.128–131.

be extended to deployment in width as well. Flank guards were mandatory for larger bodies of men.

Trench warfare did not alter the relevance of these regulations. If a commander places all his machine guns and most of his men in the front line, he is breaching *FSR*. If a hopeless piece of trench is being held just for the sake of it, as in a salient enfiladed from all sides, or if there is no prepared second line of defence, *FSR* is being breached.[52] The only exception to this principle of defence in depth with a reserve poised to counterattack if necessary is in the defence of fortifications, fixed or improvised. If it is the latter, as when new trench lines are being established, these should be converted into in-depth defences as soon as resources allow.[53]

The principle of an organised retirement is particularly well developed in *FSR*. The officer commanding the artillery may not be the most senior on the battlefield, but it is he who will control the rhythm of this manoeuvre. He selects a suitable spot with a good field of fire for a battery. Half the available infantry, covered by cavalry, retire to the line in front of his guns. The other half of the infantry march on some miles, where a second battery has set up to shelter them. The enemy marching up the road behind the infantry are forced by artillery fire to disperse into an order of battle, whereupon the forward infantry, together with the battery, retire back, again covered by cavalry, and through the new line of rearguard defence.[54] It is no coincidence that adherence to *FSR* principles was much closer in defensive, as opposed to offensive, battles in the war on the Western Front. The principle is clear and not difficult to perform if discipline is maintained.

Summary

The brevity of this section is deliberate. It is not difficult to think of more manoeuvre regulations which define principles, especially in the direction of larger forces, and it is right and proper that these be debated, as they were by senior regular officers at the time. When the war started, the relevance of every training regulation could be assessed. Most were judged to be sound. The advent of static warfare rendered some of the regulations redundant while making principles referrable to front-line communications and liaison of much more significance than they were on a battlefield where line-of-sight contact could be anticipated. But this is a short guide. More complex *FSR* principles relating to responsibilities, command, and deployment will be discussed later in this book.

Important political and financial principles are laid down, mostly in *FSR, Part II*. Reference has already been made to the requirement that a Commander-in-Chief must adhere to political guidelines as laid down by the government in his prosecution of the war. The Treasury was involved in the drafting of *Part II*, and there are a series of regulations which set out how money should be spent, and then accounted for during a campaign. General financial principles are laid down in Chapter III and developed in later chapters.[55] There is consideration of the legal position of belligerents in friendly or hostile countries, and reference is made to the Hague Convention of 1907.[56]

52 *Field Service Regulations, Part I*, p.145.
53 *Field Service Regulations, Part I*, pp.170–171.
54 *Field Service Regulations, Part I*, pp.95–97.
55 *Field Service Regulations, Part II*, see pp.43–44, 48, & Ch.VI.
56 *Field Service Regulations, Part I*, p.66.

But the main intent of this chapter is to suggest that the introduction of uniform procedures covering all basic tasks, the definition of different command structures, depending on allocated responsibilities, and a clear description of the duties of all officers, up to and including the Commander-in-Chief, make up the core of the *FSR* doctrine. It is easy to forget that these were all new concepts and that the mindset of an army without a doctrine is completely different from one with one. The change imposed on the army between 1905 and 1912 affected every aspect of it. Superimpose all arms combination and deployment in depth as defining principles on these three elements, and the detail of the regulations drafted purely to guide training becomes almost irrelevant in any assessment of *FSR*'s impact on the British Army of 1914.

5

Field Services Regulations for Cadets and Young Officers, 1909–1912

The following chapters follow the implementation of *FSR* from 1909 to 1912. These years were typical in that political and personal crises intermittently erupted, occupying the attention of those personally affected. These crises were important and significant. But, behind the scenes, the British Army, particularly in Great Britain and Ireland, was being quietly reformed and professionalised out of all recognition. Spring 1909, the date of publication of *FSR*, and the moment at which compliance with it became mandatory for all British Army officers, is a date that should be imprinted on every student of the pre-war period. Quotes and anecdotes, pertaining to the army, its ethos, and professionalism, prior to this date, refer to a quite different entity than those from after this date. It should be borne in mind, too, that no serving officer after 1909 who valued his career prospects would criticise more than the detail of specific regulations and that all officers understood that accusing a colleague of failing to observe *FSR* was tantamount to saying that he was unfit to be in the army. The absence of specific references to the term *FSR* in correspondence is understandable in this context.

If the *FSR* doctrine was going to be imposed on the British Army, then its message had to be disseminated widely and with conviction, not only to all officers but to all potential officers. *FSR* had to be taught, and, in that context, it is unsurprising that the first chapter of *Part I* is so basic that it could have been, and probably was, taken from notes for an introductory lecture to new cadets. There were two great institutions, Sandhurst Royal Military College (RMC), which trained infantry and cavalry officer cadets, and Woolwich Royal Military Academy (RMA), which, in theory, trained cadets solely for the artillery and engineers, though it did accommodate officers from other branches from time to time. The intake of both was comprised mainly of youngsters straight from school. Both institutions had had a vigorous shake-up in 1903 following severe criticism in a series of reports after the South African War. Most pertinent was the Akers-Douglas Report of 1902, tasked 'to Consider the Education and Training of Officers of the Army.' This recommended an immediate and independent review of current training establishments, further suggesting that 'the supervision and control of Military Education throughout the Army should be entrusted to a General Officer.'[1] That general officer was first Hildyard, Director of Education and Planning in 1903, then Hutchinson, Director of Staff Duties from 1904, and finally, for the purposes of this

1 Akers-Douglas Report, 'Education and Training', p.38.

section, Murray, Director of Military Training from late 1907. Both institutions were, therefore, ultimately governed by men who were well-versed in what *FSR* meant and who understood its educational requirements.

Both institutions were aware of the *FSR* debates from an early date. Colonel Gerald Kitson, commandant at Sandhurst, attended Hutchinson's staff conference in 1905, and Colonel N. Bernardiston, a later commandant, attended the 1909 staff conference at which the last amendments to *FSR, Part I* were agreed. In 1907, the main textbooks for both the RMC and RMA were *Combined Training, FSR Part I* (1905), *Infantry Training* (1905), and *Cavalry Training* (1907). There is a letter in the Sandhurst archive, dated May 1907, ordering copies of the newly published *Amendments to Combined Training* (1905),[2] and another dated October 1909, returning obsolete manuals and asking for a refund or provision of an equal value in up-to-date copies of *FSR, Part I.*[3]

Unfortunately, as Duncan says in his 2016 thesis on 'The Military Education of Junior Officers in the Edwardian Army', much, but not all, of the archives of these two cadet institutions were lost in the late 1940s.[4] Some copies of exam papers from both institutions have survived, as has some miscellaneous correspondence pertaining to Sandhurst. The curriculum changes that occurred in 1909 can be deduced from the reading lists, exam papers, and associated notes on mark allocations for different topics.[5] Of most interest are the exams on tactics set for both institutions between 1907 and 1912, since these so clearly reflect the change in reading lists which occurred on the adoption of *FSR* as the primary text in 1909. Prior to 1909, the questions are generally open. For example, the RMC Sandhurst tactics exam, December 1907, included the following questions:

1. How are the mounted troops with an army in the field divided? Explain the nature of the duties of these various bodies.
2. Describe the action of an advanced guard of all arms on coming into contact with an enemy in position.
3. By what agencies is the reconnaissance before attack effected, and upon what points is information particularly desired?
4. Enumerate the principles governing the distribution of the three arms in attack.

The given answer to these questions might be expected to reflect whether the student was training for the infantry, cavalry, or artillery. The brighter cadet might incorporate historical precedent into his answers. Question 5 asked, 'Explain the necessity for cooperation between the three arms. Why should all officers make themselves thoroughly acquainted with the principles governing the action of arms other than their own.' The ethos, even the tactical advice, given in the handbooks of the various arms, was not consistent, and that was a fact of life recognised in the training of cadets.

The RMA Woolwich tactics exam of December 1907 included:

2 *Amendments to Combined Training, Field Service Regulations Part I, 1905, 1907*, pp.9–12.
3 Sandhurst Collection Archives (SCA): Box 90, correspondence with War Office.
4 Andrew George Duncan, 'The Military Education of Junior Officers in the Edwardian Army', Ph.D. thesis, Birmingham University, 2016.
5 SCA: box 142, pre-war exam papers. RMA and RMC, 1907–1911.

An enemy is invading, and a battalion strength detachment, supported by a squadron of cavalry and two field guns is reported approaching. You are detached to deal with it, and billet for the night as the enemy force takes up a defensive position.

1. What outposts will you allot for the night? Show in the map their position.
2. Discuss the strength or weakness of the enemy's position and explain how you will endeavour to defeat him.
3. Write your orders for the attack.
4. Assuming your attack is successful and that the enemy is driven from its position, explain as far as can be anticipated, the action of your battery, i.e. the successive positions it will take up, whether its fire will be direct or indirect, and its successive targets.
5. Having regard to the nature of the country, which would you prefer to have under your command for this expedition – the two squadrons of cavalry, or an equal number of cyclists? State your reasons.'

The way operation orders were framed was not standard in 1907, albeit *Combined Training* described best practice. Indirect artillery fire, controlled by an observation officer, is assumed to be a routine skill. Even as early as 1907, the value of cyclists, instead of cavalry, in a skirmish was being debated.

In 1909, *FSR* was published, with the note that 'the training manuals of the various arms are based on [*FSR*], which, in case of any doubt arising, are the ruling authority.'[6] The problem was that in 1909, the training manuals of the various arms were not based on *FSR*. This, at a stroke, made it difficult to include single-arm training manuals in the curriculum at cadet colleges since they were not compliant. *Infantry Training* was not updated until 1911, *Cavalry Training* and *Field Artillery Training* not until 1912. All three had almost dropped off the RMC syllabus reading list for early 1912. Paradoxically, this made tactics exams easier.

The July 1911 RMC Sandhurst exam used the same scenario as for the RMA exam of 1907.

1. What measures do you take for the protection of your force while billeting? Mark on the map the positions of all troops placed on outpost duty. In Field Service Regulations it is laid down that a Commander, when halting, should first decide on his dispositions in case of attack, and then arrange the quartering of his Command and the position of his outposts accordingly. Explain how you have applied this principle.
2. A Cavalry patrol detects the approach of the enemy. Show on the map in red the manner in which you would now dispose your troops and explain your plan of action.
3. The enemy's artillery in action are in covered positions. As an artillery subaltern seeking to exactly locate these guns, mark on the map how you would approach and where you would expect to see these guns. [Only indirect fire is possible from covered positions.]
4. Mark on the map the site on which the enemy would have been likely to bring his guns into action if this fight had taken place in 1870, and explain why covered positions were not used in those days.

6 *Field Service Regulations, Part I, Operations, 1909*; *Field Service Regulations, Part II, Organization and Administration, 1909.*

Question 1 invokes *FSR* as best practice, a strong hint as to what is required thereafter. Question 3, in a Sandhurst exam, suggests that the candidate would have had the same basic tactical instruction as an artillery subaltern at Woolwich.

The RMA Woolwich tactics exam of December 1910:

1. a) Describe in general terms the object and uses of a tactical advanced guard. b) Of what arms is a tactical advanced guard usually composed.
2. With reference to outposts – a) What do you understand by a piquet? b) What are the duties of a piquet commander?
3. Bearing in mind that 'the principles of the employment of Artillery in the battle is that the greater the difficulties of the Infantry the closer must be the support of the Artillery', [a direct quote from *FSR*] explain the tactics of Artillery in the attack from the commencement of the action down to the final Infantry assault.
4. Night operations may be classified as night marches, night advances and night attacks. Describe briefly the circumstances under which these different kind of operations may be advantageously used.
5. In mountain warfare against an uncivilised enemy explain how retirements are usually carried out with special reference to the rearguard.
6. a) What do you understand by 'Standing Orders', 'Operation Orders', and 'Routine Orders'? b) Describe what is usually contained in Operation Orders.

All these questions can be answered almost verbatim by quoting *FSR, Part I.*[7] There is a right answer to every question. This last exam is unimaginative, but it was still 1910. *FSR* would have been introduced just as the cadets joined the academy. However, combining the two sets of papers gives an overview of what was being taught. All cadets, regardless of career destination, are learning the same basic procedures, as laid down in *Part I.* They would all have studied Chapter IV, for instance, which lays down regulations for billets, and Chapter V, on outposts – for the first two Sandhurst questions. Almost any chapter in *Part I* might be tested, just in this one exam.

But it is not just book learning that is demanded. In question 1 of the Sandhurst paper, the cadet is required to set up an outpost. His brief order tells him it should be an offensive outpost. He is an officer trained under *FSR*. He is expected to know how to do this. But then he has to react to changing circumstances. Question 2 of the same paper assumes that he has set up an offensive outpost, but facing the prospect of attack, he needs to convert it to a defensive one. He must demonstrate, if not initiative, then at least flexibility of thought. Examiners at Woolwich and Sandhurst were not afraid to address the most challenging complexities of *FSR*. In the December 1911 RMA exam: 'During the course of an operation a subordinate commander receives an order which, in his judgement, is unsuited to the circumstances in which he finds himself. The officer who issued the order is at a distance and there is not time to refer to him

7 *Field Service Regulations, Part I;* Successively, see Chapter V, 'Tactical Advanced Guard' pp.91–94; Chapter V, 'Piquets' pp.105–107; Chapter VII, p.128; Chapter IX, 'Night Operations' pp.176–190; Chapter X 'Mountain Warfare' pp.191–199; Chapter II, 'Orders' pp.25–33. Note that all page numbers refer to the revised edition of 1912.

for a reconsideration of the order. What action should the subordinate take?'[8] The answer is that officers in this situation should, with relevant provisos, 'take on themselves, whenever it be necessary, the responsibility of departing from, or of varying the orders they may have received.'[9] The question goes on. 'Give the reasons for your answer.' This is 'advanced' *FSR*.

The implementation of *FSR* at Sandhurst and Woolwich affected the curriculum across the board. Tactics accounted for about 40 percent of the marks in final exams, when combined with military engineering and map reading, both before and after 1909. Knowledge of sanitation (RMC) comprised less than one percent of the marks in 1907, but nearer five percent in 1912, reflecting the emphasis put on the subject in *Part I*, Chapter IV. Military Administration (*FSR, Part II*) was taught, which, together with Law, made up 15 percent. Practical skills, such as drill, musketry, and horse riding, comprise another 20 percent. Languages, geography, and military history make up the balance. The syllabus at RMA Woolwich included all the above, with additional exams in advanced mathematics, chemistry, and physics, and their application to guns, ammunition, and field engineering. Successful graduates received a remarkably complete education.[10]

It is reasonable to ask if there was a difference in the degree to which the two great cadet institutions accepted the absolute authority of *FSR*. Cadets at Woolwich were required to be proficient in mathematics and the sciences. One hesitates to generalise, but they might perhaps be more content to accept and happily implement rules pertaining to their military lives. Those at Sandhurst would have been a different cohort, more free-thinking perhaps, albeit generally from the same schools. Some may have been older, coming from university, some more entitled, some perhaps of more limited educational achievements. This dichotomy is, to some extent, reflected in the exam papers quoted. It is unfortunate that exam papers into 1912 and thereafter have been lost. Consideration of this must wait for the next chapter on older officers in service and how they coped under the new regime.

Not all officers gazetted into the British Army were educated through Sandhurst or Woolwich. A small proportion came through the Territorial Force or University Officer Training Corps (OTC). These potential officers had to demonstrate 'efficiency' by satisfactorily attending events and parades over two years and then pass a two-stage exam to achieve Certificate 'B'. Unfortunately, secondary works on the subject do not address the development of their syllabus and their programme of work on the implementation of *FSR*.[11] But examination of the records of Oxford University OTC in 1912 reveals that *FSR* was the primary text on which these exams were based. The revision course of lectures in October and November that year for Certificate 'A' takes *FSR, Part I*, one chapter at a time, through the four weeks of the course. A crammer, written by Captain Legge, ex-Prince of Wales, Leinster Regiment, as early as 1909, similarly takes Certificate 'A' students through *Part I*.[12] Certificate 'B' also had a revision course, which incorporated *FSR* principles. After passing their exams, these officers had to attend a three-week attachment with a regular battalion and be signed off as a suitable officer by the officer

8 SCA: box 142, pre-war exam papers. RMA and RMC, 1907–1911.
9 *Field Service Regulations, Part I*, pp.31–32.
10 SCA: box 142, curricula 1907 and 1912.
11 For instance, Edward M. Spiers, 'University Officers' Training Corps and the First World War', *Council of Military Education Committees of the United Kingdom*, Occasional Paper no.4, 2014.
12 R. F. Legge, *The Officers' Training Corps Examiner for Certificate 'A'* (London: Gale and Polden, 1909).

Harrow Corps at Stanmore May 1915. (Author's collection)

commanding.[13] W. Mitchinson in his *Territorial Force at War* records that 'units relied on *Field Service Regulations* for guidance and training for offensive and defence operations.'[14]

By the end of 1909, therefore, all officer recruits were receiving training based on *FSR*, and intended to prepare them for military life. The newly commissioned officers of 1909 to 1911 were somewhat handicapped in their education by the defects in the handbooks pertaining to individual arms, but these were largely rectified by 1912, when they had been revised, theoretically in line with *FSR*. Cadets commissioned after 1911, having been grounded in the principles of *FSR*, could use them to develop their military education. Once posted to battalions, batteries, or other units, the innate conservatism of the army might have made early graduates feel that what they had been taught was not completely relevant to their new work. But the cascade of new subalterns arriving, year on year, well-versed in *FSR*, and striving to impress, would have piled pressure on their immediate commanders to themselves adopt the new regulations in their entirety. Peer pressure from below.

Although not catering for cadets and young officers, the Staff College as an educational establishment fits into this chapter. William Robertson took over from Henry Wilson as commandant of the Staff College on 1 August 1910. Brian Bond, in his book on *The Staff College*, describes how he revolutionised its ethos: 'Where Henry Wilson had delighted in stimulating the student's imagination by the discussion of broad strategic and political issues, Robertson was sternly professional and non-political.'[15] Sheffield says that Robertson, as the new Staff College commandant, instructed 'students to act in accordance with circumstances and the spirit of

13 Bodleian Library, Oxford, OT 5/1/1: 'Officer Training Corps, Oxford University Contingent Part I Orders Oct 1912 – June 1913.'

14 K. Mitchinson, *The Territorial Force at War 1914 – 1916* (Palgrave Macmillan, Kindle edition [2014]) 'Pre-war Quest for Efficiency.'

15 Bond, *The Staff College*, pp.278–281.

Field Service Regulations.'[16] Ian Malcolm Brown quotes a member of Robertson's staff: 'The weakness of the instruction generally (or at least it seemed so to me,) was the tendency to take the regulations and official manuals as Bibles, and to quote them incessantly … there was an air of orthodoxy about the teaching which spread downwards from the commander.'[17] The necessity for this orthodoxy was understandable in 1910 when learning and teaching *FSR* had only just been introduced to describe the duties and responsibilities of all officers. Bond quotes Robertson speaking to his graduating cohort of 1912: 'Over and over again do our Regulations urge the importance of combination and unity of effort, but it is farcical to expect either one or the other unless staff officers display keen foresight, great activity and devote the whole of their attention to their duty.' Robertson also referred to the ethos of the *Staff Manual (provisional) 1911*, which demanded that staff be the servants of the rank and file and regimental officers and not their masters. Bond describes, quoting Harold Franklyn (later a Second World War general), the emphasis laid under Robertson's tenure at the college on the drafting of orders and messages, a key section in *FSR*, and an emphasis that continued when Kiggell succeeded Robertson in late 1913.[18] John Spencer, in his assessment of Robertson, describes him as a 'significant modernising [influence] within the British Army of the period.'[19] This is true because of the post he occupied, but he was not a pioneer in this respect. He was simply obeying orders, orders with which he agreed, from Richard Haldane and the Army Council.

16 Gary Sheffield, 'The Makings of a Corps Commander: Lieutenant General Sir Douglas Haig', in Spencer Jones (ed.), *Stemming the Tide: Officers and Leadership in the British Expeditionary Force 1914*, (Solihull: Helion, 2013), p.114.

17 Brown, *British Logistics,* p.28, referencing Brigadier General J. Burnett-Stuart, unpublished memoir, Liddell Hart Centre, King's College London.

18 Bond, *The Staff College,* pp.278–281, 289.

19 John Spencer, 'The Big Brain in the Army: Sir William Robertson as Quartermaster General', in Jones (ed.) *Stemming the Tide*, p.95.

6

Field Services Regulations, Part I, 1909-1912 in the Regular Army

It is not so easy to trace the extent to which the middle ranks of the army took up strict adherence to *FSR*. It varied, of course, from unit to unit, from command to command, and from arm to arm, but it is clear they were required to do so. References in the reports of inspectors general, in accounts of manoeuvres and staff rides, and in army memoranda dealing with training issues confirm this.

FSR was published in the spring of 1909, and it was therefore in force for most of the summer training season of that year. Two major cavalry staff rides were conducted during 1909 by Haig in his capacity as Director of Staff Duties. The first was in early March, just before *FSR* was distributed. It is difficult to interpret staff ride reports where the director is not only the commanding officer of one side but also responsible for most of the ensuing report. This criticism cannot often be levied, but a further example is the 1913 army manoeuvres, directed by Sir John French, which will be tackled later in this book. Haig is quite open in saying that he manipulates the opposing forces to set up a major cavalry-on-cavalry encounter. He controlled not only the narrative of battle but the narrative of his part in it. He described his own force as the 'strategical cavalry.' This is not a term found in *FSR*, but it is in *Cavalry Training 1907*, which is the manual that Haig refers to throughout. Strategical cavalry should 'push into the zone separating two armies' and dispose of any hostile cavalry encountered there.[1] The least *FSR*-compliant part of *Cavalry Training 1907* is in its definition of the ideal cavalry general:

> The personality of the commander is the most important factor in success. The resolute offensive, which is the essence of cavalry action, and the rapidity of movement, which is the characteristic of the arm, allow only the shortest time for consideration. Rapid decisions may therefore have to be taken under the most unfavourable circumstances. In many cases, it will be impossible for the commander of a mass of cavalry to take in correctly the strength and dispositions of the enemy, or to gauge with even approximate accuracy the strength of his adversary.[2]

1 *Cavalry Training 1907* (London: War Office, 1907), pp.192–193.
2 *Cavalry Training 1907*, p.188.

This is a very far cry from the measured assessment of risk mandated on generals and their operational staff in *FSR*, with decisions based on careful reconnaissance and collation of intelligence. Haig sees no need for a chief-of-staff aiding him in his personal decision-making, and recommends launching cavalry against enemy infantry, supporting his proposals with examples of nineteenth-century battles. It is possible to detect slight echoes of *FSR* in an acknowledgement that small patrols and communicating with the Commander-in-Chief might be desirable, but for the first three days of the ride, Haig directs his cavalry division as a totally independent force, largely disdaining all arms cooperation or overall control by a Commander-in-Chief. Incidentally, the maps he provided were still not of a scale recommended for staff rides in the regulations.[3]

It may just be a coincidence that only six weeks after this ride, on 15 April 1909, Haig received the first intimation that Haldane wanted him posted to India.[4] Nothing daunted, he conducted a second staff ride in June. The defect of inadequate maps, at least, was corrected. He ruled that the commander of an advancing cavalry division should ride 'well out in front of [the main body of] his command', and 'should be able to manoeuvre [it] with 1 brigade major, 1 orderly officer and 1 galloper' all armed with flags. There is a section on cooperation with other arms, which, in fact, proposes coordination with other arms, a quite different concept. He recommends keeping his division in reserve until he judges the enemy sufficiently destabilised that they can be overwhelmed with a charge. A section on the transmission of information collected by the cavalry suggests that the staff of the Commander-in-Chief should come and get it themselves. He uses Austerlitz in 1805 and Salamanca in 1812 to illustrate his points. Problem XI required cavalry 'to attack the enemy's artillery in order to allow the infantry to push their attack home' in a manner reminiscent of the Crimea.[5] What Edmund Allenby, Hubert Gough and Edward Fanshawe thought of these courses of 'instruction' is not recorded. All three were at both. Julian Byng was at the first. Gooch comments that the reports on these rides 'reveal an ominous faith in the effectiveness of cavalry attack on the part of the participating and directing staff', but it is difficult to agree with him when he says that Haig's teaching in them is, at least in part, consistent with *FSR, Part I*.[6] According to his own diary, Haig met up with French, Inspector General of Forces, on 11 September. French thanked Haig for taking an interest in cavalry training, but then 'gave vent to some terrible heresies' about how they should be trained.[7] Presumably, French's views on the handling of cavalry, based on *FSR*, were not the same as Haig's, based on *Cavalry Training 1907*. A month later, Haig was on his way to India. For reasons that are not entirely clear, these two staff rides are ignored by almost all those who have written on cavalry tactics between 1900 and 1914. Edward Spiers records that 'at his Cavalry Staff Rides of 1909, Haig still insisted that effects of a 'skilfully managed dismounted action' would never compare with the rare though decisive charges with the arme blanche', but he makes no comment on the differences between *FSR* and cavalry doctrine in that year.[8]

3 TNA: WO 279/27: *Cavalry Staff Ride of Director of Staff Duties, March 1909*, p.31 and text.
4 NLS: ACC 3155/2/i: Haig's personal diary, 15 April,1909.
5 TNA: WO 279/29: *Cavalry Staff Ride of Director of Staff Duties, June 1909*, pp.8, 23, 33, 34, 43–44.
6 Gooch, *The Plans of War*, p.117. There are few references to these staff rides by scholars who have traced the history of cavalry tactics. Why they have been so ignored is not clear.
7 NLS: ACC 3155/2/i: Haig's personal diary, 11 September,1909.
8 Edward M. Spiers 'The British Cavalry, 1902–1914', *Journal of the Society for Army Historical Research*, vol.57, no.230 (Summer 1979), p.75.

It is clear that French, as Inspector general, was determined, along with Nicholson, Chief of the General Staff, to ensure that *FSR* was robustly implemented during the 1909 summer training season. French even asked Brigadier General Murray, Director of Military Training, to help him with his inspections. Murray had been a principal editor of *Part I* prior to its publication, and French's final report for the year acknowledges the help he gave French in phrasing his reports. Often together, they covered almost every educational and military establishment in Great Britain and Ireland in their inspections. French is not generally complimentary about what he found:

> In the Staff tours, which formed an important part of my divisional inspections, in the written appreciation of officers of all ranks, at the conferences, and finally in the work carried out during the Army manoeuvres, I have seen evidence of a lack of knowledge of strategical principles … Many of the senior officers do not possess a sufficient knowledge of the principles and practice of war on a large scale.

He is more complimentary about middle-ranking officers. 'Inspection by this department of regimental, brigade and divisional training throughout the army, seems to show that there is generally a more uniform adherence to authorised principles.' 'Considerable improvement is to be noted' in the individual instruction of 'the section commander and the company officer.'[9] All officers were now required to ensure the training being given to, and being given by, their subordinates complied with *FSR*, so this is evidence of a general compliance at a senior level. In inspecting the cavalry, he criticises poor training in dismounted action and a general lack of proficiency in signalling. As regards the artillery, their association 'with Infantry in division … has been highly beneficial to the Artillery, who have also derived much benefit from the more extended tactical teaching pertaining to the divisional system.'[10] Although the full report was not published till 1910, feedback was provided, both to the unit commanders and their superiors, enabling immediate attention to problems identified.

Summer training, most years, culminated in major exercises and in 1909, the army manoeuvres were very major indeed, taking place between 19 and 23 September. The names of the participants are important, as they are the officers most obviously responsible for implementing *FSR* in its first year. The director was French, and on his staff were Murray and his assistant Colonel Du Cane, who was responsible for arranging manoeuvres and still responsible for collating amendments to *FSR, Part I.* Lieutenant General Horace Smith-Dorrien commanded the two divisions of the Aldershot command and London district, and two brigades of cavalry. Under him, Brigadier General William Robertson was his chief-of-staff, before he assumed command of the Staff College in 1910. Major General James Grierson commanded the 1st Division, and Brigadier General Edmund Allenby commanded the cavalry. Lieutenant General Sir Arthur Paget commanded the 3rd and 4th Divisions and two cavalry brigades from Eastern and Southern commands.[11] It seems doubtful that Paget was an early convert to the new order, though it is difficult to find objective references to him. 'Possessed of considerable wealth, Paget won renown less as a soldier than as a bon vivant; his close friendship from boyhood with

9 TNA: WO 27/508: 'Annual Reports of the Inspector General of the Forces, 1909-1913', 1909 Report, pp.5–6.
10 TNA: WO 27/508: Report of the Inspector General, 1909, pp.7–8, 59.
11 TNA: WO 279/31: 'Report on Army Manoeuvres 1909', pp.4–12. All commanders are listed.

the prince of Wales (later King Edward VII) was an incalculable asset throughout his career. Pompous and verbose, headstrong when aroused, though gallant in the field, Paget was neither cool nor clear-headed; intellectually shallow,' says the *Dictionary of Irish Biography*.[12] Travers asserts that he 'rarely visited his office in 1909, but preferred other activities', and goes on to allege that he did not even attend the 1911 manoeuvres, where he commanded, having to be briefed on them in the train to the closing conference. The writings of Travers are not always entirely reliable. The annual manoeuvres of 1911 were cancelled.

The scenario for the 1909 manoeuvres was that of war between two countries situated north and south of a mutual border running across Southern England, from Reading in the east to the Severn in the west. The two armies were based on their 'capitals', Northampton and Salisbury respectively, and both had cavalry patrols advanced. The weather that week was miserably cold and very wet. The exercise lasted three days. The introduction to the report on the manoeuvres regrets that there had not been time to ensure that they had been set up in total compliance with *FSR, Part III*.

French, in his report on them, first discusses the major options open to either force, criticising both commanders for their failure to deploy their forces in line with *FSR, Part I*.[13] He goes on to focus on other incidences where the rules of *Part I* were not being followed. He notes a failure to comply with regulations on operation orders, a failure to establish lateral communications, a failure to file copies of orders in war diaries, and a general failure to observe march discipline. 'If the right side of the road is not left clear, the difficulties of communication and control are increased, and with the increased use which is now made of motor-cars to facilitate command, this is… important.' It obviously irritated him. All 'tended to occupy the whole of the road … The men [had] to be ordered constantly to incline to the left to let traffic past.'[14] Unsurprisingly, there were many *FSR* regulations which were yet to be implemented by middle-ranking line officers. Much has to be read between the lines in these reports, but it seems that some of the confusion French describes is caused by some officers complying, leading to misunderstandings when others did not.

The Army Council, headed by Sir William Nicholson, also watched the proceedings. They were sufficiently worried by the slow progress towards conformity with *FSR* recorded by French and Murray in their inspections of units around the country before the manoeuvres, and then during them, to command the preparation of a second *Army Training Memorandum*, which was ready by 29 December 1909. The first had accompanied the issue of *FSR* at the beginning of the year. Again, collated by Murray as DMT, it starts by emphasising the general intent of the recently imposed reforms. The memorandum begins with, 'A general scheme of training was formulated by the Army Council for the year 1909'. The results of training manoeuvres and staff tours 'do not entirely accord with the principles laid down in Field Service Regulations … it is desirable to remedy [this].' 'Certain provisions (*Part I*, section 65)' on the 'Employment of Cavalry' are not sufficiently recognised. *FSR, Part I*, section 2, states that 'the full power of an army can be exerted only when all its parts act in close combination. Failure in this respect has been an unfortunate feature, [and there has been] more than one cause.' There are further long chapters on the 'conduct of a fire fight' and the 'use of reserves', each giving reasons why the advice in *FSR, Part I* should be followed. Moving on to staff duties, it noted that *FSR, Part II*

12 *Dictionary of Irish Biography*, <www.dib.ie> (accessed 25 February 2024).
13 TNA: WO 279/31: 'Report on Army Manoeuvres 1909', Director's Report, pp. pp.39–40, 41, 42, 47.
14 TNA: WO 279/31: 'Report on Army Manoeuvres 1909', Director's Report, pp.45, 50, 51, 52, 57.

had 'only been issued half way through the training season', and since it required 'a new system with which the staff had not had time to become familiar, it is not surprising that room for improvement should have become evident.'

What is remarkable about this document, which was issued in Army Orders in early 1910, is that it is not really an order. It accepts that this is still early days. This is the advice that *FSR* gives about training the army for war, it says, and these are the reasons why that advice has been formulated. We know war will be different, but the ethos behind the advice is what we want to instil. There is a spirit of almost excitement in it. We are beginning to get somewhere, it seems to be saying. We now have a plan to become a truly professional army. We are defining parameters but allowing grown-up debate on issues we know have no exact solution in a world of developing technologies and change. 'At the School of Cookery, Aldershot, some experiments have been carried out in the preservation of fresh meat, carried in mess tins, and in different methods of cooking it. The result of these experiments has been circulated to commands.' This may seem a bizarre quote to illustrate a point, but it exemplifies the attention to detail and rapid acceptance of innovation that permeate the document.[15] 'Will do better next year' is the conclusion.

The annual staff conference at Camberley was held four months after the manoeuvres, in the week of 17 January 1910, under the direction of Nicholson as Chief of the Imperial General Staff. All War Office directorates, all army commands, and all regular and territorial divisions in Great Britain and Ireland were represented, along with several Staff College delegates. The format was precisely the same as at previous conferences. The first day was devoted to debate on subjects which might lead to amendments to *FSR*, based on issues that had arisen during the training season or at the manoeuvres which followed it. Some, but not all, of the agenda items were presented by Murray and Du Cane. There is little to be gained by analysing the detailed discussion of the tactics recommended in training regulations. Two of the agenda items, however, address a command principle not yet described, this is 'lateral combination'. Officer cadets were taught that they should accept operation orders from only one officer, and that this would be their direct superior within their unit. But there were circumstances where a senior officer might wish to reinforce, say, an infantry brigade with an extra battalion. He could do this by formally ordering one brigade to release a battalion to himself, and then immediately order a second brigade to accept that battalion into its command, leaving one brigade with five battalions and the other with three. This re-shuffling was also a common necessity in the artillery, a battery being superfluous to the requirements of one brigade and better placed with another or, where its mobility in support of an infantry brigade would be beneficial, co-opted to serve under an infantry brigadier. The rapid establishment of communications within the enlarged unit was a problem that required definition, the commanding officer of the moving unit now having a new operational command hierarchy. Another command issue which needed clarification was the place of the engineers in the planning of defensive positions. What status, or indeed authority, did the Commander Royal Engineers have as he watched infantry digging poorly designed defences? Nicholson, summing up this debate and addressing infantry commanders, was characteristically blunt. 'Each man to his trade. Make use of all the expert knowledge you can get. That is my view.' More tweaks to *FSR* were required.[16]

15 TNA: WO 231/404: 'Memorandum on Army Training 1909', December 1909.
16 TNA: WO 279/496: 'Report of a Conference of General Staff Officers at the Staff College, 17th to 20th January 1910, held under the Direction of the Chief of the Imperial General Staff', p.20.

In overview, the conference was united in accepting the first task which *FSR* had set itself, which was to standardise routine procedures and actions. It accepted its second, which was to define the command structures already described. It accepted its third, which was to lay down a code of intelligent acceptance of responsibility by all officers on campaign that ensured the professional deployment and protection of their own units. It, by and large, accepted the tactical principles laid down for training, although there was scope for endless discussion on the detail. There was also near, but not total, uniformity in accepting that *FSR* was laying down correct, almost inviolate, principles applicable to forces on the battlefield. Two of these, combination of arms in manoeuvre and deployment in depth and width, are beginning to come to the fore, both emphasising the paramount importance of artillery in the close support of infantry in attack and defence.

The one major issue that remained partially unresolved by the publication and implementation of *FSR* was that of the relationship of the cavalry with the rest of the army. The chosen battlefield for debate was the make-up and actions of the advance guard, but it was more fundamental than that, with the staffing of a cavalry division a major issue. It has already been described how Brigadier General Rimington influenced the draft of *Combined Training 1905* so that *FSR, Part I, 1909* required cavalry, even in the advance guard, to combine with infantry and artillery, forbidding it to engage without support from them an enemy of all arms. Rimington was very probably influenced, as Spencer Jones suggests in his work on the British cavalry before 1914, by Robert Baden-Powell's views as Inspector General of Cavalry from 1903 to 1907.[17] Some cavalry officers privately disagreed with the perceived merging of the cavalry into a homogenous army and did not engage with *FSR*. This was not a stance that could be made explicit, with Army Council orders demanding total compliance with it. The senior cavalry officer in the army was Sir John French, but in his long report on the 1909 manoeuvres, and indeed in later reports, he echoes Army Council edicts requiring firm compliance with all regulations by all arms. But when addressing the cavalry, he selects minor issues, such as the availability of practice swords, and fails to focus on the reasons why the cavalry was not integrating into the wider army as successfully as the artillery.[18]

Progress in the routine observance of *FSR* can be seen at the 1910 manoeuvres, again directed by French, who was still Inspector General of the Forces. These comprised Lieutenant General Herbert Plumer with the 2nd Division, a half division of cavalry, and a Territorial Force taking on Lieutenant General Sir Charles Douglas with the 3rd Division, under Major General Rawlinson, the 4th Division, and the other half division of cavalry. Brigadier Generals Murray, Ellison and Kiggell were all assistant directors. Major Generals Allenby and Fergusson, both at Mons in 1914, were inspectors. Lieutenant Generals Smith-Dorrien and Paget were the chief umpires. The written summary runs to 250 pages, French, Murray, and Smith-Dorrien writing the principal reports. It is irrelevant, when assessing the army's compliance to *FSR*, that French may, in pique, have refused to have Smith-Dorrien, the Aldershot commander, as an active participant in the manoeuvres, as one respected secondary source alleges. Nicholson and the Army Council authorised the arrangements, not French, who was merely the inspector general, and it seems entirely logical to allow two new senior generals to gain experience of high command. Personal anecdotes enliven history, but they are seldom central to it. All the evidence

17 Jones, 'Scouting for Soldiers', pp.504–508.
18 TNA: WO 27/508: Reports of the Inspector General, 1910 Report, pp.8–10.

from the official report is that French and Smith-Dorrien were united in their desire to impose the professionalism demanded by *FSR* on the army.

French's report refers to *FSR* in his main narrative with a light touch. He assumes that the two generals he is assessing are following its various principles. It is not surprising, but at least impressive, the degree to which *FSR* is ingrained in the psyche of the army so soon after its implementation. French praises a tranche of officers, including the commander of the 10th Infantry Brigade (whom he later castigates for a specific breach of the regulations), for understanding the fundamental ideas behind *FSR*.

> Generally speaking, satisfactory indications were everywhere observed of the conception of an army as one organism. This spirit of close cooperation between all arms and all parts of a force is one of the best guarantees of success in war … For instance, the first attempt by the Blue cavalry to retake Castle Ditches, carried out by a few squadrons of the 4th Cavalry Brigade, unsupported, was repulsed with loss; but the second attack, in which the cooperation of the whole cavalry division and a battalion of infantry was carefully organized, was completely successful.[19]

Going on to quote *FSR, Part I*, Section 105, he states, 'In all attacks, whether hurried or not, important tactical points … must be secured as the advance goes forward, and at once be put in a state of defence, so that attempts on the part of the enemy to recapture them may be defeated, and they may be made to serve as supporting points for the [next] attack,'. This is an important, inviolate, *FSR* general principle for offensive warfare, bite and hold, as it has been termed.

French's claws do come out when he starts his concluding general remarks:

> Perhaps the most noticeable shortcomings in the tactical employment of troops were the repeated instances of failure in the service of protection. The surprise of the 10th Infantry Brigade [sic] near Manor Farm, the surprise of the blue cavalry east of Castle Ditches, the surprise and capture of three batteries near Chislebury Camp, are all conspicuous disasters for which there was no reasonable excuse… the rules [are] laid down in Field Service Regulations, Part I, Sections 64 and 90. No considerations can absolve from blame the commander who allows himself to be surprised. The habit of taking every precaution to guard against surprise should be an instinct ingrained into every commander…

The end of these remarks is almost a quote from the introduction to *Part I.* Naming and shaming the three officers who had failed to follow the regulations demonstrated that ignoring *FSR* was already not a good career move, albeit it was the responsibility of their subordinate units to ensure protection, as was taught to cadets at Sandhurst and Woolwich. The crime of the more senior officers was in not ensuring that their subordinates had been adequately taught to follow *FSR* in detail in this respect.

French finishes by praising, with certain reservations, the actions of the two commanders in their tactical conceptions near the finale of the manoeuvres:

19 TNA: WO 279/39: 'Army Manoeuvres 1910', p.63.

> The lesson may be drawn that a knowledge of principles is not sufficient to ensure victory, but that success is to be looked for in the manner with which principles are applied. Care in working out details of execution, foresight in guarding against possible dangers, and, above all, unshaken determination in carrying it out, will probably ensure the success of any reasonable plan; without these, even the best plan is likely to fail.

And this was only 1910.

French follows up his manoeuvres report with his inspector general's report for 1910. Despite having been out of the country inspecting overseas forces for much of the year, his report on general training is somewhat more critical than his manoeuvre report. The published responses by the Army Council refer frequently back to the training memorandum published at the beginning of 1910, and indeed to specific *FSR* regulations, but one is left with the impression that full compliance with *FSR* was slow in developing. The artillery, who were now training with the infantry, were ahead of the infantry in general, who were ahead of the cavalry.[20] But the 1911 conference provides evidence that *FSR* did not provide enough guidance for the artillery. John Du Cane presented the current state of training of the artillery, highlighting the problems, and the report of the subsequent discussion occupies 22 pages of animated debate.[21] Problems with the integration of the artillery into infantry divisions took some time to sort out, and there was considerable difference in opinion as to how this should be achieved. What matters is that a consensus was reached by April 1914, when *Field Artillery Training* was published by the War Office. This document has been somewhat unfairly criticised for not going further in formalising command and liaison arrangements between artillery brigades and their batteries, and infantry brigades and their battalions. It complies with *FSR* in keeping these links the responsibility of individual officers, since the circumstances in which combination or coordination might be needed might vary so widely as to make laying down firm rules unwise. It is likely that any formal arrangements that could have been agreed before the war would have been unsuitable for application in it.

The 1911 staff conference again gave an opportunity for officers to put up items for discussion which challenged specific *FSR* regulations. Nicholson, Chief of the Imperial General Staff, Murray, Director of Military Training, and Kiggell, Director of Staff Duties, in that order, led the discussion, although Nicholson was under doctor's orders and did not appear until the final day. A few minor potential *FSR* amendments were addressed on the first day. However, there is evidence of some anxiety in the middle ranks of the army.[22] To establish the context, the army was professional, and promotion was dependent on an assessment process and exams. *King's Regulations* in 1912 echoed *FSR* in stating that 'in a battalion the commanding officer, assisted by the senior major, is responsible for the systematic and efficient instruction of officers under his command in all their professional duties', and additionally 'for their due preparation for examinations for promotion.'[23] John Mason Sneddon, in his 2013 study of 'The Company Commander' in 1914, describes how this worked. 'Annual inspections and confidential reports'

20 TNA: WO 27/508: Reports of the Inspector General, 1910 Report, pp.28–31.
21 TNA: WO 279/42: Report of a Conference of General Staff Officers at the Staff College, 9th to 12th January 1911, held under the Direction of the Chief of the Imperial General Staff, pp.52–74.
22 TNA: WO279/42: Conference of General Staff Officers January 1911, pp.5–9.
23 *The King's Regulations and Orders for the Army 1912* (London: War Office, 1912), pp.20–21.

were arranged by the relevant inspector general. The 'curriculum [for promotion exams] was identical at all levels of command from 2nd lieutenant to major with candidates required to demonstrate more knowledge and experience as they progressed up the promotion ladder.' For the infantry, the core curriculum comprised regimental duties, drill and field training, and small unit tactics. The first part was a written and oral exam, in the second part the candidate was 'provided with a battalion of infantry, a battery of artillery and a squadron of cavalry' and required to resolve theoretical tactical problems. 'If an officer failed the tactical examination twice, he was required to leave the army.'[24] The tactical elements of these exams tested knowledge of *FSR* and relevant supporting manuals, and as Duncan points out, in his study of 'The Military Education of Junior Officers', there was a high failure rate.[25] Even the current handbooks for the infantry and cavalry had not been reliably updated, which made life difficult for these officers. It was during 1911 that Erskine Childers, a prominent journalist of the day, said that the differences between *FSR* and *Cavalry Training* were 'a public scandal.'[26]

It is reasonable to conclude from both French's report as inspector general for 1910 and the proceedings of the 1911 conference that middle-ranking officers, in general, lagged behind both their seniors and their recently commissioned juniors in understanding the full implications of *FSR*. It would be surprising if they did not. Nevertheless, there was a very wide range of professional books and journals that were available to this cohort and, as Duncan records, there was a big market for them.[27] Cramming for promotion exams in the army had created a minor industry, and traditional cramming textbooks did their best to keep up to date with the changes. One such was Lieutenant Colonel Layland Needham's *Solution of Tactical Problems*, which went to four editions between 1906 and September 1909. The first edition promised 'a logical and easy way of working out the tactical schemes set at examinations', and was intended to help with 'papers on tactics set at the Staff College, Promotion and Militia Competitive' examinations in 1906, with reference to advice given in *Combined Training 1905*. The preface to the fourth edition states that the 'issue of *Field Service Regulations, Part I: Operations* has necessitated an extensive revision, bringing the work up to date.' It may also now 'be useful to Officers of the Territorial Forces preparing for examination under Appendix 4, *Territorial Force Regulations*, 1908.'[28] The book is remarkably comprehensive, and as a revision text, it addresses much of *FSR* in bullet points. But it does not convey the spirit of *FSR*, and for the candidate who had not absorbed the difference between principles and rules to be followed in training, the sheer number of bullet points must have been very daunting.

A suggestion was made at the 1911 conference that the War Office might publish 'official' guidance for these exams. The request was refused. A further difficulty in 1911 for this cohort of officers was that progress in establishing the principles of *FSR* in all army training would be hindered by the coronation of George V in June. Much of the British Army at home and

24 John Mason Sneddon, 'The Company Commander', in Spencer Jones (ed.), *Stemming the* Tide, pp.320–323.
25 Andrew George Duncan, 'The Military Education of Junior Officers in the Edwardian Era', Ph.D. thesis, University of Birmingham, 2016, pp.97–98.
26 Anglesey, *British Cavalry 1816–1919*, vol.4, p.417, quoting Robert Erskine Childers, 'German influences on British Cavalry'.
27 Duncan, 'Military Education', pp.137–141.
28 Lieutenant Colonel J. Layland Needham, *The Solution of Tactical Problems, Fourth Edition Revised* (London: Hugh Rees, 1909), pp.v–vii.

abroad was involved, and meticulous adherence to ceremonial drill for several months was not conducive to absorbing the principles of independent thinking required by *FSR*. Matters were not improved by the enforced cancellation, at the last minute, of the 1911 autumn manoeuvres due to country-wide industrial action. Middle-ranking officers, vying for promotion, would have been entitled to feel some irritation that their training had effectively been held back for a year. Those officers who were posted for long periods in administration, or in isolated outposts abroad, were also particularly disadvantaged, a very real problem for officers of the Royal Garrison Artillery.

It is difficult to reconcile the testing regimen these middle-ranking officers faced and their thirst for guidance in furthering their careers with the accusations of amateurism in the officer corps that appear in publications describing the Edwardian army, often based almost solely on anecdotal evidence. Timothy Bowman and Mark Connelly are not alone in *The Edwardian Army*, in pointing out that middle-ranking officers of that era were a small and relatively homogenous group, with similar educational and social backgrounds, and that promotion was very slow.[29] However, just because this was so, it cannot be inferred that they were unwilling to professionalise as demanded by *FSR*. After all, promotion depended on it, and most officers were ambitious. Travers, and others, in framing these accusations of amateurism, all too often mislead by recounting anecdotes from early in the decade, or even in the nineteenth century, and applying them to much later, failing to recognise the watershed impact of *FSR* as published in 1905 and 1909.[30]

To complete this topic under one heading, at the 1913 staff conference, 'preparation for military exams' was again discussed. Senior officers did, as they will, bemoan the poor quality of some applicants for promotion, but a 62 percent pass rate was recorded in a tactics exam that was generally regarded, in 1912, as 'excellent' in its practicality, in that it tested adherence to current training manuals and was designed to assess fitness for promotion up to lieutenant colonel.[31] Representatives of these officers still wanted the War Office to publish what would essentially be a crammer. Their request was again refused.[32] This is one of the few occasions when J.F.C. Fuller was in complete agreement with the army hierarchy. 'The average crammer is no fool. He knows to an inch the mental measurement of the normal examiner; that is why, for tactical purposes, their cram books are totally valueless.'[33]

Since 1910, some commanding officers, through lack of intellect or traditional instinct, had been identified as failing to ensure their subordinates were adequately instructed in *FSR*, but it was said at the 1913 conference that action had already been taken to address this problem. It is not entirely clear what that action might have been, but Lieutenant Roderick McLeod, a young artillery subaltern, in a 1913 diary, describes a very pernickety battery commander failing to cope with a 5th Division exercise in fire control in Ireland. 'Shortly afterwards, he left for India, and a Major Dooner joined us. He was Staff College trained and taught us a lot

29 Bowman and Connelly, *The Edwardian Army*, pp.8–10.

30 See, Tim Travers, 'The Hidden Army: Structural Problems in the British Officer Corps, 1900–1918', *Journal of Contemporary History*, vol.17, no.3 (July 1982) pp.523–544.

31 See, *The King's regulations and orders for the army, 1912; Reprinted with amendments published in Army orders up to 1st August, 1914* (London: War Office, 1914), paras 857–895 and appendix XL.

32 TNA: WO 279/48: *Report of a Conference of General Staff Officers at the Royal Military College, 13th to 16th January 1913, under the Direction of the Chief of the Imperial General Staff*, pp.46–50.

33 J.F.C. Fuller, quoted in Bond, *The Staff College*, p.290.

about tactics.'[34] Bowman and Connelly describe, in 1912, a major being promoted to lieutenant colonel over the head of one more senior, on the grounds that the older man had 'only "passable" performance in manoeuvres and professional knowledge that was "not deep."'[35] Being passed over was essentially an invitation to retire. As Duncan says, in his review of this period, 'officers' duties included the instruction of their subordinates, and being able to impart this training properly was important.' In his paper, he praises Sir Douglas Haig for issuing instructions to the officers of Aldershot command in 1912, that they 'should give "special attention" to training their subordinates "as leaders and as instructors."'[36] But it is disturbing that he had to do so. This training had been mandated in standing orders issued by the Army Council since 1909.[37]

The staff conference of January 1912 followed the same pattern as previous annual conferences, although delegates now formally represented those directorates, commands, and divisions, regular or territorial, who were invited. Murray introduced the conference and explained the format. An officer was given 15 minutes to present a subject, and there was a brief discussion. The chairman summed up. The directors would meet that evening, decide if there were grounds for action, and 'before we re-assemble the following year, the various questions are thoroughly gone into and action taken on the points brought forward.' The responsibility for dealing with points raised was now more focused. 'I shall have to consult General Kiggell [DSD] before I answer these questions,' said Murray [DMT], during the proceedings.[38] Staff Duties was gradually taking over control of the *FSR* amendment process from Military Training, though the ultimate decisions rested with the Chief of the Imperial General Staff. Murray moved from Military Training at the end of 1912, and at the 1913 conference, it is Kiggell who is leading the discussion 'under the orders and direction' of French, the new Chief of the Imperial General Staff.[39]

34 Royal Artillery Museum (RAM): MD/1150: Lieutenant (later Colonel) Roderick Mcleod, Journal, p.13.
35 Bowman and Connelly, *The Edwardian Army*, p.36, citing a confidential report in the papers of General Sir Ian Hamilton in the Liddell Hart Centre at King's College, London.
36 Duncan, 'Military Education', pp.97–98, referencing NLS: Papers of Field-Marshal Earl Haig, ACC 3155 No91: 'Conference on Company Training, Aldershot, May 1912'.
37 TNA: WO 231/403: *Memorandum on Army Training*, 1908, p.8.
38 TNA: WO 279/45: 'Report of a Conference of General Staff Officers at the Staff College 15th to 18th January 1912, held under the orders of The Chief of the Imperial General Staff', pp.56, 69 & passim.
39 TNA: WO 279/48: 'Report of a Conference of General Staff Officers at the Royal Military College 13th to 16th January 1913, held under the orders and direction of The Chief of the Imperial General Staff', p.5.

7

Administration – The General Staff and Field Services Regulations, Part II

FSR, Part I, when it was mandated on the army in 1909, was significant in extending and defining the duties and responsibilities of all line officers, but it did not radically alter their basic job descriptions. Promotion was slow, so most officers were thoroughly familiar with their work and accepted their increased responsibilities with equanimity, comfortable with the concept of making the army more uniform and more professional. Most were familiar with *Combined Training* as a guidance document, so following an updated version as a requirement was not overly difficult. Training became more focused as senior officers observed their new duty to satisfy themselves that all their subordinates, down to the most junior, had access to compliant instruction. It is not easy to find any contemporary anecdotal references to the undoubted cultural shift that took place in the army from 1909 into 1910 and beyond. When Charteris returned from India to Aldershot in 1912, he perceived a more 'scientific' approach to soldiering, which is a good expression of the changes that were occurring.[1] In Great Britain and Ireland, the doctrine of *Part I* was being absorbed quietly without visible disruption or upheaval.

FSR, Part II, in contrast, required the administration and command structure of the devolved army to reform almost overnight. It can be argued that Richard Haldane required some introspection from the Army Council before the spring of 1909, but the full force of the reforms did not strike home until its publication. It is striking how little evidence there is of discontent in the upper echelons of the army during the early years of its implementation. Normally, major reorganisations are initially resisted. But *FSR* was not imposed on a backwards-thinking and reluctant army. Rather, it was offered to an army that wished to modernise and professionalise, in keeping with the times. It is important, while studying the detail of *Part II*, to appreciate that *FSR*, as a concept, sat comfortably on the army because it was in tune with the wider political narrative of the Edwardian era.

Very few historians address the details of the impact of the implementation of *FSR, Part II* on the army of 1909. One of the few who even mentions *FSR, Part II* is General Trythall, contributing to French and Holden Reid's, *The British General Staff*. He writes that *FSR* in 1909, 'provided a detailed delineation of the duties of the General Staff.'[2] Hew Strachan writes,

1 Charteris, *Field-Marshal Earl Haig*, pp.62–66.
2 Trythall in French and Holden Reid, *British General Staff*, p.145.

in his chapter in the same book, speaking of 1911, that 'the General Staff was a new creation … its chief had to compete with pre-existing peers, like the adjutant-general and quartermaster-general.'[3] 'New' is a relative term. In context, it is hard to know what they both mean. Both statements are true, but they beg the question: what was the General Staff? The phrase 'general staff' means everything and nothing. The term was used with great frequency in the decade up to 1914, and it is still being used now in commentaries and academic papers referring to the period. It is a term almost impossible to avoid, yet capable of wide misinterpretation in context. The evolution of staffing arrangements between the formation of the Army Council in 1904, up to the introduction of *FSR* in 1909, and then on to 1914 would be relatively simple to understand if it were not mired in terminological confusion, of which the term general staff is but one example.

At his major staff conference in January 1905, Hutchinson, Director of Staff Duties, presented an early draft of *FSR, Part II*. As previously described, he started by distinguishing between the General Staff, that is, those working in the directorates controlled by the Chief of the General Staff, and the administrative staff, those under the QMG and AG. He bases this nomenclature on the recommendations of Esher's War Office Reconstitution Committee. 'The Staff of the Army is now broadly divided into the General Staff and the Administrative Staff, the Administrative Staff being subdivided into two great branches, the Adjutant General's, and the Quartermaster General's. The General Staff dealt with all questions connected with the military defence of the Empire.' He lists, as examples of its duties, the collection and training of the troops, the preparation of offensive and defensive schemes of operations, the education and training of officers, and the planning of manoeuvres. The Adjutant General's branch, he goes on to say, deals with recruiting, organisation, mobilisation, personnel, discipline, and medical services, while the Quartermaster General's Branch deals with 'transport and supply, remount and veterinary services, barracks, stores, clothing, &c. The ruling idea' in making this distinction is to set 'one class of officers free from all cares of routine,' so as to devote all their energy to such tasks as collating intelligence, preparing operations and improving training, while other officers do the routine work.[4] That was the theory, anyway. It was by no means the practice in 1905.

In November 1906, this definition was formalised. The 'General Staff' was defined in Army Order 233, issued that month, as described in Paul Harris's 2013 thesis on the 'Men who planned the War'.[5] This order was a first response to the pressure for reform which was being exerted on the Army Council by Haldane, Ward, and Ellison, as described in Chapter 3. As Esher's report had intended, the order defined the members of the General Staff as being solely those who served under the auspices of the Chief of the General Staff at the War Office. This included all those who headed, or served in, his three major directorates, which were Military Operations, Military Training and Staff Duties. It also included those officers seconded from these War Office directorates to the various home commands to ensure the implementation of innovations in training and procedure being mandated by the Chief of the General Staff or by

3 Hew Strachan, 'The British Army, its General Staff and the Continental Commitment', in David French and Brian Holden Reid (eds), *The British General Staff, Reform and Innovation, 1890–1939* (London: Frank Cass, 2002), pp.78, 88.

4 TNA: WO 033/2747: 'Report of a Conference and Staff Ride 1905' pp.8–9.

5 Harris, 'The Staff of the British Army', pp.47–48. There is no evidence this reform was orchestrated by Douglas Haig as Harris implies.

one of his directorates.[6] The 'operational staff' of the generals responsible for home commands or expeditionary forces were not part of the General Staff.

The duties of the men who were appointed to head the QMG, AG and the MGO branches at the War Office were two-fold. The QMG, AG and the MGO did not just run their own departments. They had important advisory responsibilities as well. All three had been on the Army Council since its inception. All three were responsible for advising the Chief of the General Staff on how logistics, personnel, or ordnance issues would impinge on the capabilities of the army. They also appointed delegates, who were similarly responsible for advising the commander of any devolved force, at home or abroad, on matters relating to the vast range of their briefs. In their capacity as advisers, these administrative staff had no command functions. Their administrative duties were quite separate from their advisory function. All three also headed up powerful administrative branches of the army. Like the Department of the Chief of the General Staff (from 1909, Chief of the Imperial General Staff), the departments of the QMG, AG and MGO were subdivided into directorates, based in the War Office. This hierarchy of directorates spread out from the War Office to the various commands to supervise logistics, personnel and all the other practical and administrative tasks which were necessary to sustain the army on its various sites. Officers working in these directorates were graded as QMG or AG staff officers at levels which determined their status and level of responsibilities.

Thus, between 1906 and 1909, there were three completely distinct types of staff officer: those on the General Staff, ultimately answerable to the Chief of the General Staff; those in the administrative staff, answerable to the QMG, AG and other War Office directorates; and finally, that group of staff officers who were on the operational staff of all general officers. *FSR* was published and mandated on the army in 1909, pertaining solely to the arrangements to be made for an expeditionary force. The word 'staff' is used quite loosely in many different contexts, and the term 'General Staff' is used at least once in *Part I* to describe a general's operational staff.[7] In *FSR, Part II*, the term 'General Staff' is redefined, though it is not easy to appreciate that from the text. The officers on the personal staff of any general, be it Commander-in-Chief, corps commander, or more junior, comprised the General Staff at Headquarters. These officers could not issue orders. Their responsibility was solely to support their general in the performance of his duties. All such officers were graded with the designation GS – General Staff. However, the terminology introduced by *FSR, Part I* did not invalidate the 1906 definition of the General Staff at the War Office because that pertained to their duties at the War Office in peacetime. So, terminological overlap is inevitable.

There were now two competing definitions of 'General Staff' – those staff officers within the War Office who worked for the Chief of the Imperial General Staff, and those on the General Staff of an Expeditionary Force. At Nicholson's staff tour in 1908, testing *Part II*, the operational staff of the general commanding are called 'general staff' to distinguish them from the AG and his staff officers, the QMG and his, and the Inspector General of Communications and Railways and his. Most of these were heads of directorates with specific responsibilities. However, under the QMG, two officers are recorded as being 'general staff attached', these being from the Department of the Chief of the General Staff at the War Office.[8] In the report

6 TNA: WO 123/48: 'Army Order 233', October 1906, pp.17–21.
7 *Field Service Regulations, Part I,* p.112.
8 TNA: WO 279/22: 'Report on a Staff Tour, October 1908', pp.3–4.

on the 1909 manoeuvres, General Staff (GS) grade officers are distinguished from QMG grade and AG grade officers, all of whom are recorded as being on the Commander-in-Chief's Headquarters Staff.[9] In short, there is little consistency in nomenclature, be it in a primary source or a modern commentary. Even within single publications, the word staff is used to mean different things in different contexts.

It rapidly became clear at the army manoeuvres of 1909 and 1910 that the general principles of *Part II* pertaining to relationships at the very top of the army needed to be clarified and further defined. So, in 1910, a committee was formed, reporting directly to the Army Council, tasked with producing a *Staff Manual.* Brevet Colonel Walter Adye and Lieutenant Colonel Wilkinson Bird were both based in the Staff Duties Directorate, though other members of the committee were not. They did not report, in this work, to Temporary Brigadier General Launcelot Kiggell, their new director, though, once agreed by the Army Council, the manual was published by the War Office. The committee was charged with producing a document which should ensure coordination of 'staff work in the field' in compliance with the principles of *FSR*. Their full terms of reference were to 'examine into the conduct of staff work in the field with a view to ensuring coordination between the three branches of the Staff' and to define 'the distribution of responsibilities and duties … within each branch' in adherence with 'the general principles laid down in Field Service Regulations.'[10] Staff work 'in the field' meant on campaign, and should not be confused with staff work performed within the Staff Duties Directorate. *FSR* was not written to define the work of officers working out of the War Office under the supervision of the Chief of the Imperial General Staff, but their relationships with staff officers on campaign did have to be defined. In addition, each of the three branches at the War Office had to find, and train up, suitably competent officers to participate in the administration of an expeditionary force.

A provisional draft of this *Staff Manual* was published in 1911 and updated, still provisionally, in 1912.[11] *The Staff Manual (Provisional) 1911*, in broad terms, does little more than add detail to *FSR, Part II.* A definition of 'staff' is given, which it says adheres to that in *Part II*, noting that the term 'is often used with different meanings.' 'The Staff [of an expeditionary force]', the *Staff Manual* says, 'is composed of officers, specially appointed to assist superiors who are vested with executive authority on their own responsibility', that is, the staff of all general officers commanding. This excludes heads of directorates in an administrative branch since they are 'acting on their own responsibility in accordance with instructions issued to them by a higher authority … Officers attached to the Staff, but not actually appointed to it, are not Staff officers.' The manual confirms that the QMG and AG of any expeditionary force should work closely with the C-in-C but that they were not under his command, an anomaly that caused difficulties in 1914.[12] As might be expected, the publication of the *Staff Manual* generated a blizzard of minor proposed amendments, and the 'Committee on Staff Duties in the Field' was kept busy into 1913.[13] Despite its name, this committee neither addressed the work of the Directorate of Staff Duties nor was it responsible to it. It was an independent entity, reporting to the Army Council. The *Staff Manual* reforms had a considerable impact on very senior relationships, and

9 TNA: WO 279/31: 'Report on Army Manoeuvres 1909', pp.4–12.
10 TNA: WO 32/4730: 'Committee on Staff Duties in the Field 1911.'
11 TNA: WO 32/4730: Committee on Staff Duties in the Field, War Office, 1911.
12 TNA: WO 106/51: *Staff Manual (Provisional) 1911* (London: War Office, 1912), pp.15–18.
13 TNA: WO32/4730: Committee on Staff Duties in the Field 1911; TNA: WO 32/4731: Staff Manual, and correspondence, 1912–1914.

these will be addressed in a future chapter, but there is much in the handbook of relevance to more junior staff officers, clarifying and reinforcing the principles described in *Part II*. It starts with a firm lecture on how operational staff officers should conduct themselves. Arrogance should be avoided, particularly in contacts with line officers, and discretion should be observed. 'The relationships between officers serving on the Staff must be close and cordial.' There is even a section on the 'cultivation of friendly feelings.' 'Staff officers should never venture to criticise either superiors or inferiors to any person whatsoever. It is not within their right to do so, and nothing is more likely to cause ill-feeling.'[14]

Travers, in 1982, stated that 'the British officer corps on the eve of war was still Victorian in many of its attitudes, with an overwhelming emphasis on the influence of individual personalities and on social and regimental hierarchies.' Some of its systems 'reflected an amateur army caught in a changing world.'[15] Others have echoed these sentiments since. But it is difficult to reconcile this view on reading *FSR* and the *Staff Manual*, which preaches mutual respect, regardless of social status, and even rank. 'Victorian attitudes', whatever that means, and an 'overwhelming emphasis' on social hierarchies was not demonstrably a feature in the main body of the army by the time George V took the throne in 1910. There were exceptions, exemplified by men like Haig and Sir Arthur Paget, but the *Staff Manual* advice is the opposite of hierarchical, demanding a trusting and collegiate team of officers, whatever their rank or social standing. Not all the wording quoted above survived into the final version, but it cannot be ignored.

The next major event in the military calendar was the 1912 manoeuvres, with Sir Douglas Haig, the new GOC (General Officer Commanding) Aldershot Command, as a principal protagonist. These, and the manoeuvres of 1913, need a chapter of their own.

14 TNA: WO 106/51: *Staff Manual (Provisional) 1911*, pp.8–15; TNA: WO 32/4731: Staff Manual, uncorrected proof, War Office, 1912.

15 Travers, *The Killing Ground,* pp,6, 12: see also Travers, 'The Hidden Army', pp.523–544.

8

The 1912 and 1913 Manoeuvres

In March 1912, there was a reshuffle of the British High Command. Sir William Nicholson retired as Chief of the Imperial General Staff, and Sir John French replaced him. Sir Horace Smith-Dorrien left the Aldershot command and was replaced by Sir Douglas Haig, who had been Chief of the General Staff in India. By September, Haig was leading his corps into the 1912 Manoeuvres.

Like all manoeuvres since 1902, commanders were expected to comply with updates in the various training manuals, the most important, in 1912, being *FSR, Part I*, which had been reissued that year with amendments agreed since 1909. In addition, the *Staff Manual* had been issued in 1911, and though it was still provisional and undergoing amendment, it also reflected best practice.[1]

The manoeuvres took place in September, and the scenario of the war game was that Lieutenant General Sir James Grierson's army, on home soil in the south of England, was charged with preventing Haig's army, which had landed on the north coast of East Anglia, near Kings Lynn, from threatening London. Haig commanded the full strength of the only corps in England and had an established staff. Grierson, his opponent, commanded approximately equal numbers, albeit with less cavalry and some second-line Territorial Force units to support his regular infantry, and he had only a few days to expand his divisional staff and brief them on their new duties.

To succeed, Haig needed to defeat Grierson's forces defending London. Grierson had some assets in Cambridge, but most of his army was in Salisbury and Aldershot. The first day, 16 September, was therefore occupied by Grierson's army deploying north of London and by Haig's army marching south to confront him. Their respective forces would meet south of Cambridge, in an arc from Bedford in the west, Bishops Stortford in the south, and then across to a line about 10 miles inland from Colchester and Ipswich in the east. The two forces jockeyed for position on 17 September, and battle was joined in earnest on 18 September.

Sir John French was the director of the manoeuvres and wrote the definitive report on them. He eschews historical references and concentrates mainly on the more senior officers. He states that his assessment of their performance would be 'in conjunction with *Field Service*

1 TNA: WO 106/51: *Staff Manual (Provisional) 1911.*

Regulations.'[2] He starts with a factual narrative of the manoeuvres. The task of the first day for both commanders was to move their troops into position and, at the same time, establish where their opponents were situated. Both used air observation for nearly the first time, with only limited success. Grierson simultaneously sent his cavalry forward with orders that they should reconnoitre. With efficient collation of the reports he received, he had, by the end of the first day, a very good idea of where Haig's forces were and was, therefore, able, to some extent, to estimate his intentions. Grierson was adhering to *FSR*. 'To obtain the necessary [reconnaissance] information, the independent cavalry will dispatch such patrols as he may consider necessary. The most suitable unit ... is a patrol of from ten to twelve strong.'[3] Grierson gave the main body of his cavalry infantry and artillery support, allowing his cavalry commander to organise the reconnaissance, being careful to ensure he received any reports speedily and efficiently. A new cyclist brigade had been given to both armies, and Grierson attached his to his cavalry command to bolster their numbers, advising that they be used 'to screen the flanks of the mounted troops and to form pivots of manoeuvre.' French is very approving of his combined arm tactics and of his innovative use of the cyclists, but he is not so complimentary about Grierson's decision to keep his two infantry divisions separated, thus delaying the concentration of his forces. *FSR* advises that the main elements of a force expecting contact with the enemy should be close enough to provide mutual support; and French quotes the relevant regulations. But he concedes that no harm was done, particularly since the lack of movement of Grierson's 4th Division on the second day kept its position in well-wooded country hidden. French's narrative moves on to cover the second day, when the first contacts between the two forces occurred.

Under *FSR*, the supreme commander of a force issues brief orders to his divisions on movement and intent – he lays down the initial position each division should take up and defines their subsequent objectives, be they defensive or offensive. He issues these orders having studied reconnaissance and status reports collated by his personal staff. The divisional commander is then responsible for the deployment of his own infantry, artillery and other troops to comply with the intent of the orders he has received. If battle is joined, it is again the responsibility of the divisional commander to direct his infantry, or cavalry, brigades in the conduct of it. The Commander-in-Chief issues no fresh orders unless he wishes to adjust either the position or the intent of his divisions. The divisional commander remains responsible for the conduct of the ensuing engagement. So French is acknowledging Grierson's compliance with *FSR*, when he says that he 'wisely, and to a great extent necessarily, appears to have given his divisional commanders a very free hand', as they engaged with their opponents. 'The successful efforts of the Commander of the 3rd Division [Major General Sir Henry Rawlinson] to combine the actions of his brigades, and his energetic use of the offensive are worthy of commendation. His initiative in making use of the Territorial Force detachment at a critical juncture also proved to be justified.' Rawlinson was not the officer who showed this initiative, though his command style, in compliance with *FSR*, allowed it. A senior staff officer carrying orders to this unit saw an opportunity for them to advance and engage a flank of the 1st Division and modified their instructions. A territorial unit helping to maul a brigade of the 1st Division was the cause of considerable celebration that night. 'The Commander of the 4th Division [Major General T. D'O. Snow]', French goes on, 'carried out what was required of him [holding Haig's 2nd

2 TNA: WO 279/47: *Army Manoeuvres, 1912*, pp.52–53.
3 *Field Service Regulations, Part I*, p.115.

Division in check] with only two brigades, wisely holding one in reserve till the end.' Grierson and his senior subordinates had followed the principles of *FSR* with panache and precision.[4]

French had to walk a fine line when he came to addressing Haig's performance. He could not undermine him with blunt criticism, and he would have been aware of the King's presence at the manoeuvres and Haig's friendship with him. But he first points out that Haig ordered Allenby and his cavalry to remain concentrated, without all arms support, and to await orders. No small cavalry patrols were dispatched. As a direct consequence, Snow's 4th Division, under Grierson, managed to evade detection until late on the second night of the exercise. French comments that 'the uses to which cyclists might be put do not appear to have been realised … they were unable to take an effective part in the battle.'[5] Hamstrung by adherence to his orders, Allenby waited, at Haig's instigation, for the opportunity to use his massed cavalry in a glorious charge. The opportunity never came, and his cavalry played almost no part in the battle. French recognised what was happening. 'It must be remembered that Douglas Haig was expecting the operations of his cavalry to take effect at any moment', he says more than once. Nevertheless, Allenby is considerably criticised by French for his inertia throughout the three days.

Similarly, Lomax, commanding the 1st Division, on 18 September, was 'directed to hold his command at the disposal of the Commander-in-Chief.' He was told where to go, but not what his objectives should be, when he got there. On the final day, Haig ordered one of Lomax's infantry brigades to march five miles across the battlefield without consulting him, a grave breach of a fundamental *FSR* command principle. 'Such movements are likely to cause confusion', says French, 'and even shake confidence; they may result in troops being kept out of action at a critical time.' Later in the day, Haig joined Lomax in his headquarters and all but took over the direction of his division. Lomax, undeniably a competent general, was paralysed by Haig's orders, but French criticises him harshly, which does not seem entirely fair.[6] French finishes off his critique of Haig on the final day of the manoeuvres by observing that 'possibly if the Commander-in-Chief had not become involved in the local situation he would have been able to obtain a wider grasp of the battle.'[7] So significant were these lapses from *FSR* doctrine that French did not wait for the publication of his final report to take action.

As Chief of the Imperial General Staff, he went to the Army Council, of which he was the military head, and used his authority to persuade the council to ask the new Director of Military Training, Brigadier General David Henderson, who had only been appointed in July 1912, to collate a new Army Training Memorandum for circulation to all officers. It had not been thought necessary to issue such an update since 1909. It was issued very quickly, in December 1912. The full implications of this document will be addressed later in the chapter, but there is one short paragraph on 'Command and Direction: – Commanders sometimes fail by attempting both to command troops and at the same time to direct operations. If a commander intends to direct, he should appoint an acting commander. If on the other hand he intends to command he should do so under service conditions.'[8]

4 TNA: WO 279/47: *Army Manoeuvres, 1912*, Section III, pp.55–56.
5 TNA: WO 279/47: *Army Manoeuvres, 1912*, Section III, p.61.
6 TNA: WO 279/47: *Army Manoeuvres, 1912*, Section III, pp.54–59.
7 TNA: WO 279/47: *Army Manoeuvres, 1912*, Section III, p.60.
8 TNA: WO 279/552: 'Army Training Memorandum, War Office, 19 December 1912', p.5.

This reaffirms a basic *FSR* command principle and was a stinging rebuke to Haig's generalship at the manoeuvres. Commanders should issue brief orders and allow their direct subordinates to implement those orders. For commander, read general of any rank. Even brigadier generals should not direct the local tactics of a battalion. He could issue a new brief order if he considered the battalion had misunderstood the intent of his original order, or if he wanted it to move, but, under *FSR*, he could not assume control of, or direct, the battalion at a local level. This was especially true of the Commander-in-Chief of an army. Haig had joined Lomax at his 1st Division headquarters and started directing his brigades. This is the only instance of such an abrogation in the entire manoeuvres. This clause in the training memorandum is a reprimand, and the army would have understood it as such.

Returning to French's report on the manoeuvres, he goes on to address staffing with reference to *FSR* and the new *Staff Manual.* Crucial to maintaining 'a wider grasp of the battle' was the efficiency and efficacy of the two commanders' personal staffing arrangements. Haig's chief-of-staff was Brigadier General F.J. Davies, and Grierson's was Brigadier General R.A. Montgomerie. It is worth repeating how *FSR* defines the role of the Commander-in-Chief's personal staff: 'An officer of the staff, [even a chief-of-staff] is vested with no military command … He assists a commander … and transmits his orders.'[9] 'The commander should rely upon reports which have been … prepared for him by his general staff.'[10] These reports should be based on reconnaissance information which had been 'forwarded without delay to the nearest general staff officer', 'the means of communication so organized as to ensure rapid transmission.'[11] 'Orders must be issued in sufficient time to enable subordinate commanders to issue and distribute their own orders.'[12] 'If there be not the closest combination on the Staff, each individual giving to the others all the help in his power, there cannot be combination in the army,' added the new *Staff Manual.*[13] *FSR* demands a collegiate and efficient, non-hierarchical structure for any commander's personal staff.

When French addresses staff duties in his report, Grierson's staff arrangements escape serious criticism, though one or two mistakes are highlighted.[14] This was remarkable given that his staff was makeshift and formed at short notice, whereas the Aldershot staff had been training as a unit all summer. Grierson's report on his staff, incorporating an intelligent analysis of its function based on *FSR*, emphasises his rapport with them:

> I desire to bring to notice the extraordinarily good work done by the younger generation of General Staff officers. They are extremely well-trained, ready to take responsibility, and they are clever at interpreting the intentions of their Commander-in-Chief. To get such work out of General Staff officers, however, the most intimate relations between the Commander-in-Chief and his General Staff officers are at all times necessary.[15]

One does not think of Grierson as paternalistic, but he obviously enjoyed the manoeuvres and goes on to gleefully describe how he and his divisional commanders co-opted officers from other

9 *Field Service Regulations, Part II*, p.25.
10 *Field Service Regulations, Part I*, p.117.
11 *Field Service Regulations, Part I*, p.32.
12 *Field Service Regulations, Part I*, p.124.
13 TNA: WO 106/51: *Staff Manual (Provisional) 1911*, p.14.
14 TNA: WO 279/47: *Army Manoeuvres, 1912*, Section III, pp.61–62.
15 TNA: WO 279/47: *Army Manoeuvres, 1912*, Section III, p.172.

duties to enable all their staffs to function more efficiently. Perhaps it was a dig at Haig, whose relations with his staff were certainly not 'intimate'.

French is unrelenting in describing the poor performance of Haig's staff. He repeatedly criticises poor intelligence arrangements, slow transmission of orders, and inadequate communications. Haig and his 'commanders were far from perfectly informed as to the position … of the various portions of their own Commands. Such a situation should be impossible if staff duties are efficiently carried out.' He gives examples of several important orders which failed to reach their destination, and comments that another crucial order to the 1st Division 'cannot be said to have been fortunately worded.' Worse, there were 'frequent changes of orders'. Infantry brigades generally needed two hours to respond to an order. Changes while they were doing so could lead to hours of disruptive confusion. Haig's cavalry division failed to keep in contact with headquarters or with the 2nd Division it was supporting, and vice versa. Inadequate processing of reconnaissance information is detailed. There was 'neglect to keep in touch with the transport.' Later in the manoeuvres, orders to march arrived after the time that the troops should have set off, and on the last day, one arrived so late that the troops missed their breakfasts.[16] When, that day, Haig moved forward to join Lomax at his divisional headquarters, he did not even take his intelligence staff with him.

In mitigation, Haig, in his report, merely reports that 'the duties assigned to staff officers at their peace stations are, in many cases, widely divergent from the duties they will be called upon to perform in war.'[17] It is difficult to know who to blame for that if not their Commander-in-Chief. Captain John Charteris was on Haig's staff in India in 1911 and transferred with him to Aldershot in 1912. In his biography of Haig, written in 1929, Charteris discusses Haig's relationship with his Aldershot staff in 1912. Haig's reception 'was not altogether cordial', he says. Aldershot 'taught the latest theories of scientific soldiering', a coded reference to *FSR*, while 'India provided less scientific training.'[18] Charteris is here describing a significant doctrinal clash. It seems likely that there were also personal clashes. Haig had brought other personal staff officers, along with Charteris, from India, a contingent derisively referred to, according to Charteris, as the 'Hindoo Invasion'.

It is not as though Haig had no opportunity to hone his Aldershot staff. He directed an Aldershot command staff tour in June 1912. In his analysis, he dismissed most of his staff's 'scientific' training by stating that 'the general principles which [Clausewitz] enunciates seem quite applicable to armed forces today.' In compliance with his perception of what those general principles were, he positioned himself, at the crisis of the battle up with the leading 'echelons', with a personal staff of just three officers who 'will have to do all the drafting and interchange of orders and will be fully occupied.' He abandons not only his intelligence section but his Inspector General of Communications, his QMG and AG, and his artillery and engineer advisers further back to communicate by wire. It is not clear who was to process the information so transmitted.[19] 'Staff officers should never venture to criticise either superiors or inferiors to any person whatsoever.'[20] It is possible that this regulation in the new *Staff Manual* unwittingly

16 TNA: WO 279/47: *Army Manoeuvres, 1912*, Section III, pp.61–62.
17 TNA: WO 279/47: *Army Manoeuvres, 1912*, Section III, p.165.
18 Brigadier General John Charteris, *Field-Marshal Earl Haig* (London: Cassel & Co Ltd, 1929), pp.62–66.
19 TNA: WO 106/1453: 'Report of Aldershot Command Staff Tour 1912', pp.20, 88–92.
20 TNA: WO 106/51: *Staff Manual (Provisional) 1911*, p.13.

stifled debate on a major red flag. There had been another very similar staff dress rehearsal, orchestrated by the Staff College, then under William Robertson, just before Haig's Aldershot ride. This was meticulous in its adherence to the suggested *Staff Manual* structure, detailing responsibilities and communication pathways between a Commander-in-Chief and his staff. The chief-of-staff directed operational and intelligence sections, each subdivided to reflect areas of responsibility. Twelve principal staff officer posts are listed, excluding junior officers with specific duties, and 16 officers attached from the AG and QMG branches.[21]

It is fair to point out that some have interpreted French's criticism of Haig's performance much more benignly. Simon Batten's 2015 paper on the manoeuvres makes only one reference to *FSR*, saying 'the 1912 manoeuvres occurred at a time when the British Army was ... lacking a uniform doctrine', citing as evidence that 'all four divisions in 1912 employed very different methods of attack, with 2nd Division preferring to manoeuvre an enemy out of his position by threatening his flank and line of retreat rather than deliver a decisive blow, 3rd Division deploying on a broad front and 4th Division keeping a strong reserve in hand to use once a weak spot had been located.' He does not refer to the *Staff Manual*, though he does point out that 'one of the specific recommendations made in the manoeuvre report – that the Cavalry Division [based at Aldershot] should have a permanent staff – was not acted on, with disastrous consequences.'[22]

However, when one interprets French's report, its content is remarkable in pointing out so many departures from *FSR* and the *Staff Manual*. The Army Council and, indeed, the King were watching the manoeuvres with interest. Haig gave a completely inarticulate summation of his own performance at the closing conference, attended by many dignitaries and journalists. Anyone listening, says Charteris, would have left 'with the impression that Haig had neither ability nor military learning.'[23] It is possible to feel sorry for Charteris. The conference tried to be positive, concluding that aerial reconnaissance and cycle brigades were useful innovations, and there was much subsequent debate on tactical issues, particularly pertaining to firepower and the artillery.

But French and the Army Council saw Haig as a serious threat to doctrinal uniformity. He was preaching 'a less scientific training', which was ignoring many consensus principles that governed the training and conduct of the army in Britain and Ireland. Haig could not be sacked, so they had to give him a direct order to conform. As previously described, Henderson, the new Director of Military Training, collated an Army Training Memorandum, which was issued in December 1912.

Apart from the short paragraph on 'Command and Direction', it raised many of the points that French would make in his report on the manoeuvres, quoting specific *FSR* regulations. The cavalry came in for specific criticism. There was 'a failure to give a sufficiently definite mission to the commander of the cavalry, *FSR, Part I*, Sections 65, 90 and 91.' Again, this is a criticism levelled straight at Haig. The point is reiterated in the next clause on the 'Use of Advanced Guards', referencing Sections 65–68. The memorandum also criticises some of the

21 TNA: WO 32/4731: *Staff Manual (Provisional) 1912*, p.27.
22 See Simon Batten, 'A School for the Leaders: What did the British Army learn from the 1912 Army Manoeuvres?', *Journal of the Society for Army Historical Research*, vol.93, no.373 (Spring 2015), pp.44–46.
23 Charteris, *Field-Marshal Earl Haig*, pp.62–66.

training that year. It is implied that the training of the cavalry, as defined by *FSR*, had slipped. 'During this year's training the failure to recognise the occasions on which to employ mounted and dismounted action was again observed.' There follows a litany of criticisms. The relationship between *FSR* and the cavalry was uneasy in many ways. Tasks allocated to the cavalry did not always lend themselves easily to adherence with command regulations. Significantly, these criticisms of cavalry training were issued under French's tenure as the senior military member of the Army Council.

The training memorandum of December 1912 gives a very useful snapshot into the extent to which other aspects of the *FSR* doctrine had been instilled in the army. 'The Army Council wish it to be recognised that they are well pleased with the general efficiency of the training of all ranks of the Army.' The memorandum highlights changes made in the *Part I, 1912* update. At the 1910 staff conference, Nicholson had ordered that regulations be drafted to combine the Royal Engineers with the infantry when trench lines or fortifications were being constructed. Section 108, was now in force but had not been fully observed at the manoeuvres. Updates had also been included on the use of a newly formed 'Army Signal Service' in Section 17. 'A continued improvement in march discipline' is noted, as, less positively, were residual problems with local protection as occurred at the 1910 manoeuvres. Advice on the combination of artillery with infantry was still the subject of much debate, and it was not until *Field Artillery Training* was published in 1914 that firmer guidelines were agreed upon. As so often, it is in what is left unsaid that conclusions can be inferred. *FSR* guidelines on orders, for instance, are not addressed. The problems identified pertain to sections of *FSR*, not to whole chapters. *FSR* was well on the way to becoming a firm doctrine.

The 1913 army exercise is far less easy than the 1912 manoeuvres to analyse in terms of adherence to *FSR* and supporting manuals. There are several reasons for this. It was a huge mobilisation of troops involving six infantry divisions, two of them skeleton, and two cavalry divisions. The dispositions were complex, envisaging three participant armies. It rained and was foggy. Heavy transport, including artillery trains, struggled to climb the steep hills of the Chilterns, leading to disruptions of movements. A bland narrative, giving timings and destinations, hides rather than illuminates the tactical principles being followed. French acted both as Commander-in-Chief of the principal army and director of the exercise, which generated conflicts of interest in the conclusions published in the report. In his summing up, French is much less critical of himself as C-in-C than he was of Haig and Grierson the year before, but he does suggest that more work was needed in assessing intercommunication and staff work, since not all that he saw complied with the *Staff Manual*. Senior officers had left their headquarters, he says, losing communication with their staff.[24] French names no names, but Captain Ommanney, a junior member of French's staff did, writing a blunt report on staffing at these manoeuvres, which has found its way into an unrelated file at the National Archives.[25] 'This is dangerous ground,' it says, 'but if a connection is to be kept between the Chief [French] and his staff, it is difficult to see how it can be done if the Chief motors about to his subordinate commanders accompanied only by his four A.D.C.'s who have no direct knowledge of the orders

24 TNA: WO 279/52: Report on Army Exercise 1913, pp.29–31.

25 TNA: WO 106/51: Staff Duties in the Field, Notes by Captain Ommanney after Army Exercise 1913. Captain Ommanney was killed at Hooge in October 1914, along with Lomax and other staff officers.

and instructions given.' French had done what he had criticised Haig for doing the previous year. But even Haig 'indirectly admitted that staff work in his corps had been a problem, stating that it was "fifty per cent more effective" as a result of the exercise.'[26]

The Director of Military Training issued two more Army Training Memoranda after these manoeuvres. These memoranda were circulated to every officer in the British Army. The first, in November 1913, referred to training inspections and was intended to 'assist in the interpretation of the Field Service Regulations.'[27] The second, published in January 1914, additionally addressed the 1913 exercise, 'Although the necessity for consistent adherence to the principles laid down in Field Service Regulations is now generally recognised by all officers, it has been observed that some commanders do not give their subordinates that amount of help and guidance in the application of these principles which they ought to give.' This is criticism that goes right to the top. Senior officers were responsible for ensuring that *FSR* was taught throughout their commands. Almost the last sentence of this memorandum bemoans that 'the standard was higher a few years ago.' Admittedly, this refers to a specific activity, but it is a sentiment that endures. The letter accompanying this memorandum, which was 'prepared under the instructions of [French,] the Chief of the Imperial General Staff,' and endorsed by the Army Council, is addressed to 'General Officers Commanding-in-Chief of all Commands at Home', of whom Haig, at Aldershot, was the most senior.[28]

But time was running out. War was looming.

26 Gary Sheffield, *The Chief, Douglas Haig and the British Army* (London: Aurum Press, 2011), p.116, citing *The Times*, 30 Sept. 1913, p.4, and 20 Sept. 1913, p.10.
27 TNA: WO 279/553: 'Army Training Memorandum during the Individual Training Period 1912–13.'
28 TNA: WO 279/554: 'Army Training Memorandum 1913', pp.3, 5, 14.

9

Field Services Regulations, Part II, the Staff Manual and Politics pre-1914

Superficially, the administrative principles of *Part II* pertained only to the administration and organisation of an expeditionary force. A defining principle of *FSR* was that the Commander-in-Chief should be in command of every element of his force: 'Unity of control is essential to unity of effort. This condition can be ensured only by vesting the supreme authority in one man, the C-in-C of the forces in the field.'[1] This principle was self-evidently sensible in the direction of the operational hierarchy. In mid-August 1914, French, as Commander-in-Chief of the British Expeditionary Force to France, exercised this supreme authority, and, in his name, 'brief' operation orders were issued by the officers of his staff, headed by Murray as his chief-of-staff, who, as *FSR* dictated, should 'assist the commander in the supervision and control of the operations.'[2] So orders were issued by his General Staff, from his General Headquarters (GHQ). Perhaps 'supreme headquarters' might have been a clearer description of its function because also posted to GHQ were the senior representatives of the QMG and AG branches. *FSR, Part II* implies, in a general summary, that the C-in-C commands the QMG and AG with him on campaign.[3] But the *Staff Manual* of 1912 followed the original intent of the 1906 Army Order, which directed that the administrative directorates, including the QMG and AG branches, had an independent hierarchy, which was not controlled by the C-in-C.[4]

'The General Staff,' the manual said, 'is composed of officers, specially appointed to assist superiors who are vested with executive authority on their own responsibility' – superiors, being the commanders at army, corps, or divisional level. Excluded from membership of the 'general staff' are heads of directorates in administrative branches since they are 'acting on their own responsibility in accordance with instructions issued to them by a higher authority.' The manual confirms that the QMG and AG should work closely with the C-in-C, but that they were not under his command.[5] They had independent command functions and were ultimately answerable to their respective superiors in the War Office in London. French could not issue orders

1 *Field Service Regulations, Part II*, p.23.
2 *Field Service Regulations, Part II*, p.25.
3 *Field Service Regulations, Part II*, pp.37–38.
4 TNA: WO 106/51: *Staff Manual (Provisional) 1911*, pp.59–67.
5 TNA: WO 106/51: *Staff Manual (Provisional) 1911*, pp.15–18.

to them, but they had both an advisory function, in keeping French's chief-of-staff informed of the practicalities of supply and personnel in general, and a command function in that they had responsibility for ensuring that the needs of his fighting men were met by their sub-directorates. Attached to GHQ, in August 1914, therefore, were the directors of these various 'Administrative Services and Departments', or sub-directorates, almost all of whom were subordinate to the QMG and AG. These included directors of supplies, transport, ordnance, works, remounts, veterinary and medical services, post, and the paymaster.[6] Thus, on campaign, staff officers belonged to one of three branches. 'G' branch staff were those who served on the personal staff of the various generals in a purely operational capacity, the 'principal planners of military actions', as Harris put it. 'A' branch handled personnel, medical and other such services, while 'Q' managed supplies, quartering, transportation, and postal services.'[7] GHQ had already become a large concentration of administrative duties.

Specialist Advisers at GHQ, of whom the first two, on mobilisation in mid-August 1914, were a Royal Artillery major general and a Royal Engineers brigadier general, were also denied staff status. 'Officers attached to the Staff, but not actually appointed to it, are not Staff officers.' They were free-standing, with no command responsibilities. Their role was not only to advise the C-in-C and his chief-of-staff on operational matters, but also the QMG on relevant supplies, and the AG on relevant billeting and personnel issues. Initially, they had no staff support, since they had neither administrative nor operational command responsibilities.

GHQ would inevitably be some distance from the coastal ports where the force landed, and the lines of communication between these ports and the main body needed to be protected and supervised. *FSR* envisaged an Inspector General of Communications (IGC) who was responsible for the protection and supervision of all traffic on the lines of communication. He also had the duty to report daily to the C-in-C on the state of supply, accepting briefings from the C-in-C's chief-of-staff on impending operations that might demand extra resources.[8] The consequence of this was that the QMG and AG posted to the BEF were only responsible for moving supplies and personnel forward from holding areas or depots to the front line. They were completely dependent on the IGC to allocate them suitable premises and to decide on priorities for delivery to them on and via the lines of communication. The IGC, of necessity, had his main headquarters away from GHQ on the lines of communication, from where he could monitor who or what was arriving from England, working in tandem with an officer from the QMG's branch for supplies and the AG's branch for men.[9] The C-in-C, QMG, and AG for the expeditionary force were all at GHQ. The QMG and AG did not have the right to make routine representations directly to the C-in-C, but were required to take problems to the IGC in the first instance. *FSR* also assumed that the IGC would control and run the railways between the port of disembarkation and the front line. The first dress rehearsal for this arrangement was run by Sir William Nicholson in 1908.[10] But it was also tested less rigorously on other exercises, including the first day of the 1912 manoeuvres. The complexity of these arrangements and the

6 Brigadier General J.E. Edmonds, *History of the Great War, Military Operations, France and Belgium 1914: Volume 1, Mons, the Retreat to the Seine, the Marne and the Aisne, August-October 1914* (London: MacMillan, 1933), pp.471–472.
7 Harris, 'The Staff of the British Army', p.27.
8 *Field Service Regulations, Part II*, pp.32–34.
9 *Field Service Regulations, Part II*, p.41.
10 TNA: WO 279/22: 'Report on a Staff Tour, October 1908', pp.6–11.

potential for confusion and conflict were recognised rather belatedly, after the *Staff Manual* had been published in its final form in 1912.

At the staff conference of January 1914, Sir Horace Smith-Dorrien, then the General Officer Commanding, Southern Command, sponsored a presentation by Major General Altham, who served under him, on the relationships of the IGC with those based at GHQ, as defined in *FSR*. The conference was chaired by French in his capacity as Chief of the Imperial General Staff. Altham drew attention to the complexity of these arrangements and recognised a possible stop-gap solution of simply putting the IGC under the command of the QMG, but then went on to suggest a complete rethink of the senior relationships at GHQ to provide a more stable and permanent solution. Summarising the ensuing debate, others, supporting him, went on to suggest that the posts of QMG and AG at GHQ could be merged. At this point, Brigadier General Du Cane got very tetchy, accusing Altham and others of wanting to rewrite *FSR* altogether; Brigadier General John Gough, representing Aldershot, said he had not done his homework and did not really understand the problem, but that he was sure that Haig saw no necessity for change. Major General Macready, from the Adjutant General's department, tried to calm the debate by supporting a rethink of the relationships, and French was left to sum up what was clearly a very important problem with no solution that would unite all parties. He had little choice but to defer the issue for further consideration.[11]

Probably it is as well that he did. Going to war halfway through an *FSR* rewrite might have been worse than going to war with regulations that were already recognised as flawed, with a debate on possible solutions on record. French, Murray, Robertson, and Macready, respectively C-in-C, Chief of the General Staff, QMG and AG in the BEF of August 1914, were all at the conference. The only absentee from the five men who had to live with the problem later that year was Frederick Robb, who was to become IGC. This is a somewhat simplistic overview of an important debate, but this was neither the first, nor the last, time that two of the most influential officers in the British army, Haig, and Smith-Dorrien, took different stances on a major *FSR* issue, with French between them as an indecisive referee. It was to be a recurring theme over the next year.

Brown, in his book *British Logistics*, not only gives a valuable account of this debate, but also gives an overview of *FSR, Part II* in 1914. It 'set out the means by which the British Field Armies would be organized and administered … The document had some inherent strengths, the greatest [being] its inherent simplicity.' Those drawing up the regulations 'in 1909 could not have predicted the scope of Britain's next war, [thus] … general principles provided a very sound basis for field regulations.'[12] Another strength, for a reference handbook, was the range of subjects with which it dealt. Many of these benefited from being succinctly described so that the details of the arrangements to be made were left flexible enough that the regulations could apply whatever the infrastructure, terrain, and climate of the country to which the expeditionary force was to be deployed.

A good example is the provision of medical services, as described in Chapter XI. The basic structure of the service is laid out. A single medical officer is attached to each battalion, or

11 TNA: WO 279/495: 'Report of a Conference of General Staff Officers at the Royal Military College, 12th to 15th January 1914, held under the Orders and Direction of the Chief of the Imperial General Staff', pp.29–38.

12 Brown, *British* Logistics, chapter 2 'War Plans and Reality' pp.41–46.

similarly sized unit, with his medical supplies in a 'maltese cart' (essentially a pony and trap). His role is to apply first aid and to supervise his stretcher bearers. A daily wastage rate of three men per thousand is estimated, but 'after a general engagement, the number of wounded to be dealt with is not likely to be more than twenty per cent, nor less than five per cent of the troops engaged.'[13] Field ambulances, the organisation of these being 'very elastic,' would transport wounded from a 'collection zone' behind the fighting, chosen by this one medical officer, and take them to the 'evacuation zone', which comprised 'clearance hospitals' and 'ambulance trains'. Finally, casualties would reach the 'distributing zone', being allocated to one of five types of medical facility, including hospital ships and convalescent depots for the lightly wounded. 'In practice, all three zones must overlap somewhat.' Although a brief outline is given of front-line arrangements and procedures for the guidance of medical officers, much is left to the initiative of the medical sub-directors at the various locations.[14] By 1914, a further handbook entitled *Regulations for the Army Medical Service* and a pamphlet on training had been published.

A battalion stretcher bearer's post in 1915. (Author's collection)

However, it is notable that the *FSR* section on sanitation is far more directive than the section on medical services. The lessons of the South African War had been well-learnt: 'The commander of every unit and formation is responsible for the sanitary conditions of the quarters or localities occupied by his command, and for taking all measures necessary for the preservation of the health of those under him.' He is required to seek the advice of the medical officer if

13 *Field Service Regulations, Part II*, p.123.
14 *Field Service Regulations, Part II*, pp.116–125.

in doubt, and he could expect sanitary inspections from the district 'specialist sanitation officer', who commanded 'sanitary squads' which acted as 'sanitary police' invested with the authority of military police, wearing badges of due authority. Like the medical arrangements, this much more tightly defined bureaucracy was administered by a directorate of the AG's department.[15]

In practice, problems arose in 1914 and thereafter because some of *FSR*'s general principles pertaining to command arrangements were too well defined. Certain of its detailed provisions, particularly concerning transport, proved unworkable in 1914 and 1915, and adjustments had to be made. Most of these adjustments were obvious and self-evidently desirable, although senior officers always took a deep breath before jettisoning specific *FSR* regulations. In most cases, the problem regulations were referred to the War Office, which took a pragmatic attitude in not meddling with adjustments that worked.

A major problem not foreseen was that of artillery command. Almost from the first month of the war, it became increasingly clear that the command hierarchy for the artillery was not fit for purpose. An almost inviolate principle of *FSR* was that the divisional commander fought any battle, having been directed on movement and intent by more senior commanders. The divisional commander should, therefore, have total control of all the military assets that he intended to use in carrying out his orders. This meant that the artillery command essentially stopped at subdivisional level, with the brigadier general, Royal Artillery, being the most senior officer to control artillery in battle. With the precipitate growth of artillery, particularly heavy artillery, in France, there was no formal method of coordination. Artillery Advisers, who were attached to GHQ and corps commands but were not on the staff of either, had no operational role and were forbidden from interfering in the artillery direction of a division. There was no leeway on this point in *FSR*. It was established in the principles of *Part I* on training for war and all arms combination, and it was backed up by command regulations in *Part II*.

As the command status quo became increasingly stressed by the realities of battle, there was no time and no mechanism for considered amendments to *FSR*. The solutions that were found and the fervent doctrinal debate that they engendered will be addressed in the second half of this book. Just as with operational research, the study of the administration and organisation of the British Army at war requires an understanding of basic, and evolved, *FSR*.

However, it is not enough to regard *FSR* as merely being intended, as Michael Hunzeker put it in 2021, 'to provide officers with precise instructions designed to meet every wartime contingency.'[16] It may be read that way on a superficial study. But its early drafts had served as a facilitator and driver of the debate which characterised the pre-war professionalisation of the British Army, a process which started in the aftermath of the South African War at the turn of the century and was accelerated by the Haldane reforms from 1906. Haldane was a philosopher politician, and any major policy document produced under his watch incorporated principles which reflected both political realism and ideological direction. *FSR* represented a major step in the professionalisation of the army, and that was an ongoing process. No draft of *FSR* was intended to be the last word. Nobody advocated rigid adherence to tactical training guidance that was not informed by recent developments in warfare.

15 *Field Service Regulations, Part II*, pp.111–116.
16 Michael A Hunzeker, *Dying to Learn, Wartime Lessons from the Western Front* (Ithaca: Cornell University Press, 2021), p.100.

So, if a historian writing on operations alleges that a specific tactical training regulation is demonstrably unsuited to trench warfare, it is unreasonable for him to conclude that the whole document was obsolete. Just as it is unreasonable that an earlier generation of historians dismissed the relevance of *FSR*, except as a Haig-centred affirmation of nineteenth-century ideas on how to conduct war. *FSR* shaped the army with some principles that are quite inflexible. These had a very significant impact, not always beneficial, on the way the war was conducted. But within both parts of *FSR*, there are drivers which encourage and guide change, and there are administrative arrangements that allow organic growth, even allowing unconventional solutions. *FSR*, in 1909, was as much a political manifesto as a prosaic handbook.

When Richard Haldane became Secretary of State for War in late 1905, the army was poorly administered and hardly under political control. It answered first to the King, and politicians were reactive, rather than proactive, in their dealings with it. The army was seen as a deterrent force ready to be deployed to trouble spots around the Empire, a home defence force in case of invasion, and, in the last resort, a force to aid the civil authorities in the event of unrest on home soil, but how it would set about performing any of these functions was not clearly defined. By 1909, however, when *FSR* was published, Haldane had usurped much of the King's responsibilities and defined exactly how he wanted the army to respond in case of war. By 1914, there were plans as to how their other functions could be implemented.

FSR is often dismissed as a document, nebulously defining the staff reforms that transpired in the army in the years before 1914. It is barely mentioned in David French and Brian Holden Reid's book on *The British General Staff* of that era.[17] John Gooch, in *Plans of War*, is similarly reticent, though his Haig centrism disrupts the narrative of his chapter on these years. He does say that, 'in other areas of the General Staff besides that concerned with strategic planning, there were signs of development which corresponded to the supposed needs of war', and this in 1910. He goes on to say that, by 1914, 'manuals [had] played a vital part in the preparation of the army', while making the point that they 'had not been thoroughly revised or refined.'[18] Brian Bond, in his chapter on the 'General Staff' in his book on the *Staff College*, makes much the same points: 1910 'marked the beginning of the General Staff's preoccupation with practical planning for war', he says, and that, at least by 1911, 'the General Staff was making a serious effort to educate the Army for war.' By 1914, the General Staff 'had established definite training principles by means of the staff manuals … and provided a fairly efficient "thinking department" at the War Office.'[19] He does not credit the publication of *FSR* in 1909 as the catalyst that, at the least, spurred on this sequence of events.

During 1908 and 1909, the Army Council, the General Staff (correctly defined by Bond as those officers in the War Office under the Chief of the General Staff), the QMG and the AG had been devoting their full attention to the detail of *FSR, Part II*. *FSR* was a detailed study of the best way to organise the prosecution of an expeditionary war. So, it seems unsurprising that in 1910, those at the War Office who had devoted the last year or two of their lives to ensuring *FSR* was fit for its narrow purpose would move on to ensure that the structure of the peacetime army was such that its provisions could be supported in the transition to war. The preparation and implementation of *FSR* by the Army Council, at the instigation of Haldane, from 1907,

17 Trythall in French and Holden Reid, *British General Staff*, p.145.
18 Gooch, *The Plans of War*, pp.119, 126.
19 Bond, *The Staff College*, pp.234, 239 in Chapter 7, pp.213–240.

enabled the changes in army thinking that allowed them to achieve this. *FSR* kick-started the cultural reform of the War Office.

By 1910, senior officers and Haldane himself could present *FSR*, particularly *FSR, Part II*, as evidence that the army had a very clear idea as to how they would fight any war. It also had a wider vision of what the army required from the state to facilitate that purpose. Wilson, for instance, because his role has been most thoroughly documented, was able to go to the Committee of Imperial Defence (CID) and present a concise expression of how the army could respond to any political demands that were put on it. Senior officers could be confident that they commanded a small, but nevertheless very professional, army, organised and trained to fight any type of war. Famously, a Royal Navy delegation to the CID in August 1911 was unable to present a coherent analysis of their role in any future conflict. Hew Strachan briefly describes this meeting and goes on to say that the 'CID's attention between 1911 and 1914 was focused, not on the BEF and its possible deployment, but on the Royal Navy, blockade and home defence.'[20] This statement can be challenged. The CID endorsed a focus on mobilisation, as well as the facilitation of a wider role for the army at home in the event of a political crisis. But, before examining the specific ways in which the CID did this, it is instructive to consider the decision-making processes in Edwardian Britain.

Change in the Edwardian era did not necessarily emanate from democratic, or even bureaucratic, processes. Many ambitious and very able individuals had a quite disproportionate impact on major institutions, up to and including the state itself. As in every era, including our own, there were currents of change and reactions to perceived threats that drove the body politic onward. The changing relevance of Empire, the challenges of industrialisation and bureaucratisation, and the rapid development of new technologies, all vied with unfounded fears of invasion and a burgeoning market for scaremongering spy stories that shaped the era. Unelected individuals took it upon themselves to engage generally or specifically with perceived problems or threats. New ideas, and new solutions, some with military implications, were often adopted after informal proposals by individuals, followed by consensus implementation with the agreement of senior figures in the organisation addressed. Viscount Esher, for instance, wielded extraordinary influence. Relying only on a carefully nurtured friendship with the King, he had no democratic mandate for the responsibilities he was handed. It was his committee which had mandated *FSR*. On a smaller scale, within the army, Gerald Ellison had no formal right to continue editing his early draft of *FSR, Part II* between 1904 and 1906. He never worked within Hutchinson's Directorate of Staff Duties. Similarly, Charles Callwell and David Henderson acted alone in writing their books on *Small Wars,* and *Field Intelligence*, respectively. Both were subsequently taken up by the War Office and published as semi-official guidance for the army after the end of the South African War. Reforms, or new ideas that were perceived as deserving attention by an influential elite, were implemented with only semi-formal authorisation.

FSR should be read, not with a modern analytical approach, but with an awareness of these Edwardian conventions as regards the genesis of ideas and their implementation in practice. *FSR* describes a framework, which is accepting of innovation and embellishment. It is both rigid and malleable. The ideas in *FSR* embraced far more than military detail. *FSR* defined a doctrine for the British Army, compliant with the national mood. It was not just an instruction manual

20 Strachan, 'The Continental Commitment', p.77.

for the management and deployment of an expeditionary force. Richard Haldane personified this slightly anarchic, paternalist approach to organisational change.

He was an elected representative and had specific responsibilities as Secretary of State for War, but he was also a man of his time. Once he had settled into his job in 1906, he embraced this spirit of exploration and cooperation and set the tone for army reform. Two distinct types of men are needed for different purposes in the army, he asserted. There is the 'fighting man', and there is 'the man charged with administrative duties of a civilian nature, who needs only enough military knowledge to conform to military requirements.' He pointed out that these two cohorts have different training and educational needs.'[21] He knew that the 'Staff College trained future generals and chiefs of staff, not future quartermasters or adjutants', as Ian Brown, amongst others, asserts.[22]

Aimée Fox, in *Learning to Fight*, describes how Haldane made a determined effort to improve administration skills in the army as early as 1907, acting alone and only semi-officially. He arranged for a cohort of officers to attend the London School of Economics (LSE) to join a 'Course for the Training of Officers for the Higher Appointments in the Administrative Staff of the Army.'[23] G. Sloan, in his 2012 article in *War in History*, describes this initiative in more detail. Since 1902, Haldane had been a member of a semi-formal group of 12 distinguished men who met for dinner to discuss political and economic issues from a Fabian viewpoint. They called themselves the Co-Efficients. 'Haldane was the expert in Law and Mackinder was the expert in Liberal Imperialism. Other prominent members were Sir Edward Grey, Bertrand Russell, Leo Amery, George Bernard Shaw, Sidney Webb, and H. G. Wells.' Halford Mackinder became director of the LSE in 1903, and as soon as Haldane became Secretary of State for War in 1906, he asked Mackinder to design a course for army officers. Mackinder immediately proposed a six-month course in economics and business administration, starting in January 1907, and suggested that it be repeated annually. Haldane instructed the Army Council to release 30 officers, mostly colonels and majors, to attend this external tuition. Mackinder, in his opening address, said 'that the British army was the greatest single business in the United Kingdom. He then went on to argue that both the Army Council and the Lords of the Admiralty were in fact two boards of business directors.' Seven of these comprehensive courses in business administration had been run by 1914.[24] If committees were involved, Haldane made it clear that their function was merely to rubber stamp the proposals.

Haldane inherited an organisation that was already aware of the rapid innovation and technological change of the first decade of the twentieth century. This awareness is epitomised by the ethos of *FSR, Part I*, with its annual conference at which specific regulations could be challenged and amended, encouraging officers to keep themselves actively informed on military developments abroad and on civilian developments that might have military applications. It took little more than tacit approval from Haldane and the Army Council to allow informal contacts between soldiers and civilians in such fields as cartography, communications, and aviation. This

21 TNA: WO 33/3379: Richard Haldane, 'Further Note,' December 1906, p.1.

22 Brown, *British Logistics*, p.17.

23 Aimée Fox, *Learning to Fight, Military Innovation and Change in the British Army, 1914–1918* (Cambridge: Cambridge University Press, 2018), pp.164–184.

24 G. Sloan, 'Haldane's Mackindergarten: a radical experiment in British military education', *War in History*, 2012, 19 (3). pp.322–352. Gooch wrongly attributes this initiative to Haig; Gooch, *Plans of War*, pp.108–109.

is to ignore the many more formal links necessitated by the introduction of new weaponry, particularly artillery pieces, for the army, the manufacture and design of balloons, and a host of other developments in aeronautics.

Aimée Fox, in her chapter on 'Civilian Expertise' in *Learning to Fight*, describes in detail the army's many semi-formal pre-war links with civilian bodies. It was recognised from quite early in the decade that 'soldiers, particularly those in the technical branches of the army, could derive further benefits from training in, and exposure to, civilian skills. This took place in a number of fora from lectures to formal courses.' The British army's pre-war Field Survey assets were seconded to the Ministry of Agriculture and Fisheries. The Institute of Civil Engineers developed close ties with the School of Military Engineering at Chatham, and a particularly strong link was forged between military and railway specialists, such that an officer-only 'Engineering and Railway Staff Corps' was incorporated into the Territorial Force in 1907.[25] Christopher Phillips, in his book *Civilian Specialists at War* also describes 'the army's willingness to seek out and exploit expertise from civilian sources, concentrating on links with the railway industry.'[26]

There were other links. 'The Queen Alexandra's Imperial Nursing Service supported the regular army and had 463 trained nurses in 1914', says Charles Messenger in his book, *Call-to-Arms*. Apart from the Territorial Force Nursing Service, there were three established voluntary organisations. The First Aid Nursing Yeomanry and the Women's Sick and Wounded Corps were both active from 1907. 'In 1909, the War Office drew up a scheme open to both sexes for providing voluntary aid to the sick and wounded. This became known as the Voluntary Aid Detachments, which were formed under the auspices of the TF County Associations but were managed by the British Red Cross Society and St John's Ambulance.'[27]

FSR, Part II was clearly influenced by this modus operandi. It was a product of a specific moment in Edwardian history. There are many ways that civilian influences are acknowledged in *FSR, Part II*. The whole ethos of it is that army administration should follow a civilian model of directorates to manage its functions. Chapter VII on Supplies, Chapter VIII on Transport, and Chapter XI on the Medical Service all acknowledge that civilian expertise will shape the organisation of them in the circumstances of a campaign. More specific examples of direct civilian involvement are not hard to find. Accountants are attached to an expeditionary force for the first time, a decision not particularly welcomed by the Army Council. In the provision of medical services, there are explicit arrangements made for accepting civilian help from those charitable sources just described to augment arrangements made within army resources. For example:

> All voluntary offers of assistance in aid of the sick and wounded made in the United Kingdom on the outbreak of war or during the progress of hostilities, other than those coming from the Ambulance Departments of the St. Andrew's Ambulance Association for the provision of personnel, must be submitted, in the first instance, to the British Red Cross Society, who will communicate them to the Army Council if they are likely to be of practical value.[28]

25 Fox, *Learning to Fight*, pp.164–184, 196.
26 Christopher Phillips, *Civilian Specialists at War: Transport Experts and the First World War* (London, University of London Press 2020) p.24.
27 Charles Messenger, *Call to Arms, The British Army 1914–18* ([2005] Cassell, London, 2006), pp.243–246.
28 *Field Service Regulations, Part II*, pp.126–128.

Many new charities sprang up, and the principle of the army being prepared to accept useful civilian assistance was extended to include, amongst other skills, interpreters and volunteer drivers from motoring organisations on the outbreak of war.

Superficially, it might appear that *FSR, Part II,* merely laid down the command structure, administration and associated notes required for the direction, supply, and support of an expeditionary force. But it also acknowledged that, in the twentieth century, the army could not work in isolation. It needed civilian input, civilian ideas, and civilian methods to function to its full potential. *FSR* says almost nothing about the structure, ethos, or duties of those working at the War Office in London, but those who worked on *FSR* recognised that what was true for a small part of the army, an expeditionary force, had to apply to the wider army and, in particular, the War Office. *FSR, Part II* required the War Office to rethink and redesign its role on many fronts, but most significantly on mobilisation.

FSR, Part II from 1909, says, somewhat airily, that 'the prescribed military authorities are responsible that preparations are made in peacetime in accordance with Regulations [for Mobilisation] for either general or partial mobilization as may be ordered.'[29] This begged the question as to who the 'prescribed military authorities' were. 'The Adjutant General to the Forces', *Part II* continues, 'is responsible to the Army Council for the provision and maintenance of personnel [and for] coordination of mobilization arrangements and orders. The Quartermaster General' for issuing supplies and equipment and for 'providing horses.'[30] This is restating the understanding of the arrangements prior to 1909, when mobilisation plans were the responsibility of the AG, and a mobilisation committee was a fixture at the War Office. Necessarily, some mobilisation responsibilities were devolved. In 1908, according to the *War Office List*, the Military Secretary supervised the placement of officers, and the QMG dealt with stores, with separate arrangements being made for the artillery and engineers. The AG had overall responsibility for coordination.[31] There is no record of a coordinated transport plan and seemingly little overview responsibility.

In 1908, the military duties of Major General John Spencer Ewart as Director of Military Operations are defined as relating almost exclusively to the British Army overseas.[32] By 1912, Henry Wilson, Director of Military Operations, though only a temporary brigadier general, was devoting most of his time and energy to the detail of mobilisation transport arrangements in the United Kingdom. His interest may have dated from when he had acted, somewhat bruisingly, as Inspector General of Communications and Railways, in the dress rehearsal of *FSR, Part II* run by Sir William Nicholson in October 1908.[33] Keith Jeffery, in his biography of Wilson, quotes General Sir Percy Radcliffe as saying of M.O.1 in 1912 that 'having been a rather sterile and academic branch, living in a rarefied atmosphere of its own, it became the mainspring of all our preparations for war.'[34] This is somewhat of an overstatement, but it does illustrate how the demands of *FSR*, intelligently interpreted, precipitated such a startling change of culture at the War Office. As so often in Edwardian Britain, the innovations were generally organic, driven by individuals who were in tune with the national mood and responsive to political concerns

29 *Field Service Regulations, Part II*, p.21.
30 *Field Service Regulations, Part II*, p.185.
31 H. Moggridge, *The War Office List 1908*, pp.xiii–xiv.
32 H. Moggridge, *The War Office List 1908*, p.41.
33 TNA: WO 279/22: 'Report on a Staff Tour, October 1908', pp.6–11.
34 Jeffery, *Field Marshal Sir Henry Wilson*, p.101.

about the country's readiness for war. Wilson exemplifies this quality, but he was merely one of a cohort of officers, and it is his superior, William Nicholson, Chief of the Imperial General Staff, who deserves the credit. It was in another context, but Nicholson's comment at the 1910 staff conference sums up the spirit of the army between 1909 and 1914. 'Each man to his trade. Make use of all the expert knowledge you can get. That is my view.'[35]

By 1914, the *Regulations for Mobilization* allocated a great deal of the responsibility to the general officers commanding all the various commands in Great Britain, Ireland and even the Channel Islands. They had to maintain registers of all local reservists, amongst other duties.[36] The peacetime structure of the War Office, and the duties delegated to army commands, including Aldershot, were little by little, but significantly, amended so that the whole army could seamlessly transfer onto a war footing. *FSR, Part II* implied rather than defined the necessity for this change, but it can be regarded as one of the catalysts that precipitated these reforms.

The extent of civilian involvement in these plans and the role of the Committee of Imperial Defence (CID) in allowing them to be implemented is relatively well known. This secretive committee comprised, from 1903, the 'Lord President, the Prime Minister, the Secretary of State for War and the First Lord of the Admiralty' with non-cabinet members 'the First Sea Lord, the Commander-in-Chief, the Head of the Naval Intelligence, and the Head of Military Intelligence.'[37] 'It theoretically formalised inter-service cooperation.'[38] The Prime Minister could coopt additional members if he deemed it necessary. It had a secretariat and supported a host of sub-committees that reported back to it. The Prime Minister could, and did, refer many contentious issues to these sub-committees, whose reports were never published, but whose conclusions and recommendations were adopted and implemented by extra-parliamentary decree on the outbreak of war, or before.

There was an acceptance across the spread of what, for want of a better phrase, can be described as the 'establishment' in Britain, that a major continental crisis, even an invasion, was a realistic possibility and that steps needed to be taken to plan for war. Although this debate was open, consequent decision-making was often not. Different parts of the establishment identified specific problems or risks and then worked out their own contingency precautions or solutions, often without reference to higher authorities or each other. Many of these 'plans' were never agreed in cabinet, let alone Parliament.[39] Some were presented to, or appropriated by, the CID, which 'supported the cause of state action', in contrast to most politicians who did not.[40] They addressed a wide range of issues, civil and military. For instance, Britain's trading and business community, so vital for its prosperity, depended on the international banking system, of which the City of London was a major hub. After an uncomfortable flight of capital from London during the Morocco crisis in 1911, the Treasury and senior bankers disagreed on how to address

35 TNA: WO 279/496: 'Conference of General Staff Officers 1910', p.20.
36 *Regulations for Mobilization 1914* (London: The War Office) pp.8,16.
37 Dunlop, *The Development of the British Army*, p.215. This was the constitution of the Committee of Defence, set up in 1903. Its name was later changed to the Committee of Imperial Defence.
38 John Sweetman, 'Towards a Ministry of Defence: First Faltering Steps, 1890–1923', in French and Holden Reid (eds), *The British General Staff*, p.33.
39 Cameron Hazlehurst, 'Asquith as Prime Minister, 1908–1916', *The English Historical Review*, vol.85, no.336 (July 1970), p.510.
40 David French, *British Economic and Strategic Planning, 1905–1915* (London: George Allen and Unwin, 1982), p.77.

the problem in the future, but draft legislation was mooted to give ministers the power to react and stabilise the financial system. During a series of earlier crises, just at the smallest threat of war, the availability of insurance for shipping and cargo had dried up. Without it, ship owners briefly stopped their ships from sailing. Longer hiatuses in imports to Britain would have led to a shortage of food and raw materials for industry, leading, potentially, to famine and mass unemployment. Government guarantees to ship owners were mooted but then scotched.[41] Both issues were noted by sub-committees of the CID, which took notes and then sat on them. This is a simplistic summary of wider issues, but it illustrates the almost laissez-faire philosophy of the pre-war years and sets the scene for an increasingly proactive role for the state.

Even before 1909, the CID was instrumental in authorising, with the full cooperation of industrialists and local authorities, measures to facilitate the army's perceived role in time of crisis, and how, it and the state should react in the event of war. In 1908, local authorities were instructed, as part of their statutory duties, to develop plans to impose internal military control, including censorship and internment, in an emergency, though it was 1913 before a register of aliens was prepared. There was no democratic legitimacy to this. In 1908, an *Emergency Powers Act* to allow activation of these arrangements was mooted but never enacted.[42] In 1910, Wilson, as Director of Military Operations, obtained permission from the CID, with Prime Minister Herbert Asquith and Secretary of State for War Richard Haldane concurring, to devote the resources of his directorate, for the foreseeable future, to planning in detail the mobilisation of the 'Expeditionary Force', so scantily described in *FSR*.[43] In 1910, the CID had set up a standing committee to address the 'Co-ordination of Departmental Action on the Outbreak of War.'[44] According to Gooch, this committee reported in April 1911. Actions to be taken in the run-up to war 'chiefly relating to the provision and protection of transport and communications', although 'there are many instances in which the responsibility of taking the requisite action has not yet been allotted to individuals or sections.'[45] Maurice Hankey, who was assistant secretary to the CID from 1908 and full secretary from 1912, took responsibility for the preparation of a *War Book*, which formally, from 1911, allocated these responsibilities, mostly pertaining to railways and ports.[46] In tune with these pronouncements, Wilson was able to invoke the authority of the CID to obtain full cooperation from the merchant shipping and railway industries and by November 1912, he had worked out a two-week timetable.[47] To facilitate his project, the CID issued further guidance to local authorities, building on the 1908 directives.

Wilson's mobilisation plan was kept up to date and annually rehearsed on random units. The CID sponsored other plans, too. The fledgling Labour Party and increasingly militant trade unions were mooting a general strike at even the threat of war.[48] This, combined with

41 French, *British Economic and Strategic Planning*, p.76.
42 French, *British Economic and Strategic Planning*, p.76.
43 McDermott, J. 'The revolution in British military thinking from the Boer war to the Moroccan crisis', in Paul Kennedy (ed.), *The War Plans of the Great Powers 1880–1914* (Abingdon: Routledge, 2014 [1978]), p.107.
44 TNA: CAB 38/16/21: 'Co-ordination of Departmental Action on the Outbreak of War.' Committee of Imperial Defence, November 1910.
45 Gooch, *The Plans of War*, pp.119–120.
46 See also; French, *British Economic and Strategic Planning*, ch.2.
47 Jeffery, *Field Marshal Sir Henry Wilson*, pp.87–102.
48 Alan Simmonds, *Britain and World War One* (London: Routledge, 2011), pp.15–17.

gloomy forecasts of a financial crash, followed by famine and unemployment, fostered the belief that civil unrest, even insurrection, was a real possibility. In 1913, the War Office agreed to a Home Office and Metropolitan Police request that troops be provided to guard key buildings, including food distribution centres, in London in the event of potential civil unrest.[49] But, there was still no *Emergency Powers Act* to legitimise these provisions. With a European war at least a possibility, the CID had taken on itself, without parliamentary scrutiny, the task of developing measures to be imposed on the civilian population of Britain if war should break out. Many industrialists and politicians tacitly approved or cooperated with the arrangements. When war did break out, a cabinet subcommittee was immediately set up, which appropriated and actioned many of the CID contingency plans – with questionable legality and without keeping minutes. As an example, it authorised a Rail Executive Committee to take control of the railways.[50]

It is up to the reader to decide whether *FSR* was a mere footnote to these military and civil preparations or whether its implementation was a prerequisite to the arrangements the army was able to make in terms of War Office reform, legitimising the formation of partnerships with civilian authorities and businesses to enable efficient mobilisation and other increasingly tightly defined reactions to any crisis. It can certainly be argued that the ethos of *FSR*, that of an acceptance of the army's interrelationship with civilian developments and civilian concerns, was integral to the arrangements made.

The adoption of *FSR* by the army was merely one of the measures that was accepted in what can retrospectively be termed the build-up to war between 1908 and 1914. The mood of the times encouraged the military to engage with civilian experts, to accept their ideas, and vice versa. The implementation of *FSR* within all parts of the army, not just those parts that would make up any expeditionary force, was all the more thorough and complete because its philosophy was completely in tune with the pre-war political climate.

49 French, *British Economic and Strategic Planning*, pp.85–86.
50 French, *British Economic and Strategic Planning*, p.88.

10

The Historiography of Field Services Regulations pre-1914

Conventionally, the historiography of a subject is presented at the beginning of a book, but in truth, there are no books in the literature which address the subject of *FSR* as a primary theme. There is mention in passing. There is some acknowledgement of its existence. But there is no analysis of its content. There are very few assessments of its impact over time, and these are unsupported by more than very brief summaries of its genesis. It can reasonably be asked if there is a historiography of a subject that has never been seriously studied. Any historiography of *FSR* must consist of plucking brief sentences or paragraphs from publications devoted to what their authors regard as broader themes. Many of these authors are of great stature. So, where to start?

Field Service Regulations, 1909 constituted a general doctrine for the British Army of 1909. As an anonymous author (thought to be Major Richard Pope-Hennessey) stated in the *Edinburgh Review* in April 1911: 'It is among the first duties of the General Staff of a great modern national army to indoctrinate it with a clear conception of the basic principles of war', and he accepted that the intent of *FSR* was to 'indoctrinate'. He rejected the idea that *FSR* constituted a military doctrine since this required a commitment to a particular tactical shape when deploying for battle, nor was it a tactical doctrine, due to its deliberate operational flexibility. The author was critical of *FSR* in consequence. Definitions of doctrine in a military context have changed, but it seems reasonable to distinguish, as he does, between general, military, and tactical doctrines. He does not address command principles as comprising a doctrine. Douglas Haig wrote to Launcelot Kiggell in 1911, saying that 'I have tried to preach 'the doctrine' as laid down in *FSR*… and have quoted chapter and verse so that the General Staff here may interpret the regulations in the way in which I believe is intended.'[1] But he had opined the previous year that 'Field Service Regulations and Manuals are in themselves of little value unless their teaching is connected by a general common doctrine inculcating initiative and cooperation.'[2] It is difficult to interpret this statement. Initiative and cooperation are at the heart of *FSR*, but Haig is implying that something is missing. It suggests that it was his personal view that *FSR* was not quite a doctrine.

1 Haig to Kiggell, 27 April and 15 June 1911, (I/11 & I/15) quoted in DeGroot, *The Military Career of Douglas Haig*, pp.329.
2 TNA: WO 279/526: *Reports on Staff Tour, held by the Chief of the General Staff, India, 1910*, p.34.

This goes to the heart of how a doctrine was defined before 1914. All historians look for continuity, and almost the only area in which *FSR* has been extensively discussed is in responding to the question as to whether it constituted a doctrine in 1914. In that context, it is doubly surprising that no academic study has set out to analyse what it says across the full range of subjects it covers. It is easy enough in a document as long as *FSR* to cherry-pick quotes that suggest one view of war or another, as Pope-Hennessey did in 1911. So, what are academic historians looking for?

Any officer who had attended the Staff College in the last years of the nineteenth century would have seriously studied the 'art', or even 'science', of war, based on the work of a succession of nineteenth-century military theorists. This was not only true of most senior officers in 1909, but it is also true of academic historians, most of whom have steeped themselves in the military campaigns of the eighteenth and nineteenth centuries. 'In the years before 1914 … it is important to understand that a Jominist conception of general principles rather than tightly constricting rules was the intellectual atmosphere', say Bowman and Connelly in *The Edwardian Army*.[3] 'FSR continued to reinforce the lessons of [Haig's] Staff College years, with an emphasis on Clausewitz', says Tim Travers in his book, *The Killing Ground*.[4] It is thus impossible to make an objective assessment of *FSR* and its historiography without an awareness of the impact of the old masters on both serving soldiers pre-war, and on the historians that study them. Adam Dighton, who wrote an article in 2020 entitled 'Jomini versus Clausewitz: Military Thought in the British Army, 1866–1933', demonstrates that this approach is still considered relevant.[5]

But Dighton is joining Hew Strachan in this arena, and such is his stature, it is as well to start a review of the literature on the origins of *FSR* with his thoughts. His masterly summary of the impact of European military writers, such as Jomini and Clausewitz, on the development of doctrine in the British Army prior to 1909 describes the importance that he felt was attached to establishing continuity of doctrinal thought. Strachan quotes from Jomini's *Précis*: 'Jomini saw his subject not as an art but as a science', and 'said that war consisted of five parts: strategy, grand tactics, logistics, tactics of the different arms, and the art of the engineer; operations, his discussion of which was subsumed under strategy, was not one of them.' In contrast, 'Clausewitz defined strategy as the use of the battle for the purposes of the war. He saw much of the tactical activity of his own day as indecisive and went on to argue that it was the aftermath of battle, the pursuit, that determined its wider outcome.' Tactics 'is that part of war in which theory can develop most fully into positive doctrine.' Strachan goes on to argue, with hypnotising erudition, the influence of both on Henderson's teaching at the Staff College in the 1890s, linking that to the principles in *FSR, Part I*. He sees *Part I* as a logical successor to these masters, citing Hamley's book, *The Operations of War*, which has been discussed in a previous chapter, as an intermediary.[6] In another publication, he credits Robertson and Haig, in 1907, as influenced by Henderson, with moulding the final shape of *Part I* along Clausewitzian lines.[7] *FSR* 'was drawn

3 Bowman and Connelly, *The Edwardian Army*, p.76.
4 Travers, *The Killing Ground*, p.92.
5 Adam Dighton, 'Jomini versus Clausewitz: Hamley's Operations of War and Military Thought in the British Army, 1866–1933', *War in History*, vol.27 (2) 2020, pp.184–185.
6 Strachan, 'Operational Art', pp.3, 5, 8.
7 Robertson was chief-of-staff at Aldershot, under Horace Smith Dorrien. He contributed to debate on the content of *FSR*, but there is no evidence he challenged his commander's views. Robertson had been sponsored by Henderson, going with him to South Africa in 1900. He never forgot his debt.

up under the supervision of Douglas Haig, while he was DSD', he says, and 'reflected ideas which Haig had formulated in 1896–1897.'[8] Strachan is writing in support of a thesis, first put forward in the 1960s by John Terraine, and developed by Tim Travers in the 1980s, that puts Douglas Haig at the centre of events. Since he commanded the British Army for three of the four years of the war, guiding it to victory in 1918, this is not an unreasonable stance to take for those years. But these three historians assert Haig's centrality to events right back to the 1890s, based on a theoretical intellectual continuum in military thinking.

Before addressing this issue further, the question must be asked as to how Haig came to be credited as the original thinker behind *FSR*. Going back to the immediate aftermath of the First World War, there are important books which address *FSR* principles but not the origins of it.[9] The first oblique reference in secondary sources to the origins of *FSR* comes in a 1929 biography of Haig by John Charteris, one of his staff juniors. He claims that Haig was Haldane's 'right hand man', being the director charged with arranging the 'details of the … organization of the Expeditionary Force', in 1906, implicitly crediting him with revising *FSR, Part II*, for publication in 1909.[10] As Director of Military Training in 1906 and most of 1907, Haig had no responsibility for *FSR*, and there is no evidence to support the narrative that Charteris asserts. In 1935, Haig's more official biographer, Sir Alfred Duff Cooper, later Secretary of State for War and then First Lord of the Admiralty, records that when, in November 1907, Haig 'was transferred from Director of Military Training to that of Director of Staff Duties … except for office routine, his real work [setting up the Territorial Force] remained very much the same, for he arranged that several of the duties hitherto performed by his former office should be transferred to his latter one.' He retained responsibility for 'questions of policy and war organization'. Duff does not enlarge on this statement, going on to describe how the strain of his work on the Territorial Force contributed to his collapse from exhaustion in April 1908.[11] In 1938, Brigadier John Dunlop, the former Assistant Adjutant General of the Territorial Army, wrote in his influential book, *The Development of the British Army 1899–1914*, that '*FSR, Part I, Operations*' was approved as a consensus document, and '*Part II, Organization and Administration*' was ratified as a political necessity, both in 1909, while Haig was DSD. It is possible to infer from the following paragraphs that Dunlop thought that Haig had an influence on both, though a misprinted date and muddled wording make this moot.[12]

There matters rested until, in 1961, a military historian, Alan Clark, published *The Donkeys*, so titled in reference to the phrase 'lions led by donkeys.' This castigated Haig and his fellow generals of 1915 for unimaginative tactics that resulted in huge loss of life, and it ignited a wave of anti-Haig sentiment, which was further fuelled by *Oh! What a Lovely War*, a 1963 stage play that was released as a film in 1969. Aware that this presentation of events had entered the national consciousness, a group of mainly British historians were appalled at the way Haig was

8 Strachan, 'The Continental Commitment', p.92.
9 S.W.H. Rawlins, *History of the Development of the British Artillery in France 1914–1918, from records in the Office of the Major General Royal Artillery at General Headquarters* ([privately published, 1918] <www.theogilbymuster.com AMOT039_WW1_MD.1162>); Alexander H.C. Kearsey, *1915 Campaign in France, The Battles of Aubers Ridge, Festubert and Loos, considered in relation to the Field Service Regulations* (Sussex: Naval & Military Press, 2007 [Gale & Polden, 1929]).
10 Charteris, *Field-Marshal Earl Haig*, pp.37–39.
11 Cooper, *Haig*, p.116.
12 Dunlop, *The Development of the British Army*, p.292.

being lampooned and in 1963, John Terraine, who worked on military topics for the BBC as a journalist and screenwriter, published *Douglas Haig, the Educated Soldier*, which credits Haig with learning from experience in the Sudan, followed by South Africa. Making little of his spell at the Staff College in 1897, he goes on to note that Haig thought deeply on cavalry tactics, publishing both officially and unofficially before being appointed to the War Office in 1906:

> South Africa had exposed the want of a general doctrine of war in the British Army, a system of thought and organization, laid down by a General Staff … General De Pree, who was on Haig's staff at the time, has left an account of Haig's policy in action, in the teeth of reactionary opposition to such an un-British concept.

He then cites the anecdote previously told by Duff Cooper in his biography of Haig, pertaining to:

> …a staff conference in January 1907, where a 'Member of the Army Council got up and in a most amusing speech poured ridicule on [the draft *FSR, Part II*]'. The assembly was greatly amused till Haig rose with a face of intense anger and, in a cutting voice, said 'If General X—— will tell us what we ought to do instead of pulling everything to pieces, we shall get on much better. Let us have some system to start with, and if it is not perfect, we can improve it.' General X—— despite his seniority and high position made no rejoinder … After this, there was very little opposition to the reforms of the General Staff, and the Army which fought the Great War was administered and organized on the lines laid down in this book.[13]

This conference happened in 1908, not 1907. Apart from Lyttelton, who chaired the conference, there was no member of the Army Council present. The anecdote presumably refers to Major General H. Miles, a future Quartermaster General. In the discussion after Adye's lecture on the ideas in *Part II*, Miles seems to have specifically challenged proposals which related to lines of communication. Neither Lyttelton nor Haig were sufficiently familiar with the document to counter the detail of Miles' argument, and Lyttelton regretted that the author of the papers Adye had presented, presumably Ellison, was not present to clarify the issues raised. Haig then said, Lyttelton agreeing, that he believed that the army 'must start with these regulations and give them a trial. If they were found not to work, they could be modified as experience dictated.' This measured account of the proceedings may have glossed over some heated words.[14] Haig exhibits no familiarity with the detail of *Part II*, but is loyally following Haldane's policy, which had been adopted by the Army Council some weeks previously, of getting the document ready for future publication. Having asserted that Haig had scotched opposition to reform, Terraine goes on to assert that 'the final value of this achievement … need hardly be stated; coupled with a similar approach to Operations in *Field Service Regulations Part I*, it constitutes a major, but almost forgotten, contribution to final victory.'[15] This is the totality of the evidence offered by

13 John Terraine, *Douglas Haig, the Educated Soldier* (London: Leo Cooper, 1990 [reprint: Cassel, 1963]), chapter 3, pp.42–43.
14 TNA: WO 279/18: *Conference at the Staff College, 1908*, p.27.
15 Terraine, *Douglas Haig*, p.43.

Terraine that Haig was closely involved with the final editing and implementation of both parts of *FSR*. His narrative is quite openly an attempt to re-establish Haig's intellectual reputation.

Brian Bond, in his 1972 book, *The Victorian Army and the Staff College*, does not refer to *FSR*, except in occasional mention of 'regulations', although he does credit the three staff college commandants of this era, Rawlinson, Wilson, and Robertson, with influence. He does not address the impact of Staff College conferences on the evolution of British Army doctrine.[16] In 1974, John Gooch wrote in *Plans of War, 1900-1916* that three staff officers, Colonels Henry Wilson, Sir Henry Rawlinson, and Gerald Ellison, co-wrote an early draft of *FSR, Part I*, but he credits Haig with editing *Part II* for publication during the late summer of 1908, as previously described, and suggests, with no supporting evidence beyond his organisation of the two cavalry staff rides, also previously described, that Haig participated in the implementation of both parts of *FSR* in 1909.[17] In 1980, Edward Spiers, in his biography of Haldane, reaches the conclusion that Haig almost single-handedly forced the army to accept *Part II*. He mentions neither Ellison nor Nicholson in his analysis. He does not trace *FSR* through committees, and he sets the scene for the uninformed and remorseless Haig centrism of many of the books and papers that characterise the next 20 years.[18]

Probably the most influential book in cementing the belief that Haig and *FSR* were almost indivisible is *The Killing Ground*, by Tim Travers, published in 1987. Like Spiers, he is relentlessly Haig-centric, barely acknowledging other military thinkers in the British Army. He says that because Haig learnt certain ideas at the Staff College in 1897, this reflected what the army was learning. He goes much further than Terraine, Gooch, or Spiers in his chapter on 'Douglas Haig, the Staff College and the continuity of ideas.' He credits Haig with developing ideas at the Staff College in 1897 that 'stayed with him to the First World War and beyond.'[19] As Director of Staff Duties in 1907, he 'was responsible for preparing the Field Service Regulations and for attempting to inculcate a sense of uniformity in the army regarding strategy, tactics and staff organization … FSR continued to reinforce the lessons of his Staff College years, with an emphasis on Clausewitz.' Once at war, in 1916, 'Haig was not alone in attempting to apply an earlier ideal to twentieth century warfare. A host of senior officers maintained the same attitude … as might be expected, since they were following *FSR* doctrine.'[20] Travers is claiming that *FSR* was based on Clausewitz and that Haig embodied *FSR* and the doctrine of the British Army in its prosecution of the war, that it thought and acted as he did. This is the hypothesis that Hew Strachan supported so articulately in 2002 and thereafter.

A digression is required. It is undeniable that Haig accepted Clausewitzian theory as his creed. His book, *Cavalry Studies, Strategical and Tactical*, published in 1907, his cavalry staff rides in 1909 as Director of Staff Duties, and his two major rides in India in 1910 and 1911, all include long essays drawing lessons from the writings of Clausewitz and others. In a letter to Kiggell in 1910, just after *FSR* was published, Haig criticised the 'talkers' at the War Office, Aldershot, and Camberley who 'know not what war really is, nor Clausewitz' fundamentals.'[21] In June 1912, at an Aldershot command staff ride, he wrote that 'the general principles which

16 Bond, *The Staff College*.
17 Gooch, *The Plans of War*, pp.113–117.
18 Edward Spiers, *Haldane, An Army Reformer* (Edinburgh: Edinburgh University Press, 1980), pp.151–154
19 Travers, *The Killing Ground*, pp.92, 96.
20 Travers, *The Killing Ground*, p.92.
21 Brown, *British Logistics*, p.27, referencing Haig to Kiggell, 14 July 1910, Kiggell Papers, I/8, LHCMA.

[Clausewitz] enunciates seem quite applicable to armed forces today'. Especially is his conclusion true that 'if an army is formed into two principal corps, each of which has its special commander, that is to neutralise the Commander-in-Chief.'[22] Haig is here contradicting almost the key principle of *FSR*. 'Unity of control and effort can be ensured only by vesting the supreme authority in one man, the C-in-C of the forces in the field.'[23] It is not difficult to find other assertions by Haig which fundamentally contradict both the letter and spirit of *FSR*. Cavalry should enjoy 'the greatest independence of other arms in every kind of duty', he says, not for the first or last time, in 1909.[24] So, are Travers and Strachan right in asserting that the military theorists who undoubtedly guided Staff College teaching before the South African War continued to inform army thinking into the twentieth century?

The practice of analysing strategic and tactical deployment in terms of historical precedent was waning throughout this period. At Hutchinson's 1906 staff conference, a veteran Colonel Lonsdale Hale, spoke up 'For Teaching and for Studying Military History', aware that cadet colleges and the Staff College were beginning to limit the amount of time in the curriculum that was devoted to the theories of Jomini, Clausewitz and military history in general. His lecture was a plea for the status quo.[25] But since Roberts had ordered that *Combined Training* be used as the principal tactical guide for analyses of manoeuvres or staff rides in 1902, fewer and fewer officers were citing historical precedents in their reports. There are no historical references at all in the analyses of the 1904 manoeuvres.[26] There were two staff rides in 1907, under Lyttelton as Chief of the General Staff. The first was coordinated by Hutchinson, Director of Staff Duties, and there is one very brief reference to Jomini, and another to Moltke by Lyttelton in a 75-page report, but the relentless emphasis is on compliance with *Combined Training*.[27] In the second, coordinated by Haig, Director of Military Training, 'a deep study of military history is the best guide' to the problems raised, and historical precedent is repeatedly referenced in the commentary.[28] Nobody but Haig, and perhaps Lyttelton, seems to have this view. It is a surprise when French produces a short paragraph citing Clausewitz in his long report on the 1909 manoeuvres.[29] As an aside, the only mention the current author has found, of historical precedent in diaries on active service, though doubtless there are more, is a Captain Mowbray, on the divisional staff under Haig in the confusion of I Corps retreat from Bavai and Mauberge on 25 August 1914. 'The 2nd Corps cannot be nearer than Le Cateau – a dangerous division of force. This situation reminded one of British and Prussian retirement after Quatre Bras by forest of Soignies.'[30] One doubts Mowbray shared this observation with Haig.

Perhaps, the last word on the subject should be given to William Robertson, commandant of the Staff College, speaking to graduating students in 1912:

22 TNA: WO 106/1453: 'Report of Aldershot Command Staff Tour 1912' Aldershot 1912, p.20.
23 *Field Service Regulations, Part II*, p.23.
24 TNA: WO 279/27: *Cavalry Staff Ride of Director of Staff Studies, March 1909*, p.31.
25 TNA: WO 279/9: 'Conference and Staff Ride, January 1906,' p.131.
26 TNA: WO 279/8: 'Report on Army Manoeuvres, 1904,' pp.8–11, 76–90.
27 TNA: WO 279/14: 'Staff Ride held by Director of Staff Duties May 1907' pp.37, 42.
28 TNA: WO 279/17: 'Staff Ride held by The Chief of the General Staff October 1907,' p13. Also pp.10, 19, 46, 48, 49.
29 TNA: WO 279/31: 'Report on Army Manoeuvres 1909' Introduction, Director's Report and p.42.
30 RAM: MD/931: Captain, later Major, J L Mowbray, RFA, Untitled diary, 24 Aug 1914, p.7.

> It will further assist you to keep on the right lines if you remember to study with the definite aim of obtaining guidance for future use in war, and not merely for the sake of amassing … knowledge of past wars. …[If we adhere] to this viewpoint, we shall not be likely to waste time in fascinating, but valueless, hair-splitting dialectics; we will not make too frequent use of stereotyped phrases which may mean one of several things or even nothing at all; we shall not burden our minds with too many historical parallels and will not be so apt to form conclusions which, however attractive they may appear on paper, have little or no connection with the rough and bloody work of masses of men trying to kill each other.[31]

This statement from a man at the forefront of change in the British Army suggests that he believed that the study of the past masters of warfare lacked relevance in a new industrial age. He, and other disciples of Henderson who had experienced the South African War, and then digested reports from the Russo-Japanese War in Manchuria in 1904, saw nothing to gain from studying principles of warfare that had evolved from Napoleonic and subsequent campaigns. The impact of so many new technologies – railways, telephones, motor cars, machine guns, smokeless rifle cartridges, quick-firing artillery, aeroplanes, and balloons – looked to have changed the face of warfare forever. It is difficult to argue, too, that the adoption of modern business management techniques by the administrative branches of the army, as defined in *Part II*, was a legacy of the past.

In common with the assertion that the British Army laid a disproportionate emphasis on historical precedent, Travers also teaches that 'the British officer corps on the eve of war was still Victorian in many of its attitudes, with an overwhelming emphasis on the influence of individual personalities and on social and regimental hierarchies.' Its promotion system 'reflected an amateur army caught in a changing world.'[32] It is possible to question whether Travers is talking about the world in which Haig moved, and the attitude that Haig displayed, since he concentrates with such intensity on him in his commentaries, or the actuality of life in the army, where royal patronage and self-indulgent study did not penetrate. His approach ignores the professionalism engendered by compliance with the principles of *FSR*. With *FSR* denigrated and inextricably linked with Haig's ideas, it is hardly addressed by the next generation of historians.

In 1988, Peter Simkins, in *Kitchener's Army*, says that 'many retired officers [returning to command in 1915] found they could not adapt to the changes wrought by the introduction of the new Field Service Regulations', but this is the only mention of *FSR* in the book.[33] This fascinating observation deserves at least a modicum of further analysis, but alas, there is none. At least, Simkins introduces a subject for further work. Thoughtful mentions of *FSR*, even cryptic mentions, are rare. Books that mention *FSR* only to emphasise Haig's association with it can be disregarded. In 2002, General Trythall, contributing to French and Holden Reid's, *The British General Staff*, says that *FSR* 'provided a detailed delineation of the duties of the General Staff.'[34] It is frustrating that he does not amplify what he means by this statement, beyond describing the red tabs that General Staff officers were entitled to wear.

31 William Robertson, quoted in Bond, *The Staff College*, pp.279–280.
32 Tim Travers, *The Killing Ground*, pp.6, 12: see also Tim Travers, 'The Hidden Army', pp.523–544.
33 Simkins, *Kitchener's Army*, p.217.
34 Trythall in French and Holden Reid (eds), *The British General Staff*, p.145.

Those historians who tackled operational or biographical subjects pertaining to the Western Front in the 1990s had no guidance beyond their diligence in reading *FSR* for themselves. Their output is characterised by agreement with Travers. Most assume that Haig's leadership embodied *FSR*. Even the distinction between *Parts I* and *II* is blurred in most publications. With varying emphasis, most of this generation of historians either ignore *FSR* altogether or do so after asserting that Haig 'supervised' or 'wrote' *FSR*. There is one conspicuous dissenting voice. Gerard De Groot's 1988 biography of Haig states that Haig has 'been given too much credit for *FSR*' and did not create it.[35] Most papers and books suggest that he did. Amongst the most prominent during the 1990s are Dennis Winter's *Haig's Command, a Re-assessment*,[36] Michael Howard in the *London Review of Books*,[37] Paddy Griffith's *Battle Tactics of the Western Front*,[38] and Sanders Marble's PhD thesis, *The Infantry cannot do with a gun less*.[39]

An unfortunate side-effect of this was that *FSR* continued to be ignored or misunderstood in operational and biographical publications. It was assumed that because Haig wrote the regulations, they must conform to his thinking. In a further logical contortion, it was further assumed that Haig must have followed them in his command methods after their publication and that Haig's military thinking and *FSR* were one and the same. This was the teaching passed on to the next generation of academic historians at the millennium. The 1999 edition of Brian Bond and Nigel Cave's *Haig, a Re-appraisal*, mentions *FSR* only once, despite the assumption made by most of its contributors that Haig was instrumental in its genesis and implementation.[40] A new century did not lead to a reappraisal.

Since then, many important studies continue to assert that Haig was instrumental in the development of *FSR*. For some papers, it is a fundamental premise. Haig 'played a major role in formulating doctrine … in the form of Field Service Regulations 1909, for the whole army', says Gary Sheffield.[41] Sometimes, there is some academic analysis of what *FSR* says, but almost always focusing on just one aspect of it. Timothy Bowman and Mark Connelly, co-authors of *The Edwardian Army*, assert that *Part I* 'was largely written by Haig.' Having confined their analysis and discussion of *FSR* to tactical training regulations, they unsurprisingly conclude that *FSR* was not 'a rigorous system' that defined the army in 1914.[42] The following are some more important works that continue to assert Haig's association with *FSR* into the twenty-first century. Albert Palazzo's *Seeking Victory on the Western Front*; J.P. Harris's *Douglas Haig and the First World War*, and Ian Beckett, Timothy Bowman, and Mark Connelly's *The British Army and the First World War*.[43] These are only a representative sample, and there is little to be gained by

35 Gerard De Groot, *Douglas Haig*, p.128.
36 Denis Winter, *Haig's Command, A Reassessment* (Barnsley: Pen & Sword Books, 2005 [1991]), p.34.
37 Michael Howard, *London Review of Books*, vol.13, No. 8, 25 April 1991, p.5.
38 Paddy Griffith, *Battle Tactics of the Western Front* (New Haven: Yale University Press, 1994), p.77.
39 William Sanders Marble, 'The infantry cannot do with a gun less: the place of the artillery in the BEF, 1914–1918', Ph.D. thesis, King's College, London, 1998, p.157.
40 Brian Bond and Nigel Cave (eds), *Haig, a Re-Appraisal 80 Years On* (Barnsley: Pen & Sword, 2009 [reprint, 1999])
41 Gary Sheffield, 'The Makings of a Corps Commander', in Jones (ed.), *Stemming the Tide*, p.114; see also Gary Sheffield, *The Chief*, p.60.
42 Bowman and Connelly, *The Edwardian Army*, pp.66, 74, 77, 87, 95, 105.
43 Albert Palazzo, *Seeking Victory on the Western Front, The British Army and Chemical Warfare in World War 1* (Lincoln: University of Nebraska Press, 2000), pp.17–19; J P Harris, *Douglas Haig and the First*

addressing, at this juncture, the papers debating the learning curve theory, which are dependent on this assumption but hardly mention *FSR*.

However, early in this century, some historians encountering *FSR* in their research began to question, implicitly rather than explicitly, whether one man could have shaped such a complex set of regulations and whether its importance to the British Army of 1914 had been underestimated. Certainly, Spencer Jones, in his thesis on the *Tactical Development of the Regular British Army, 1902–1914*, in 2009, and subsequent works raises these questions. Without allocating any credit to Haig, he addresses in detail concepts which, after debate, were accepted into *FSR* and other training handbooks. He states categorically that 'while Field Service Regulations was an important advance in British military thinking, it did not represent the creation of a formal written [tactical] doctrine.' The reasons for this pronouncement are as compelling now as they were in 1911, when Pope-Hennesey first voiced them. 'Faced with the need to remain flexible to face a variety of enemies around the globe, the British Army was neither willing nor able to develop a formal operational doctrine prior to the First World War.'[44] Jones is referring to the tactical elements in *FSR, Part I*, not the entirety of the document, when he rejects it as a formal doctrine. He makes no effort to address the command or administrative principles described in *FSR, Part II*.

Niall Barr, who has taught at both King's College London and Sandhurst, wrote in 2004 that 'the regular officers of 1914 had had many years of experience of command and took [*FSR*] for granted.' He further describes its general impact on ethos, tactics and command.[45] Andrew Simpson in his important paper on corps command in 2001, acknowledges the importance of *FSR, Part II* in determining operational hierarchies, and Tony Vines' 2015 paper on management also recognises the centrality of *Part II* in determining administrative hierarchies. Both assert that Haig had written the document, sticking to this belief with such certainty that their conclusions are questionable.[46] Ian Malcolm Brown's masterly study of *Logistics on the Western Front*, deserves special mention. It was published in 1998 and stands almost alone in emphasising the impact of *FSR, Part II* on the British war effort from beginning to end – without allocating any credit to Haig for formulating it.

Aimée Fox, in her 2018 book on *Learning to Fight*, addresses all aspects of *FSR*, including the duties and responsibilities of officers. She reaffirms that 'Haig was one of the key architects of FSR'. She agrees with Travers that 'the lack of an authoritative doctrine pre-1914 resulted from the social and organizational structure of the army, including the formal and informal power of the regiments and of principal generals.' She agrees with Jones that *FSR, Part I* was not a doctrine and goes on to say that neither was *Part II*, despite, or because of, its 'inherent simplicity'. In the first chapter, she decides that the British Army had an 'ethos' in 1914 of which

World War (Cambridge: Cambridge University Press, 2008), p.45; Beckett, Bowman and Connelly, *The British Army*, p.41.

44 Jones, 'Tactical Development of the Regular British Army', pp.44, 46.

45 Niall Barr, 'Command in the Transition from Mobile to Static Warfare, August 1914 to March 1915', in Gary Sheffield and Dan Todman (eds), *Command and Control on the Western Front, The British Army's Experience 1914–18*, (Staplehurst: Spellmount, 2004), pp.14–15.

46 Andrew Simpson, *The Operational Role of British Corps Command on the Western Front, 1914–18*, Ph.D. thesis, University College, London, 2001; Anthony Vines, T*he Heroic Manager: An Assessment of Sir Douglas Haig's Role as Military Manager on the Western Front*, Ph.D. thesis, King's College London, 2015.

FSR was an essential component, but that *FSR* did not constitute a doctrine which defined that ethos. Her book is very wide-ranging, and she refers to *FSR* regularly. She concludes that 'fundamental to the army's learning effectiveness was the influence of [a] two stranded pre-war ethos, comprising the social and the intellectual, [which] provided an important and enduring framework throughout the First World War.'[47] She does not, in her conclusion, revisit the difference between a doctrine and a strong multi-faceted ethos.

Michael Hunzeker, in his book *Dying to Learn: Wartime Lessons from the Western Front*, in 2021, takes a different approach. He hails *FSR* as 'a landmark in British military thinking', but then says that 'the FSR manuals were [merely] intended to provide officers with precise instructions designed to meet every wartime contingency', and that it was, therefore, not a doctrine. If *FSR* had been a doctrine, he says, it would have standardised army training, educated 'junior leaders' to cope with war, created a source of 'institutional memory', and fostered debate. Apparently, it did not achieve these objectives. He then seems to have second thoughts about whether the British Army had a doctrine, saying, of 1914, that 'professionalism alone cannot account for the BEF's tactical acumen', and that 'the BEF's moderately centralized command structure also deserves credit'. His analysis then drifts, and he fails to develop the very pertinent concept of institutional memory with respect to the British Army, *FSR* and 1918.[48]

Some historians writing on 1914 to 1918 come close to agreeing with Fox's continuity of 'ethos' for want of a better word at this juncture. Jim Beach, in his paper on 'Doctrine Writing' from 1917 to 1918, observes that official Stationery Service [SS] guidance issued to all officers in 1916 genuflects 'towards the pre-war Field Service Regulations (FSR), with the earlier guidance being noted in regard to [its] general principles'. The fact that 'references to FSR had appeared in earlier doctrine manuals … is more than just an accidental continuity.'[49] Jonathan Boff, in his book *Winning and Losing on the Western Front*, quotes *FSR, Part I*, before observing that, 'in theory, therefore, the British Army of 1914 was firmly alive to the value of a combined arms approach.' In the subsequent narrative, he describes how the best units of the Third Army were replicating this approach in their fighting at the very end of the war.[50]

There is a small group of relatively recent papers which ignore *FSR* altogether, leading to simplistic conclusions. Simon Robbins, a research fellow at the Imperial War Museum in 2005, ignores *FSR*'s impact on conduct and relationships, the ethos, of pre-war regular officers in his book on *British Generalship*.[51] Andrew Duncan's 2016 thesis on the 'Military Education of Junior Officers', and Simon Batten's 2015 assessment of the '1912 Manoeuvres' are potentially useful studies that seem incomplete without consideration of the impact of *FSR* on their chosen subjects.[52]

47 Fox, *Learning to Fight*, pp.34, 43, 241.
48 Hunzeker, *Dying to Learn*.
49 Jim Beach, 'Issued by the General Staff: Doctrine Writing at British GHQ, 1917–1918', *War in History*, 19 (4) 2012, p.489.
50 Jonathan Boff, *Winning and Losing on the Western Front: The British Third Army and the Defeat of Germany in 1918* (Cambridge: Cambridge University Press, 2012), Ch.5, 'British Tactics, the True Elixir', pp.126–135.
51 Simon Robbins, *British Generalship on the Western Front, 1914–18: Defeat into Victory* (Taylor and Francis e-library, 2005), pp.1–17.
52 Duncan 'Military Education'; Batten, 'The 1912 Army Manoeuvres'.

Far more surprising is the lack of mention of *FSR* in pre-war biographical assessments of almost every senior general of 1914 except Haig. Neither Keith Jeffery's biography on *Sir Henry Wilson*, nor Robin Prior and Trevor Wilson's on *Sir Henry Rawlinson*, refer to *FSR*.[53] This seems an extraordinary oversight. There is no mention of *FSR* in *Haig's Generals*, edited by Ian Beckett and Steven Corvi, despite the impact acceptance, or otherwise, of its principles had on their command styles.[54] Spencer Jones, and contributors to the compendiums he edited addressing 1914 and 1915, are more aware. 'Field Service Regulations laid out important principles that proved of value in 1914', he says in the first of them.[55] Following the lead of Andrew Simpson's pioneering work on corps command, others are beginning to draw attention to the difference in command styles that can be attributed to the pre-war influence of the principles of *FSR*.[56] The importance of different command styles amongst the various generals at the Somme is beginning to be analysed in more detail, usually with conscious awareness of *FSR* principles.[57] But this is encroaching on the impact of *FSR* on the British Army at war on the Western Front, and the second half of this book will address these issues in more detail.

53 Jeffery, *Field Marshal Sir Henry Wilson*, p.63; Prior and Wilson, *Sir Henry Rawlinson*, p.9.
54 Ian Beckett and Steven Corvi (eds), *Haig's Generals* (Barnsley: Pen & Sword Military, 2020 [reprint: 2006]). The chapter on 'Hubert Gough' by Gary Sheffield and Helen McCartney refers usefully to Gough's non-compliance with *FSR*, albeit without referencing or appearance in the index.
55 Jones (ed.), *Stemming the Tide*, p.21; Spencer Jones (ed.), *Courage without Glory, the British Army on the Western Front 1915* (Warwick: Helion, 2019 [2015])
56 Andrew Simpson, *British Corps Command*, Ph.D. thesis.
57 See, for instance, David Tattersfield, 'British Corps Commanders in the Great War', https://www.westernfrontassociation.com/world-war-i-articles/british-corps-commanders-in-the-great-war/, accessed 17 March 2022.

Part II

Preface to Part II

'The necessity for consistent adherence to the principles laid down in Field Service Regulations is now generally recognised by all officers.'

Memorandum 'issued to every officer at Home, in the Regular Forces, Special Reserve, and Territorial Force,' January 1914.[1]

'If all officers act in accordance with these regulations the whole army will work in harmony, and economy of force will result; but if, instead, officers act on the inspirations of the moment, however brilliant these flashes of genius may be, discord will arise through misinterpretation of intention, and the army will act inarticulately, and wear itself to pieces by the friction of its parts.'

J.F.C. Fuller in *Training Soldiers for War*, published in 1914.[2]

'It is not intended that this pamphlet should in any way take the place of existing training manuals.'

Introduction to *Notes from the Front,* issued to all officers in February 1915.[3]

'The general principles laid down in our training manuals hold good.'

Sir Launcelot Kiggell, Haig's chief-of-staff at GHQ, in SS 109, *Training of Divisions for Offensive Action*, published May 1916.

To 'a steady adherence to the principles of our Field Service Regulations are our successes to be attributed'.

Sir Douglas Haig, in September 1918, to Sir Henry Wilson, a principal pre-war author of them.

'There has been a tendency during the present war to look upon trench warfare and open warfare as two separate things. This has led to a disregard of many of the fundamental principles, laid down in the training manuals issued before this war, as being inapplicable to trench warfare… We have now, however, resumed our allegiance to principles of training employed before the war.'[4]

SS 135, *The Division in Attack, November 1918.*

1 TNA: WO 279/554: 'Memorandum on Army Training during the Collective Training Period, 1913'.
2 Captain J.F.C. Fuller, *Training Soldiers for War* (London: Hugh Rees Ltd., 1914), p.45.
3 Central Distribution Section (CDS) Number 4, *Notes from the Front, Part III, and Further Notes on Field Defences, Collated by the General Staff,* February 1915, p.31.
4 Stationery Service (SS) Number 135, *The Division in Attack, issued by General Staff, November 1918*, pp.3–4.

The first half of this book argues that *FSR* did constitute a professional doctrine for the British Army of 1914 – a doctrine, moreover, that had evolved by consensus, shaped by the views of a host of senior officers over many years. Most historians agree that the British Army of 1914 fought with awareness of *FSR* in some shape or form. The question now to be answered is whether the army adhered to it once the war started, and if it did, how significant the implications of that adherence were.

This section of the book will argue that *FSR* was of seminal importance. No analysis of the British army's command structures, operational or administrative, no assessment of its tactics, small scale or large scale, and no appreciation of its expansion and reorganisation can be complete without an understanding of what *FSR* had to say on these different subjects. It will suggest that some of its tactical and command principles were ignored but not forgotten in the middle year of the war, before being readopted, and that the best parts of the British Army were adhering to *FSR* principles in 1918 as determinedly as the BEF had in 1914. Given that it is being suggested that the influence of *FSR* was all-pervading, there are many strands that must be followed.

What is meant by the term *FSR*? It refers simply to a set of manuals, but, in context, it may refer to just a single regulation, a set of regulations, or a principle described in the body of the document. 'This officer did, or did not, follow *FSR*.' 'This reform did, or did not, comply with *FSR*.' These statements should always be qualified. *Part I* and *Part II* are sometimes wrongly regarded as unrelated texts. Assertions made about *Part I* may be generalised to apply to *Part II* or vice versa. The most informative use of the term is when it is employed to describe compliance, or otherwise, with a quite specific principle. For instance, *FSR* requires that if infantry have taken a strong point at the limit of their artillery support, they should then pause, consolidating their gains to allow time for the artillery to come far enough up to support the next phase of the advance.[5] In this example, a specific regulation is being followed, but this is also a tactical process in compliance with a major *FSR* principle, in this case, all arms combination at every stage of the battle.

In analysing military developments, it is the principles, not the details, of specific training regulations that are important. For instance, when tanks were introduced, there was controversy as to whether they should be used in combination with infantry or whether they should be an independent strike force. Obviously, there are no specific regulations in *FSR* relating to their employment. *FSR* principles support combination, but there were many who argued they should be used primarily as an independent strike force. Almost every debate, on almost every subject, during the First World War, has a doctrinal element, often multiple doctrinal elements, which can be referenced to *FSR*. This does not mean that adherence to *FSR* principles is necessarily the correct course of action. It merely defines the debate.

An additional complication is that, although individual principles can be identified and categorised, every principle is dependent on the application of others. *FSR, Part I* and *FSR, Part II* describe the doctrine from two different angles, each adding layers of meaning to the other. They are both separate and indivisible. The regular British Army of 1914 followed *FSR* principles. There was no guarantee these principles would stand the strain of war, and adherence to them was a state of mind as much as a professional duty. By early 1915, it is possible to distinguish between units in terms of their degree of adherence to *FSR*. Right from the start

5 *Field Service Regulations, Part I*, pp.51, 137–140.

of the war, it is possible to judge the performance of individual officers with respect to their compliance with its key principles. The gradation is relatively sharp because *FSR* principles are so interdependent. The follow-up question to be answered is whether a strong awareness of *FSR* principles helped an officer and his men to stay alive, and whether *FSR* compliance led to relative success on the battlefield. Did *FSR* define a framework doctrine and an ethos that was fit for purpose in a modern continental war? If the answer to that question is no, then the whole *FSR* experiment can be deemed a failure and consideration of it becomes less relevant as the war progresses, and as the army struggles to readjust to a new reality without a relevant doctrine. This is the essence of the learning curve theory, which will be discussed in more detail later in the book. If, however, it is demonstrated to be fit for purpose, then compliance or otherwise in successive battles becomes an ever more important factor in operational assessments.

How can those questions be answered? It is impractical to follow every one of the principles of *FSR* in detail. It is, however, possible to take some major elements of *FSR* and assess adherence to them in broad terms year on year. The first element is that every officer should be trained to perform basic tasks in the same way. He should, after basic training, be able to move from one unit to another and find it easy to adjust since the way orders are framed, the way billets are organised, and the way all the routine tasks of army life are performed are standardised. A second element is that the division should be the fighting unit. The divisional commander should be responsible for the achievement of the objectives given to him. He should be in control of all the assets he needs to use in the achievement of his objectives. A third element is the ethos of being an officer under *FSR*. The duties and responsibilities of every officer require that he be personally responsible for the training and protection of his men. Without specific orders, an officer, whatever his rank, should organise his unit in defence, or in offence, liaising closely with neighbouring units, laterally and vertically, communicating with them, both relying on their support and providing support for them. In practice, this is easiest to follow in the relationship between field artillery and infantry within a division. A fourth element is the command hierarchy, which is tightly defined in *FSR*: brief, strictly hierarchical orders to the fighting man, a collegiate consultative structure in the personal staff of general officers, up to and including the staff of the Commander-in-Chief, and a clear distinction between these styles of command and the essentially civilian organising bureaucracy of the administration of the army. There are also two absolutely fundamental principles that are either followed or not. There should be all-arms combination at every stage of the battle, whatever that means when new weaponry is added to the equations of battle. The army should deploy in-depth, with flank guards in place, at all stages of war, whether static or moving, whether in defence, offence or passivity.

It is helpful to break the analysis down into two overviews, one from the viewpoint of the junior hierarchy of the army, up to divisional command, and the other from the viewpoint of the very senior officers commanding at corps and army level, or with major responsibilities for administration and organisation. These two overviews are essential, but they are not enough. For *FSR* to be judged a significant factor in the year-on-year evolution of the army's tactics and structure, it should be demonstrated that *FSR*'s influence on specific commanders significantly determined their style of leadership, that *FSR* was relevant in laying down the basic education of all officers, not just before the war started, and that the principles of *FSR* as they relate to the duties and responsibilities of junior officers remained relevant despite the tribulations of trench warfare, and the impact of new technologies, such as gas, tanks and aeroplanes. A full analysis of the influence of *FSR* on evolving operational tactics at sub-divisional level, on logistics, on the adoption of new technologies, on the organisation of the artillery, on command at multiple levels, and on both major and minor strategic intent, would be an enormous project, completely beyond the range of this book.

Individual aspects of some of these factors have already been covered by a succession of inspired historians. There are some, like Ian Malcolm Brown, Spencer Jones, Niall Barr, and Jonathan Boff whose theses hint at the continuity of influence of *FSR* over years of warfare. There are a few that have grasped the nettle and wrestled with its influence year-on-year as the war progressed, usually more implicitly than explicitly. The current author cannot begin to emulate the erudition and volume of research that goes into their major works. Jim Beach on doctrine writing, Aimée Fox on learning, and Andy Simpson on corps command are merely examples of major works which have shaped the second half of this book. But it is primary sources that should drive any narrative. A major source to which the current author is indebted is the archive of letters left by his grandfather and other relatives. It is the backbone on which all his research has been based. In the absence of meaningful reference to *FSR* in almost all secondary sources, this has provided him with many anecdotes to illustrate *FSR* in action, or *FSR* ignored. The next two chapters demonstrate *FSR* in action at Mons. Subsequent chapters follow the influence of *FSR* on administration and command, and on defence and offence in Western Front battles, with particular reference to the guidance issued throughout the war by the War Office and GHQ.

11

Smith-Dorrien, II Corps, and the Mons Campaign August 1914

The narrative that follows is a factual account of the Mons campaign by operational analysis, based on a previous publication.[1] The account given in Edmond's *Official History* contains so many serious factual errors that it cannot be used for reference purposes. For instance, it states that 'the concentration [of the BEF] was virtually complete on the 20th.'[2] This was not true, and largely invalidates the succeeding narrative. John Terraine's *Mons*, is equally flawed, a basic premise of his being that French and GHQ played almost no part in directing the battle.[3]

Operational analysis with reference to *FSR* divides all actions and decisions into two camps: compliant or non-compliant. There can be no assumption that compliance and success go together; it may be that the reverse is true, but this approach does provide an objective measure by which to assess the events of any one day on any battlefield of the First World War. It is convenient to undertake operational analysis at corps or divisional level. Orders received by them can be identified, and there is a finite number of subordinate units to follow in assessing the impact of those orders on them. The exact timings given in this account are from unit diaries, usually cross-referenced to neighbouring or subordinate units.[4] Timings given in staff records of the receipt of orders are likely to be more accurate than those in unit diaries written up retrospectively.

This chapter will follow II Corps, from 20 to 23 August, with particular attention to the role played by General Sir Horace Smith-Dorrien in response to his orders from GHQ. By 20 August, most of the BEF had arrived at their concentration areas in northern France. Lieutenant General Sir James Grierson, commander of II Corps, had died on 17 August and Smith-Dorrien had been nominated to replace him, despite being technically too senior for the role, outranking both his fellow corps commander, Lieutenant General Sir Douglas Haig (I Corps), and Lieutenant General Sir Archibald Murray, chief-of-staff to Field Marshal Sir John French. Smith-Dorrien was still in England on the morning of 20 August and did not arrive in

1 David Hutchison, *Mons, an Artillery Battle* (Warwick: Helion, 2018).
2 Edmonds, *Military Operations, France and Belgium 1914*, p.50.
3 John Terraine, *Mons, the Retreat to Victory* (London: Batsford, 1960).
4 The reliability of such timings is discussed by Major A.F. Becke in *The Royal Regiment of Artillery at Le Cateau, 26 August 1914* (Woolwich: Royal Artillery Printing House, 1919), pp.1–2.

France until that evening. He boarded a train to take him to his corps headquarters in the early hours of 21 August.

Operation Order 5

On 20 August 1914, French issued Operation Order 5 to his army, which consisted then of two corps and a cavalry division. This order detailed the route of advance for the BEF from its concentration area in northern France up into Belgium. The advance was to start on 21 August. On the first day, II Corps, under Fergusson, was to advance from around Landrecies to Bavai, and I Corps, under Haig, from around Wassigny to Landrecies, both within northern France. The cavalry division, under Major General Edmund Allenby, was to advance into Belgium, reconnoitring to the east.

The plan was simple. The advance would take three days. At the end of the third day, the right wing – Haig's I Corps – would be in touch with the left wing of the French 5th Army, but where the French army was facing north, the British forces would be angled out to the north-west, facing north-east. I Corps would be on the right of the British line; II Corps would be on the left. The contact between the two corps on completion of the deployment would be a few miles northeast of Mons. The idea was that the German 1st Army would attack the French from the north, allowing the British to attack their exposed western flank. It was anticipated that the first two days of the advance would be through friendly territory, giving time for the troops to adapt to the routines of war. So, at 4:00 a.m. on 21 August, the advance began. The advance is described as a 'peace march' in GHQ records, that is a march through friendly territory with no possibility of hostile attack.[5] If any hostile contact was anticipated, *FSR* regulations for protection on the march would have been observed.

That same morning of 21 August, Smith-Dorrien was on a train from Boulogne, having crossed the Channel from Harwich the evening before. He was on his way to Landrecies to take up command of II Corps. The first battalions of II Corps arrived in Bavai at around midday, but it was not till 3:00 p.m. that Sir Horace arrived in Landrecies. There, he found a staff car waiting for him, and he too joined the crowded road from Landrecies to Bavai.

Sir Horace arrived at his new staff headquarters in Bavai at 4:00 p.m. and immediately went into conference with his chief-of-staff, Brigadier General George Forestier-Walker. II Corps staff had been organised in strict compliance with *FSR*, and as he expected, his staff had the reports he required immediately to hand. British regulations defined in detail the ethos and requirements of a general's personal staff, and Sir Horace expected perfection. He got it. His first requirement was for a briefing on the state of his two divisions. He learnt that the 3rd and 5th Divisions had only two artillery brigades between them when they should have had eight. Neither division had its heavy batteries or its divisional ammunition columns. It was not known where the missing artillery units were or when they would arrive.[6] Nor did they have any Field Ambulances and some smaller units.[7] II Corps was far from concentrated.

5 TNA: WO 95/1/2: General Staff, War Diary entry, 21 August 1914.
6 TNA: WO 95/1375: 3 Division, 21 August 1914; TNA: WO 95/1521: 5 Division, 21 August 1914.
7 TNA: WO 95/1/2: General Staff, 20 August 1914.

His second request would have been for a briefing on potential hostile threats. He was told that enemy cavalry was known to be at Soignies, some 20 miles north of Bavai, eight miles beyond Mons, that small cavalry patrols had been reported on or over the Condé canal, just west of Mons, and that a force of infantry, supported by cavalry and artillery, was reported at Nivelles, about eight miles east of Mons. The proximity of these threats was such that any advance into Belgium might lead to contact with the enemy. These observations are recorded in the corps intelligence diary.[8]

He then reviewed the next day's advance, which was due to start in less than 12 hours – at 4:00 a.m. on 22 August. Operation Order 5 gave specific destinations for his divisions at the conclusion of their day's march. He learnt that this was assumed to be another 'peace march', moving to billets in small hamlets a few miles south of the Condé canal. The slag heaps and industrial mining belt between these hamlets and the canal would obscure observation to the north. There was no provision for outposts to give warning of an enemy advance. There would be no cavalry ahead of his corps and no flank guard to the west. Once in possession of these three reports, Sir Horace immediately called for his staff car and made his way to meet with Sir John French and his staff in their GHQ at Le Cateau.

He arrived there at about 7:00 p.m. and presented his assessment. British regulations in 1914 were very clear on the dispositions required of an army advancing into potentially hostile territory. An absolute requirement was that the army should consist of all arms.[9] Sir Horace had almost no artillery. A second was that an advancing force should always have flank guards.[10] II Corps had no flank guard to the west, a serious matter since it was known that the German High Command used encirclement as its strategy of choice. A third was that an army under the slightest threat must post outposts at the end of a day's march to guard against surprise. If defensive, these outposts were posted to detect the approach of any enemy force, resist it if practical, and retire back to the main body if hard pressed. If, however, a further advance was planned the next day, the outposts would be offensive, more substantial, and invariably supported by artillery, to constitute the advance guard of the force for the next day.[11] There was no easy way to arrange outposts on the dispositions mandated for the conclusion of the next day's advance under Operation Order 5.

Sir John French and his staff immediately recognised the validity of the points that Sir Horace made. Operation Order 5 was torn up, and Operation Order 6 was prepared to replace it, drafted in meticulous compliance with the British regulations on the precautions required in the event of the advance of an army towards an enemy. Since Operation Order 6 superseded Operation Order 5, a clause was inserted advising I Corps that its order of advance on 22 August should be as described in Operation Order 5. There were now no orders from GHQ valid for 23 August. The preparation of the new order took less than two hours, and Sir Horace returned to Bavai with a copy of it in his pocket. The official draft of Operation Order 6 was not issued to I Corps and the cavalry division until 11:00 p.m. that night, an hour after Sir Horace reached his headquarters.[12] It took time for new orders to diffuse down through the corps. For instance, it was

8 TNA: WO 95/629/4: II Corps staff intelligence diary, 21 August 1914.
9 *Field Service Regulations, Part I, Operations, 1912*, p.14. 'Every force that takes the field against an organized enemy should be composed of all arms.' See also p.51 on order of march.
10 *Field Service Regulations, Part I, 1912*, p.91–93. Another fundamental principle.
11 *Field Service Regulations, Part I*, pp.98–111. Outposts, etc.
12 TNA: WO 95/1/2: General Staff, Operation order 6, 21 August 1914.

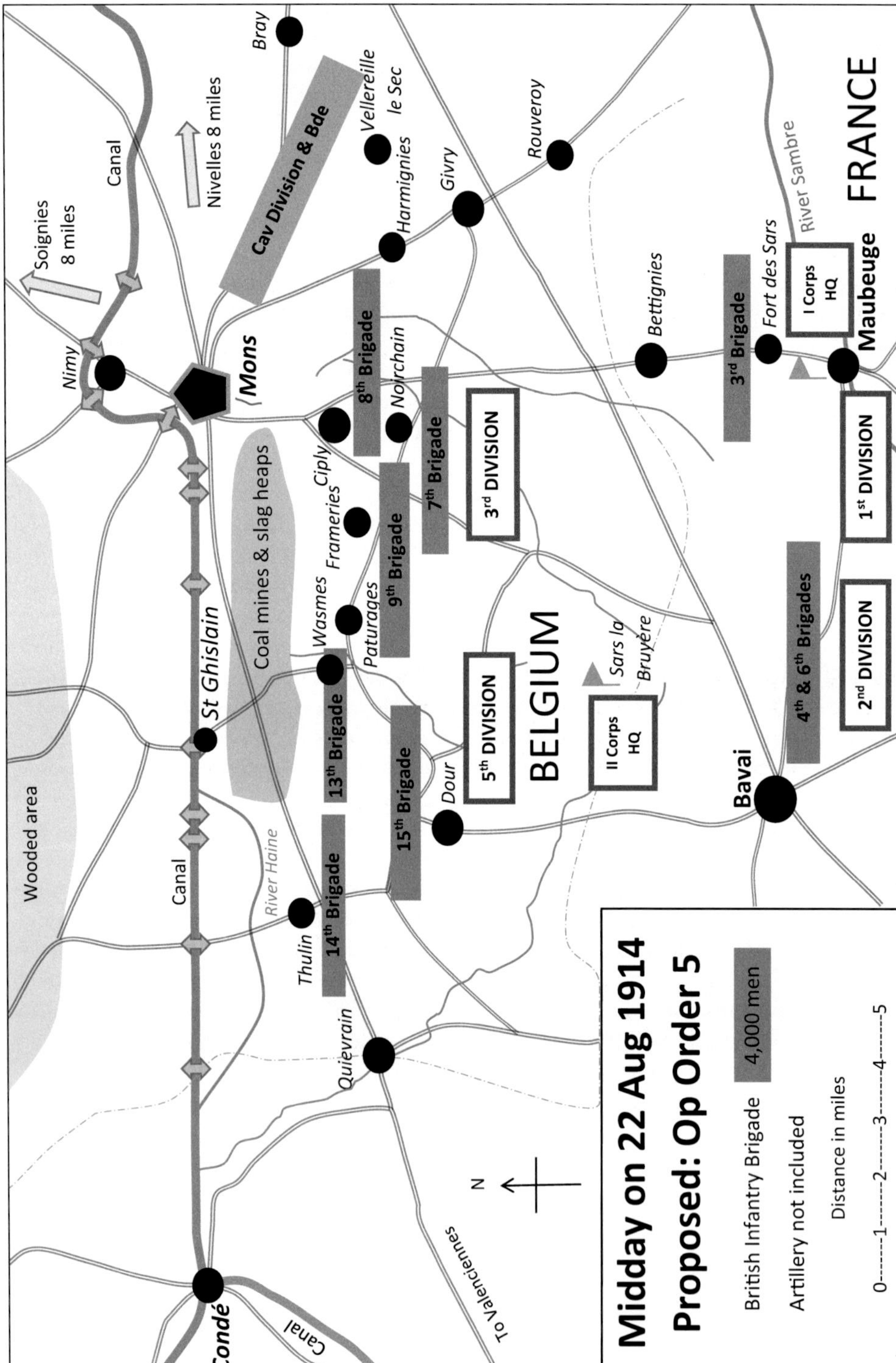

Proposed II Corps dispositions for 22 August 1914 under GHQ Operation Order 5.

not till 8:00 a.m. the next morning that the 9th Infantry Brigade, 3rd Division, received 'verbal orders', revising their destinations, 'news of the enemy advance on Mons' having been received.[13]

II Corps was now instructed to establish defensive outposts on the Condé canal, north of Mons, as far east as the Obourg bridge, and then southeast for some miles down to Givry, a total length of 21 miles. At least one unit diary expresses concern at the length of this front, since 'if the frontage occupied in battle is so great as to reduce the force kept in hand for the ultimate assumption of the offensive much below half the total force available, the position may be considered as too extended to be held with a view to decisive action.'[14] Few realised at this stage that II Corps now had no orders to advance on 23 August. Four infantry brigades and a battalion, out of the six infantry brigades in II Corps, took up outpost positions. Their brief was to give warning of the approach of hostile forces; and, if attacked, to hold the enemy up to give time for the depleted main body of the army behind them to organise its defence and, specifically, to enable II Corps to deploy its arriving artillery. This main body was much smaller than recommended in *FSR*, but Sir Horace judged that the unusual strength of his defensive outpost line was necessary. As usual, under *FSR*, local commanders made their own arrangements according to the terrain. Some pushed piquets forward, and some did not. Some cleared a field of fire; others saw no need. All would have ensured local communications and local protection. Every unit would have prepared 'confidential' instructions for retirement from their positions if it became necessary.[15] 'Orders for a possible retreat should always be thought out beforehand, in case of need.'[16] There was just one artillery battery in the front line, and that against the wishes of the 5th Division artillery commander. Turning it back round, and getting it out, would have been difficult, and it was covering a vital bridge at St Ghislain, so the over-eager battery commander was allowed to stay where he was. All other artillery was deployed in covered positions well back from the outpost line. II Corps settled into its defensive deployment, waiting for both its own artillery and the enemy to arrive. Most of this, but not the divisional ammunition columns, would arrive at the II Corps reserve line, after very long forced marches, by the evening of 22 August. They immediately went into billets.

In addition, under Operation Order 6, the cavalry division was ordered to traverse through the advancing II Corps that afternoon and take up station as flank guard to the west of II Corps, leaving only the weak infantry flank guard to the east, behind the one remaining British cavalry brigade. This major revision of strategic deployment ensured that II Corps now complied, as far as was possible, with *FSR* tactical advice. If Smith-Dorrien had arrived 24 hours later than he did, the history of the Mons campaign might have been very different.

GHQ Orders for 22 August

On the morning of 22 August, I Corps, II Corps and the cavalry division all moved as planned, I Corps complying with their advance to Maubeuge, still within France, as laid down in

13 TNA: WO 95/1425: 9 Infantry Brigade, 22 August 1914.

14 *Field Service Regulations, Part I*, p.141.

15 See, for example: TNA: WO 95/1425: 9 Infantry Brigade, 22 August 1914, p.52.

16 *Field Service Regulations, Part I*, p.32.

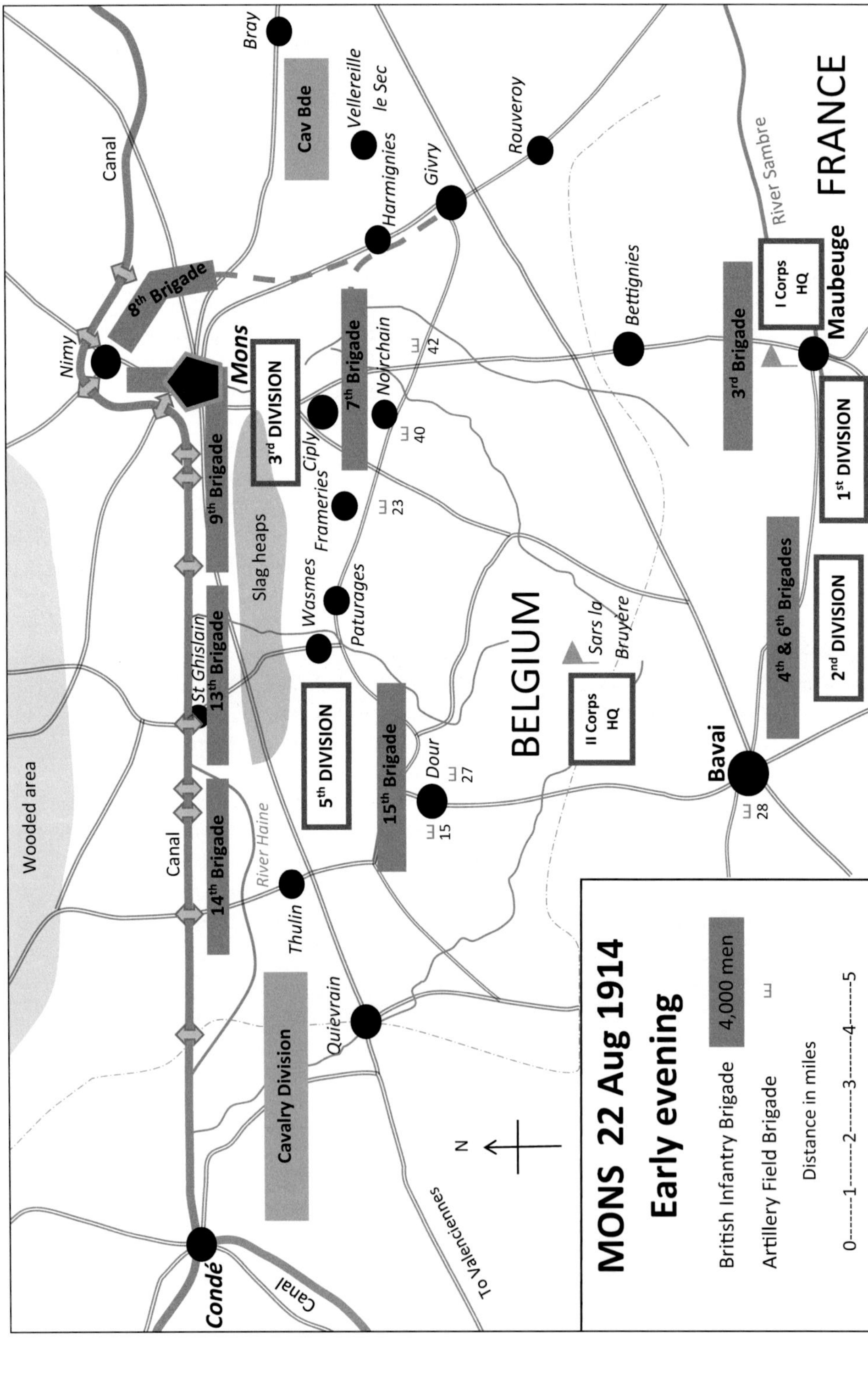

II Corps dispositions on 22 August 1914 in compliance with GHQ Operation Order 6.

Operation Order 5, II Corps and the cavalry complying with Operation Order 6. All three units liaised with French units to minimise congestion on the roads.

The GHQ intelligence diary for these dates has been lost, but GHQ transmitted intelligence to both its corps as required by *FSR*. Through the night of 21 into 22 August, that of II Corps records that the strength of enemy forces at both Soignies, north of Mons, and Nivelles, east of Mons, had been underestimated.[17] This implied a greater risk that II Corps could be attacked from the east or face an encirclement manoeuvre from the west. Smith-Dorrien reacted to the latter threat by instructing the flank of the 5th Division to drop back to face north-west, rather than due north.[18] GHQ also needed to react. So near to the enemy, *FSR* required that the two corps be close enough to provide mutual support. This was not only desirable on general grounds. The frontage occupied by II Corps was too long, and could only be decreased if GHQ arranged for I Corps to take over a proportion of it.[19] GHQ issued order Army Order 57 (OA57) to I Corps at about midday.[20] This urgent order instructed both the 1st and 2nd Divisions of I Corps to immediately continue their advance, with a view to relieving those II Corps units posted east and south-east of Mons. The order was brief, and did not require I Corps to perform the whole of this advance that day, but it did state that I Corps should be in position by 6:00 a.m. the next morning at the latest. OA57 was received at I Corps HQ at 1:00 p.m., and was copied to II Corps. GHQ can be criticised for this order arriving so late in the day, but its intent, and the rationale for it, under *FSR*, are very clear.

GHQ issued a follow-up order, OA62, at 5:00 p.m., clarifying the exact demarcation line between I Corps and II Corps at Mons. I Corps was to be responsible for the defence of Mons from the east, right up to the canal bridge at Obourg.[21] II Corps also received a copy of this order, which was passed to the 3rd Division. Its 8th Brigade was ordered to continue preparing positions on the eastern flank of the salient, but to retire when relieved, or by 6:00 a.m. at the latest, to act as a reserve.[22] This would allow II Corps to draw in its eastern flank and reinforce its main body.

Smith-Dorrien and Major General Hubert Hamilton, commanding the 3rd Division, assumed that I Corps was complying with these orders. If Haig or either of his two divisional commanders chose to modify or ignore the order, their staffs 'should at once inform the issuer of it, and the commanders of any neighbouring units likely to be affected.'[23] French and Murray also believed that I Corps was complying, despite an enigmatic update from I Corps, which is summarised in GHQ records as order 'was not received (?) till late (6 pm? see message files) and involved a night march.'[24] The message files would have confirmed that the time the orders were sent out was much earlier than this, and receipt of them would have been acknowledged.

17 TNA: WO 95/629/4: II Corps staff intelligence, 21–22 August 1914.
18 RAM MD/1150: McLeod, with the 15th Brigade, RFA, Journal, 23 August 1914.
19 Terraine, *Mons,* p.82. French 'issued no written orders between 11.55 pm on August 21st and 8.25 pm on August 24th.' This is untrue. GHQ issued more than 30 orders in this time.
20 TNA: WO 95/588/4: I Corps staff, OA57, 22 August 1914.
21 TNA: WO 95/630/1: II Corps staff, OA62, 22 August 1914.
22 TNA: WO 95/1400: 8 Infantry Brigade, 23 August 1914.
23 *Field Service Regulations, Part I,* 1912, pp.31–32.
24 TNA: WO 95/1/2: General Staff, 22 Aug 1914.

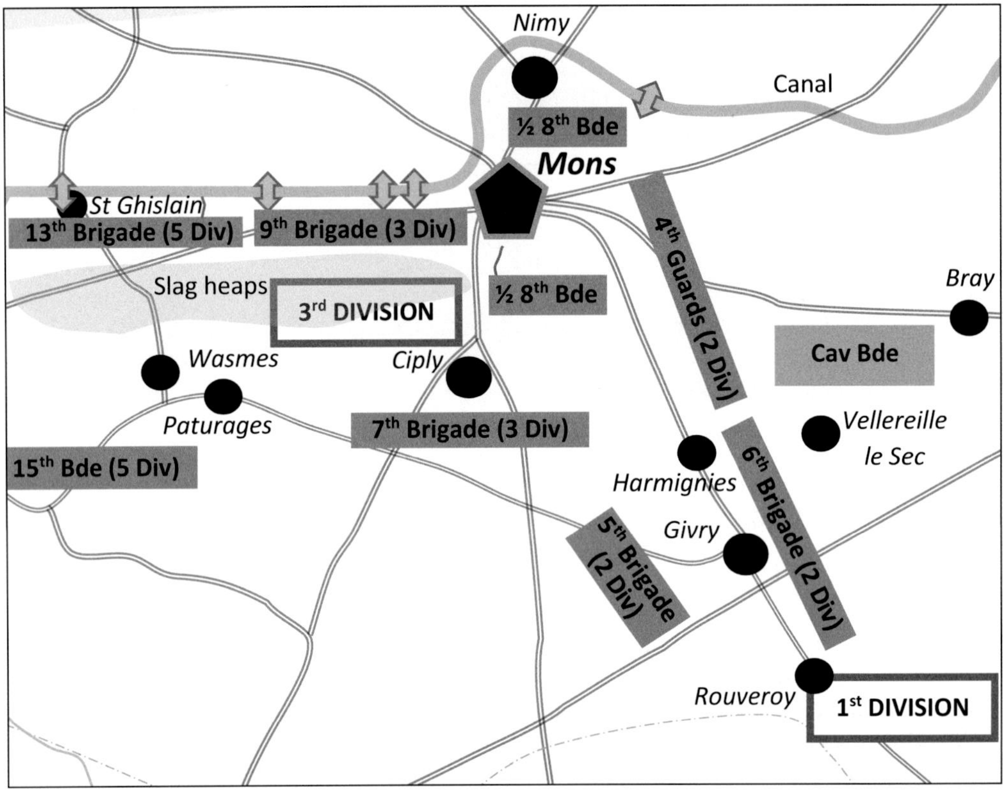

Salient positions mandated by GHQ orders for 6:00 a.m., 23 August 1914.

At midnight, Smith-Dorrien sought and received permission from GHQ to withdraw those 3rd Division units deployed east and southeast of Mons, on the line from the Obourg bridge to Harmignies, in expectation of the arrival of the 2nd Division.[25]

The Meeting at Sars-la-Bruyère at 6:00 a.m. on 23 August

French came up to Smith-Dorrien's II Corps headquarters, at Sars-la-Bruyère, at 6:00 a.m. on 23 August. Smith-Dorrien, Haig, Allenby, Murray, and various other staff officers were all summoned for a general conference. It is not reliably reported in contemporary documents, but it was brief, and later accounts suggest that French gave an oration rather than entering a dialogue. He did not remain long at Sars-la-Bruyère. He took Allenby and departed for Valenciennes. This was not unreasonable, though Allenby's absence from the subsequent discussion of Murray and the two corps commanders was unfortunate. The western flank of II Corps was an obvious danger point in the event of an encirclement manoeuvre by the approaching Germans. The

25 TNA: WO 95/630/1: II Corps Staff, 22–23 Aug 1914.

'commander even of a large army should rarely omit to reconnoitre personally.'[26] French wanted to liaise with the French divisions in that sector. In addition, his lines-of-communication defence troops, four battalions under the command of Major General L.G. Drummond, had just arrived there. French constituted them into the 19th Infantry Brigade and ordered them to advance to the Condé canal to combine with the cavalry division and its horse artillery. Once they were in position, he ordered Allenby to take command of the combined force.[27] The flank guard to II Corps was now an all-arms force, as required by *FSR*.

Meanwhile, back at Sars-la-Bruyère, Murray had gone into conference with Smith-Dorrien and Haig. This meeting is summarised in II Corps records, timed at 7:00 a.m., as 'General arrangements in case of attack', and it incorporates a plan for the retirement of both I and II Corps if that should become necessary. Smith-Dorrien appears to have chaired the meeting. He was the senior officer present. He summarised his positions and announced that he was already establishing a defence line between Harmignies in the east, about five miles southeast of Mons, to Dour in the west, a similar distance south of the Condé canal. If his, and by his understanding, the 2nd Division's defensive outposts around Mons did not hold, and he did not expect them to, all units should fall back to that line, where the main body of the artillery awaited them. That line would be firmly held to cover any further retirement. Murray agreed with this plan, with the stipulation that 'the retirement to the Bavai position, if it ever takes place, is to be a matter for General Headquarter orders.' Haig also agreed to the plan, insisting that he would need exclusive use of the main Mons to Bavai road for the retirement of his 2nd Division from east of Mons.[28] Neither Smith-Dorrien nor Murray had any reason to believe that the 2nd Division was not already in position near the canal, east of Mons.

By the time these arrangements had been made, the battle of Mons had started. It was not Smith-Dorrien's responsibility to direct the detail of this battle, which initially involved no more than his defensive outposts already in position. He had no reason to believe that I Corps had not occupied the line east of Mons. II Corps intelligence diary records 16 status reports received from the two divisions that day.[29] There are also 27 entries in its war diary.[30] Smith-Dorrien was responsible for ensuring that his two divisions synchronised their retirements, maintaining contact and protecting their flanks at Dour and Harmignies, respectively. His initial task was to check that his 'main body' defensive line was adequately prepared, and urgent orders were issued in that respect by II Corps staff to both divisions.[31]

The German attacks to the east of Mons started to develop at about mid-morning, and this is when Hamilton of the 3rd Division first registers disquiet at the absence of the 2nd Division from the defence line east of Mons. It was not till midday that II Corps received any news of the whereabouts of the 2nd Division. The 4th (Guards) Brigade had arrived at Ciply, south of Mons, at 10:30 a.m., but they then marched back south, offering no support to II Corps. The 6th Infantry Brigade had taken over the outpost line between Harmignies and Givry to the

26 *Field Service Regulations, Part I*, p.117.
27 TNA: W 95/1096: Cavalry Division, 23 August 1914.
28 TNA: WO 95/630: II Corps Staff, 23 August 1914, p.75.
29 TNA: WO 95/629/4: II Corps Intelligence, 23 August 1914.
30 TNA: WO 95/630/1: II Corps War Diary, 23 August 1914.
31 See, for instance, TNA: WO 95/1375: 3 Division, 23 August 1914, order issued just after 7:00 a..m; TNA: WO 95/1401: XLII Brigade RFA, 23 August 1914, orders at 10:00 a.m.; TNA: WO 95/1521: 5 Division Artillery, 23 August 1914, and associated brigade diaries.

southeast. At about 2:00 p.m., Smith-Dorrien sent Hamilton to make a personal appeal to I Corps headquarters, asking Haig to at least allocate some troops to the defence of the line north of Harmignies, even if they were too late to help nearer to the canal. At 3:00 p.m., II Corps believed that this help was imminently forthcoming.[32]

Between Mons and Harmignies, a distance of four miles, the 2nd Royal Scots (Lothian Regiment) of the 3rd Division held a long line of outposts, which was now being threatened by a German advance. Following a personal appeal by their CO (Commanding Officer) to the CO of the 2nd South Staffordshire Regiment, 6th Infantry Brigade, 2nd Division, the latter sent his reserve company to bolster the line north of Harmignies. This meant that the Staffordshires were now disobeying orders by deploying out of their allotted sector. Their CO, if challenged, would have invoked his right, under *FSR*, to modify orders on his own initiative. Simultaneously, Brigadier General Davies, his immediate superior, was asking Major General Charles Monro at divisional headquarters why his left flank was not being supported by the 4th (Guards) Brigade. Davies was not the only officer asking where the Guards' battalions were. Brigadier General Doran, commanding the 8th Infantry Brigade of the 3rd Division, and indeed Hamilton and Smith-Dorrien, all of whom, under *FSR*, expected to be informed if dispositions were changed, were all asking the same question.

Meanwhile, limited retirements from outpost positions, particularly at Nimy, the northernmost point on the canal within the Mons salient, were performed by battalion COs, monitored, and coordinated by brigade commanders. Divisional commanders coordinated the general fighting retirement to the main body line. At no point did Smith-Dorrien issue a general retirement order, although he kept his divisional commanders aware of their relative positions in the middle of the corps line. As dictated by *FSR*, senior officers defined intent, and subordinate officers controlled the battles in their own sectors.

At 6:15 p.m., two battalions of the 4th Guards finally arrived to deploy north of Harmignies, and by sometime after 7:00 p.m., they were in position.[33] Smith-Dorrien could do no more about this gap, and by now, he was far more worried about the gap in his defence line at Paturages. Because the 3rd Division still had to defend to the east and to the north of Mons, it only had sufficient men to man the defence line as far as Frameries, and the 5th Division to the east only had sufficient to fortify between Dour and Wasmes. This left a one-mile gap at Paturages. As early as 2:00 p.m., Smith-Dorrien had made Monro of the 2nd Division aware of his need for reinforcements in this sector, and Monro ordered the 5th Infantry Brigade to concentrate. He asked I Corps for permission to dispatch them into the gap. Permission was refused. II Corps was not informed.

At 5:30 p.m., the risk became critical when the 1st Dorsetshire Regiment, 15th Infantry Brigade, deployed at Wasmes, the eastern end of the 5th Division's second position, reported that they were watching the 9th Infantry Brigade falling back towards Frameries, with a German battalion 1,000 yards behind them.[34] The expected reinforcements to fill the gap had not arrived. At 7:00 p.m., Smith-Dorrien contacted GHQ to ask for permission to order an

32 TNA: WO 95/630/1: II Corps Staff, 23 August 1914.
33 TNA: WO 95/1342: 1 Irish Guards, 23 August 1914.
34 TNA: WO 95/1572/2: 1 Dorsetshire Regiment, 23 August 1914.

immediate withdrawal from his defensive line if a German attack started to penetrate this gap.[35] French refused permission, but in an order copied to II Corps, he immediately ordered I Corps to cooperate with II Corps in filling the gap.[36] At about 8:00 p.m., Smith-Dorrien saw Haig in person to ask for the necessary reinforcements and was assured that they would be provided. Happily, the German advance stopped at nightfall. The last II Corps infantry battalions to fall back to the defence line did not arrive until nearly midnight. The gap at Paturages was still wide open. The 5th Infantry Brigade arrived to fill it at 2:30 a.m.[37]

Summary

Having established the sequence of events and the timelines of the various orders and movements, a clear picture of events has been drawn. From the arrival of Smith-Dorrien at Bavai at 4:00 p.m. on 21 August to midnight on 23 August, II Corps acted in strict compliance with *FSR*. The performance of its staff under Forestier-Walker was particularly impressive, with reports collated and measured orders issued promptly.

French and his GHQ staff have had a very bad press. Much has been made, in almost every account of the campaign, of disagreements at GHQ on the perceptions of enemy strength in the days before Mons. If there was disharmony at GHQ, there is no objective evidence of it in the war diaries. Of course, there was uncertainty at GHQ that week; of course, there was discussion. But on evaluation of the orders issued after that discussion, and despite the uncertainty, perfectly defensible conclusions were reached, and appropriate action was taken on that basis. The requirement that 'systematic arrangements must always be made to ensure that every possible source of information is fully utilised, that all information received is immediately transmitted to the proper quarter, and that it is carefully sifted before any conclusions are formed' being the 'duties of the general staff,' seems on the evidence to have been observed.[38] On the evidence, GHQ followed *FSR*. French had no right, under *FSR*, to interfere with the dispositions of his subordinates once he had communicated positions and intent to them. He did not.

On the front line of battle, two additional factors affected the outcome. The first is that, in this, almost the first battle of the war, neither army felt the need to fight once dark fell. At dusk, almost to a man, the advancing Germans found suitable spots to slump down, eat some emergency rations and try to rest. Some of the British artillery even retired into billets. An uneasy silence fell over the battlefield, and the two British divisions of II Corps were enabled to consolidate their hold on Smith-Dorrien's defensive line and prepare for the early morning attacks that would ensue.

The second factor is that the German field artillery was quite astonishingly ineffective. Its fire was accurate and unremitting, but it caused almost no casualties. The reasons for this have been described elsewhere, but briefly, the shell used was a complex multi-purpose one. In high-explosive mode, its charge was too small to cause damage, and in shrapnel mode, the shell was

35 Smith-Dorrien, *Memories of Forty-Eight Years' Service*, p.385, reproducing G 271 from II Corps to GHQ, timed at 7:15 p.m.

36 TNA: WO 95/630/1: II Corps Staff, 23 August 1914. GHQ OA90, received 8:00 p.m.

37 TNA: WO 95/1343: 5 Infantry Brigade, 23 August 1914.

38 *Field Service Regulations, Part I, 1912*, p.112.

unstable so that the shot sprayed up and then dropped to the ground relatively harmlessly. If the German field artillery had been as effective as the British, the outcome of the battle might have been very different.[39] The German field howitzers were very effective but did not come into action until relatively late in the day. Both sides absorbed the lessons. British troops did not fear the enemy field artillery, and in subsequent battles, the German howitzers were in the forefront of the battle, coming into action much more quickly.

So, II Corps was lucky. The heavy field artillery bombardment did not cause casualties. This chapter has been kept deliberately factual. It has addressed material inaccuracies in previous accounts. But it has not addressed morale. Some mention has been made of uncertainty in II Corps unit diaries at the wisdom of advancing without artillery, and then of taking up such a long outpost line. But once the decision was made, with Smith-Dorrien firmly in control, scrupulously adhering to *FSR* in his control of both staff and peripheral units, this uncertainty evaporated. Outpost battalions and brigades refer to heavy artillery fire, but factually. They did not let it interfere with their duty to hold the line and then fall back in an orderly fashion. French conscript units had broken in the face of it. The professional British Army did not. Even when some battalions came under heavy howitzer fire and sustained serious casualties, this is still a fact. If one takes the analysis further into the campaign, the steadiness of II Corps staff and the units they were directing is remarkable.

On 24 August, the 3rd Division was initially ordered to retire from the defence line south of Mons to Bavai, where it would deploy and dig in, while the 5th Division was directed further west, in the same relative position to the 3rd Division as it had been on the Condé canal. However, in practice, the 5th Division was delayed in its retirement by enemy attacks and the lack of good roads on which to retire, particularly when the German capture of Élouges threatened the most direct route to their planned destination. The 5th Division had no choice but to retire on Bavai. II Corps staff not only recognised that this would happen at an early stage but issued a change of orders to both divisions. The 3rd Division, already arriving at Bavai, was instructed to move west and take up the positions allocated to the 5th Division; the 5th Division, when it arrived in Bavai, was instructed to remain there and take up the positions allocated to the 3rd Division. This complex cross-over was organised while both divisions were engaged in fighting withdrawals. Yet no confusion is recorded; both divisions retained cohesion, and both were ready to move at 5:30 a.m. the next morning.

All II Corps unit diaries are upbeat at that stage. The 3rd Division, which GHQ feared had been badly mauled, conducted a classic retirement on 25 August – *FSR* to the letter, orders were hardly needed – and a decisive rearguard action was fought at Solesmes. General Von Kluck, commanding the German 1st Army, considered this a significant reverse. 'The IV. Corps was able to attack the British troops at Solesmes, but they did not evacuate the village till after nightfall, after putting up an obstinate resistance.'[40] So routine was this action considered that it is barely mentioned in division or brigade diaries. It was a far more important action than the battle at Landrecies, fought by I Corps, which Von Kluck does not even mention. He might have done so if it had similarly held up the 7th Division of IV Corps in its advance on Le Cateau

39 David Hutchison, 'The Effectiveness of German Field Artillery at Mons and during the Retreat in August 1914', *Journal for the Society of Army Historical Research*, vol.95 (2017), pp.331–337.

40 Alexander Von Kluck, *The March on Paris, the Memoirs of Alexander Von Kluck, 1914* (Barnsley: Frontline Books, 2012 [1923]), pp.59–60.

from the east. But just when the battle at Landrecies was beginning to hold up the German advance, Haig ordered the 4th Guards to retire precipitately, allowing the 5th Division to be taken on their vulnerable flank about six hours later.

In summary, II Corps, in its entirety, followed *FSR* to the letter. Generals, their staff, brigade and regimental commanders and even the most junior of fighting officers complied with it. Occasionally, excessive adherence caused problems. One battery commander was cut off from his direct superior and so received orders to retire from a neighbouring infantry brigade. He refused to comply, as was his right. The two battalions on either side of his battery, one from each infantry brigade, refused orders to retire that would abandon the battery. They waited until an order from the correct superior reached the stubborn, and arguably misguided, battery commander. All three units report the incident factually, without comment, in their war diaries.

So, what of I Corps?

12

Haig, I Corps, and the Mons Campaign August 1914

This chapter will follow I Corps, from 20 August to 27 August, with particular attention to the role played by Lieutenant General Sir Douglas Haig. Both I Corps and its two divisions commissioned staff to write summaries of the Mons campaign after the events. The I Corps summary is supported by Haig's diary. These summaries cannot, and should not, be relied on since they are robustly contradicted by entries in subordinate diaries that are convincing and consistent. It is particularly helpful to cross-reference infantry war diaries with those of their supporting artillery to discern the intent of various manoeuvres. By 20 August, most of the BEF had arrived at their concentration areas in northern France.

Operation Order 5

As previously described, on 20 August 1914, French issued Operation Order 5 to his army, which consisted then of two corps and a cavalry division. This order detailed the route of advance for the BEF from its concentration area in northern France up into Belgium. The advance was to start on 21 August. Haig, commanding I Corps, had an opportunity to influence the planning when French held a three-hour conference of 'army commanders and G.O.C. Cavalry Division' on 18 August to discuss and finalise the plan of advance.[1] Like II Corps, the 1st and 2nd Divisions of I Corps had not completed their concentration on 20 August, though Haig makes no reference to any missing units in his notes on a final planning meeting at I Corps headquarters on 20 August.[2] The timing and speed of I Corps' advance were such that most such units were able to catch up, but not all did. The 2nd Division ammunition column did not reach I Corps until the afternoon of 23 August.

On the first day, II Corps, under Fergusson, was to advance from around Landrecies to Bavai, and I Corps, under Haig, from around Wassigny to Landrecies, both within northern France. The cavalry division, under Major General Edmund Allenby, was to advance into Belgium, reconnoitring to the east. By the end of the third day, it was anticipated that the two corps would have wheeled to the east, facing northeast, linking just east of Mons, with the cavalry in

1 TNA: WO 95/1/8: General Staff, Commander-in-Chief BEF, diary, 18 August 1914.
2 NLS: Acc.3155/98: Douglas Haig Papers, 20 August 1914, pp.69–70.

front of them. It was also anticipated that the first two days of the advance would be through friendly territory, giving time for the troops to adapt to the routines of war. So, at 4:00 a.m. on 21 August, the advance began, being described as a 'peace march' in GHQ records.

On the afternoon of 21 August, Haig took the opportunity to join French at Allenby's cavalry division headquarters at Givry and to reconnoitre the ground that his corps was due to take up at about midday on 23 August under Operation Order 5.[3] He was accompanied by his Artillery Adviser, Brigadier General Henry Horne, and they discussed where the guns should be sited. Technically, the siting of the artillery was, under *FSR*, a purely divisional responsibility, but this reconnaissance, strongly recommended, if not mandated by *FSR*, proved its value only 36 hours later, when the divisions arrived on this line and had to deploy in the dark.

Also, on 21 August, Haig met with the commander of the French forces around the powerful, and crowded, frontier fort of Maubeuge. This was on the line of march of the 1st Division and, coming up from Landrecies on the afternoon of 22 August, they would need to billet around Maubeuge. As a result of this meeting, the billets for the lead infantry brigade of the 1st Division the next day were moved to Fort des Sars, three miles north of Maubeuge, right on the border with Belgium.[4] Two brigades of artillery were attached in support, providing an all-arms balance to this advance guard, which would be covered by the whole cavalry division. GHQ were informed.[5] In contrast to the dispositions planned for II Corps under Operation Order 5, these comply with *FSR*.

At 11:00 p.m. that evening, I Corps received a copy of Operation Order 6. Though this replaced Operation Order 5, it stated that its orders to I Corps for 'tomorrow ... will hold good.'[6] Thus, the 1st Division would advance to Maubeuge and the 2nd Division to Bavai. This advance, again under peace conditions, except for the advance guard already mentioned, started at 4:00 a.m. on 22 August. I Corps headquarters moved to Maubeuge, and at about midday, Haig left it and motored to inspect the 3rd Infantry Brigade at Fort des Sars. Following this inspection, he set off for Beaumont, 18 miles east, to visit General de Mas-Latrie, commanding the French 18th Army Corps and, after that, a French divisional headquarters closer to the battle.[7] It is not clear who accompanied him. He may have taken his chief-of-staff, Brigadier General John Gough. Haig did not comply with *FSR* at this point. 'If a commander intends to leave the main body of his command for any length of time, he should detail an officer, who should be provided with the necessary staff, to act for him in his absence.'[8] Major General Samuel Lomax, commanding the 1st Division, was in Maubeuge. By 1:00 p.m., Haig was completely out of contact with his headquarters.

At about 1:00 p.m., OA57 was received by I Corps at Maubeuge.[9] This urgent order instructed both the 1st and 2nd Divisions of I Corps to immediately continue their advance, with a view to relieving those II Corps units now posted east and southeast of Mons under Operation Order 6. The order was brief and did not require I Corps to perform the whole of the advance that day, but it did state that I Corps should be in position by 6:00 a.m. the next morning at the latest.

3 TNA: WO 95/588/4; I Corps Staff, 21 August 1914.
4 TNA: WO 95/1274: 3 Infantry Brigade, 21 August 1914.
5 TNA: WO 95/1/2: General Staff, War diary, 22 August1914.
6 TNA: WO 95/1/2: General Staff, Operation Order 6, 21 August 1914.
7 NLS, Acc.3155/98: Douglas Haig Papers, August 1914, p.82.
8 *Field Service Regulations, Part I*, 1912, p.21.
9 TNA: WO 95/588/4: I Corps staff, OA57, 22 August 1914.

Immediately, a car was dispatched to find Haig. Simultaneously, I Corps staff at Maubeuge called a General Staff meeting at 3:00 p.m. to discuss this urgent order.[10] Divisional staff officers attended, and in Haig's absence, the decision was made that both divisions should prepare for an immediate advance. Already dispersed into billets and needing at least two hours' notice, the 1st Division agreed to march at 6:00 p.m. and the 2nd Division at 7:00 p.m. Meanwhile, Haig is recorded as receiving a copy of OA57 at '3.22 pm.'[11] If this is so, he had time to peruse it as he drove back to his headquarters. He did not arrive until after 5:00 p.m. He immediately cancelled the proposed advances, sending Horne off urgently to the 1st Division. He arrived too late. By 6:15 p.m., when he arrived, the whole division was already marching and Lomax refused to stop it.[12] Similar orders to the 2nd Division arrived just in time to cancel their advance. 'Under instructions just come from I Corps, 2nd Division movement from billets postponed till early tomorrow. Orders follow later.'[13] Monro's understanding of the timing of the next day's advance is critical. Not only did this order not comply with best practice in its clarity, as defined by *FSR*, I Corps staff also did not inform 'the issuer of [OA57], and the commanders of any neighbouring units [II Corps] likely to be affected' of his decision to disregard the order.[14]

FSR was not being followed. Most importantly, Haig, in cancelling a GHQ order, is not acknowledging French, his Commander-in-Chief, as the supreme authority with strategic responsibility. For 'unity of control', says *FSR*, 'supreme authority' must be vested 'in one man, the C-in-C of the forces in the field.'[15] Any 'subordinate commander issues orders' only on 'the execution of the duties allotted to him.'[16] Haig is very publicly rejecting this subordinate role and is refusing to accept the intent of GHQ orders. He has also ignored other important lesser regulations. He has certainly not paused to receive reports from his staff before issuing his orders.[17]

Haig and I Corps received OA62 from GHQ at 5:00 p.m. This gives exact details of the intended demarcation line between I Corps and II Corps at Mons: I Corps was to be totally responsible for the defence of Mons from the east from 6:00 a.m. on 23 August at the latest.[18] Necessarily, since 2nd Division was not advancing, this order from GHQ was ignored at the time of receipt. I Corps sent an ambiguous message to GHQ reporting a delay in its receipt, but, presumably after Haig and his staff had assessed the situation, I Corps issued, at 9:30 p.m., a new order (G63) to the 2nd Division. It was ordered to advance immediately with a view to arriving at Mons by 6:00 a.m.[19] This highly significant and important order was acknowledged by the 2nd Division staff and then totally ignored.[20] They had been led to understand, only two and a half hours earlier, that their advance had been 'postponed till early tomorrow.' Now, back in billets, an immediate advance was impossible. It took two hours for an infantry brigade to collect in order of march. Already that day, the men had marched since 4:00 a.m., billeted from

10 TNA: WO 95/1283; 2 Division, 22 August 1914.
11 TNA: WO 95/588/4: I Corps staff, 22 August 1914.
12 TNA: WO 95/1274: 3 Infantry Brigade, 22 August 1914.
13 TNA: WO 95/1283: 2 Division, 22 August 1914, order to 5 Infantry Brigade, received 7:00 p.m.
14 *Field Service Regulations, Part I*, pp.31–32.
15 *Field Service Regulations, Part II*, pp.23, 22, 28.
16 *Field Service Regulations, Part II, 1913*, p.29.
17 *Field Service Regulations, Part I*, p.117.
18 TNA: WO 95/630/1: II Corps staff, OA62, 22 August 1914.
19 TNA: WO 95/588/1: I Corps Staff, G63, 22 August 1914, p.14.
20 TNA: WO 95/1283: 2 Division, 22 August 1914.

about 1:00 p.m., been fed and dispersed by 3:00 p.m., and mobilised from 4:30 p.m. to parade at 7:00 p.m. They had then returned to billets to bed down for the night by 9:00 p.m. The 2nd Division ignored this order and arranged for their advance the next morning to start at 4:00 a.m. In a further breach of *FSR*, neither I Corps, II Corps, nor GHQ was informed of this decision.

By midnight, the 1st Division was taking up its positions, between Givry and Rouveroy, south and a bit east of Mons, and had made touch with the independent 5th Cavalry Brigade, which was then ordered by GHQ to come under Haig's orders. Surprisingly, there is no record of any orders from I Corps to 5th Cavalry Brigade until Horne took charge of them after midnight on 23 August.[21] II Corps, meanwhile, was withdrawing those 3rd Division units deployed east and southeast of Mons in expectation of the arrival of the 2nd Division.[22]

Just after midnight, Haig discovered that the 2nd Division had not responded to G63. He sent an urgent order to them to march within the hour. This timescale was simply impossible, and Gough, Haig's chief-of-staff, would have known this: the 2nd Division's staff responded with an exasperation unprecedented in other unit diaries.[23] The three brigades marched from 2:45 to 3:15 a.m., much later than Haig anticipated, reaching their destinations from 11:00 a.m. The 6th Infantry Brigade linked with the 1st Division and occupied the line up to Harmignies at midday, covered by their divisional artillery. The 5th Infantry Brigade went into reserve positions behind the 6th.

Haig's Artillery Adviser, Brigadier General Henry Horne, who had selected artillery positions at a forward reconnaissance on 21 August, had accompanied the 1st Division on their advance. Despite having no executive responsibility under *FSR*, he spent the night advising the artillery commander of the 1st Division, then of the 2nd, where to site their guns. Horne's tact and expertise were such that they were happy to comply with his suggestions. Sound placement of the artillery was a feature of I Corp's deployment at Mons, being much better thought out than II Corps, whose Artillery Adviser had been incapacitated in a road traffic accident in France and not replaced.

The 2nd Division's remaining infantry brigade, the 4th (Guards) Brigade, was directed by an Operation Order 4.[24] Two battalions of the Guards marched for Mons, with orders that their attached artillery should deploy at Bois la Haut, which dominated the eastern approaches to Mons. These guns were to cover the two battalions that were to move in front of them, facing east. They would arrive far too late for this to be possible. The other two battalions marched directly to Harmignies, one to remain in reserve, the other to deploy beyond the northern flank of the 6th Infantry Brigade, linking up with the first two battalions. Meanwhile, Haig was required by French to attend a meeting at II Corps Headquarters, Sars-la-Bruyère, at 6:00 a.m.

At this point, it is necessary to explain the difficulties of an operational analysis of the movements of Haig, I Corps and its constituent parts during this campaign. Both I Corps and its two divisions compiled summary reports on the campaign, and Haig later revealed that he had kept what he said was a contemporaneous diary. This diary supports the narrative given in the I Corps summary report. There is absolutely no doubt that Haig was at Sars-la-Bruyère at

21 TNA: WO 95/1138/1: 5 Cavalry Brigade, 22–24 August 1914.
22 TNA: WO 95/630/1: II Corps Staff, 22–23 August 1914.
23 TNA: WO 95/1283: 2 Division, 23 August 1914; TNA: WO 95/1343: 5 Infantry Brigade, 23 August 1914.
24 TNA: WO 95/1283: 2 Division, 23 August 1914, p.44. It is not clear who issued this order.

6:00 a.m. GHQ, II Corps and the cavalry division war diaries all confirm it. But both Haig's personal diary and the I Corps summary report say that he was not. In addition, there are so many other instances where the narrative given in these three reports, and Haig's diary, is positively misleading that they can only be used as evidence of an attempt to disguise the failings of I Corps. The narrative of the day's events is further obscured by the inexplicable loss of the war diary of the 4th (Guards) Brigade, which necessitates greater reliance on this brigade's battalion diaries and those of its supporting artillery. The brigade's battalions received orders, but without the brigade diary, it is difficult to know whether these orders emanated from the 2nd Division or directly from Haig at I Corps. Surprisingly, it is Haig's own diary that confirms he was issuing orders directly to Brigadier General Scott-Kerr, commander of the 4th (Guards) Brigade. At 11:00 p.m. on 23 August, Scott-Kerr found Haig and asked him whether he should be accepting orders from corps or division, since he could not obey both at the same time. Haig appears not to understand that *FSR* required Scott-Kerr to identify the one superior he should accept orders from.[25] The 4th (Guards) Brigade was by no means the only infantry brigade which received orders directly from Haig, bypassing both Monro and Lomax at division and his own staff at I Corps.

So, despite what is said in I Corps documentation, Haig was present at a meeting with French at Sars-la-Bruyère, in company with many other staff officers, at 6:00 a.m. After French and Allenby departed for Valenciennes, he went into conference with Murray and Smith-Dorrien at 6:30 a.m. to agree 'General arrangements in case of attack.' This meeting was minuted, with a copy deposited in II Corps records.[26] It incorporates a plan for the retirement of both I and II Corps if that should become necessary. Haig is recorded as insisting that his corps would need exclusive use of the main Mons to Bavai road for the retirement of his 2nd Division from east of Mons. Both Murray and Smith-Dorrien assumed that the 2nd Division was already in position. For the next several hours, the 3rd Division was still expecting them.

At about 10:30 a.m., the 4th (Guard) Brigade battalions arrived at a point less than a mile short of their destinations. They waited while contact was made with the 3rd Division. The I Corps staff diary reports, wrongly, that they had deployed into position after midday. But by then, all four battalions of the Guards, together with their accompanying artillery, had received counterorders, instructing them to rendezvous at Quevy, about seven miles south of Mons, and for the full brigade to concentrate there, south of the reserve 5th Infantry Brigade, both in support of the 6th Infantry Brigade on the front line between Harmignies and Givry.[27] Only Haig or Monro had the authority to issue these orders. The orders are not recorded in the divisional diary. At 2:00 p.m., the 6th Infantry Brigade asked 2nd Division HQ where the Guards battalion they were expecting was.[28] Yet again, affected units were not informed, as *FSR* requires, about a change in orders.

From this point the narrative of battle, established by operational analysis, diverges ever wider from the narrative given by the *Official History*, which is dependent on the veracity of the report in I Corps records, written by Haig, and supported by his papers. As previously

25 NLS: Acc.3155/98: Douglas Haig Papers, 23 August 1914, p.94.
26 TNA: WO 95/630: II Corps Staff, 23 August 1914, p.75.
27 TNA: WO 95/1326: XLI Brigade RFA; TNA: WO 95/1342: 3 Coldstream Guards; both 23 August 1914.
28 TNA: WO 95/1283: 2 Division, 23 August 1914.

described, between 2:00 and 3:00 p.m., Hamilton, commanding the 3rd Division, contacted Haig, through the 2nd Division, to request the reinforcements planned by GHQ for east of Mons.[29] It is probable that he suggested that his 3rd Division was in considerable peril, beginning a retirement from Nimy to Mons, with a detachment at Obourg bridge, east of Mons, in danger of being cut off, and German forces pressing on his weakly held eastern flank. German artillery fire on his positions was intense, and wounded troops were being evacuated only with difficulty.

Haig's response was first, at 3:50 p.m., to warn the 1st Division that they should prepare for an immediate retirement to Maubeuge.[30] The 1st Division was still anticipating that this order would be activated at 6:00 p.m., though they failed to understand the rationale for it.[31] His second response, at 4:00 p.m., was to order the Guards, who had just reached Quevy, to turn round and march three miles back north again, to the tiny hamlet of Harveng, two miles south-east of Harmignies. Simultaneously, he ordered the 5th Infantry Brigade to march from their reserve positions at Genly, three miles east of Harveng, to the same destination. Both units had supporting artillery. Arriving 'in consequence of alarming reports, the utmost confusion seemed to prevail, the flat plateau above Harveng was crowded with artillery, the village and street were equally crowded, and no-one seemed to know whither to go or what to do.'[32]

Monro was taken by surprise by this concentration of his brigades but, presumably after consultation with Haig, took responsibility for planning the defence of the hamlet. He put the 5th Infantry Brigade to work digging a defence line to protect the hamlet from the north, and the 4th (Guards) Brigade to work digging a defence line to the east. This new line of defence, which can be termed the Haig Line, was situated less than two miles from the defence line already constructed by II Corps to the north, and less than two miles from the line of the 6th Infantry Brigade, running south from Harmignies, to the east. The heavy battery of the 2nd Division and other artillery units were deployed to the southwest of Harveng to cover any assault on it. At 4:30 p.m., the German artillery opened a heavy and accurate barrage on the 6th Infantry positions. However, due to the ineffectiveness of their field artillery projectiles, there were no casualties. Two batteries supporting them were engaged by German howitzers and do record losses.

At about 6:00 p.m., two battalions of the Guards were ordered to move forward, with supporting field artillery, and to extend the 2nd Division's 6th Infantry Brigade line north of Harmignies, thus relieving the overextended 3rd Division battalion in that sector.[33] There is no transparency in the records as to who issued their orders. Horne was certainly involved. In the confusion at Harveng, and having little else to do, he participated in the redeployment of the 2nd Division artillery. The howitzer brigade was sent to reinforce the artillery behind the 6th Infantry Brigade and he seems to have persuaded Haig, or simply used the authority of being on Haig's staff, to allow him to take control of two 2nd Division batteries of the 41st Brigade RFA, which were not needed in the defence of Harveng. Ever tactful, he liaised with Monro and suggested that he take them to the heights north of Harmignies, since this portion of the

29 TNA: WO 95/630/1: II Corps Staff, 23 August 1914.
30 TNA: WO 95/1227: 1 Division, 23 August 1914.
31 TNA: WO 95/1274: 3 Infantry Brigade, 23 August 1914.
32 TNA: WO 95/1342: 3 Coldstream Guards, 23 August 1914.
33 TNA: WO 95/1326: XLI Brigade RFA; TNA: WO 95/1342: 1 Irish Guards, both 23 August 1914.

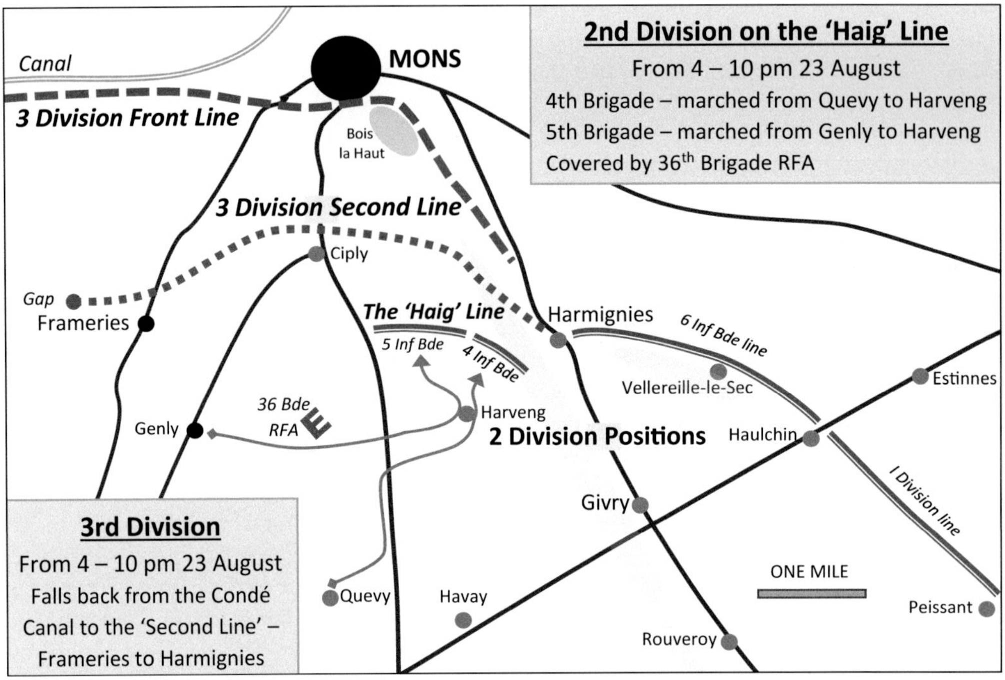

A defence line is constructed by the 2nd Division around the hamlet of Harveng.

line had no artillery support. *FSR* requires that all batteries should have a nominated escort, and the 2nd Division diary implies that Monro authorised the release of the two battalions for that reason.[34] In marked contrast to II Corps records, there is no clarity in the origin of orders reaching infantry or artillery units at this stage of the battle. It seems likely that Horne and Monro took matters into their own hands.

At 8:00 p.m., Smith-Dorrien visited I Corps headquarters, presumably invoking GHQ order OA90, which I Corps had just received. This required I Corps to support II Corps if it asked for aid. Monro was ordered to send three battalions to 'the occupation of ground which had been abandoned', at Paturages.[35] This order was not based on intelligence and implied the 3rd Division was giving way. Monro hesitated to obey this order, since he had been ordered to hold Harveng in strength, and he had just released the two 4th (Guards) Brigade battalions to deploy north of Harmignies. He ordered them back. But, certainly, the two batteries of the 41st Brigade RFA, and possibly the infantry as well, considered that they were obeying orders from Horne at I Corps. As mandated by *FSR*, they refused to withdraw without his authorisation. So, Monro moved one of the two remaining Guards battalions digging in east of Harveng to relieve three of the four 5th Infantry Brigade battalions digging in north of Harveng.[36] It was not till 10:00 p.m. that the three battalions of the 5th Infantry Brigade started their march from the Haig Line north of Harveng. Monro now had only three battalions holding a line to

34 TNA: WO 95/1283: 2 Division, 23 August 1914.
35 TNA: WO 95/1283: 2 Division, 23 August 1914.
36 TNA: WO 95/1283: 2 Division, 23 August 1914.

which Haig had allocated eight battalions. By the standards of the day, the three 5th Infantry Brigade battalions did not move slowly, in that they covered less than eight miles in four and a half hours, arriving at Paturages, mildly demoralised and very tired, at 2:30 a.m., but nor did they hurry.[37]

Summary

Haig does not emerge from this narrative with much credit. Some of this reputational damage is self-inflicted. Conventional accounts of the Mons campaign rely heavily on Haig's writings, be they his diary or his report in I Corps records.[38] Operational analysis, in some cases very simple operational analysis, reveals significant discrepancies between his diary and report, and actual events. Haig denies his presence at the planning meetings at Sars-la-Bruyère at 6:00 a.m. on 23 August. He says that he did not meet with Smith-Dorrien until 10:30 a.m. that morning, but 10:30 a.m. is the time that the 4th (Guards) Brigade received orders to march from Mons to Quevy, abandoning their orders to support II Corps up from Harmignies. I Corps records that the Guards did take up these positions. The records of the Guards battalions and their supporting artillery say they did not. It is inconceivable that these three war diaries have been doctored. The war diary of the 4th (Guards) Brigade has been lost, the only such loss in the whole campaign. To suggest that a deliberate attempt has been made to hide the true version of events is mere speculation. Operational analysis evaluates the reliability of evidence. Understandably, some timings given are inaccurate. Some orders are assumed to have been carried out when they were not. It is sometimes not easy to distinguish between genuine misunderstandings and deliberate fallacies. It is sad that one has to do so.

Operational analysis should address the questions of outcomes and how the actions of senior officers influenced these. The outcome that GHQ planned for II Corps was achieved, and it was achieved as a consequence of rigid adherence to *FSR*. Haig did not follow *FSR*. He considered himself an independent commander, not constrained by the strategy laid on him by his Commander-in-Chief. He did not rely on advice or intelligence reports collected by his staff. He repeatedly issued orders and counter-orders to his subordinates without observing conventions on command pathways or informing those affected by his orders. Many of these orders were verbal, and those that were written were often spontaneous and poorly drafted. This makes operational analysis much more dependent on the reactions of subordinate units since the main body of I Corps staff was often not informed of changes in the plan.

It is tempting to allege that Haig was so shaken after watching the French falling back to the east that he reverted to a cavalry commander who had to make rapid decisions on the information available to him. But in June 1912, Haig had directed an Aldershot command staff ride. In his report, for no obvious reason in the context, he discusses 'the problem of the organization of the whole of the Expeditionary Force into armies.' 'The general principles which [Clausewitz] enunciates seem quite applicable to armed forces today'. Especially as his conclusion is true that 'if an army is formed into two principal corps, each of which has its special commander, that is to neutralise the Commander-in-Chief.' He cites Gyulai in 1859 and Benedek in 1866

37 TNA: WO 95/1343: 5 Infantry Brigade, 23 August 1914.
38 TNA: WO 95/588/4: I Corps staff diary, 23 August 1914.

to support this conclusion, arguing that they both lost control of the constituent parts of their armies.[39] He quotes *FSR*, 'When several divisions are mobilized they may be grouped in two or more armies, each under a separate commander but all under the supreme command of the C-in-C'.[40] Haig ignores the last inconvenient phrase of this regulation. 'Napoleon I, who of all generals of the past had most experience in the command of armies, laid this number [two divisions] down as suitable for independent command.' Haig follows by quoting Napoleon in saying that a corps, 'well led, can fight or avoid battle, and manoeuvre according to circumstances without any misfortune happening to it.' He supports this conclusion by citing Rudolf von Caemmerer, who wrote the *Development of Strategical Science* in 1905. 'The army corps is found to be the natural strategic unit.'

Summing up on the constitution of an expeditionary force, Haig opines that 'there will be considerable advantage in grouping two of our divisions into an 'army', although the grouping together of two parts is open to all the objections mentioned by Clausewitz.'[41] This was written before Haig participated in the manoeuvres of 1912 and 1913, so it is impossible to assert that this remained his view in 1914. But just like a knowledge of *FSR* was invaluable in interpreting the operational analysis of II Corps, so knowledge of Haig's adherence to certain aspects of Clausewitzian theory may inform operational analysis of I Corps at the Battle of Mons.

Furthermore, a feature of Haig's strategic thinking was that an army should never be afraid to refuse combat. Charteris records that in India, in 1910, Haig:

> …foresaw the situation with which the British Army was actually confronted in 1914, and the whole of one tour was devoted to the problem of how a small force, faced with the advance of an overwhelming enemy, should direct its operations: whether it should accept battle if a favourable but fleeting opportunity offered, or whether it should devote its whole energies to disengaging itself from the threat by a rapid and skilful withdrawal.[42]

The 1912 Aldershot staff ride set up a scenario in which this tactical dilemma is revisited. In discussing whether to send a division forward to hold Cold Ashby, a village in Northamptonshire, which was about to be taken by large forces from the north, Haig discusses the pros and cons. If the advance was likely to buy useful time for further concentration, or if the village was of great strategic value, the advance might be justified. But if these conditions were not met, then the risks of such an advance become too great. The division 'may become so involved as to be unable to extract itself and become overwhelmed … if attacked and driven back, even if not annihilated, it will have a bad effect on morale … to hold out just long enough and then retire from such a position would require a very exceptional commander.'[43] He concluded that such an advance should not be made,

If it was Haig's intention to follow his own advice and avoid battle, he succeeded. I Corps suffered well under 100 casualties in the two days of advance to, and retirement from, Mons, most of those in the artillery. The unexpected problem that Haig faced was the severe drop in morale

39 Ferencz Gyulai, an Austrian commander, lost the battle of Magenta in the Second Italian War of Independence. Ludwig Benedek lost the Austro-Prussian war, commanding for Emperor Franz Josef.
40 *Field Service Regulations, Part II,* p.26.
41 WO 106/1453: 'Report of Aldershot Command Staff Tour 1912' Aldershot 1912, pp.20–22.
42 Charteris, *Field Marshal Earl Haig*, p.54.
43 TNA: WO 106/1453: 'Report of Aldershot Command Staff Tour 1912' Aldershot 1912, pp.17–19.

that was the consequence of his command style. At divisional level and below, *FSR* was generally being followed in I Corps. Lomax and Monro were both firm adherents to it, and as required, expected their subordinates to comply. This meant that their orders were brief and issued strictly on hierarchical lines. They ran efficient and compliant staffs with good intelligence collation, such that they appeared better informed than their commander. But when *FSR* was not followed, officers of all ranks became disoriented. The near mutinous fury repeatedly recorded in both I Corps divisional diaries during the campaign is unprecedented, and contrasts very unfavourably with the calm professionalism of II Corps unit diaries, despite their much greater endurance of uncertainty in battle. Monro's 2nd Division diary makes particularly uncomfortable reading. Their only respite from order counterorder sequences came when Haig allowed Horne to draw together the fractured units of the 4th (Guards) Brigade, two artillery brigades and the 5th Cavalry Brigade and to start the process of a rearguard action, in compliance with *FSR*, to cover the retirement of the 2nd Division. In doing so, he temporarily usurped Monro's and Scot-Kerr's authority, but he relinquished command as soon as the units had steadied. He was the only I Corps officer who serenely weathered Haig's style of command while demanding *FSR* adherence in subordinates who should not, under *FSR*, have been under his command in the first place. On the next day, 25 August, life got even more difficult for Lomax and Monro. Haig elected to completely ignore Operation Order 7 from GHQ that mandated a retirement 'to the neighbourhood of Le Cateau.'[44] Instead, he issued G122 at 10:00 p.m. on the 24th to his divisions. This order required his corps to cooperate with the French in defending bridges over the River Sambre, and billet overnight between seven and 15 miles from Le Cateau.[45] The complexity and confusion of this day of retreat led to several instances of panic and disintegration in 2nd Division units.

Lomax managed to keep a tight hold on his division, but even he was reduced to apoplectic fury at midnight on 25 August, cancelling Haig's orders, which had gone direct to his infantry brigades, and subsequently adhering to another unnecessary order with studied and meticulous disdain, marching his entire division through the tiny hamlet of Le Favril, just south of Landrecies, without stopping. Haig had ordered all three of his brigades to occupy it.[46] Monro, by then, simply records trying to regain touch with his three brigades, which had been dangerously scattered by Haig's impulsive and ill-informed orders to them, without his consent, during 25 August.[47]

II Corps and GHQ, meanwhile, in a reprise of the situation at Mons, were waiting for the 2nd Division to fall into line between Le Cateau and Landrecies. It seems unlikely that the regular officers of the 3rd and 5th Divisions ever forgot or forgave their betrayal in it not doing so. 'Staff officers should never venture to criticise either superiors or inferiors to any person whatsoever. It is not within their right to do so, and nothing is more likely to cause ill-feeling.'[48] This Staff Manual statement was observed by all concerned during the long retreat from Mons. Sir John French could have reacted with much more than the gentle reprimand he issued to Haig on 29 August.[49]

44 TNA: WO 95/1/2: General Staff, Operation Order No 7, 25 August 1914.
45 TNA: WO 95/588/1: I Corps Staff, G122, 24 August 1914. See also copies of French operation orders in these records, dated 22, 28 and 29 August.
46 TNA: WO 95/1227: 1 Division, 25 August 1914.
47 TNA: WO 95/1283: 2 Division, 23–26 August 1914.
48 TNA: WO 106/51: Staff Manual (Provisional) 1911, p.13.
49 Cooper, *Haig*, pp.160–162.

13

The Historiography of Field Services Regulations on the Western Front

There are few references to *FSR* in contemporary reports, unit diaries, journals, and letters from the Western Front. It is not difficult to understand why this is so. Paradoxically, the more firmly *FSR* was regarded as a doctrine generally applicable to all officers in the pre-war army, the less likely it was to be cited or referred to. As Professor Niall Barr puts it, 'the regular officers of 1914 had had many years of experience of command and took the information contained in Field Service Regulations for granted. They carried out procedures almost instinctively', thus contributing to a 'dearth of official evidence' of their thought processes, 'in the early months of the war.'[1] Part of the definition of a doctrine is that it is totally accepted by most of the population to which it applies. There were other doctrines similarly accepted by the British Army officer corps in 1914, including a belief in Christianity and a patriotic respect for the authority of the King. Under normal circumstances, no officer would feel the need to draw attention to these beliefs, and few do. *FSR* was also a doctrine, and adherence to it can be regarded as a quality defining the behaviour of all officers of the British Army of 1914.

These officers had been required to study and follow *FSR* and teach it to their subordinates. An officer could expect to be refused promotion and sanctioned by the inspectorate if he did not apply it to his work. There was a general expectation that he would be familiar with its details. J.F.C. Fuller said, in his *Training Soldiers for War*, published in 1914, that:

> If all officers act in accordance with these regulations the whole army will work in harmony, and economy of force will result; but if, instead, officers act on the inspirations of the moment, however brilliant these flashes of genius may be, discord will arise through misinterpretation of intention, and the army will act inarticulately, and wear itself to pieces by the friction of its parts.[2]

This was a general view. Inevitably, however, in a significant army, a small number of maverick officers did not follow *FSR* in all respects. However, the conventions of the day were such that fellow officers almost conspired to disguise these lapses. Accusing another officer of not

1 Barr, 'Command in the Transition', in Sheffield and Todman (eds), *Command and Control*, pp.14–15.
2 Captain J.F.C. Fuller, *Training Soldiers for War* (London: Hugh Rees Ltd), p.45.

'Some poor back wire'. This was the original caption by an infantry subaltern in 1915, illustrating the lack of a strong reserve line as required by FSR. (Author's collection)

understanding *FSR* was tantamount to saying that he was not fit to be in the army. *FSR* itself forbade criticism of a superior officer. The current author's own grandfather vented several times in letters home to his mother about the behaviour of his senior officers in their disregard of pre-war conventions and practice. Often, his next letter would ask her not to share its content on the grounds that he might be sanctioned or even court-martialled if word got out. While he is happy to name officers whom he respected, he is silent on the names of those he did not. He never mentions Haig once, in about 800 letters from the front line, covering every year of the war.[3]

All regular officers knew the rules of their profession very thoroughly. So, if a senior officer failed to follow *FSR*, the lapse was recognised at once. Several examples of comment have already been cited in the unit diaries of lesser units in the advance to, and retreat from, Mons. These comments are not referenced to *FSR*. But every serving officer who read the entries would have immediately recognised them for what they were.

Similarly, although there are very few references to *FSR* in post-war books written by veterans of the conflict, this does not mean that they are not referring to it. Sir Horace Smith-Dorrien's book, *Forty-Eight Years Service*, mentions *FSR* only twice, and that in relation to his own conduct, not anybody else's. But he is not above a sly dig at French, writing of before Mons, that 'the French were so insistent on our moving forward to cover their left flank that, although short of guns, field hospitals and Engineer Units, the C-in-C decided to go without them, as the news of the enemy was that they had left Brussels and were advancing west and south of that town.'[4] Every regular officer reading that would have known that *FSR* forbade any advance

3 Hutchison, *The Young Gunner*, pp.46, 234.
4 General Sir Horace Smith-Dorrien, *Memories of Forty-Eight Years' Service* (London: John Murray, 1925), p.376.

towards an organised enemy without artillery and engineers. Sir Hubert Gough, in his book, *The Fifth Army*, does not mention *FSR* at all, despite the fact that he is writing partly in response to accusations that, at the Somme, he issued orders direct to junior formations, ignoring intervening levels of command, in breach of *FSR*.[5]

The evidence that *FSR* is being followed by junior officers is often hard to pick up without an understanding of it, but letters and journals are a good source for judging their degree of adherence. Lieutenant Edmond Schreiber, later a Second World War general, was with the 115th Battery RFA, 25th Brigade, which was supporting the 2nd Infantry Brigade, 1st Division, I Corps at Mons and thereafter. He describes his retirement on 25th August. 'The march started again at dawn, a long weary day, very hot at times and heavy showers of rain … I was sent ahead to reconnoitre positions for the batteries of our brigade. I rode many miles on this task and chose many positions, none of which we occupied.'[6] Under *FSR*, it was the duty of a battery on rearguard duty to identify lines of resistance that could be occupied to delay a pursuing enemy. He does not point out that he is observing *FSR*.

Similarly, Lieutenant Hutchison describes to his mother what he was doing in the days after the arrival of his battery at Ploegsteert Wood south of Ypres, in June 1915.

> We have had to make ourselves a gun position and dugouts … I talked with infantry officers in the first line trenches … went for a long ride this afternoon to have a look at our second line of defence position … went for a ramble amongst our support trenches, chiefly discovering where there weren't any. [We looked] for new observation stations, and laid wire to them … [and] reconnoitred roads to GHQ position [the reserve line] for the brigade.[7]

This is spread over several letters, but he documents almost every duty and responsibility of a junior officer on active duty with a detached unit under *FSR*. Lieutenant Marshall, with a 35th Division battery, was lucky enough to have a regular commander when they arrived on the front line at Maricourt during the Somme Battle:

> Although I wanted to sleep in my tent, the skipper absolutely objects to sleeping above ground, so that ever since we came in, we have spent all our time digging holes for ourselves to sleep and crawl into … Our neighbours, a 60-pounder battery, have taken no precautions; indeed, their mess is a tent. This accounts for the very heavy casualties they are having.[8]

Arranging protection for one's men, without specific orders, is a fundamental duty laid on officers by *FSR*.

Most books written during the war or in the immediate aftermath of it were intended for a general readership, and they are unhelpful in assessing the impact of *FSR*. The patriotic, rose-tinted inaccuracies of, for instance, Ernest Hamilton's, *The first Seven Divisions, being a detailed*

5 Sir Hubert Gough, *The Fifth Army* (London:, Hodder and Stoughton, 1931).
6 RAM: MD/425: Journal of Lieutenant Schreiber, 25 Aug 1914.
7 Hutchison, *The Young Gunner*, pp.78–79.
8 Hutchison, *The Young Gunner*, pp.157–158.

account of the Fighting from Mons to Ypres, first published in 1916, and Sir Arthur Conan Doyle's *A history of the Great War. Volume 1.: The British Campaign in France and Flanders, 1914,* also published in 1916, are of interest in that they got through the censors but is of little use to the academic researcher except as social history. Ian Hay's *The First Hundred Thousand* describes with delightful irreverence the training and experience of a Highland Yeomanry Regiment as it went to war in 1915:

> Struthers owed [his rank] to the fact that in the far back ages, he had held a commission in a University Corps. He was a scholar of his College, and was an expert in the art of accumulating knowledge in quick time for examination purposes. He knew all the little red manuals by heart, was an infallible authority on buttons and badges, and would dip into the Field Service Pocket Book as another man might dip into the Sporting Times. Strange to say, he was not very good at drilling a platoon.[9]

But some books were written for a professional readership. Becke's *Royal Regiment of Artillery at Le Cateau*, published in 1919, is a meticulous history, making good use of personal testimony and unit war diaries. Major Becke had previously written on Napoleonic military history, and he wrote this book using the resources of the Historical Section (Military Branch) of the Committee of Imperial Defence. He wrote it, almost as an experiment, 'to show Officers of the Regiment what use would be made of their War Diaries.' Few would have had access to these documents during the war itself. It must be almost the first operational analysis of a First World War engagement based on objective research. He devotes five of its 80 pages to a tactical analysis with reference to *FSR*, suggesting that the placement of the 5th Division artillery so close to the front line at the battle, was not only consistent with *FSR*, as an exception to a general rule that they be posted in covered positions to the rear, but required of it in the circumstances. Since the book was being written while the war was progressing, this focus on *FSR* implies that he considered that it remained relevant. 'The delaying action fought by the Second Corps at Le Cateau is a teaching example which will well repay the diligent study by all gunners.'[10] He also knowledgably discusses the reliability of unit war diaries, pointing out the dangers of excessive reliance on any one of them.

A further book, albeit published in 1929, is Alexander Kearsey's *1915 Campaign in France, considered in relation to the Field Service Regulations.*[11] Colonel Alexander Kearsey entered the army in 1896 and served in the South African War from 1899, winning a DSO. Between the wars, he married into the aristocracy, attended the Staff College, and, in August 1914, served on the Embarkation Staff at Southampton. He fought at First Ypres with the 7th Cavalry Brigade in November 1914 and subsequently in the Dardanelles and Palestine campaigns, being wounded in 1917. In 1918, he was appointed to the command of a cadet college, having been mentioned in dispatches twice. He was a conventional and respected regular army officer, and he retired after the war as a lieutenant colonel.[12] His book analyses the battles on the Western Front in 1915 with

9 Ian Hay, *The First Hundred Thousand* (Edinburgh and London: Blackwood, 1915), p.39.
10 Becke, *The Royal Regiment of Artillery at Le Cateau*, pp.v, 76–80.
11 A. Kearsey, *1915 Campaign in France, The Battles of Aubers Ridge, Festubert and Loos, considered in relation to the Field Service Regulations,* (Sussex: Naval & Military Press, 2007 [Gale & Polden, 1929])
12 Lieutenant Colonel Alexander Kearsey, Biographical detail <www.vlib.us/wwi/resources/egyptiancampaign.html> (accessed 15 April 2024).

respect to *FSR*, following the battles of Aubers Ridge, Festubert and Loos with forensic precision, quoting specific regulations at each point. He is writing primarily for a professional audience that was familiar with *FSR*. He is at pains to be 'impartial', recording the details of departures from *FSR* without emotion, leaving it to his reader to decide whether the departure was built in to the plans, was avoidable in the course of carrying out those plans, or unavoidable in the heat of battle. In his narrative of the Battle of Loos, he identifies 26 occasions when *FSR* supplied appropriate guidance, which can be broken down into 12 instances where the British army complied and 14 instances where they did not.[13] He even points out a further six instances when the Germans successfully followed British *FSR* in their reactions to events. The main interest in the book is that it was written at all. His 'Introduction' makes it clear that it is a reactive book, responding to the 'interesting' account of events given in the recently published volume of '*Military Operations*', (James Edmond's *Official History of the War*), which covered the 1915 campaign on the Western Front. Kearsey is writing to crystallise points made in the debate about these events within his social circle. He makes no attempt to define the doctrine of *FSR*, assuming that his audience already has that knowledge. Nor does he attempt to apportion blame. The book is a compelling testament to the importance with which middle-ranking regular soldiers regarded *FSR*, even years after the war. Many were still angry that *FSR* had, during significant battles, been ignored. As late as 1937, Ferrers-Guy was writing to Edmonds, the official historian, saying that the staff 'cannot say that their orders were always framed on sound tactics based on Field Service Regulations (FSR) Part I', and that this failure had required 'brave men to do what was impossible'.[14] Edmonds' *Official History*, in all its volumes, avoids reference to doctrine throughout, purporting to record what did happen rather than why it happened. Even Andrew Green, in his book on *Writing the Great War*, does not pick up on its failure to address doctrinal differences in the higher command. However, he does emphasise the tightrope Edmonds was walking with many senior generals still alive and the War Office anxious to present a somewhat sanitised version of command controversies.[15]

Another meticulously referenced book, the *History of the Development of British Artillery in France*, written by Brevet Colonel Stewart Rawlins in 1918, follows every development in the organisation and command structure of the artillery in France with reference to the command principles laid down in *FSR*. He was on the staff of, and had access to all the records of, the major general Royal Artillery at GHQ in 1918. He served in the Royal Field Artillery earlier in the war, winning the DSO and being appointed Companion of the Most Distinguished Order of St Michael and St George. His book contains a long chapter on 'Tactical Development':

> It is scarcely possible to trace the development of artillery tactics with the same detail and accuracy as has been possible with [Commands, Staff and Organization] dealt with in preceding chapters … Tactical changes naturally sprang from the line and in many cases were gradually and generally adopted without reference to G.H.Q. … The British Artillery was of course trained for war on [*FSR*] and 'Field' and 'Garrison Artillery Training' [and these] proved a remarkably sound guide to the main principles of artillery in action.[16]

13 Kearsey, *1915 Campaign in France*, pp.39–62.
14 Simon Robbins, *British Generalship on the Western Front, 1914–18: Defeat into Victory* (London: Taylor and Francis, 2005), p.21, M.C. Ferrers-Guy to Edmonds, 29 July 1937, PRO CAB45/116.
15 Andrew Green, *Writing the Great War: Sir James Edmonds and the Official History 1915–1948* (London: Frank Cass, 2003).
16 Rawlins, *British Artillery in France*, pp.88, 162.

All three of these books will be referenced in the following pages, but for most historians attempting operational analysis, their main sources will be the unit diaries available from the National Archives in London. There are literally thousands of them. They vary in reliability for reasons that Becke sets out. Some are written by men dazed and confused, some are written up after the event (sometimes long after the event), some, a very few, have been doctored or severely culled. Many report selectively or put a debatable interpretation on events. They are written by real people, often with cheap pencils, some with good handwriting, others in an almost illegible scrawl, some verbosely, some so briefly as to be virtually useless. They have to be interpreted within these very human parameters. No single such diary should be relied on. Cross-referencing with neighbouring units of all arms, and up and down the hierarchy, is mandatory for a complete account, and support from personal letters or journals, written at the time, is highly desirable. Battle summaries, written after the event and stored in divisional or corps diaries, should be treated with caution. The reports on a trivial trench raid in June 1916 provide an example of coordinated falsification with arguably benign intent. 'A very successful raid was carried out on this day by 14th Gloucesters, one machine gun being captured.'[17] Second-Lieutenant Duke Marshall, serving with the artillery of the 35th Division, wrote home to his sister the next day:

> Our bantams raided the Hun line last night and brought back a machine gun, but no prisoners [this being the principal aim of the mission]. They claim to have killed many Germans. Colonel Roberts and Captain Butt were killed with about 10 other casualties. I wonder at it being called a great victory. Bit of a failure I would have thought![18]

It is recorded factually in the associated war diaries. There is no mention of reconnaissance, planning or cooperation with the artillery to suggest compliance with *FSR*. It was written up as a success in the London *Times* of 9 June. Nobody wanted to tell the relatives of Colonel Roberts, or a division with already dubious morale, that their losses had been in vain. Research into any war is difficult.

Hutchison gives a lively account of a similar trench raid mounted by the Canadian Division on 17 November 1915:

> The Canadians next door had a splendid show the night before last. It started with a subaltern asking permission for himself and three men to creep out and in the night throw a lot of bombs at a particular bit of the German trench. The company commander said 'let's make it a company show' and went and asked his battalion commander's permission. The battalion commander said 'good idea, let's make it a battalion show' and went to ask his brigade commander's permission, who said 'no, we will have a brigade show' and asked the divisional commander's permission who said 'excellent plan, we will make it a divisional show', and permission was asked of the corps. They approved of it, and arranged for the divisions on either side to cooperate. So, two nights ago the Canadians shelled the German front trenches about 1 am. They then lifted off the front trench to allow two bombing parties of 20 men apiece who bombed with the greatest of ease into the trench

17 TNA: WO 95/2471/1: 35 Division Artillery, 8 June 1916.
18 Hutchison, *The Young Gunner*, p.301.

> selected, killed 30 to 40 Germans and took 12 prisoners. They then quickly evacuated the trenches again, taking the prisoners with them and losing only one man. Then they waited while the Germans organized their bombing parties and proceeded to retake their own empty trenches by bombing them in force. When they had done this and had again crowded into their front trenches, a very heavy fire was again opened on them – with good effect we hope.[19]

Andrew Iarocci, in his book on the 1st Canadian Division, describes from the war diaries the meticulous preparations for this raid involving careful reconnaissance, rehearsal, all arms combination, and brief orders on movement and intent to the raiding party. Yet even so, it was nearly derailed by a planning lapse, when the Canadian artillery staff ordered 'A' battery, Royal Canadian Horse Artillery, to cut barbed wire, where 'a line of trees blocked the target from the gunners' view.' The wire was cut by hand.[20] All would have learnt from the experience. There is naturally no mention in primary or secondary sources of *FSR*, but on this day of battle, the planning and execution were *FSR* compliant.

It has been asserted that because the training regulations in *FSR, Part I* were written mainly for open warfare, they became irrelevant when static trench warfare supervened. This is to miss the point. The aim of basic training was to teach officers to firmly adopt *FSR* principles with respect to protection, reconnaissance, liaison, the issue of operation orders, all arms combination and the formulation of relevant training for specific operations. It is jumping the gun, but SS 135 (November 1918) *The Division in Attack*, states, as a GHQ pronouncement at that date, that:

> ...there has been a tendency during the present war to look upon trench warfare and open warfare as two separate things. This has led to a disregard of many of the fundamental principles, laid down in the training manuals issued before this war, as being inapplicable to trench warfare ... We have now, however, resumed our allegiance to principles of training employed before the war, and must be careful not to depart from them again.[21]

But despite this retrospective justification, it is right to point out that one cannot assume that following *FSR* tactical advice, or observing its principles, was relevant to conditions in 1915, let alone 1918. In the war years, *FSR* doctrine was never officially updated. Some details in *Part II* were updated in 1914 and 1917, but no changes were made to *Part I*. There are advisory updates in the Central Distribution Section (CDS) and Stationery Service (SS) publications, produced both by the War Office and by GHQ, throughout the war. Orders were issued at the highest level that consigned specific regulations to effective oblivion, particularly relating to command hierarchies. But *FSR*, as a set of principles, remained as it was. Individual regulations might be found inapplicable, but they were not formally struck out. Principles in it might, by some, have been deemed inapplicable to modern warfare, but that does not stop them from existing. It is relatively easy to elucidate whether any individual action during the war followed *FSR*

19 Hutchison, *The Young Gunner*, pp.94–95.
20 Andrew Iarocci, *Shoestring Soldiers, The 1st Canadian Division at War, 1914–1915* (Toronto: University of Toronto Press, 2008), pp.260–261.
21 SS 135, *The Division in Attack, issued by General Staff, November 1918*, pp.3–4.

Routine crowding of trenches in 1915. (Author's collection)

principles or not. Haig chose at Mons to disregard *FSR* by issuing orders directly to infantry brigades. That is a fact. There is no moral judgment to be made. There can be no assumption that observing *FSR* in this respect is better than not doing so. If following this command principle was not applicable to modern warfare, then no sensible soldier would observe it.

There is much evidence that some very sensible soldiers did believe that this and many other core *FSR* principles should be followed, even late into the war. Jim Beach's analysis, in his article on 'Doctrine Writing' from 1917 to 1918, is one of very few papers on any subject pertaining to the Western Front which benefits from its lack of reference to *FSR*, because it allows him to remain objective on Haig's influence on it. It is not until page 24 of 26 that he observes that SS guidance in 1916 genuflects 'towards the pre-war Field Service Regulations (FSR), with the earlier guidance being noted in regard to the "general principles" of an attack, advanced guards, reconnaissance, operations orders, and frontages.' The fact that 'references to FSR had appeared in earlier doctrine manuals … is more than just an accidental continuity.'[22] This begs the question as to whether anybody read and took notice of doctrinal pamphlets, a subject Beach addresses earlier in his paper. However, it does suggest that some *FSR* principles remained relevant over the long term.

Attempting to find evidence of this continuity in operational books and theses is not an easy task. Combination of arms in every stage of battle is the single most important tactical principle laid down in *FSR*. Consider an article, written in 2010 by Jonathan Boff, on 'Combined Arms', during the last three months of the war in 1918. This quotation is from the abstract. 'Pre-war regular officers continued to dominate the army of 1918', which is undeniably true, but then: 'Their culture, rooted in the attitudes of the nineteenth century or even earlier, militated against the coherent dissemination and application of a single doctrine.' In fairness, there is much in the paper that is valuable and insightful, but this sentence dismisses the British Army's unified

22 Jim Beach, 'Doctrine Writing', p.489.

professionalism in 1914, which was defined by *FSR*, as no more than an ethos at best. In this article, he does not mention *FSR*, except bizarrely, to record that one officer in 1918 asked for written guidance on how to follow it.[23] But Boff returns to the subject of all arms combination in his book *Winning and Losing on the Western Front* two years later, and his tone is very different. He quotes *FSR, Part I* on the necessity for all arms combination, and goes on to say that 'in theory, therefore, the British Army of 1914 was firmly alive to the value of a combined arms approach.' In the subsequent narrative, he describes how the best units of the Third Army were following *FSR*, or SS documents based on it, in close fighting, right at the end of the war.[24] Beach and Boff are both acknowledging a continuity of awareness of the principles of *FSR* in the senior ranks of the army.

FSR is not just about tactical principles. What it says on command and administration is at least as important. *FSR*, in all its detail, can be defined as a general doctrine, not a tactical doctrine, nor a military doctrine, for reasons that have already been discussed. Its command principles, however, are laid down in such detail that they constitute a doctrine. 'The pre-war Field Service Regulations were models of clarity which made the relationship between commanders and staff plain', says Professor Niall Barr.[25] All officers are allocated to one of three different organisational structures. General staff officers serve the generals on their General Staff. Line officers obey direct and brief orders from their immediate superiors. Administrative staff slot into a civilian-based enterprise that manages logistics and paperwork, issuing and receiving detailed orders and reports within directorates.

Barr was writing in *Command and Control*, edited by Gary Sheffield and Dan Todman, published in 2004. Since this book purports to 'seek actively to examine the issues of command and control' on the Western Front and Barr introduces the importance of *FSR* in an early chapter, one might expect useful assessments of the impact of *FSR* on command at war.[26] But Andy Simpson, in a chapter on 'Corps Command', is the only other of the remaining seven contributors to even mention *FSR*, despite its demonstrable relevance to command and control. Even Simpson does not address the whole *FSR* doctrine on command. 'It is important to clarify the theoretical basis for the BEF's operations. This was embodied in *Field Service Regulations, Part I, Operations*.' This is a surprising statement. It is *FSR, Part II,* and its off-shoot, the *Staff Manual*, which define command relationships.

> This volume [*Part I*] sets out the principles under which the army should operate … [It] specifically avoided going in to too much detail, assuming that those applying them should, through experience and training, know what actions to perform within their framework. This modus operandi reflected the general reluctance within the British Army to accept a formal doctrine – defined as 'a set of beliefs about the nature of war and the keys to success on the battlefield … It is important to emphasise that *FSR* reflected Douglas Haig's views on warfare.'

23 Jonathan Boff, 'Combined Arms during the Hundred Days Campaign, August–November 1918', *War in History*, 17 (4), 2010. Quotation from abstract. Also p.476.

24 Jonathan Boff, *Winning and Losing on the Western Front: the British Third Army and the Defeat of Germany in 1918* (Cambridge: Cambridge University Press 2012), Ch.5, 'British Tactics, the True Elixir' pp.126–135.

25 Barr, 'Command in Transition', in Sheffield and Todman (eds), *Command and Control*, pp.14–15.

26 Sheffield and Todman (eds), *Command and Control*, p.4.

Simpson's argument, as presented above, encapsulates all the intellectual difficulties consequent on fallacious assumptions. If Haig, at the least, approved *FSR* between 1909 and 1914, then presumably, he was following its tactical principles in 1914. *FSR*, Simpson implies, was first and foremost a tactical handbook, with *Part II* a mere appendix offering advice on the administration of the BEF. Simpson's following analysis sets out other preconceptions that have informed academic historians for the last 50 years. 'It is difficult to see how *FSR* could be applied at all, as trench warfare rendered redundant most of its assumptions about an attack', although he goes on to say that 'all the offensives of 1915 were to some extent in accordance with *FSR*.' Like many before him, Simpson tries to dismiss *FSR* but then suddenly finds it to be relevant. As he says later, 'corps greater control of artillery led them to breach *FSR*, in that they tended to leave less and less scope for the exercise of initiative, despite the view of *FSR* that the man on the spot knows best.'[27] This is not a tactical principle. It is a principle falling under the category of the duties and responsibilities of junior officers. There is much to agree with in both Simpson's original thesis and his chapter in *Command and Control*, but, in both, he dwells at length on Haig's alleged association with the production of *FSR* and assumes that he is following it.[28] His whole presentation is based on this factual fallacy. It is sad, because there is much good, solid work in it, and his work opens a new area for debate. An understanding of command at the corps level is mandatory for the general historian trying to get to grips with how the infantry and artillery worked together (or not) in any one battle.

Timothy Bowman and Mark Connelly, co-authors of *The Edwardian Army*, also confine their discussion of *FSR* to tactical concepts, and assert that *Part I* 'was largely written by Haig.'[29] Even when Ian Beckett joined their team to publish *The British Army and the First World War*, *FSR* is still regarded mainly as an advisory tactical handbook. Addressing command, and disagreeing with Barr on the clarity of the concepts it expressed in *FSR*, they say that 'it might also be argued that command itself was not sufficiently well understood in finding the balance between guidance and control of subordinates … Pre-war Field Service Regulations had implied decentralisation in command but had not defined it clearly.'[30] Decentralisation is an imprecise word that means different things in different contexts. It is used at least once in *FSR, Part II*: 'The essence of all efficient organizations lies in due sub-division of labour and decentralisation of responsibility among subordinates, each individual being given duties which he can perform adequately.'[31] This is simply describing delegation, a universal necessity. But perhaps they are referring only to *FSR, Part I, Operations*. Delegation is certainly a feature of *Part I*. The Commander-in-Chief directs the position and intent for his divisions, and the divisional commander is responsible for actioning the movement and achieving the aims given to him. This seems a clear concept, albeit it does not admit of a senior general micromanaging his brigades and divisions, as Haig and Gough were prone to do. Beckett, Bowman and Connelly repeat the fallacy that Haig 'oversaw the writing of' *FSR* in 1908.[32] For a balanced assessment

27 Andy Simpson, 'British Corps Command on the Western Front', in Sheffield and Todman (eds), *Command and Control*, pp. 98–101, 103.
28 Simpson, *British Corps Command*, pp.8, 16, 23–26; Simpson, 'British Corps Command' in Sheffield and Todman (eds), *Command and Control*, pp.98–100.
29 Bowman and Connelly, *The Edwardian Army*, pp. 66, 74, 77, 87, 95,105.
30 Beckett, Bowman and Connelly, *The British Army*, p.210, this statement being referenced to five other papers.
31 *Field Service Regulations, Part II*, pp.23–24.
32 Beckett, Bowman and Connelly, *The British Army*, p.41.

of the impact of *FSR* on the British Army in the First World War, it must be disassociated from Haig. Their statement should perhaps read that 'it might be argued that Haig did not understand the necessary balance between guidance and control of subordinates, as defined by *FSR*', because he certainly did not accept the concept of delegation to divisional commanders, either in 1912, or during the Mons campaign. Again, it is unfair to select this one generally useful book for criticism when so many books and articles make equally debatable Haig-centric observations, quoting the same erroneous assumptions about Haig's relationship with *FSR*.

Paul Harris and Marble Sanders are another team which assumes that Haig's views and British Army doctrine are one and the same. Saying that 'it was Haig who had drawn up the pre-war Field Service Regulations', they analyse the planning failures at Neuve Chappelle in 1915. They quote Major General John Du Cane, Artillery Adviser at GHQ, who wrote a critique of the battle, mainly pertaining to the handling of reserves. Du Cane, who helped edit *FSR, Part I* for publication in 1909, finishes by paraphrasing one of its key principles. 'The first assault should be prepared and delivered as at NEUVE CHAPELLE, but it should not be pressed so far as to carry the infantry beyond the range of our artillery support. The first step should then be consolidated, counter-attacks repelled and a fresh advance prepared for.'[33] Harris and Marble say that this addendum 'muddies the waters' of the previous analysis.[34] Anything but. It is a statement which almost every regular infantry and artillery officer would have thought self-evident, hardly worth stating. Asking infantry to advance without artillery support was an unthinkable and fundamental breach of *FSR*. Why, DuCane is saying, very forcibly, is the army not following *FSR*? Harris and Marble go on to discuss the differences in operational strategy advocated by Haig, who wanted 'to break the enemy's line in a continuous violent push' and by William Robertson, who, forcefully, in a letter to Launcelot Kiggell, Chief of the General Staff at GHQ on 5 July 1916, advocated a step-by-step approach, with all arms combination and fire-power, in line with *FSR*. But Robertson, they say, judged that Haig 'was the slave of pre-war military ideas', suggesting that what Haig did, and what *FSR* said, were one and the same. If Robertson made any judgment at all of Haig, he would have judged him to be a slave to nineteenth-century Clausewitzian ideas, with some justification. If anybody was a slave to 'pre-war' military ideas in 1915, it was Rawlinson, trapped in the *FSR*-compliant belief that divisions should be responsible for the detailed planning and execution of battle at a time when the corps was being advocated as the level at which battles were planned.[35] The insistence that Haig was the conventional doctrinaire in all tactical matters is a recurring theme. Like Simpson, and Beckett, Bowman and Connelly, Harris and Sanders believed that '*FSR* reflected Douglas Haig's views on warfare', while simultaneously describing the ways he repeatedly departed from *FSR* in his military planning.[36]

It is important to emphasise that the impartial historian should not assume compliance with *FSR* is better than non-compliance, or vice versa. There is no doubt that Haig challenged *FSR* principles, and a good case can be made to argue that he was right to do so. But any paper that assumes that Haig's military philosophy and *FSR* are one and the same can only seriously

33 See *Field Service Regulations, Part I*, pp.51, 137–140.
34 Paul Harris and Sanders Marble, 'The "Step-by-Step" Approach: British Military Thought and Operational Method on the Western Front, 1915–1917', *War in History*, 15 (1) 2008, p.23.
35 Harris and Marble, 'The "Step-by-Step" Approach,' pp.28–31, 34.
36 Simpson, 'British Corps Command', in Sheffield and Todman (eds), *Command and Control*, p.99.

mislead. Once, however, historians start dealing with the last year of the war, the problems generated by this assumption become less relevant. As Boff and Beach both hint, GHQ's operational thinking, if not Haig's, began to align itself with the principles of *FSR*.

A branch of the literature which should not be overlooked is the impact of *FSR* on the development of administrative services through the First World War. *British Logistics on the Western Front* was published as long ago as 1998, but it remains a definitive study. Written by Ian Malcolm Brown, it says that *FSR, Part II*, 'set out the means by which the British Field Armies would be organized and administered … The document had some inherent strengths, the greatest [being] its inherent simplicity.' Those drawing up the regulations 'in 1909 could not have predicted the scope of Britain's next war, [thus] …general principles provided a very sound basis for field regulations.'[37] He goes on to describe some of its inherent weaknesses and how these were addressed, but he leaves the reader in no doubt that the principles laid down in *FSR, Part II*, and the *Staff Manual* were of relevance at every stage of the war and that post-war rewrites of it owed a great deal to earlier manifestations of the document.

Perhaps the most important impact of *FSR*, in general, was its influence on learning, an aspect recently addressed by Aimée Fox in her important 2018 book, *Learning to Fight*. She addresses all the main principles of *FSR*, including the duties and responsibilities of officers. Her initial analysis is flawed by the supposition that 'Haig was one of the key architects of FSR', but, as previously described, she agrees that *FSR, Part I*, had a great impact on the teaching and evolution of tactical ideas. *FSR* was 'used throughout the war, and, where possible, regular army instructors were sought to run training schools.' She concludes that 'fundamental to the army's learning effectiveness was the influence of [a] two stranded pre-war ethos, comprising the social and the intellectual, [which] provided an important and enduring framework throughout the First World War.'[38] Having associated Haig and *FSR*, it is impossible for her to conclude that FSR constituted a true doctrine.

Michael Hunzeker's book *Dying to Learn, Wartime Lessons from the Western Front*, written in 2021, also previously described, hales *FSR* as 'a landmark in British military thinking.' However, he goes on to say that 'the FSR manuals were [merely] intended to provide officers with precise instructions designed to meet every wartime contingency', and thus did not constitute a doctrine. A doctrine, he says, must, amongst other things, create a source of institutional memory.[39] This idea resonates with Fox's concept of a persistent and powerful ethos driving the evolution of all aspects of military activity on the Western Front.

Certain concepts must be addressed in a book focusing on the details of British Army doctrine since they are of theoretical importance to academic historians. The first is the learning curve theory. The learning curve is an attractive concept, and there is no doubt that it reflects our own personal experience in life and work. It can be applied with considerable justification to the increasing professionalism of every individual who fought or served on the Western Front, right up to Haig himself. However, applying the term to the whole British Army on the Western Front makes a fundamental assumption that that army did not start with a set of relevant principles to inform the way it should conduct the war. Few papers discussing the concept even mention *FSR*. In its initial presentation, the learning curve theory referred only

37 Brown, *British Logistics*, pp.44–45.
38 Fox, *Learning to Fight*, pp.34, 43, 241.
39 Hunzeker, *Dying to Learn*, p.100.

to the British Army's evolution in tactical practice from the first day of the Somme until 1918. William Philpott's 'Beyond the Learning Curve', published in 2009, offers a sober reflection on the theory. Quite rightly, he says that 'the problem to date has been that the Great War's battles have usually been studied as isolated tragic events, rather than stages in a progressive continuum.' But even in 2009, he cannot avoid questionable generalisations. 'It needs to be recognised that by 1918 the British Army was not just much better at what it did, but that it was doing something entirely different – if not from July 1916, then certainly from August 1914.'[40] The only way in which that statement can be tested is to compare the practice of the army of 1914 with that of 1916 and 1918 against a common standard. The standard which provides the most comprehensive set of criteria is *FSR*. Philpott does refer to doctrine:

> Haig's army remained a tool – a much sharper one – in the hands of a military genius, and the narrower parameters of the British army's own doctrinal evolution must be acknowledged. The persistent conception of warfare at GHQ as a phased 'manoeuvre' for advantage – through stages of engagement, wearing out, decisive attack and exploitation – seems, as Tim Travers has argued, to be a 'late nineteenth-century ideal of war' which no longer fitted the sort of war that the army was fighting on the western front.[41]

Is this true? Did the army's 'doctrinal evolution' from 1914 really start as being a 'late nineteenth-century ideal of war'? A study of *FSR* suggests that it did not.

There are equally pertinent questions to be posed in assertions made in support of the concept of a 'Revolution in Military Affairs' (RMA), by Brigadier Jonathan Bailey in 1998.[42] 'My contention' he says, 'is that the most significant RMA in the history of warfare took place between 1917 and 1918. It amounted to the birth of modern warfare with the advent of artillery indirect fire as the foundation of planning at the tactical, operational and strategic levels of war – the invention of deep battle.' Discussing artillery indirect fire, he says that 'warfare in 1914 was linear with prevailing doctrines emphasizing flanks, envelopments and annihilations. It was based on the contact battle of physical encounter where maneuver forces were supported by artillery firing directly, generally at short range.' Moreover, 'the British experimented with indirect fire during the Boer War and concluded that in mobile warfare it was not practical.' The principles of indirect fire were being taught at Woolwich even before 1907,[43] and an effective indirect fire sight was introduced in 1913. 'The prime reason for the failure to exploit indirect fire ... was lack of imagination and doctrinal laziness', he asserts.[44] Indirect fire, 'fire from covered positions', is repeatedly advocated in *FSR* and is clearly described in *Field Artillery Training, 1914*. Bailey argues that 'artillery indirect fire' was not used in 'planning at the tactical' level of war in 1914. Only a study of 1914 battles can confirm whether the artillery was following its own guidelines and using them, where they had the opportunity. Artillery, throughout the ages,

40 William Philpott, 'Beyond the "Learning Curve", The British Army's Military Transformation in the First World War', *RUSI Analysis*, 10 November 2009, <https://rusi.org/commentary/beyond-learning-curve-british-armys-military-transformation-first-world-war>, accessed 4 June 2020.

41 Philpott, 'Beyond the "Learning Curve"', quoting Travers, *The Killing Ground*, p.86.

42 Brigadier Jonathan Bailey, 'Deep Battle 1914–1941: The Birth of the Modern Style of Warfare', *FA Journal*, US Field Artillery Association, July–August 1998, pp.23–35.

43 SCA: box 142, pre-war exam papers. RMA and RMC, 1907.

44 Bailey, 'The Birth of the Modern Style of Warfare', pp.23–25.

has always tried to engage targets that damage the enemy, whether its infantry, its artillery, or its command personnel. To describe what was merely an incremental increase in the range of indirect fire as a revolution overstates the case.

William Philpott and Jonathan Boff revisit these theories in 2019 in an article in the *British Journal of Military History*.[45] It is not an easy read. 'Although the existence of a western front Revolution in Military Affairs (RMA) is now generally acknowledged in studies of the "trench warfare" that epitomises the First World War, some scholars still position their analysis of the conflict's military developments within a dated meta-narrative of inefficiency and military ineffectiveness.' Philpott and Boff refer repeatedly to the British Army's military culture. 'It is empirically unquantifiable; it is not unitary; it constantly shifts shape; and its effects are often tacit and extremely complex.' Despite this, they go on to say that

> … the British Army's culture and adaptation is the most studied, within the parameter of the long-running 'learning curve' debate … British and Commonwealth historians of the western front have built up a considerable body of literature charting the changes in warfare that occurred, and especially the British response to them, primarily in terms of technology, tactics, operations and command. These studies take an empirical approach rather than employing any sort of theoretical framework, and collectively have argued that the British Army was far from being the reactionary institution of myth, led by 'butchers and bunglers', which never got to grips with the realities of modern industrial warfare. Instead, it progressively climbed a 'learning curve', or underwent a 'learning process', which took it from disaster on the first day of the Battle of the Somme to leading the Allied armies to victory over Germany during the 'Hundred Days' campaign of August to November 1918.[46]

An alternative view might be to suggest that a theoretical framework, delineated by *FSR*, does exist, that this framework can be usefully employed to link the learning process of the British Army and its higher command to its doctrine and that it is possible to follow both the evolution of that doctrinal framework and the degree of adherence to it, in the different armies, corps and divisions that participated in that war. Given the variations in practice that will be described in the following chapters, this will not always give a full picture, but it is a thesis on which to build, with much of the spadework already done by historians such as Andy Simpson and Aimée Fox.

45 William Philpott and Jonathan Boff, 'Introduction: Transforming War, 1914–1918', *British Journal for Military History*, 5.2 (2019), pp.1–18.

46 Philpott and Boff, 'Transforming War, 1914–1918', pp.2, 11–12.

14

Administration and Command 1914–1915

'The essence of all efficient organizations lies in due sub-division of labour and decentralisation of responsibility among subordinates, each individual being given duties which he can perform adequately.'[1] Never was this pronouncement more important than when the British army went to war in 1914.

In the chapter on the pre-war impact of *FSR, Part II*, it was suggested that regulations that seemed to pertain exclusively to an expeditionary force of the army reflected the political and business administration beliefs of the Edwardian period; that its philosophy reflected the ethos of the wider army, and society in general. Prior to the preparation of the final draft of *Part II*, the responsibilities of the administrative branches of the army on campaign had been agreed in outline, and the subsequent detail of the document had fleshed out the practical details of these responsibilities, defining the duties and responsibilities of the officers involved, under the watchful eye of both the Quartermaster General and Adjutant General in 1908. *FSR*, therefore, offered no formal guidance to the working of the War Office and did not define the duties and responsibilities of the officers who were serving there. But this does not mean they were unaffected by, or unresponsive to, the reforms. On the contrary, the duties and responsibilities of those at the War Office changed and evolved at speed. *FSR, Part I* authorised initiative to junior officers in changing circumstances of battle where previous orders are no longer applicable. This ethos suffused Edwardian society and the army. Modernisation and professionalisation could not, and did not, wait for a democratic mandate or formal definitions of areas of responsibility. An example given in an earlier chapter was the rapid evolution in the duties and responsibilities of Henry Wilson, the Director of Military Operations, from 1910 onwards with respect to preparations for war. Abrogation of powers, and cooperation with, and coordination of, civilian enterprises for military ends came before the formalisation of processes.

Field Service Regulations, both volumes of it, but mainly *Part II*, defined in outline the organisation and administration of a British Expeditionary Force to be sent abroad to any destination. From the start, it is explicit in defining its own remit: 'A system of organization must be suitable to the character and armament of the forces and to the nature of the proposed operations … the

1 *Field Service Regulations, Part II*, pp.23–24.

system must be sufficiently elastic to meet all the varying conditions which may arise, and which it is impossible to foresee.'[2] Furthermore:

> ... when a force is to be mobilized for a campaign to be fought under special conditions, certain modifications of organization will become necessary ... Should the C-in-C during the course of a campaign consider it necessary to modify the organization of any unit, the amended war establishment of the unit, revised in accordance with his wishes, will be notified to all concerned.[3]

FSR authorised initiative, including administrative initiative, if it was required.

The definitive book on this system of organisation is undoubtedly Ian Malcolm Brown's masterly study of *Logistics on the Western Front*, published in 1998. It was ahead of its time in acknowledging from the outset the importance of *FSR* and in recognising the administrative advantages of *Part II*:

> The greatest strength of the British system of organization and administration lay in its inherent simplicity ... Administrative officers knew exactly where they stood in the chain of command and how it had been laid out ... Extensive sub-division of the administrative organization, combined with effective central control, resulting in one administrative officer managing a large number of subordinates in various departments.

But he then says that:

> ...in August 1914, the BEF went to war with an administrative structure at best only marginally suited to its needs; however, the flexibility of *Field service Regulations, Part II*, and the professionalism and pragmatism of its administrators allowed it to overcome the obstacles ... Most of the decisions made in 1914 revolved not around how to change the system, but [first] how to adapt the general regulations to the needs of a continental army, and [second] how best to use the latent administrative talent in Britain that had run the Empire before the war.[4]

Brown then goes on to address the major specific difficulties that arose in 1914. However, addressing the generality of *FSR*, it proved to be superbly suited to the needs of the BEF. To develop this argument, the order of Brown's two decision-making processes needs to be reversed. Harnessing of 'latent administrative talent' came before any consideration of how to adjust the regulations or the details of the army establishment. Charles Messenger's book, *Call to Arms*, describes the mobilisation process in minute and fascinating detail.[5] Where possible, vacancies in the expeditionary force were filled from within the army, but this was not always possible. Colonel George Macdonogh, who had headed a branch within Military Operations at the War Office, was appointed 'to head the BEF's intelligence branch.' Macdonogh identified a few

2 *Field Service Regulations, Part II*, p.23.
3 *Field Service Regulations, Part II*, pp.26–27.
4 Brown, *British Logistics*, pp.44–46, 67.
5 Charles Messenger, *Call to Arms*, pp.15–37.

officers with language skills, 'but the majority of officers for the fledgling Intelligence Corps had to be drawn from civilian life.' He found 13 suitable regular and reserve officers and identified 'forty-two scout officers' who were civilian volunteers. Scotland Yard detectives manned his security duties section. He crossed to France on 23 August.[6] The place for intelligence within the command structure of the BEF was already established, and its unforeseen massive expansion, even at this early stage of the war, could be administratively accommodated and its unconventional manning tolerated. As already emphasised, flexibility within the C-in-C's headquarters is a principle of *FSR*. The constitution of all directorates was laid down in war establishment documentation within the War Office, but during and after mobilisation, all that was necessary, under the regulations, to expand an existing section within the staff was that the C-in-C should ask that its war establishment be amended to accommodate the change.[7] Expansion came first. The administrative detail was then quickly put in place. These clauses were used freely throughout the war, in all branches of the army, all formally signed off by the C-in-C.

Recruitment of an intelligence section for the cavalry division was similarly haphazard. Edmund Allenby found 'Lieutenant Colonel George de Symons Barrow of the Indian Army in the corridors of the War Office, and commandeered him.' Barrow then recruited a civil engineer, an Indian Army subaltern, a Dutchman, and a Swede as interpreters 'and two police detectives with bicycles.' Again, the pre-ordained structure of a division could accommodate this disparate party, even though, prior to the outbreak of war, funding had not been made available to establish a cavalry divisional staff.[8]

Similar evidence of bolt-on expansions can be found in many areas of the army's activity. There was a map crisis during the retreat from Mons. 'Luckily the Ordnance Survey had a comprehensive collection of printing plates, and MO4 was able to deliver new maps within twenty-four hours. The Printing Company RE deployed with the BEF also helped to make good the shortfall.'[9] Fox describes how this minimal 'provision for a printing depot in the field as part of the BEF's mobilisation plan', grew exponentially as the war progressed.[10]

The use of civilians within the expanding army rapidly became routine. Unsurprisingly, the army had insufficient interpreters, and many came from unconventional sources. The Royal Engineers Signal Service was short of motorcycle dispatch riders and recruited informally. Messenger also describes the adventures of the 'gentlemen chauffeurs and their cars.' Including Toby Rawlinson, brother of Henry, and the Duke of Westminster, they were named the RAC Corps of Volunteer Motor Drivers and looked to the Inspector General of Communications for instruction.[11]

While some of these examples stretch the definition of 'latent administrative talent', the principle of inclusion of civilians to help solve military shortages and problems is clear. There are many examples of bolt-on developments of this nature, some totally new, some expanding exponentially from very small beginnings.[12] As well as the arrangements for printing already

6 Messenger, *Call to Arms*, pp.48–50.
7 *Field Service Regulations, Part II*, pp.26–27.
8 Jones, 'Scouting for Soldiers', pp.510.
9 Messenger, *Call to Arms*, pp.51–54.
10 Aimée Fox-Godden, 'Beyond the Western Front: The Practice of Inter-Theatre Learning in the British Army during the First World War', *War in History*, vol.23 (2), 2016, p.196.
11 Messenger, *Call to Arms*, pp.51–54.
12 Messenger, *Call to Arms*, pp.48–54.

mentioned, Fox cites the British army's minimal Field Survey assets, with their members being seconded to the Ministry of Agriculture and Fisheries in 1914. However, capabilities evolved and grew very rapidly. By 1915, an ex-Ordnance Survey employee was commanding the 1st Ranging and Survey Section, and by 1917, there was a headquarters in France with topographical, map, observation, and sound-ranging sections, all staffed by men actively recruited for having the relevant civilian skills.[13]

As Major General Sir Nevil Macready, AG to the BEF in 1914, said in his autobiography, 'as time went on the increase of the Army in the field and the requirements necessitated by trench warfare caused not only an unprecedented inflation of existing services, but constant new developments in every direction.'[14] The various responsibilities of the QMG and AG, he explains, are divided into defined hierarchical directorates, each of which imposes a relevant bureaucracy on their subordinate sub-directors. While the QMG 'has his stores and workshops for the upkeep of the fighting troops, the Adjutant General has to keep the equivalent in the shape of a large office in rear of the armies.'[15] There was a considerable shortage of regular officers in the British Army with the skills needed to run either the 'stores and workshops' or the 'large offices' required in late 1914. But, as Brown says, there was a large reserve of 'latent administrative talent' in Britain and the Empire, very well versed in the principles of running a bureaucracy and adhering to the necessary legal and accounting regulations, even in the stress of active warfare.

Macready recognised right from the beginning of the war that there were certain tasks that well-qualified civilians performed better than regular army officers. 'One of the matters for which the Adjutant General's Staff is responsible is the burial of the dead and record of graves.' During the Battle of the Aisne, Macready realised the scale of the problems and, in October 1914, first met Fabian Ware, who went on to become the permanent vice-chairman of the Imperial War Graves Commission in 1917. Macready learnt that Ware had edited the *Morning Post* for five years before the war, spoke French fluently and had administrative experience with the Red Cross. At that first interview, Macready 'booked him to create an organization to supervise and record the graves of our soldiers.'[16] He then asked the War Office if he could set up this 'separate organization.' Though still under contract with the Red Cross, Ware, a civilian, 'collected a dozen gentlemen with whom he was acquainted … and thus started an organization which developed into the Graves Registration and Inquiries Department, with Headquarters at Winchester House, St. James Square, working under the Adjutant General at the War Office.' Acting major from February 1915, Ware was promoted to lieutenant colonel only a year later, reflecting the size of the organisation he was setting up.

Similarly, amongst Macready's other responsibilities was a duty to 'regulate the clergy, who were by no means so peaceably inclined towards each other's denominations as one might reasonably expect … Regular officers had tried their hands at it, not altogether successfully…' A visiting dignitary recommended a mature territorial major, and Macready wired the War Office and asked for his services. Major Auckland Geddes, brother of the better-known Sir

13 Fox-Godden, 'Inter-Theatre Learning in the British Army,' p.196.
14 General The Rt. Hon. Sir Nevil Macready, *Annals of an Active Life* (New York: George Doran, 1925), vol.1, p.223.
15 Macready, *Annals*, vol.1, p.200.
16 Macready, *Annals*, vol.1, pp,219–221.

Eric, proved to have the necessary 'firmness and tact', and 'within not many days of his arrival, I heard nothing more of any trouble in that department', despite the huge expansion of the army, and the arrival of Empire forces with yet more denominations and cultural requirements.

These problems were dwarfed by the demands of the medical and ambulance services Macready was responsible for providing. He recruited two very senior doctors with wide administrative experience. Sir George Makins, President of the Royal College of Surgeons, and Sir Anthony Bowlby, Surgeon-in-Ordinary to the King, took up posts at GHQ and on the Lines of Communications, respectively.[17] He passes quickly over the volunteer help the army received in the care and transport of the wounded in 1914, but Messenger, in his chapter in *Call-to-Arms* on 'Women in Khaki', covers it in much more detail. As referred to in the chapter on pre-war administration, there were three well-established women's nursing organisations, separate from the regular army's Queen Alexandra's Imperial Nursing Service, and the Territorial Force Nursing Service, who both deployed to France within weeks of the war starting. Voluntary Aid Detachments, under the auspices of the Red Cross, comprising both sexes, were soon serving abroad, and this was the main route by which volunteers served the army during the war.[18] The First Aid Nursing Yeomanry was refused recognition, but this did not stop a few of their members from going to France, and their organisation was later recognised after doing good work for the Belgian Army.[19]

However, in less obviously 'civilian' areas of duty, the principle of employing skilled civilians as staff officers was viewed with some suspicion. Brown says that 'as early as late October 1914 … a partial and highly practical response to the lack of staff officers' in the Supplies Directorate, commanded by Brigadier General Frederick Clayton, suggested 'that civilians from large firms, such as Harrod's, might be either loaned by their firms or enticed into volunteering … Civilians from such firms possessed practical experience in moving consumer goods around Britain … The employees of the numerous British railway firms had expertise in moving freight and passengers.' Clayton pointed out that age was not a handicap, and their lack of military experience would be relatively easy to address. 'While there is no evidence to suggest that [his] request was carried out, it is clear that the idea that former businessmen could help administer the BEF had taken hold.'[20] Rather than 'taken hold', it had simply persisted. Perhaps it is also relevant that Clayton was a graduate of Haldane's LSE course on business administration, run in 1907.[21] But there was a long-standing rule that all staff officers should have experience of regimental service. Macready expresses this view very clearly in his memoirs:

> It is well that those who desire to draw comparisons between the regimental and the Staff officer should remember that success on the Staff can only be attained after a thorough preparation as a regimental officer both in peace and war, so that when removed from amongst those with whom his earlier life has been passed the Staff officer is able to sympathise with the needs and limitations of his former comrades in their daily and hourly peril.[22]

17 Macready, *Annals*, vol.1, pp.221–229.
18 *VAD – Red Cross*, <https//vad.redcross.org.uk/volunteering-during-the-first-war> (accessed 1 July 2024).
19 Messenger, *Call to Arms*, pp.243–246.
20 Brown, *British Logistics*, p.85.
21 Phillips, *Civilian Specialists at War*, p.50.
22 Macready, *Annals*, vol.1, p.216.

Even later in the war, this remained the official policy within the QMG and AG branches.[23] Brilliant intellects and politicians, volunteering, served first in the trenches. Too many of them died before they could contribute according to their ability.

Even before the war, if there was an innovation that could, with benefit, be introduced into the army, nobody tried to alter the structure of the army first and then introduce it formally. It was trialled, often at the instigation of quite junior officers, with the acquiescence of local commanders, and if the new ideas seemed to have merit, was introduced by consensus to the rest of the army, at which point regulations and establishments might be adjusted to make room for it. One of the great beauties of the regulations is how the detailed duties and responsibilities of a set of officers, pertaining to a specific innovation, could be both influenced by civilian input and legitimised with a simple signature from the C-in-C. If a new unit within the divisional hierarchy or a new staff sub-directorate was needed, even a new arm of the army, the development could be managed at speed. The mechanism, as laid down in *Part II*, has already been described. Some staff examples have already been cited, relating to intelligence, cartography, and more, but it applied to operational developments too.

One example, of many, which illustrates this narrative with respect to operations, is the development of the machine gun as one of the key weapons of war on the Western Front. Its early semi-formal development was followed by bolt-on developments in army structure, without disrupting the balance of the army. The Vickers machine gun blog provides much information on the attempts by quite junior officers, mainly based at the School of Musketry in Hythe, to persuade the British Army to increase its pre-war complement of machine guns.[24] Their arguments fell on deaf ears. Hythe was under the jurisdiction of the Director of Staff Duties until 1909 and then the Director of Military Training. When the BEF went to war, each infantry battalion and cavalry regiment had a machine gun section of just two guns. Casualties were heavy, and the need not only to replace trained machine gun officers but also to augment them was soon seen as a priority. The problems became more pressing when the War Office authorised a doubling of the number of machine guns in each section. There were some local training initiatives since responsibility for 'the training and efficiency of all officers and men in a unit belonged to the commanding officer.'[25] But for obvious reasons, there was a difficulty in finding instructors.

Lieutenant Colonel G.S. Hutchison describes, in his 1938 history of the *Machine Gun Corps*, how the first machine gun school in France accessible to men of diverse units was formed. In November 1914, the subject of machine guns was discussed by staff officers after dinner at a restaurant in St Omer, at which one of the owner motor drivers of the RAC Corps of Volunteer Motor Drivers was present. The driver, C. D'A. Baker-Carr, was a former Captain in the Rifle Brigade, and he had served as an Assistant Instructor at the School of Musketry, Hythe. After the discussion, he was asked if he would undertake the work of training machine gunners to replace casualties at a school to be established at G.H.Q.[26] The school opened on 2 December

23 Brown, *British Logistics*, p.147.

24 Vickers, 'Machine Gun,' *Vickers MG Collection and Research Association*, <www.vickersmg.org.uk> (accessed 2 July 2024).

25 Fox, *Learning to Fight*, p.86, paraphrasing *FSR*.

26 Lieutenant Colonel G.S. Hutchison, *Machine Guns: Their History and Tactical Employment (Being also a History of the Machine Gun Corps, 1916–1922)* (London: Macmillan, 1938), pp.130–131.

1914, and within a few months, according to Hutchison, not necessarily the most reliable of sources, over 600 men were attending its weekly courses.

Simultaneously, in 1914, the case for a mobile machine gun capability had been made; and as early as 26 October, Army Council Instruction 289 authorised a 'Motor Machine-Gun Battery' to be added to the war establishment of every division, to be handled under the auspices of its artillery. The units were to be raised and trained in England. There were different routes, with different levels of formality, to innovations. In early 1915, every battalion formed a machine gun section, distinct from the infantry. In October 1915, the Machine Gun Corps was formed, recognising its disparate uses and its need for specialist training. It had three branches. For the infantry branch:

> ...machine-gun sections were withdrawn from Infantry battalions and formed into machine-gun companies, one of which was attached to each brigade. At the same time, a Machine-Gun Training Centre was formed at Grantham for the purposes of training and supplying reinforcements for machine-gun companies in the field, and raising new machine-gun companies. In March, 1918, it was decided to attach one machine-gun battalion to each division.[27]

As Aimée Fox in her book on *Learning to Fight* says, within 'the army's ethos, formations were encouraged to innovate and learn within broader institutional parameters. This applied to all levels of command.'[28]

Leaving aside the generality of how *FSR* enabled the British Army to expand so smoothly within a broad administrative framework, and returning to Brown's assertion that 'in August 1914, the BEF went to war with an administrative structure at best only marginally suited to its needs', it is true that some of the detailed regulations on the duties and responsibilities of specific officers, did not prove fit for purpose.[29] Some problems could have been foreseen. *FSR* assumed that any expeditionary force would be enabled to take control of its own transport arrangements, and its administration was defined on that basis. Phillips, in his book *Civilian Specialists at War*, describes the problem:

> The pre-war conversations between the French and British general staffs had resulted in an arrangement whereby the BEF's transport requirements were to be manned and controlled by the French. The BEF's hosts undertook to complete the work of construction, repair, maintenance, traffic management and protection necessary to maintain the British troops on the western front.

This unwillingness on the part of the French authorities to relinquish control of their own rail network in August 1914, made it impossible to follow *Part II* regulations with respect to rail transport in supplying the British Army. 'The duties nominally assigned to a British director of railway transport (DRT) were almost entirely assigned to the French army.'[30] Additionally,

27 Vickers, 'Motor Machine Gun Service' (accessed 2 July 2024).
28 Fox, *Learning to Fight*, pp.58, 86.
29 Brown, *British Logistics*, p.67.
30 Phillips, *Civilian Specialists at War*, p.97.

Transport for the machine gun school at St Omer. (Author's collection)

Machine-gun section, Queen's Westminster Rifles, February 1915. (Author's collection)

British practice was to run frequent small, fast trains. The French, in contrast, ran much larger trains, carrying sizeable units in their entirety, which ran much more slowly.[31] There was also a pre-war arrangement in which the French promised adequate facilities and labour at the ports. In August 1914:

31 Messenger, *Call-to-Arms*, pp.55–57.

> …the IGC Sir Frederick Robb was dismayed to discover that the French 'had not kept their promises about the dock employees, they can only furnish 1000 stevedores out of the 3000 [and] they propose not to work at night. I have had to be very firm about this, they have now promised to try and get some more.' This inauspicious beginning to the practical operations of the Franco-British coalition set a pattern that continued once the fighting commenced.[32]

Despite this, 'the efficiency with which the BEF moved overseas [in 1914] is quite astonishing, especially when the flaws in the regulations under which it operated once it arrived are considered.'[33] These flaws were rapidly tackled where they threatened the integrity of the army, but they were not addressed by formal regulation change. There was no time for that. 'Latent administrative talent', with its origins within the army itself, was the key to the pragmatic manipulation of the administrative structure of the army that stabilised its upper areas of command.

The events of August and September 1914 dictated that the position of GHQ changed rapidly and often. The precipitate retreat from Mons would have severely stressed any system of transport. The line of retirement was not initially clear, and Robb, the IGC, initially believed that the retreat would be to the Channel ports for evacuation rather than to the east of Paris. The bases at Le Havre and Rouen were partially evacuated and then had to be reopened.[34] Robertson authorised his subordinates to abandon paperwork and show initiative in delivering supplies to units on the march during the retreat. This was a recognition that regulations on independent initiative in *Part I* might, in exceptional circumstances, become applicable even to administrative officers.[35]

There had always been a question mark over the pivotal role of the Inspector General of Communications (IGC) and his overlapping responsibilities within the BEF administrative hierarchy, as described in Chapter 9. The issue had been flagged up as a potential problem at the 1914 staff conference by a group of senior staff officers, including Major General Sir Nevil Macready, who was now AG to the BEF. In retrospect, it was fortunate that their warnings were ignored since the amendments suggested would have required significant revision of *FSR Part II* and the *Staff Manual*, only months before hostilities started, and there was much disagreement on the details. However, the problems rapidly became evident.[36] Phillips describes the consequences in August 1914:

> The British divided responsibility for transport and supply between two officers. [Frederick Robb], the IGC, maintained stocks at the bases and controlled traffic on the lines of communications from his headquarters at the BEF's advanced base. [Sir William] Robertson, the QMG, worked alongside Sir John French at GHQ and took charge of the administrative arrangements between Robb and the units at the front.[37]

32 Phillips, *Civilian Specialists at War*, p.98.
33 Brown, *British Logistics*, p.44.
34 TNA: WO 95/3949/1: Staff Diary of Inspector General of Communications, August 1914.
35 Phillips, *Civilian Specialists at War*, p.99.
36 TNA: WO 279/495: 'Conference of General Staff Officers January 1914', pp.29–38.
37 Phillips, *Civilian Specialists at War*, p.105.

Despite the crucial role of the IGC and the necessity that he liaise closely with senior staff of all designations at GHQ, the IGC is not even mentioned in the official list of those deployed to France in August 1914.[38] Phillips continues:

> Under the guidelines laid down before August 1914 the General Staff was to identify priorities for movement, Robertson to issue instructions to the relevant units and Robb to coordinate the move. The system collapsed on contact with the enemy. Between 25 August and 1 September GHQ changed location five times … which made contact between Robb and Robertson almost impossible to sustain.[39]

Hew Strachan, amongst others, credits Robertson with finding a solution: 'The situation was saved when Robertson, then the Quartermaster General in the BEF, subordinated himself to' French as Commander-in-Chief.[40] It was not as simple as that. As Brown explains, there were other problems as well. Despite being far from battle, the IGC was technically responsible for transporting wounded from the front line, using ambulances controlled by the AG, Macready. The Director of Works, Brigadier General Andrew Stuart, was technically subordinate to the QMG but, in practice, responded to requests from the IGC.

'Had Sir John French not had three consummate professionals as his QMG [Robertson], AG [Macready], and IGC [Robb], he might have had a terrible problem on his hands', Brown says. 'In spite of the flaws in *FSR, Part II* their professionalism let them work towards solving problems.' But he also draws attention to the forbearance of the Army Council in general, and General Sir John Cowans QMG of the Forces, in particular. They allowed their subordinates free rein in finding informal solutions. Brown writes, 'Robb agreed to a pseudo-subordination to Robertson (and Macready) on questions that affected command of the various directors from the railheads forward, without removing himself from the direct authority of the C-in-C.'[41]

One of the main additional problems was that the French controlled all aspects of rail transport. Robertson as QMG, as early as 26 August, appointed Major Marr Johnson, a regular army officer who was familiar with French railway practices, to act as an expert conduit between himself and the French authorities to coordinate the movements he ordered. Johnson 'had created railway timetables and worked alongside the French to develop the BEF's concentration inland from the ports [and] … was fully conversant with the technical aspects that governed French railway operations.' An assessment by Sir Ronald Maxwell, who took over from Sir Frederick Robb as IGC on 19 September, of the rail arrangements at Boulogne later in the year also concluded that the detail of *Part II* could not be used alongside the French systems, and another liaison officer with knowledge of the French railway system was appointed there.[42]

FSR, Part II then, was no more than a template for the organisation and administration of the British Army into the war. Those sections which worked well were followed; those that did not, like rail transport, were modified after assessments by specialists in the field. Macready, as AG, writes that 'once G.H.Q. was established at St Omer it was possible to reorganize methodically,

38 Edmonds, *Military Operations, France and Belgium 1914*, p.471.
39 Phillips, *Civilian Specialists at War*, p.105.
40 Strachan, 'The Continental Commitment', pp.78, 88.
41 Brown, *British Logistics*, pp.46–56.
42 Phillips, *Civilian Specialists at War*, pp.105–106.

in the light of experience already gained, the various services for which I was responsible.'[43] As a further example of significant alteration, *Part II* allocated responsibility for the movement of heavy supplies on canals and rivers to a Transport Directorate, while heavy goods moved by train were the responsibility of a Railway Directorate. In December 1914, Robertson transferred waterborne transport, in its entirety, to come under the Director of Railways.[44] Sir William Robertson is rightly regarded as one of the most brilliant generals in the senior hierarchy of the British Army of 1914–1918. His professionalism and pragmatism, as QMG in the first months of the war, were partly the consequence of his pre-war career trajectory. He was chief-of-staff at Aldershot when *FSR* was first implemented and followed this with tenure as commandant of the Staff College when it, and the *Staff Manual*, were being adopted as the primary guidance to relationships and procedure in the upper reaches of the army. This meant that he had an encyclopaedic awareness of both its general principles and its detail. His temperament and knowledge made him ideally suited to becoming the first QMG to the BEF, and he can be credited with preventing the BEF from imploding into administrative chaos in its first major test of continental warfare. With regard to *FSR* principles, Robertson's action in taking control over some of the functions of the IGC meant that he accepted some orders directly from French as C-in-C. This complied in spirit with *Part II*, acknowledging the primacy of the C-in-C. on campaign over all elements of his army, but departed from the principle of the QMG being responsible primarily to the QMG in London. The regulations were never formally amended in this respect under French's tenure as C-in-C. The Army Council did not want to interfere with a system that was functioning pragmatically. That this was a conscious decision is suggested by the Army Council's decision to formally require a rewrite of chapter XV of *FSR, Part II*, dealing with money and accounts, which was implemented in September 1914, as Army Order 359.[45]

The contribution that Sir John French made to the evolution of the administration of the BEF is difficult to quantify. Brown says that:

> ... on 1 January 1915, Sir John French found himself in command of an army in transition ... However, the administrative infrastructure put in place in August 1914 – based on the Field Service Regulations and pragmatism – remained intact. The new year would see GHQ doing its best to cope with the BEFs expansion ...The flexibility in the regulations that had been evident in 1914 began to break down as pressure brought on by the growing expeditionary Force compelled the administration to face new problems with inadequately defined specifics ... The Administration continued to make effective ad hoc changes to overcome new problems as they arose, but it did not consider the future.[46]

In a later chapter Brown discusses French's failure to address administrative issues. In December 1914, French turned down Robertson's request to consult the French on increasing access to ports, despite a follow-up request from Maxwell, the IGC: 'The time had clearly arrived, indeed it had passed, when the French must be approached ... Perhaps Sir John did not understand the task being demanded of his administrators.' In February 1915, 'the problems for the ICG and

43 Macready, *Annals*, vol.1, p.222.
44 Spencer, 'Sir William Robertson', in Jones (ed.), *Stemming the Tide*, p.105.
45 *Army Orders, 1914* (London: War Office, 1914), p.74.
46 Brown, *British Logistics*, p.75.

QMG did not rank highly on Sir John's list of priorities … Operational (G branch) concerns rated far more attention than administration – at a time when the converse should have been true.' Brown points out that British and French lines of communication and supply ran across each other. In exchanges 'between Sir John and Joffre, the needs of the IGC and QMG, and their French counterparts were not raised – and they should have been … The first order of business should have been to put the rear area into a better state to support the fighting formations', this after Aubers Ridge. Finally, in summary, 'the manner in which the BEF faced and overcame the administrative hurdles of 1915 illustrates a typically pragmatic and British approach to the solution of difficult problems. There was at best minimal input from the C-in-C.'[47]

Brown goes on to say that the problems were 'because of *Field Service Regulations*.'[48] He says that *FSR* prevented French from addressing administrative problems, since the QMG and AG were answerable to the War Office. This is simply wrong. Section 8 of *FSR, Part II* states that:

> …the authority of the C-in-C is supreme in all matters within the theatre of operations on land. He is responsible for the efficiency of the forces in the field, for the control and direction of their operations as a whole … He issues such orders on all matters connected with the efficiency and maintenance of his forces in the field as he considers necessary for the execution of his plan of operations, for the success or failure of which he is responsible.

This section goes on to say that 'the C-in-C is relieved of direct responsibility for the conduct of the business of providing the requirements of the forces in the field, unless he sees fit to interpose.' The circumstances in which he should interpose are fully described in a section, which first defines in broad terms 'administrative services and departments' as those parts of the army without which the fighting troops cannot be maintained in a state of efficiency. The C-in-C is required to act if the 'efficiency' of his forces is being compromised by administrative deficiencies, and even if that is not already the case, he has the duty to interpose 'when important questions are referred by the [QMG and AG] for the decision of the C-in-C or I.G.C.' The main circumstance in which such questions would be raised was when these senior administrators had insufficient authority to tackle the problem. The section goes on to say that if the C-in-C should fail to act, whether asked to or not, when administrative deficiencies were threatening the efficiency of the force under his command, 'the responsibility is his.'[49]

In other words, the C-in-C has almost unlimited powers, and just as he is directly responsible for failures in battle, so he is similarly responsible for failures in the support services that maintain his army in the field. The tenure of Sir John French can be assessed in the light of these regulations and in his refusal to engage cooperatively with Joseph Joffre, Commander-in-Chief of the French Army, in relation to issues arising from the irrational organisation of port facilities or the problems arising from having lines of communications which intersected with those of the French, causing log-jams and delays. This lack of engagement fuelled mutual suspicion. In the autumn of 1915, the British were even refused permission to install a dedicated phone line from Boulogne to Britain, which would warn them when incoming ships could be expected.[50]

47 Brown, *British Logistics*, pp.80, 98–104.
48 Brown, *British Logistics*, p.103.
49 *Field Service Regulations, Part II*, pp.28,44.
50 Phillips, *Civilian Specialists at War*, p.155.

Quite why French refused to engage with Joffre at an administrative level, despite the problems limiting the BEF's offensive potential, is not clear. *FSR* laid a duty on him to do so.

Haig took over as Commander-in-Chief on 19 December 1915, so Brown's verdict on Haig during that year can be included here: 'Haig certainly appreciated the value of solid administration – this would become very clear when he took over from Sir John – but he had found little time [for it] while commanding I Corps.' When he took over First Army, he wanted 'for the present not to touch administration.' And further, 'Haig's desire to steer clear of administration is likely nothing more than a misguided belief that he, as an army commander, might actually be able to influence battles in progress.' Brown thinks administration far more important than heroic leadership, and he quotes Archibald Wavell's *Generals and Generalship* in support of this contention. 'It is knowledge of the mechanics of war, not the principles of strategy that distinguishes a good leader from a bad.'[51]

51 Brown, *British Logistics*, p.77, referenced to Haig's diaries of December 1914, and p.231.

15

Operational Review 1914 to mid-1915

The following documents are covered in this review:

CDS 2, 3, 4 and 53	*Notes from the Front*, December 1914 to May 1915
CDS 5	*Trench Warfare, Notes on Attack and Defence*, February 1915
CDS 50	*Tactical Notes*, July 1915

All armies must adapt from the outset of any war, and even their mode of adaption must adapt as well. Few would dispute that the BEF at Mons knew how to fight, but did the expanding British armies of 1915 know how they should fight? This, and the following chapters, look at the guidance given to all officers on their duties and responsibilities at war, and traces the guidelines that senior officers were required to follow in their prosecution of it. The advice emanated mainly from the War Office in the early years, but GHQ in France started issuing its own guidance in mid-1915. The ideas presented in this guidance tell us far more about the views of those who wrote or issued them than they do about the views held by recipients. They are an endorsement of what the War Office, and later GHQ in France, considered best practice at the time they were issued.

Nikolas Gardner, in his book on *Command in 1914*, says that Henry Wilson, while the Battle of the Aisne was still underway, asked the three corps commanders to provide general advice 'for the benefit of newly arriving formations based on experience gained in the first part of the war.'[1] Behind this request was a query: was British training and command doctrine, as defined by *FSR*, applicable to the conflict in which the British Army now found itself? One 'General Officer', presumably, but not certainly, Smith-Dorrien of II Corps, said that it was, and that 'the essential thing is to pay attention to the sound principles on which our training is based.' A much more detailed response came from Lieutenant General William Pulteney. Written in September 1914, it is reproduced in *Notes from the Front*, published in December. 'Undoubtedly, one of the chief lessons of this war has been the necessity for the closest cooperation between'

1 Nikolas Gardner, *Trial by Fire, Command and the British Expeditionary Force in 1914* (Westport: Praeger, 2003), p.92. It has not proved possible to trace and verify his reference.

the infantry and artillery. He generally endorses all the other principles of *FSR*.[2] But he did highlight the single most important concept in *FSR*, that of all arms combination. Other principles, such as defence in depth and operational command relationships, are significant, but if all arms combination was not applicable to this new war, then many *FSR* training regulations would have become null and void. This chapter will examine adherence to this principle in the first year of war. In practice, in the first year of war, all arms combination meant the close cooperation of infantry and artillery. The cavalry seldom deployed as such on the Western Front.

The baseline guidance in August 1914, when the BEF went to war, was *FSR*. As the mobile warfare of 1914 settled into the static warfare of 1915, it was widely perceived that the training needs of new officers required reconsideration, especially if it was to be truncated. The command structure that *FSR* mandated was generally perceived as sound, although that pertaining to the artillery was creaking and would be revealed as requiring reform. Best practice for new junior officers, as the lessons of the war were learnt, was addressed by means of a series of Central Distribution Section (CDS) publications, later designated Stationery Service (SS) updates, which started providing tactical and practical advice, based on *FSR*, in late 1914. They were initially collated by the General Staff in the War Office in London and then approved by Lieutenant General Sir James Wolfe Murray, the new Chief of the Imperial General Staff. Aimée Fox, in her book *Learning to Fight*, provides a particularly helpful description of the development of this service.[3]

CDS 2, 3, 4 and 53

Four editions of *Notes from the Front* (CDS 2, 3, 4 and 53) were issued between December 1914 and May 1915. Right from the earliest days of warfare, not only corps commanders but also other trusted officers of all ranks were approached, and their views were sought on the applicability of *FSR* and the manuals of the other arms based on it in the current war. The *Notes* candidly record their observations, often offering advice on the performance of routine tasks to avoid accidents and improve protection. They were practical guides: 'A copy of these notes should be handed to every officer … It is not intended that this pamphlet should in any way take the place of existing training manuals.'[4] Some authoritative advice, for instance, on the design of fortifications, did develop the advice given in *FSR*, but only 'in amplification of' other manuals, in this case, that of field engineering.

Following the advice given in *FSR*, as it pertained to fighting soldiers, provided certainty in a very uncertain world. *Notes from the Front, Part I*, merely re-emphasised established training principles. For instance, its first paragraph restates the importance of defence in depth, one of *FSR*'s fundamental principles. It was issued in December 1914, and *Part IV* was issued in May 1915. All four parts of *Notes from the Front* take pains to reinforce the importance of the more general regulations. Many of the specific tactical regulations in *FSR* had been written

2 TNA: WO 95/668/1: III Corps Staff, 'Tactical' note, late September, 1914; CDS 2 *Notes from the Front, Part I, Collated by the General Staff*, December 1914, pp.2–10.
3 Aimée Fox, *Learning to Fight*, pp.78–85.
4 CDS 4, *Notes from the Front, Part III, and Further Notes on Field Defences, Collated by the General Staff*, February 1915, p.31.

with open warfare in mind, but they were training regulations and guidance on how to practice for war. Updating these had been a priority at the annual General Staff conferences since 1909 and before, but with the outbreak of war, all such conferences were cancelled. Since *FSR* defined a set of principles, which was recognised as separate from the details of training, this was not seen as a problem. As *Notes from the Front, Part III,* noted: 'At the beginning of the war [artillery] operations took place in open undulating country where methods learnt at practice camps were found suitable. Lately, operations have taken place in flat enclosed country, [and this] …together with the advent of the German heavy howitzer, has necessitated modifications, not in principle, but in practice.'[5] Not unnaturally, training exercises needed to be modified to reflect the new reality of war.

'Battery HQ with sapper walking past', a photograph taken by an infantry subaltern in 1915. (Author's collection)

Since 'one of the chief lessons of this war has been the necessity for the closest cooperation between' the infantry and artillery, this required that other *FSR* principles, facilitating it, be taught.[6] 'Closest cooperation' could not be achieved without the continuing implementation of principles relating to command structure and to the duties and responsibilities of junior officers. Modifications in command structure as the army expanded were not addressed in the early CDS and SS pamphlets, but the duties and responsibilities of junior officers were. In 1914, liaison, on personal initiative, was the duty of every officer, as laid down in *FSR*. Without this liaison, infantry and artillery combination was impossible.

Notes from the Front, Part III, issued in February 1915, addresses this *FSR* principle in detail with reference to junior artillery officers. The Forward Observation Officer (FOO):

> …is a direct link for co-operation between the infantry and the guns behind them. Usually, the best place for this officer in a protracted engagement is in the infantry trench itself … The company commander in the trench is often in telephonic communication with the battalion commander and if the artillery telephone be placed in the 'dug-out' next to the infantry telephone, messages can be sent direct from the battalion to the battery commander.

5 CDS 4, *Notes from the Front, Part III,* February 1915, p.29.
6 CDS 2, *Notes from the Front, Part I, Collated by the General Staff,* December 1914, pp.2, 7.

It further recommends that the FOO shares the detail of 'ranged' points with the local infantry commander so that he can inform the battery directly if he wants one of these points attacked.[7] Later in the document, the difficulties of maintaining communications are discussed and 'best practice' variations in wire layout for the division generally are described, suggesting doubled wires in all exposed areas.

CDS 5

A follow-up document, CDS 5, *Trench Warfare, Notes on Attack and Defence*, also from February 1915, enlarges on the necessity for 'close cooperation between infantry and artillery …in defensive organization.' There should be 'a sufficient force of artillery in close support of the infantry line, and ready at short notice to open rapid burst of fire on any part of the ground between the two trench lines.'[8] CDS 5 'prescribes no hard and fast methods', but 'so far as general principles are concerned, the doctrine [sic] described in field service regulations holds good.' Its strictures on attack emphasise thorough preparation and 'the vital importance of the most intimate cooperation between artillery and infantry.'[9]

It is easy to overemphasise the relevance of these publications. They were certainly widely distributed, but whether they were widely read is another matter. Experienced regular officers would very likely have assumed that they knew it all already, and if they were well-versed in *FSR* principles, the pamphlets offer little that is new. Very callow officers would likely have found the advice given in them difficult to absorb. They would have relied much more on personal instruction within their units. But *FSR*'s advice on all arms combination was demonstrably applicable to static warfare.

Doctrine in Defence

As Stewart Rawlins said in his *History of the Development of British Artillery in France*, *FSR* and *Field Artillery Training 1914* 'contained irreproachable matter with reference to all that concerns the defence.'[10] *FSR* is a doctrine of communication and liaison, all arms combination at a sub-divisional level. There is no provision in it for very senior officers to direct the artillery – 'It is of the utmost importance that communication should be maintained between the artillery and infantry commanders.'[11] Some commentators allege that this principle was merely an aspiration. Bowman and Connelly, for instance, say that 'the British went to war without a formalised method for infantry and artillery cooperation.'[12] Travers goes further in saying that 'pre-war cooperation between artillery and infantry was largely absent.'[13] Travers, at least, is wrong. It is

7 CDS 4, *Notes from the Front, Part III*, February 1915, p.31.
8 CDS 5, *Trench Warfare, Notes on Attack and Defence*, collated by the General Staff, February 1915, pp.16–18.
9 CDS 5, *Trench Warfare*, February 1915, p.2.
10 Rawlins, *British Artillery in France*, p.89.
11 *Field Service Regulations, Part I*, p.21.
12 Bowman and Connelly, *The Edwardian Army*, p.85.
13 Travers, *The Killing Ground*, p.72.

true that generals at corps and GHQ level did not, in 1914, organise that cooperation, but even that statement is called into doubt by the effectiveness of Horne in marshalling I Corps artillery during the Battle of Mons. It is also true that *FSR* and *Field Artillery Training 1914* did not lay down a universal template for this liaison, saying that 'the actual method by which this co-operation should be obtained will vary in accordance with the general nature of the operation.'[14] This was prescient in that nobody foresaw trench warfare, and any formal regulations drafted before the war would almost certainly have been unsuitable for it. But *FSR* did demand that all front-line commanders understand the liaison procedures for any operation, be it static or mobile. It was part of their job description under *FSR*. If there is strong evidence of such cooperation, it is also evidence that other major *FSR* principles were being followed. Infantry artillery combination within a division cannot be achieved unless the subdivisional command structure allows it. Nor can it be achieved unless individual subdivisional officers are willing to actively liaise with neighbouring units as defined in their personal responsibilities on the battlefield. Infantry artillery combination is, therefore, a good marker of *FSR* compliance. The purest, indeed only, way of assessing all arms combination at this level is to look at unit diaries, preferably together with personal letters or journals of participants in the action. In defence, it is relatively easy to recognise.

The principles of a defensive retreat had been debated and rehearsed before the war. Brian Bond wrote that, 'The most unorthodox and most useful training concept that Robertson introduced at Camberley [in his tenure as Staff College commandant from 1910 to 1913] was the practice of staff duties connected with retreats,' though Bond's use of the word 'unorthodox' might be challenged, given the emphasis given to retirements in *FSR*.[15] The aim of many a Victorian campaign on the edges of the Empire involved an offensive advance, a decisive battle, and a controlled retirement; the Tirah Expedition of 1897 is just one example.

The principles of an organised retirement are described in *FSR*.[16] To recap, the officer commanding the artillery may not be the most senior on the battlefield, but he controls the rhythm of the manoeuvre. He selects a suitable spot with a good field of fire for a battery, and half the rearguard infantry battalions, covered by cavalry, retire to the line in front of these guns. The other half marches on some miles, where a second battery has set up to shelter them. The enemy marching up the road behind the infantry are forced by artillery fire to disperse into an order of battle, whereupon the forward infantry battalions, together with the battery, retire back, again covered by cavalry, and through the next line of defence. This describes mobile warfare in retirement, as practised in the retreat from Mons in 1914. But in static warfare, under *FSR*, the same principle of the primacy of artillery in the defensive arrangements applies, whether the forces deployed are under attack or simply in readiness for an attack. *FSR* principles of the defensive use of artillery were followed into 1915.

Major F. Lambarde had retired from the army as a captain in 1910 after a long and notably undistinguished career in the Royal Garrison Artillery. In April 1915, he was commanding the four guns of 458 Battery, of the 118th Howitzer Brigade, attached to the Canadian Division on the opening day of Second Ypres. Two days before, he had taken over an exposed gun position from the French, as the Canadian infantry took over the lines in front. He had immediately,

14 *Field Artillery Training* (London: General Staff, War Office, 1914), pp.235–238, 247.
15 Bond, *The Staff College, 1854–1914*, p.286.
16 See *Field Service Regulations, Part I*, pp.95–97.

on his own initiative, moved his guns into covered positions. On the edge of the chlorine gas cloud, which heralded the start of the infantry battle, Lambarde was ordered to retire. That evening, he moved his battery, not, as ordered, to a position behind the Canadians, but, at the request of a British officer, he diverted his battery to cover the left wing of the thin British line of the Geddes contingent, four British reserve battalions, which moved forward, without artillery support, to cover the left flank of the beleaguered Canadians on the first day.

'Ascertained we only had a small body of the Middlesex Regiment in front of us and no other battery near us,' reported his subaltern Colin Hutchison. 'We waited anxiously for dawn.' In an excellent covered position, with well-sited observation posts, the battery was not moved for 26 days as the British line where it met the Yser Canal was held, despite heavy shelling and frequent attacks. 'Of course, being nearest to the infantry we are called on by them to shell snipers and little gatherings of Germans they imagine they see,' wrote Hutchison in early May. In a later letter, he wrote that their targets are 'chiefly observation posts or lairs used by snipers and machine guns,' chosen 'at the request of infantry brigades.'[17] This is clear evidence of liaison between 458 battery and the local infantry at both brigade and front-line level. Lambarde had received brief orders to support the troops in front of him. He had already chosen his battery position, set up his own observation posts, made his own arrangements for local liaison, and was now firing, at the request of infantry, not necessarily on orders from his own command hierarchy, selecting the targets himself to best support them. He had taken responsibility for managing his own ammunition supply. The infantry commanders liaised with the artillery, either at brigade level or directly with the forward observation officer, to suggest targets for attack. There was almost no input from senior officers outside of coordinated offensives. Lambarde had followed the defensive principles of *FSR* to the letter.

The second source by which this action can be judged is from the war diaries of the units involved. For this battery, on those days, the record confirms the eyewitness summary. On 29 April, '458 knocked down a length of strong parapet at the request of the infantry. 458 demolished two cottages containing machine guns,' and so on. On 3 May, 'enemy's trenches were reported to be filling up. 458 was immediately turned onto these trenches and expected attack did not develop. 458 Battery shelled two houses at request of infantry, where machine guns were located … 458 Battery fired a few shell at 4 batteries reported by aeroplane.'[18] This is evidence of a more sophisticated liaison. The report on aerial reconnaissance must have come through the corps to the division and brigade commanders who were now tasked with the counter-battery work of the howitzer brigades.

As a broad generalisation, such close artillery cooperation with the infantry was regarded as essential in defensive battles. The advantages to the infantry are clear from the example given above. This was more a last-ditch stand than a retirement, but during 1915, the army established more permanent trench lines, as both bulwarks of defence and springboards for attack. This did not negate the need for infantry-artillery cooperation, rather the reverse. Combination between the forward infantry and its supporting artillery was highly desirable. In August 1915, Brigadier General J. Rotton, on appointment as Commander Royal Artillery of the regular 7th Division, presided over the issue of orders on 'Artillery Cooperation in Defence.'

17 Hutchison, *The Young Gunner*, pp.58–62.
18 TNA: WO 95/3744: 118 Brigade, Royal Field Artillery, 29 April to 3 May 1915.

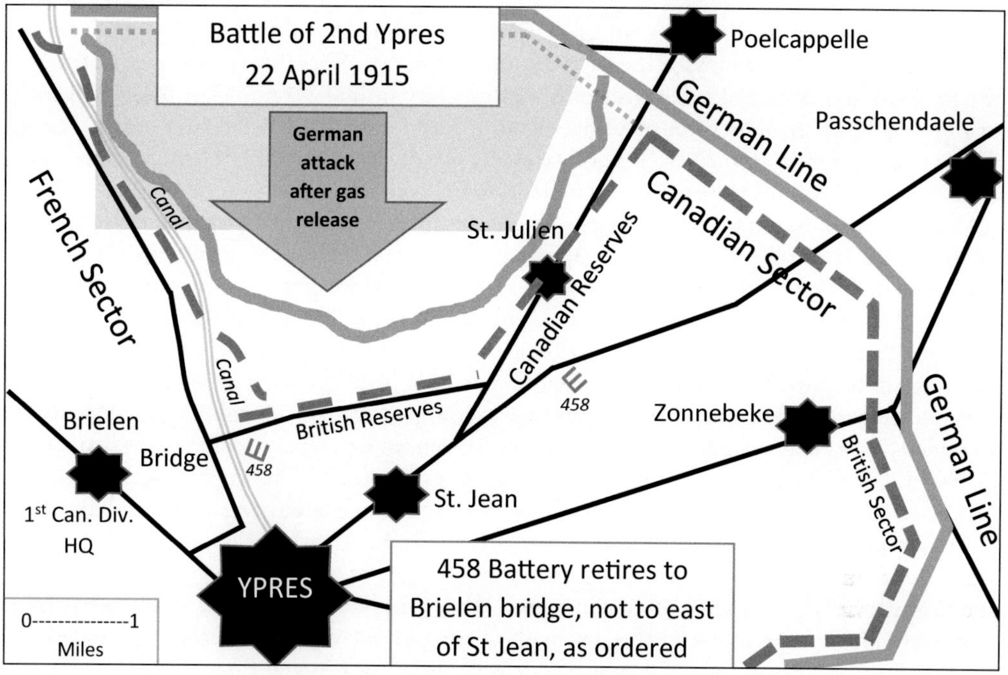

2nd Ypres Battle, evening of 22 April 1915.

> As a rule, one artillery brigade should be detailed to each infantry brigade. The artillery brigade Commander will be responsible for the defence of that front and have a telephone line to maintain close touch with the infantry brigadier whose front he supports. As far as possible, each battalion front is covered by one or more batteries. Each battery should appoint a forward observation officer (FOO) whose duty is to assist the infantry by personal observation of the front, and by being a channel of communication between battery and battalion, communicating to his battery requests for Artillery assistance against targets, etc. The necessary telephone lines [should be set up.] …In addition, the FOO should be able to listen in to the Infantry telephone system; and there should be an additional unmonitored wire from the front-line trench to battery for use in an emergency.[19]

The order also instructs that the FOO should sleep in battalion headquarters at night; that every battery should register points on, or just behind, the enemy front lines, and that all guns should be aligned on these targets at night, ensuring that artillery support could be provided quickly in the event of a surprise attack. This sophisticated template ensured that liaison pathways were clearly defined, and that any artillery response to an attack would be commensurate to the threat posed. Rotton was doing no more than defining his version of best practice – with reference to *FSR* and CDS updates.[20]

19 TNA: WO 95/1638/4: 7 Division, Artillery Cooperation with Infantry, 11 August 1915, pp.32–34.
20 CDS 2, CDS 3, CDS 4, *Notes from the Front, Parts I, II & III,* (London: Collated by the General Staff, War Office, 1914–1915).

Not all officers in the British Army of 1915 were well enough versed in *FSR* to produce such a comprehensive plan. Many of the urgently commissioned officers sent out as replacements, in late 1914 and early 1915, had had only rudimentary military training in the complexities of *FSR*. If they had come through Officer Training and Territorial Force units, their training varied considerably in its quality. The ability of any one division to absorb the professionalism of *FSR* compliance in this respect was dependant on the competence of their officers.

'This place is a training ground for raw troops, and we have got three officers from the 37th Division attached to us for instruction', reported Hutchison from his new positions at Ploegsteert Wood in late June 1915.[21] New divisions were given an induction period, shadowing established units in the line, though, as Rawlins noted, during 1915, the 'low establishment of Territorial [divisional artillery] proved a serious drawback', meaning 'additional artillery from regular divisions had to be provided.'[22] Both these factors may have benefited such divisions in their drive for professionalism. Most new divisions had a leavening of regulars returning to war after being wounded. Lucky was the subaltern who had an experienced regular as his mentor, be it an officer or NCO. But not surprisingly, the subtleties of infantry artillery liaison, as described in *FSR* and associated publications, were too much for most of the newly arriving Territorial divisions.

On arrival on the front line in France in April 1915, the 47th Division, previously the 2nd London Division, also issued standing orders on countering an attack, a copy of which is in their artillery diary. It starts with a command: 'The front line is to be held at all costs.' There were certainly strong reasons for this, particularly early in the war when all the effort of defence construction went to the forward trenches. It was initially envisaged that a trench line would consist of a series of small strongpoints connected by trenches. These strongpoints comprised 'improvised fortifications' as defined in *FSR, Part I*, and, as such, were required to be fiercely defended.[23] However, *FSR* advises that improvised fortifications in open country should be reorganised as time and resources allowed. They should be converted into defensive outposts in front of a main line of defence and a fall-back line in case of necessity. The presence of a second trench line behind the first is evidence of *FSR* compliance. Exposed salients should be withdrawn, and indefensible ground should be left vacant.[24] In practice, these were difficult concepts for inexperienced troops and activation of them was seen by some high up in the BEF hierarchy as evidence of defeatism. John French took the opportunity of Smith-Dorrien suggesting just such a rationalising retirement to force his resignation in May 1915.[25]

To continue with the 47th Division's standing orders on countering an attack, written in April 1915: 'At the first sign of an attack, our artillery will bombard the enemy's trenches. To open fire satisfactorily the closest touch must be kept between the forward trenches and the batteries by a pre-arranged signal. Red rockets have been provided for this purpose. …Counter-attack to be effective must be immediate.' The instructions given lack focus. 'Commanders are to have a plan ready for all eventualities. 'Infantry Brigade Commanders will consult with officers commanding the supporting artillery.' Despite this, the artillery is not mentioned in defining 'general principles' of defence, but it goes on to say that 'close cooperation with the infantry, the support

21 Hutchison, *The Young Gunner*, p.79.
22 Rawlins, *British Artillery in France*, p.29.
23 *Field Service Regulations, Part I*, pp.170–171.
24 *Field Service Regulations, Part I*, pp.98–111, 128–131, 142, 145.
25 Beckett, Bowman and Connelly, *The British Army*, p.253.

of whom is their primary function, is essential for all battery officers. Their observing stations should be made known to the infantry and their requirements for observation explained.' 'Plans for action in the event of attack, prepared by Infantry Brigade Commanders, should include details of artillery support. The CRA is responsible for complete and accurate registration.' In this war diary copy, there is a pencilled addition, '? Telephone Communications.'[26] It is a fair question. The liaison described falls far short of that required in *FSR*, *Field Artillery Training*, and *Notes from the Front*. Battalion commanders are not in the loop, and lines of responsibility for the intensity of any artillery response are not clear. The FOO, in his observation post, is not directed to liaise with front-line infantry and is useless at night. This guidance does not, in many respects, conform with either common sense or *FSR*, but as a basis for improvement in the light of experience, it is a reasonable starting point. Enlightened Territorial and 'New Army' artillery and infantry officers would have learnt much from taking over the positions of regular units, finding sophisticated communications in place. In this division, in 1915, compliance with *FSR*, with respect to professional liaison, was an aspiration, not a fact.

The Artillery Command Structure as it Developed from August 1914

In 1914, the British Army was in no doubt, under *FSR*, that it was the divisional commander who had the primary responsibility for the local tactical management of a battle. He was responsible for converting intent into results. He had total control over his own artillery and handled his division as an all-arms force. French and his corps commanders in 1914 had no authority to direct the artillery. No directive was issued from any source in the senior hierarchy of the army to challenge this position in 1914 and 1915. The problems of artillery direction at the corps or army level became manifest in late 1914, although the first Artillery Advisers were appointed to French's GHQ, and both corps HQs, before the BEF even departed to France. The Army Artillery Adviser was required to advise not only French and Murray, his chief-of-staff, but also William Robertson, the QMG, and Nevil Macready, the AG to the BEF, on operations, logistics and manning respectively. He was allocated staff support later in the year when the first heavy guns started to arrive, but the War Office gave him an officer from the QMG branch, reflecting his role in advising on the provision of guns and munitions.

Haig wrote a personal report covering the performance of I Corps on the Aisne in 1914. He addresses the subject of infantry-artillery cooperation: 'On the 18th [September] General Horne returned to Corps Headquarters and at my request undertook the organization of the artillery fire.' This was not the first time he had made this request. At Mons, Haig had acted on a principle advocated in German infantry regulations but not in *FSR:* 'Artillery forms the skeleton of battle … the commander must reserve for himself the choice of the artillery position and indicate to the artillery commander what cooperation he expects from him.'[27] Horne was his de facto artillery commander for the Battle of Mons. A month later, Haig described

26 TNA: WO95/2708/1: 47 Division Artillery, April 1915.

27 *Drill Regulations for the Infantry, German Army, 1906, translated for US War Department by Francis Behr* (Washington: Government Printing Office, 1907) p.72. The 'iron framework of the battle' as proposed for the British Army in CDS 98/4, *Artillery in Offensive Operations April 1916*, will be addressed in the next chapter.

in detail the benefits of giving Horne, who, under *FSR*, had no executive powers whatever, the authority to command within his corps operational hierarchy. Horne was enabled to issue orders designed to improve infantry-artillery combination both within and between divisions, to improve protection of the guns by demanding covered positions with associated observation posts, and to coordinate air observation to direct the fire of batteries.[28] In addition, he had the authority to impose zones on the divisional artillery to avoid the accidents and confusion which are vividly described by Gardner in the early stages of the Aisne battle.[29] There were very few senior artillery officers with Horne's experience. He had already demonstrated great tact in managing Haig's inappropriate 'rapidity of decision' at Mons and in managing divisional CRAs who were very aware of the command intricacies of *FSR* that vested all responsibility on themselves. Doubtless, he had to use his tact and charm in his new role at the Aisne.

The good sense of this appointment by Haig was self-evident, but Haig made no attempt to legitimise it. Gardner describes how Haig's corps headquarters had become increasingly independent of GHQ.[30] Beyond this battle report, there is no record that he advised French, or Du Cane, French's Artillery Adviser at GHQ, of the arrangement or that he contacted the War Office to formally request authorisation from them to create the post of Commander Royal Artillery at corps level. As Stewart Rawlins, in his invaluable book on the *British Artillery in France*, explains, he should have done so. If he had, and it had been agreed by French, a clear explanation of his duties and responsibilities, allocating him staff support, would have been formally drafted. Without this, Horne's position was irregular, and he could not legally be allocated any staff.[31] Many problems might have been avoided if this amendment had been made, because it was a question that never went away, becoming ever more pressing when heavier guns started to arrive in France.

By January 1915, Du Cane had also become convinced of the desirability of an artillery commander at corps level. But by then, the mechanism by which it could be legitimised was becoming more complex, though French, as C-in-C, could have demanded it. The War Office was already wrestling with the staffing problems arising from the creation of two armies under French at GHQ. Now, a further layer separated Du Cane from corps Artillery Advisers. He issued a consultation document that month, an unsigned copy of which found its way into the war diary of IV Corps, probably inappropriately. He repeats Haig's argument: 'Each division has its divisional artillery and a small' number of heavier guns. 'Their fire is distributed and fire control is decentralised.' If, 'an attack is contemplated it will be necessary to concentrate the fire of the heavy guns … For this purpose, a Corps Artillery Commander with a Staff Captain and sufficient means of communication are necessary.' He should 'be termed the C.R.A.' and should 'command such portions of the artillery as not placed specifically under divisional commanders … It will in some cases be desirable for tactical reasons to place some of the artillery of one or both divisions directly under' his orders. 'Occasions also may arise when it is desirable to place some of the artillery of one division under the other Divisional Commander. There has hitherto been far too much rigidity in this respect, which has been by no means conducive to the provision

28 TNA: WO 95/588/1: I Corps Staff, 'Operations of the 1st Corps on the River Aisne, September 1914' p.17.
29 Gardner, *Trial by Fire*, p.93.
30 Gardner, *Trial by Fire*, p.208.
31 Rawlins, *British Artillery in France*, pp.1–2.

of efficient artillery support.'[32] But this letter, presumably written to garner support for a formal request to the War Office to recognise a new post, never gathered sufficient backing. By severely curtailing the absolute authority vested with divisional CRAs, it doubtless generated some resistance at the divisional level, and with French taking no view, no further progress was made.

Rawlins quotes a further letter issued by GHQ in April 1915, which confirms the lack of progress. It re-defined the status quo: 'As the duties of Artillery Advisers are not laid down in the Staff Manual or Field Service Regulations… they should be defined in order that possible misunderstandings should be avoided. Except as provided for below the duties of an Artillery Adviser are purely advisory. He is not a commander nor is he a Staff Officer.'[33] The exception provided for was if an army or corps commander asked him to assume command over any part of the artillery for a specific operation. Naturally, this opened the floodgates, and, unsurprisingly, different army and corps commanders had different views as to which part of the artillery he should assume control of and what constituted a specific operation. He was still not entitled to operational staff support.

Commentary on Defensive Doctrine in 1915

The varying extent to which very senior officers used their powers to direct divisional artillery officers inevitably stressed the very clear operational hierarchical command structure defined in *FSR*. But the whole concept of front-line infantry-artillery liaison in passive conditions, when neither side was attacking the other, was further threatened in 1915. It is surely self-evident that every infantry brigade commander, every battalion commander, and every man in the trenches would have wanted a battery at their disposal to engage tiresome snipers, machine guns or artillery posing a threat in their sector of the line. It is equally self-evident that every battery in a forward role would have wanted to provide this support. The FOOs of forward batteries spent a lot of time with their infantry counterparts. They became friends. There was much discussion on the role of the field artillery in the upper echelons of the army, and a future chapter will address the issues raised, but there were local reasons why this invaluable liaison was suppressed through 1915. The main driver was a shortage of ammunition. Regular battery commanders were trained to husband their supplies of shells. In mobile warfare, the ammunition columns were not always to hand. A battery without ammunition was completely useless, so commanders would fire only on targets that justified the expenditure. Due to the command hierarchy under which they worked, only their immediate superior could order them to fire. No infantry officer could order a battery to fire unless he had formally assumed command of it. He could only request it. Battery commanders provided only the support they could afford to give. But in 1915, the batteries of the new divisions were very inexperienced. They needed more shots to hit a target. They lacked judgment in selecting targets. Their observation posts were often inadequate, and many batteries were poorly sited.

The combination of these factors meant that staff officers, mainly from the QMG's branch, saw it as necessary to impose rationing on the use of ammunition supplied to batteries. Any

32 TNA: WO 95/707/1: IV Corps General Staff diary, 'Memorandum on Artillery Organization in Corps, 18 January 1915.'
33 Rawlins, *British Artillery in France*, p.2.

surplus ammunition had to be stockpiled for the offensives that were planned. The detail of how this rationing was enforced varied from division to division, but generally, the divisional artillery was required to maintain a local reserve for use in the event of a surprise attack. The use of any surplus ammunition that was allocated on a week-by-week basis was not determined by the batteries. They were under orders to fire only on targets agreed upon, or selected by, more senior officers in the artillery hierarchy. 'This morning I stayed in and got properly roasted by the Brigadier for ordering one of our batteries (the colonel being out) to retaliate to an annoying German battery that was making a nuisance of himself', wrote Captain Ralph Blewitt RFA, serving with the 1st Division in February 1915.[34] Some of this direction even came from corps artillery commanders, though most was orchestrated at the divisional level. The perception of the front-line artillery commanders was that they were being emasculated, and that their local knowledge of the front line was being ignored. They perceived that they were receiving orders to withhold fire based on logistical, not operational, criteria, based on advice from staff officers, who were seldom as qualified to select targets as they were. 'Unfortunately, our ammunition being limited, we are not allowed to make ourselves as objectionable as we would like', observed Hutchison from his battery on 9 June 1915. Then, later in the month, 'we are saving up our weeks supply of ammunition to give them a really healthy dose somewhere. Personally, I don't agree with this. I think we ought to use it in little bits for the benefit of the infantry.'[35] In short, the ethos of *FSR*, in which more junior officers took responsibility for their actions in liaison with their infantry or artillery counterparts, was under sustained attack. One result of this was a breakdown in trust between staff and regimental officers.

Much has been written on the rancour which developed between staff and front-line officers during 1915. Paul Harris quotes Keith Simpson in saying that 'unfortunately, the country-house lifestyle of many generals and their staffs and the incestuous nature of their self-promotion did not endear them to the regimental soldier.'[36] It was much more visceral than that. Those divisional officers of all ranks who adhered to the principles of *FSR* in respect of infantry-artillery combination found their terms of reference amended without consultation. Batteries looked on helplessly as infantry died. They blamed the staff, particularly those who did not understand the difference between operational orders and administrative directives. Interference with respect to the interface between these two sources of instruction became increasingly intrusive. Hutchison quotes one trivial example: 'There is a new scheme for testing our stock of ammunition devised by some worry somewhere in some office. The batteries now have to count their ammunition at 8 pm, when it was at 2 pm. It is simply extraordinary how difficult it is to count ammunition in the dark.'[37] In his division, administrative staff officers of the QMG branch were given the job of enforcing rationing.

So, up to mid-July 1915, all the guidance emanating from the War Office was endorsing *FSR*, while inexperience, intrusive rationing and an increasingly civilian staff preparing detailed, rather than brief, orders, seems to signal that *FSR* was perhaps not entirely suitable as a doctrine for static trench warfare, being applicable only in active defence.

34 IWM: 92168: Captain Ralph Blewitt RFA, letter, 4 Feb 1915.
35 Hutchison, *The Young Gunner*, pp.77, 83.
36 Harris, 'The Staff of the British Army', p.17.
37 Hutchison, *The Young Gunner*, p.89.

Commentary on Offensive Doctrine in 1915, Excluding Haig's First Army

CDS 5, *Trench Warfare, Notes on Attack and Defence*, issued in February 1915, endorses *FSR* principles in attack, as did CDS 2, 3, 4 and 53, *Notes from the Front*. CDS 5 restates the necessity of thorough reconnaissance and collation of intelligence. Its strictures on attack emphasise 'the vital importance of the most intimate cooperation between artillery and infantry.' Since 'the capture of trenches is generally easier than their retention … the most careful consideration and preparation in advance' is needed.[38]

Michael LoCicero describes 'an almost unknown brigade level attack … conceived to improve an unsatisfactory' length of line in July 1915. 'Limited in scope, and relatively successful in outcome, this small-scale enterprise was indicative of what could be achieved by meticulous planning, and, as generally articulated in *Field Service Regulations*, close cooperation between various arms of the service (artillery, engineers, infantry, etc.) during this still transient period of position warfare.'[39]

Later that month, on 30 July 1915, the British lost ground at Hooge following an attack on the 14th Division with flamethrowers. Plumer ordered the 6th Division on a front of 1,000 yards to retake the lost ground. Thomas Marden, in his *History of the 6th Division*, describes the attack on 9 August: 'The attack was completely successful; all objectives were quickly gained … Not only was all the ground lost on the 30th July regained, but an important spur north of the Menin Road, which had hitherto been in German occupation, was included in the final position consolidated.' This attack was:

> …the first attempt made to follow the barrage really closely. The barrage did not, however, "creep" up to the German front line, but was placed directly on it at once at zero and lifted back from there, the 6-in. howitzers lifting slightly before the Field Artillery. The infantry lay out as close to the barrage as possible below zero, and moved in on time as soon as the Field Artillery barrage lifted. The attack was looked upon for some time as a model of really close co-operation between infantry and artillery. The casualties were 70 officers and 1,700 other ranks.[40]

Artillery FOOs were ordered up at least as far as battalion headquarters for the attack. 'Yellow screens will be used to indicate that our troops have gained a certain position and cannot advance further without artillery support. Blue and yellow flags will be waved by selected N.C.O.s to indicate that our shells are falling short.'[41] Marden's account is somewhat rose-tinted, and casualties were relatively heavy, but it illustrates, like the smaller attack that LoCicero describes, remarkable compliance with *FSR*.

It is not infrequently asserted that the lifting barrage was a First World War invention. Rawlins, in his *History of the Royal Artillery*, written in 1918, disagrees. *FSR* and *Field Artillery Training* (*FAT*) 'proved a remarkably sound guide to the principle of artillery in action.' 'FAT

38 CDS 5; *Trench Warfare*, p.2.

39 Michael LoCicero, 'A Coda to the Second Battle of Ypres: International Trench 6–10 July 1915', in *Courage without Glory*, pp.312–313.

40 Thomas Owen Marden (ed.), *A Short History of the 6th Division* (London: Hugh Rees 1920), pp.13–16.

41 TNA: WO 95/1581/1/2: 6 Division Artillery, Operation Order 27, 5 August 1915.

foresaw the lifting barrage, from which the creeping barrage sprung; insisted throughout on the paramount importance of observation of fire, a principle which fell somewhat into disregard during the trench warfare regime; [and] emphasised the necessity for the close artillery support of infantry at all stages in a battle.'[42] The claim by the 6th Division that this was the first time it had been used is debatable, since the technique of a lifting barrage is described minutely in *Field Artillery Training 1914*:

> Whether the artillery can continue its fire until the assaulting infantry is actually on the point of closing with the enemy, or whether it should increase its range on the first signs of the commencement of the assault, must depend on the circumstances of each case ... The advantages of artillery support at this period are so great that the danger from a few shells falling short must not be allowed to prevent the artillery from continuing their fire till the latest possible moment.[43]

The main difference between a lifting barrage as envisaged pre-war and that which became routine later in the war was, as Rawlins says, that the former insisted that artillery fire be directed under close observation, while the latter was often pre-ordained, based on an expectation of the needs of the infantry, rather than their actual needs in real time – cooperation, not necessarily combination.

It is obviously difficult to compare these attacks by a single brigade or division with that of two or more divisions working together, such as was occurring in Haig's much bigger attacks further south but the planning of these attacks reflects the ethos of Plumer's Second Army. Involved in all the battles of 1915 were battalions of the Territorial Force, which had been individually incorporated into regular divisions. As early as February 1915 French praised the competence of these units, who were 'fast approaching, if they had not already reached, the standards of efficiency of the regular infantry.'[44] The narrative in this chapter has largely concentrated on the exploits of Smith-Dorrien's, later Herbert Plumer's Second Army. But, going back to 1914, and the travails of II Corps at First Ypres, Gardner describes how Smith-Dorrien tried to obey GHQ's orders on maintaining an offensive momentum during that battle, even when his troops were almost unable to comply, and when he was deeply unhappy at not having sufficient time to prepare attacks.[45] Fighting under *FSR*, he saw no choice but to obey orders that were not compliant with it.

However, Steven Corvi, in his 2006 analysis of Smith-Dorrien's conduct into 1915, opines that his notes in War Office reports show that he believed that 'pre-1914 notions of the war and its execution were completely false.' Influenced by Travers, Corvi bases this last statement on the assumption that the British Army was complying with an 'offensive tactical doctrine of the pre-war days', a Clausewitzian ethos that articulated 'the conviction that the moral effect of a strong offensive doctrine would prevail over any circumstances.' He portrays Smith-Dorrien as

42 Rawlins, *British Artillery in France*, pp.88–89.
43 *Field Artillery Training 1914*, pp.250–252. See also *FSR, Part I*, section 106.
44 K. Mitchinson, *The Territorial Force at War 1914 – 1916* (Palgrave Macmillan, Kindle edition [2014]) 'Pre-war Quest for Efficiency,' p.116.
45 Gardner, *Trial by Fire*, pp.132–137.

a maverick in believing that 'the modern battlefield did not follow this predetermined order.' Smith-Dorrien said that:

> ...the closest possible co-operation between infantry and artillery is an absolute necessity... He often displayed tactics that were contrary to GHQ thinking, and even questioned ... the consistent ordering of offensives. He wanted to employ fire and movement tactics and was even a proponent of defensive retreat ... This was viewed by GHQ as defeatist in nature, and ... in the end, doctrinal rigidity and the 'system' with its inherent personalised command structure, destroyed his career.[46]

Corvi implies that it was Smith-Dorrien's refusal to accept the pre-war doctrine of the army that led to his dismissal. In fact, it was his insistence on following the principles of *FSR* that did so. It was ironic that it was Plumer who succeeded Smith-Dorrien as the commander of the Second Army because he immediately performed the defensive retreat his former chief had suggested and which *FSR* mandated. Plumer's supervision of the little offensives described in this chapter suggests that he, too, expected planning based on collated intelligence, allowing time for all arms combination to be organised for attacks with limited and defined objectives, all in compliance with *FSR*.

46 Steven Corvi, 'Horace Smith-Dorrien, Second Army, 1914 – 1915', in Beckett and Corvi (eds), *Haig's Generals*, pp.201–203.

16

Operational Review mid-1915 to 1916

The following documents are covered in this review:

CDS 24 *Object and Conditions of Combined Offensive Action*, June 1915
CDS 50 *Tactical Notes*, July 1915
Preparatory Measures before undertaking Offensive Operations, February 1916
SS 101 *Notes for Infantry Officers on Trench warfare*, March 1916

The War Office in London issued the early CDS pamphlets. These were highly compliant with the principles of *FSR*. The next question is whether the *FSR* doctrine could survive the extraordinary scale of losses incurred by I, II and III Corps during the latter months of 1914. If the army generally perceived that their casualties were because of, rather than in spite of, *FSR*, then many elements of it would have been abandoned. It is often asserted that the regular army of August 1914 was effectively destroyed by the end of the year. The National Statistics of the Military Effort, published in 1922, records that there were 10,938 officers in the army of 1914, with a further 2,882 on the reserve. By the end of 1914, 2,119 officers had been lost: killed, died of wounds or prisoners. A further 2,098 had been wounded, but this last figure includes minor wounds and could count the same officer more than once. One can only guess, but it seems likely that at least 1,000 of these would have returned to active service, excluding those fit only for home service. The regular army was undoubtedly severely mauled, losing many of its best officers, but it was not destroyed. The principles inherent in *FSR* could still potentially be taught and followed by regular officers, particularly in the artillery and engineers, since their losses killed as a percentage of total officers available were less than those of the infantry. The question persists as to whether front-line officers continued to base their soldiering on *FSR* principles, as advised by their senior generals at GHQ and the War Office.[1]

The year 1915 is extraordinarily difficult to assess in this respect. Spencer Jones has performed a great service in addressing the subject in *Courage without Glory*, first published in 2015, but he would be the first to admit that its content merely scratches the surface in addressing the many

1 *Statistics of the Military Effort of the British Empire During the Great War 1914 -1920* (London: War Office, 1922), pp.30, 253. The figures are acknowledged as approximate.

issues. It was, as he says, the forgotten year. First, the British Army was reeling from its losses. Secondly, the army was expanding extremely fast, swollen first by the arrival of the Territorial divisions, and then later in the year, by the first divisions of Kitchener's New Army. 'The British Army's operational and tactical development,' that year, 'was uneven,' he says.

> Some lessons were learned, but others were misinterpreted, forgotten or simply ignored. Commanders struggled to understand the battlefield problems of the war, and were forced to solve them with an army that was lacking in both equipment and training. Poor generalship greatly compounded these difficulties, but even skilful commanders found that their plans could be undone by the limitations of their own forces and the effectiveness of the German defences.[2]

As his next chapter in the book makes clear, this is a very understated analysis. His description of the barely tolerable stresses caused by loss of command expertise, a near absence of competent staff officers, the inexperience of even regular reinforcements, lack of guns and ammunition, and the relentless attrition demanded by politicians, compounded by the 'mercurial', to put it kindly, behaviour of John French, leave one in awe that the British Army survived the year at all.[3] Everybody was running on instinct. Those who had accepted *FSR* as their military doctrine, like Smith-Dorrien, used it to guide their day-to-day operations and tactics. Those who had not used whatever resources their personal education provided.

FSR-based publications, augmented by updated advice in *Notes from the Front*, remained the backbone of the often inadequate training that officers new to the front received. But in the near chaos of 1915, young officers found themselves expected to comply with *FSR* in active defence and limited offensives, but required to forego the meaningful liaison *FSR* demanded at a sub-divisional level due to the bureaucratisation of trench life, exacerbated by the shell shortage. There was a need for new guidance. In mid-1915, GHQ in France started issuing its own guidance.

CDS 24

CDS 24, *Object and Conditions of Combined Offensive Action*, was issued in June 1915. This was a translation of an edict issued by General Joseph Joffre, Commander-in-Chief of the French in April 1915:

> The object of an offensive action is not merely to gain possession of a line of enemy trenches but actually to drive the enemy from his entire position and to defeat him, without giving him time to reorganize … It appears advisable to give the attacking units as their objective points in rear of the enemy's fortified position, the possession of which will be a guarantee that the preliminary result to be obtained, i.e. the piercing of the enemy's line – has been secured. In aiming at the possession of these points, the attacking units must regard the

2 Jones, 'Introduction: The Forgotten Year', in Jones (ed.), *Courage without Glory*, p.xxix.
3 Jones, 'To make war as we must, and not as we would like: The British Army and the Problem of the Western Front', in Jones (ed.), *Courage without Glory*, pp.31–55.

> enemy's trenches not as an end in themselves, but as a series of barriers which must be penetrated before reaching the objective laid down.[4]

On 22 August 1914, Joffre had issued this advice:

> Attacks have been carried out, without close cooperation between infantry and artillery. Every combined operation includes a series of detailed actions aiming at the capture of the point d'appui. Each time it is necessary to capture a point d'appui, the attack must be prepared with artillery. The infantry must be held back, and not launched to the assault until the distance to be covered is so short that it is certain that the objective will be reached. Every time the infantry has been launched to the attack before the artillery has made its effect felt, the infantry has fallen under the fire of machine guns, and suffered losses which might have been avoided. When a point d'appui has been captured, it must be organized immediately, and artillery must be bought up.[5]

This general order is close to a précis of *FSR* regulations. It demands that artillery combine with infantry at every stage of battle.

Joffre had not completely changed his mind as outlined in CDS 24. He proceeds on the assumption that most of the preparatory work had been done by the artillery before the initial assault:

> The artillery opens the path for the infantry … It will have been the role of the artillery, by systematically directing its fire on the successive lines of the enemy's positions, to destroy his defences, and to break up his dug-outs, communication trenches and flanking works. It will have lowered the morale of the defenders by repeated shock and will be in readiness to afford effective support to the infantry attacks, throughout their duration, not only on their original but also on their ulterior objectives.

He is advocating artillery support from inception to the conclusion of the offensive.

He acknowledges that 'artillery fire is effective only when it has been possible to register with extreme precision', a process that took some hours in 1915. The conditions under which this was possible could only exist if FOOs could find suitable observation posts, with the requisite communications, close enough to their targets to direct their own guns. Since there existed a 'risk of seeing the whole line of attack halt to reorganize in the captured trench, and subsequently await the enemy's counter offensive', he said that 'the assaulting troops, at all distances, will be imbued with the idea of breaking through, of going beyond the first line of captured trenches, and of continuing the attack without inter-mission till the final result is obtained.' His attack plan assumed artillery dominance and the effective destruction of most of the enemy defences:

4 CDS 24, *Object and Conditions of Combined Offensive Action*, issued by the General Staff, GHQ, June 1915, copy of proclamation issued by J Joffre, General Officer, Commanding-in-Chief, General Headquarters, Eastern Armies, 16th April, 1915.

5 Edmonds, *Military Operations, France and Belgium 1914,* p.75.

> The complete preparation of the attack being an indispensable condition for success, it follows that its execution must be regulated by the completion of this preparation, and must especially depend upon the securing of the results aimed at in the artillery preparation. Higher commanders must satisfy themselves that all the precautions laid down have been complied with, and the necessary results obtained. The responsibility is theirs.[6]

In other words, infantry attacks should not proceed if the artillery has failed to destroy the enemy defences.

It is unlikely that British generals would have read Joffre's remarks with any more than passing interest since the organisation and ethos of the French army was so different to that of the British Army, but the publication of CDS 24 does suggest that there were those at GHQ who agreed with the sentiments expressed. Joffre proposed breakthrough as the primary objective of battle, based on artillery dominance, albeit implicitly accepting that artillery support would tail off for the attacking force in the later stages of the battle. CDS 24 was very quickly followed by a similar edict from GHQ that pertained to British Army thinking.

CDS 50

CDS 50, *Tactical Notes*, was issued in July 1915. This can be taken as more definitely reflecting the views of French, Haig, and the senior leadership of the BEF since it incorporated the experience of the first offensive battles of 1915, fought by Haig's First Army, at Neuve Chapelle, Aubers, Festubert and Givenchy. Earlier pamphlets issued by the War Office in London never challenged the primacy of FSR and referenced it frequently. In contrast, there is no reference to *FSR* in *CDS 50*, nor does it engage with *FSR* principles. It is not an impressive document. It lacks any overview of the tactical ideas that might lead to success, concentrating on detail. Many of these details address the poor initial planning and poor initial reconnaissance of previous 1915 offensives: 'Any attempt to crowd troops into a confined space, in immediate proximity to the front line, leads to heavier casualties than an advance from lines in rear.' The lack of guns, particularly heavy artillery, which was a fact of life in these battles, is acknowledged in passing: 'A heavy bombardment on the first line and support trenches, both on the front of attack and on the flanks, appears to offer the best chance of destroying [machine guns]; while a barrage of H.E. shell on both flanks of the Infantry attack, directed on the enemy's trenches and tactical points in rear, will probably neutralise their fire.' There is no mention of any bombardment of the second line trenches, which the infantry was expected to carry on and attack: 'Artillery barrages should be directed on to the enemy's supporting points and communications, and not on open spaces of ground, which leads to waste of ammunition.'[7] The reasons why this wasteful fire was occurring are not addressed. Accuracy could only be guaranteed by registration in 1915, and registration for any battery required some hours and good observation.

Forward liaison between infantry and artillery in attack is ignored. Its section on communications refers only to the infantry, except to suggest that infantry officers might consider using

6 CDS 24, *Combined Offensive Action*, appended notes.

7 CDS 50, *Tactical Notes*, issued by the General Staff, GHQ, 31 July 1915, sections 8, 9.

the telephones of FOOs to pass information back to their brigades.[8] This lack of emphasis on the importance of infantry and artillery working together at the sharp end of an attack is significant. This is reflected in the detailed analyses of the planning of the battles of 1915. Even in Spencer Jones's book on the battles of 1915, it is difficult to find any reference to FOOs or the role of the artillery after its initial bombardments. As Jones says, 'the capture of the first line of trenches – often at a high cost in lives – was merely a precursor to a chaotic assault on the second or third German line which would take place without benefit of close artillery support.'[9]

There is no doubt that Haig wanted a decisive battle along the lines of Joffre's scheme proposed in CDS 24. Nick Lloyd, in his paper on 'Haig's Command of First Army' sums up Haig's views:

> In the absence of a clear, guiding hand from Sir John [French], Haig approached the battles of 1915 with one eye on the past ... The enemy would be engaged on a wide front, his reserves drawn in and then exhausted, before the decisive blow was struck by one's own reserves. A cavalry pursuit would then scatter the foe. Alongside this emphasis on the decisive offensive came a fundamental view of warfare that de-emphasised technology and firepower and stressed the continuing relevance of human factors, including the need for discipline, high morale, and 'pluck' on the battlefield ... [In] 1915, Haig still thought of battle in ... traditional, almost Napoleonic, terms.[10]

As Haig told the Prime Minister, Herbert Asquith, in June, 'With such changed conditions [of war on the Western Front] it might be thought that the old principles of war had also changed. But I do not think that is so... The difficulty is to apply these great principles under the changed conditions.'[11] He is talking here of Clausewitzian principles, not *FSR* ones. Before that, in February, he had given French warning of his impatience with small operations and his desire for decisive action: 'The advance to be made is not a minor operation. It is to be understood that we are embarking on a serious offensive movement with the object of breaking the German line, and consequently our advance is to be pushed vigorously. Very likely an operation of considerable magnitude may result.'[12]

Spencer Jones, in his chapter on the Western Front battles of 1915, discusses the two schools of thought on offensives, albeit without referencing *FSR*: one which 'sought to maintain the momentum of the original attacks to such a point that the Germans would have no time to recover'; the other 'a methodical approach which sought to capture limited, manageable objectives.' 'There is a temptation, born of hindsight,' he says, 'to view bite and hold as an operational panacea ... However, it must be emphasised that at this stage of the war, [views on how to conduct bite and hold] were nebulous and informal.' On the contrary, *FSR* laid down a clear template on how it was to be conducted. Plumer, who ordered or approved several such operations, such as the counterattack, using the 6th Division, in July 1915, ensured that *FSR* was followed with respect to reconnaissance, planning and implementation. Even Haig, as noted above, does not dismiss the feasibility of 'a minor operation', or limited attack. More pertinently,

8 CDS 50, *Tactical Notes*, section 3.
9 Jones, 'Introduction' to *Courage without Glory*, p.xxv.
10 Nick Lloyd, 'With Faith and without Fear: Sir Douglas Haig's Command of First Army during 1915', *The Journal of Military History*, vol.71, no.4 (October 2007), pp.1059–1060.
11 Lloyd, 'Haig's Command of First Army', p.1060.
12 Haig to GHQ, 12 February 1915, quoted in Lloyd, 'Haig's Command of First Army', p.1062.

View From trench loophole of no-man's land and the German lines, 1915. (Author's collection)

Jones goes on, 'by definition, [bite and hold] would not provide clear cut victories suitable for public consumption.'[13] There was almost intolerable pressure on French to deliver a decisive success. Politicians like Asquith wanted to hear that total victory was possible, and Haig assured them that it was. The blame for the disastrous battles of 1915 can be spread widely. *FSR* does not spread blame widely. If the army fails in battle, the C-in-C is totally responsible.

French gave Haig almost exclusive rights over the offensives of 1915. Patrick Watt's analysis of Haig's approach to the planning for the Battle of Neuve Chapelle confirms his vision of divisions moving as one unit under his corps commanders and artillery controlled at a senior level.[14] This is not *FSR*. All the evidence suggests that few in the senior ranks of the British Army supported Haig's decision to abandon the *FSR* principles of infantry-artillery combination at every stage of an attack in the pursuit of victory, and of giving up the division as the unit devising its own preparations for attack. Rawlinson is one of the most studied corps commanders, and attention is repeatedly drawn to his propensity to ask divisional commanders for their views before coordinating a corps attack. That is *FSR*, and so is his championing of 'bite and hold', also addressed in Robin Prior and Trevor Wilson's assessment of his command capabilities.[15] Robertson and Du Cane, even Kiggell, all express views consistent with *FSR* in their various critiques of the battles of 1915. A belief in the

13 Jones, 'The Problem of the Western Front', in Jones (ed.), *Courage without Glory,* pp.52–53.
14 Patrick Watts, 'Douglas Haig and the Planning of the Battle of Neuve Chapelle', in Jones (ed.), *Courage without Glory*, pp.192–194.
15 Prior and Wilson, *Sir Henry Rawlinson*, pp.25,79.

necessity of adherence to *FSR* seems to have permeated the senior ranks of French's advisers. How could it not when the pre-war careers of Robertson, Wilson, Du Cane, Rawlinson and Kiggell, amongst many others based in England for the pre-war period, had been shaped by its centrality to their professionalism?

An instinct to adhere to *FSR* permeated the junior ranks as well. Alexander Kearsey's book, written in 1929, as a response to James Edmond's *Official History* of the Western Front battles of 1915, has already been discussed. His book, which, such was the interest, went to a second edition in 1930, gently challenges Edmond's bland accounts of these battles, with a forensic analysis of them with reference to *FSR*.[16] If *FSR* was still considered relevant by those who lived through these battles 15 years after the events described in them, it is difficult to argue that they were not relevant at the time. Kearsey confines himself to tactical regulations. In his book, he addresses the battles of Aubers Ridge, Festubert and Loos. In his narrative of the Battle of Loos, he identifies 26 occasions when *FSR* supplied guidance, which can be broken down into 12 instances where the British Army complied and 14 instances where they did not.[17] The book is non-judgmental, and he names no names, but he implies that, in his view, the attacks should have complied more closely with *FSR*.

The debate about the battles of 1915 is key to Haig's operational reputation. Was Haig right to jettison much of the baggage of *FSR* in his conduct of the battles? Possibly. Did he ask for changes to be made to the binding regulations that determined the way the army worked in 1915? No, he did not. Without question, his offensives failed, and they failed badly. Partly, they failed because he did not, indeed could not, implement his own belief that artillery 'forms the skeleton of battle', and should be directed by the Commander-in-Chief on the field. There were too few guns and too little ammunition, but, more significantly, the structure to implement this ambition was not in place. Haig was not afraid to challenge existing command structures. He had already done so in illegally giving Horne operational responsibilities and appointing him Commander Royal Artillery in his First Corps, but there is no evidence that he was aware that many of the officers he was working with were very uncomfortable about him doing so.

The Artillery Command Structure in 1915

As Major General Noel Birch, Haig's Artillery Adviser at GHQ, put it in July 1916, and it was a process that started in 1915, the *FSR* regulations laid down that the corps:

> … Artillery Adviser, though it is distinctly laid down that he is neither a Staff Officer nor a Commander, has become a fighting officer, and has had to assume a position that he … is not entitled to. He allots his guns, controls his ammunition, supervises the artillery fights, etc … Corps Artillery Commanders …[have] already assumed these duties … to a great extent … through the personality of individuals and not from GHQ direction.[18]

16 Kearsey, *1915 Campaign in France, in relation to the Field Service Regulations.*

17 Kearsey, *1915 Campaign in France*, pp.39–62.

18 Noel Birch, Uniacke Papers, RAI, U/III/13, memos to Kiggell of 8/6/16, as referenced in Marble, 'The infantry cannot do with a gun less', Ph.D. thesis, Appendix, pp.192–195.

In practice, this meant that every divisional Commander Royal Artillery (CRA) had a different relationship with his counterpart at corps level. The problems of artillery command were compounded in February 1915 when heavy artillery started to arrive in greater quantity. The 60-pounder batteries of four guns, which had gone to France with each of the first six divisions, were no longer under divisional control as a permanent arrangement. The Army Artillery Adviser was charged with maintaining them, in line with his QMG advisory function, and then he allocated them to those divisions which would most benefit from having them. The first medium-heavy howitzers were allocated to corps and theoretically similarly allocated. But the heavy tractor-drawn guns (8 inch and above) were collected into Heavy Artillery Reserve (HAR) Groups by the War Office and allotted, after consultation with GHQ, to the army where they could best contribute. Brigadier generals, commanding these groups, were based at the army HQ, but were outside the army commander's operational staff.[19] This unsatisfactory arrangement arose because the War Office, guided by *FSR*, saw no alternative but to create these groups in this fashion. French, as C-in-C, did not dictate a desirable artillery command structure, as, under *FSR*, he had the right and duty to do, despite the oft-expressed anxieties of his Artillery Adviser.

Rawlins systematically records the stop-gap orders that were issued during 1915 to commanders and advisers alike, without reference to the impact that any one order would have on artillery arrangements elsewhere. Thus, counter-battery operations, for instance, were given to the Heavy Artillery Reserve Groups – without reference to divisional CRAs who, at the time, were doing most of this work. HAR commanders took over responsibility for collating reconnaissance information from the Royal Flying Corps, their attached balloon companies, and survey companies that were locating hostile batteries. But many enemy field batteries were close to the front line, known to the divisional field artillery, and best attacked under local control. The general confusion is summed up by Rawlins:

> Thus, there came about the vicious system whereby the responsibility for artillery direction on the front of a corps was vested partly in the divisional artilleries (nominally, but only nominally, under corps direction) and partly in those H.A.R. groups which were entirely outside corps direction. The inevitable result was that any intended operation brought about a whole series of artillery conferences at which were present each divisional C.R.A. and H.A.R. Group Commander concerned. The Corps Artillery Adviser (or Advisers) attended and also the Army Artillery Adviser; but as these senior officers' status was purely advisory, it naturally followed that these conferences were usually marked by long discussions, sometimes amicable, sometimes heated, between a host of independent artillery officers.[20]

Sanders Marble, in his thesis on *the Place of the Artillery in the British Expeditionary Force, 1914-1918*, is less measured: 'Bureaucratic infighting dogged every change (those that happened and also those that were only proposed) in the artillery chain of command, and it must be said that this was a complete waste of effort.'[21] Waste of effort it may have been, but the debates were a direct consequence of attempting to force a new and necessary command level into a structure

19 Rawlins, *British Artillery in France*, p.45.
20 Rawlins, *British Artillery in France*, pp.91–92.
21 Marble, 'The infantry cannot do with a gun less', Ph.D. thesis, p.181.

that had already been fixed by the regulations of *FSR, Part II*, and by the implications that any suggested changes might have on the operational principles laid down in *Part I.* Marble, despite basing some of his work on Rawlins, consistently understates the impact of *FSR*, both on command and tactics. In Sheffield and Todman's *Command and Control*, he presents an analysis of the military career of General Herbert Uniacke, an early HAR commander and one of very few artillery generals who preserved useful papers. Marble's account not only describes the dangerously divided responsibilities in the artillery hierarchy but also the frustrations Uniacke endured throughout the war. He was side-lined by Rawlinson in preparations for the Battle of Loos and for a long period was prevented from signing off his own orders. Based in army HQ, he had clear views on how counter-battery work should be conducted, and he aligned with Gough in his belief that the heavy artillery, for which he was responsible, and by extension, the lighter artillery as well, should be directed at corps, if not army level.[22] Ignoring *FSR* in this article, Marble misses an opportunity to generalise his personal story to other commanders who experienced similar command constraints and similar resistance from divisions as they tried to utilise their skills and resources in ways that sometimes adhered to, sometimes challenged, *FSR* rules and principles on both command and tactical deployment.

CDS 50, *Tactical Notes*, records the ineffectiveness of many artillery barrages in 1915, saying that they were frequently directed 'on open spaces of ground', thereby wasting ammunition.[23] But there is no analysis as to why this should have happened. Rawlins explains that while it was recognised that all the guns of a corps, that is, those of its two divisions, needed to cooperate in the initial barrage, it was then desirable for each divisional commander to direct his own guns in a way that maximally supported his own infantry. *FSR* did not admit the possibility of two divisions working in tandem in a single attack. In the absence of a defined artillery command structure, there was no mechanism by which artillery cooperation between two divisions could be satisfactorily achieved. At Neuve Chapelle, a coordinated artillery timetable, according to Rawlins, 'was introduced' for the first time. 'The artillery of the 7th Division was placed under the orders of the C.R.A. 8th Division for the preliminary bombardment and for the original assault, reverting to the command of the C.R.A. 7th Division when his division attacked … This did not work well.'[24] At the Battle of Givenchy, 'the CRA, 7th Division' retained the responsibility for controlling the artillery of several divisions, so that he 'was, in practice, required to "exercise control" over a very large concentration of guns.' This did not work well either. Hutchison, observing with the Canadian divisional artillery at Givenchy, graphically describes the chaos and confusion that the slow communications consequent on another division directing the targets for his division's guns engendered. When they were ordered to fire on new targets, they were given no time for the necessary registration.[25] Unsurprisingly, their fire landed 'on open spaces.'

Du Cane, French's Artillery Adviser, in writing to William Robertson, his chief-of-staff, noting the problems engendered by asking divisional commanders to act up, observed that

22 Sanders Marble, 'Command of Artillery: the case of Herbert Uniacke', in Sheffield and Todman (eds), *Command and Control,* pp.195–209: see also Jackson Hughes, 'The Monstrous Anger of the Guns, the Development of British Artillery Tactics, 1914 – 1918', Ph.D. thesis, Adelaide University,1992, which also ignores *FSR* entirely.

23 CDS 50, *Tactical Notes,* July 1915, sections 8, 9.

24 Rawlins, *British Artillery in France,* p.94.

25 Hutchison, *The Young Gunner,* pp.72–78.

'IV Corps operations demonstrated the need of an [overall] artillery commander.'[26] Problems were not confined to the direction of the field artillery and field howitzers supporting divisional infantry attacks at these battles. The heavy guns which had arrived on the Western Front, directed by commanders, based at, but independent of, army headquarters, needed to be included in corps planning. Andy Simpson, in his thesis on corps command, goes into the detail of Haig's arrangements for these battles, fruitlessly trying to equate them with *FSR*.[27] But, with command responsibilities inappropriately arranged by compliance with *Part II*, and Haig ignoring the strictures on divisional control laid down in *Part I*, like many before and after him, he fails to understand the multiple roots of the problems. Haig was not following *FSR*. He neither wrote it nor believed in it. He abrogated French's responsibility for the ultimate control of battles. He demanded corps, not divisional, planning of attacks. He accepted that there was, anyway, too little artillery. Of necessity, and by inclination, he ignored the *FSR* principle that infantry required artillery support at all stages of battle.

Haig believed, with some justification, that the artillery ought to be coordinated on a corps front, in breach of *FSR*. He also believed that the divisions should be firmly directed in the detail of their manoeuvres by orders from above, again in breach. Haig's style forced both French and his senior subordinates to adopt a military philosophy which was at odds with their own. Their personal duties and responsibilities were being challenged and modified. *FSR* required French to clearly define intent and final positions with his operation orders. Haig abrogated the right to decide both intent and final positions. *FSR* required that divisional commanders be directed to prepare their own plans of attack. Haig demanded that his corps commanders, such as Rawlinson, usurp their authority and come up with coordinated plans involving more than one division, without ensuring that this was feasible, given the artillery command structure and ammunition deficiencies of 1915.[28]

French was guided by *FSR* in his thinking, but had a relaxed approach to its detail. It has already been shown that he refused to take the responsibility he should have taken in addressing logistic and artillery command inefficiencies. He tolerated Haig's independent approach to command at Mons during the first days of the war. And now, in the battles of 1915, he seems to have given up on trying to direct Haig. But most of his staff and most of Haig's subordinates, including Rawlinson, were highly aware of the strictures of *FSR* and uncomfortable with significant deviations from it.

Preparatory Measures

Following the obvious failure of Haig's offensives, a report was put together by the General Staff at GHQ. In early February 1916, *Preparatory Measures to be taken by Armies and Corps before undertaking Offensive Operations on a large scale* was issued.[29] This was not distributed in the SS

26 Rawlins, *British Artillery in France*, p.5.
27 Simpson, 'British Corps Command', pp.37–38.
28 Simpson, 'British Corps Command', pp.37–38.
29 Brigadier General J. E. Edmonds, *Official History of the Great War, Military Operations France & Belgium, 1916, Volume 1, Appendices* (London: MacMillan, 1932), Appendix 16, 'Preparatory Measures to be taken by Armies and Corps before undertaking Offensive Operations on a large scale' General Staff GHQ, February 1916, pp.91–124.

series and is directed just at senior officers for planning purposes. However, in its detail and scope, it seems to represent a determined attempt not to repeat the mistakes of the 1915 battles. A great deal of work is suggested on communications and protection. Reserve and support arrangements should be planned in the greatest detail. Reconnaissance is emphasised, on both sides of the line, to ensure good fields of fire and observation for artillery. Unsurprisingly, in a document addressed to senior officers, *FSR* is not specifically invoked, but, notably, the division is regarded as the primary unit, and not the corps: 'A divisional commander, to whom a definitive objective is assigned, should have under his orders the artillery which is necessary to enable him to carry out his task. This will include not only the normal divisional artillery but such other guns as are detailed to prepare his objective for assault.'[30] Divisions were also told to make provision for an early artillery advance over both sets of trenches, the limits of artillery support for the infantry without such an advance having been determined before the battle started. All this was *FSR* compliant. It is a long document, with appendices describing arrangements made by Haig's First Army for the opening day of the Battle of Loos in September 1915. It seems likely that most of it was written while French was still Commander-in-Chief, and that Major General John Du Cane, French's Artillery Adviser, was involved since there is more than usual emphasis on the artillery.

Jim Beach's article on 'Doctrine Writing at British GHQ' in 1917 and 1918 is authoritative and invaluable. As he observes: 'Surveying the 1916 output, one is struck by the relatively small number of pamphlets and their low-level focus', and how they genuflect 'towards the pre-war Field Service Regulations (FSR), with the earlier guidance being noted in regard to the "general principles" of an attack, advanced guards, reconnaissance, operations orders, and frontages.'[31] He makes no attempt to describe CDS 50, *Tactical Notes*, issued by GHQ in July 1915, which is not compliant with *FSR*. He is referring principally to SS 101, *Notes for Infantry Officers on Trench warfare*, which, significantly, was issued by the War Office, not GHQ, only a month after *Preparatory Notes*.

SS 101

SS 101, *Notes for Infantry Officers on Trench warfare*, issued in March 1916, was, as its title implies, advice for infantry officers, principally, presumably, for officers of the new divisions now being deployed into action. It is almost a stand-alone document for junior officers, describing their duties in a front-line trench and emphasising how front-line officers should always work closely with their artillery counterparts, establishing communications and observation points and then liaising closely with them in both defence and attack, although not even once does it reference *FSR*.[32] The exact command structure of the batteries in close support of battalions and brigades is not laid out, allowing divisional CRAs to make that decision for themselves in line with *FSR*, but advice is given for artillery support of an infantry attack, which is worth quoting in full.

30 Edmonds, *Official History, 1916 Appendices*, p.93.
31 Beach, 'Doctrine Writing', pp.468, 489.
32 SS 101, *Notes for Infantry Officers on Trench Warfare March 1916* (London: War Office, 1916), pp.44–45, 52–55, 59–61, 71–72.

Action of Artillery during the Assault: At the moment fixed for assault, artillery fire must lift from the actual places to be assaulted, but must be kept up on the immediate flanks of the attack. Once the assault has been launched, the duty of the artillery is :

a) To keep down the fire of the hostile artillery. This is done by the counter-batteries.
b) To prevent the enemy bringing up supports and reserves, by keeping up steady fire on his communication trenches and other lines of approach and places in rear where troops might collect for counter-attack.
c) To give continuous support to the infantry during their advance and to deal with obstacles, strong points, &c., which may be holding them up.

The difficulties of this latter task are almost entirely those of observation and intercommunication. It is often impossible owing to smoke, dust, &c., to see exactly where the infantry have got to, and what is stopping their progress. The obtaining of timely information from the advanced troops presents great difficulties, and will depend largely on the efficiency of our counter-battery work. If the enemy guns are not silenced, they will form a barrage behind our attacking troops which will make the sending back of information exceedingly uncertain. The measures to be taken to ensure, so far as possible, continued artillery support to the infantry during the advance are as follows

a) A proportion of field guns dug in close to our front trenches are useful to cover the flanks and give close support to the infantry.
b) Battery commanders must place themselves where they can best see the general situation and keep touch with their batteries, and must be prepared to act on their own initiative, in the absence of information and orders from above.
c) Each battery must have a forward observing officer, whose duties are to keep in touch with the infantry commander whom the battery is supporting, to keep the battery commander informed as to the exact position of the infantry, and to assist him in ranging onto anything that is checking the progress of our infantry. The forward observing officer must be provided with telephone and signalling equipment.[33]

This, in describing the duties and responsibilities of divisional officers, is, as Beach says, completely compatible with *FSR*. *FSR* does not envisage the artillery concentrating on counter-battery work during an infantry advance. But this update is entirely logical, assuming that some medium-heavy guns are attached to the divisional artillery. It describes with great clarity the duty of battery commanders to use their initiative in helping the infantry out if they encounter difficulties in their advance.

33 SS 101, *Notes for Infantry Officers March 1916*, pp.60–61.

Summary

Making general conclusions about *FSR* compliance during 1915 is complicated by the existence of doctrinal differences between Smith-Dorrien's command and Haig's, against a background of inexperience and lack of training which permeated all levels of the army. A lack of uniform doctrinal leadership from French adds to the difficulties. Later, in 1914, Haig led his corps and, into 1915, his army, almost independently of his Commander-in-Chief. As Gardner, in *Trial by Fire*, describes of 1914, and Nick Lloyd, in his article on 'Haig's Command of First Army' confirms, Haig had great autonomy from Field Marshal French and GHQ.[34] French was exhausted by his responsibilities and apparently happy for Haig to assume independence in the direction of his First Army. French found Smith-Dorrien hard work and his assertive compliance with *FSR*, in contrast to Haig's alternative and politically popular ideas, was becoming a divisive influence, which was impinging on French's authority. One of them had to go. It was Smith-Dorrien's proposal to give up some ground in a damaging salient, in line with a pragmatic regulation in *FSR*, that gave French the opportunity to force Smith-Dorrien's departure.[35] He promoted the much more emollient Herbert Plumer in May 1915, despite him holding very similar views to Smith-Dorrien.

In early 1915, and particularly in II Corps, III Corps and the Second Army, *FSR* was the defining doctrine followed, as recommended by the War Office in London, albeit it did not, in passive trench warfare, appear entirely suitable for the existing conditions. Inexperience and ignorance mitigated its universal observation, and the bureaucratisation of industrial warfare, coupled with shell shortages and rationing, nearly caused its demise. However, it was so obviously applicable to defensive and small offensive encounters that most new line officers were happy to learn from their more experienced regular colleagues and apply it to their jobs. French allowed Haig to deviate very significantly from its principles and conduct a series of large offensives based on his own vision of warfare. Those at GHQ had little choice but to go along with the experiment, but by the end of the year, there was a strong feeling in the War Office, and perhaps at GHQ too, that French and Haig had gone too far in rejecting some key *FSR* principles. This narrative is supported in the CDS and SS documentation issued up to the Spring of 1916.

34 Lloyd, 'Haig's Command of First Army', pp.1051–1076.
35 See *Field Service Regulations, Part I*, p.145.

17

Operational Review 1916 to 1917

The following documents are covered in this review:

CDS 98 1–4	*Artillery Notes,* January to April 1916
SS 109	*Training of Divisions for Offensive Action*, May 1916
SS 119	*Preliminary Notes on Tactical Lessons,* July 1916
SS 135	*Instructions – Training of Divisions for Offensive Action*, December 1916
SS 143	*Instructions – Training of Platoons for Offensive Action*, February 1917
SS 148	*Forward Inter-communication in Battle*, March 1917

In the first few months of 1916, *Preparatory Measures before Offensive Operations* and SS 101 had seemed to re-impose tactical thinking as defined by *FSR*, but developments in the command structure of the artillery were incompatible with the concept of divisional integrity in an offensive. The principle of a divisional artillery commander directing his own artillery to support divisional objectives was all very well, but with brigades of artillery, and even batteries, allowed to switch targets on their own initiative, and with heavier guns being an intrinsic factor in a division's ability to achieve its objectives, it was obvious that corps artillery commanders should, at least to some extent, have a command function. However, any modification of command responsibilities away from that laid down in *FSR* had a direct impact on the duties and responsibilities of front-line officers, also as defined by *FSR*.

By early 1916, the command responsibilities for the various arms of the artillery had been somewhat clarified. In late 1915, Corps Artillery Advisers were designated General Officer Commanding, Royal Artillery (GOCRA), although their duties were not officially redefined.[1] It was still true, as Major General Noel Birch, Haig's Artillery Adviser at GHQ, said at the time, that 'though it is distinctly laid down that he is neither a Staff Officer nor a Commander, [he] has become a fighting officer, and [now] … allots his guns, controls his ammunition, supervises the artillery fights, etc. … through the personality of individuals.'[2] This meant that every divisional CRA still had a different relationship with his counterpart at corps level, largely

1 Rawlins, *British Artillery in France*, p.46.
2 Noel Birch, memo to Kiggell of 8/6/16, as referenced in Marble, 'The place of the artillery in the BEF, Appendix, pp.192–195.

depending on the army commander's views on the artillery. It was not until June 1916 that Haig seems to have turned his attention to the direction of his artillery. He authorised a letter to the War Office, asking that they recognise the actual state of affairs; that the divisional artillery had '48 – 18 pdrs. & 16 4.5in Hows.', that corps artillery 'consist of medium artillery', and that army artillery should 'consist of the heaviest artillery, including all that on railway mountings.' Heavy Artillery Groups (HAR) would continue to operate entirely outside of corps direction.[3] It is in that context that the CDS and SS documentation addressing tactical practice in 1916 needs to be interpreted.

CDS 98 Artillery Notes

It is not clear who issued the four volumes of CDS 98. *Number 1, Close Shooting in the Field* (January 1916) is highly technical and was required reading for all battery commanders. It describes innovations in practice that allowed far quicker registration.[4] It is likely that *Numbers 3 and 4* were issued by GHQ in France. *Number 3, Counter-Battery Work* states that 'just as the artillery forms the main support of the offensive, so also is it the strongest weapon of the defense', and is best discussed after consideration of *Number 4*.[5] *Number 4, Artillery in Offensive Operations* (April 1916) echoes SS 101 in demanding 'complete cooperation between the artillery and the infantry', going so far as to say that 'care must be taken to avoid cramping the initiative of the subordinate artillery commanders ... Normally, divisional artillery [that is, field guns and howitzers] will remain, both tactically and administratively, under the orders of the divisional commander.' The importance of reconnaissance, forward liaison, and close support of infantry attacks, by advancing some field artillery in their support, are all emphasised along the lines of *Preparatory Measures* of February, *SS 101* of March 1916 and *FSR Part 1*. 'Battery commanders ... once the attack has been launched must be prepared to act instantaneously on their own initiative.' As Jim Beach says, in his article on 'Doctrine Writing at British GHQ', all of this is consistent with achieving infantry-artillery combination by appropriate deployment of the artillery to support the attack and by demanding close liaison at divisional level, as recommended in *FSR*. But there is a kick in the tail. CDS 98/4 goes on to describe four possible scenarios of attack – 'an infantry brigade with artillery attached, a division, a corps, or an army.'[6]

> The principle that a divisional commander, to whom a definite objective is assigned, should have under his orders the artillery which is necessary to enable him to carry out his task, may often be inapplicable, as for instance where a corps attacks in depth and divisions succeed each other on the same front; for experience shows that any attempt to apply this

3 Rawlins, *British Artillery in France*, pp.50, 91–92.

4 CDS 98, *Artillery Notes. Number 1, Close Shooting in the Field* (January 1916), as reprinted in *Field Artillery Notes, No 1*, issued by the Army War College, Washington DC, May 1917.

5 CDS 98, *Artillery Notes. Number 3, Counter-Battery Work* (1916), as reprinted in *Field Artillery Notes, No 1*, issued by the Army War College, Washington DC, 1917, p.37.

6 CDS 98/4, *Artillery in Offensive Operations April 1916* (France: GHQ, 1916), IWM SS/CDS Pamphlets collection, as reproduced in William Sanders Marble, 'The infantry cannot do with a gun less: the place of the artillery in the BEF, 1914–1918', appendix 11.

> principle of attack in depth to the artillery is foredoomed to failure. Now, more than ever, the guns form the 'iron framework of the battle'; and all recent operations have proved the necessity for a carefully elaborated scheme for the employment of the whole of the artillery, involving a methodical allotment of tasks from the outset, and depending for its successful execution on an effective chain of artillery command.[7]

The next section allocates tasks for the various classes of the artillery, stating that after the initial attack, the divisional field guns and howitzers should confine their attention to 'counter battery work.'[8] In other words, in this document, it is proposed that the *FSR* defining principle of infantry artillery combination at the sub-divisional level be abandoned in major attacks.

The 'iron framework of battle' or as the German Regulations of 1906 put it, the 'skeleton of battle' was a feature of Haig's thinking at Mons and at the Aisne.[9] The problem then was the command structure that it required. It depended, as CDS 98/4 says, 'on an effective chain of artillery command.' Haig had needed, when in command of I Corps, a highly competent artillery commander, grounded in the detail of *FSR*, who could interpret his ideas on artillery and use tact and reasoned argument to persuade his divisional artillery commanders to comply with them. In 1914, he had found such a man in Henry Horne, his immediate subordinate. But sequentially in command of an Army in 1915, and all British forces on the Western Front in 1916, Haig did not find it so easy to direct his artillery according to his vision.

CDS 98, *Artillery Notes, Number 3, Counter-Battery Work*, makes a determined effort to define artillery command structure: 'The general officer commanding Royal Artillery of the army is charged with the coordination of all artillery action in both offense and defense.' Not quite so, since 'the general officer commanding Royal Artillery of the corps' is 'at all times, responsible … for the counter battery work of the corps.' Again, not quite so, since 'whenever hostile batteries can be seen active from ground observing stations, they should be promptly engaged', which would be within the sphere of divisional, or even brigade, artillery commanders.[10] Despite the highly specific definition of the different responsibilities of these individual commanders with respect to the coordination of intelligence from different sources such as air observation, balloons and survey company reports, in practice there was so much variation between command arrangements, at all levels, that trying to impose a consistent structure on the whole army in a mere guidance document was never going to work. It is worth repeating again the point Major General Noel Birch, Haig's Artillery Adviser at GHQ, made in July 1916 – 'Corps Artillery Advisers' had morphed into fighting officers, 'through the personality of individuals … and not from GHQ direction.' Technically, they were not even on the General Staff at either corps or army level. It was the personality of individuals that continued to define artillery command, not *FSR*, not GHQ directives, and not CDS pamphlets.

7 CDS 98/4, *Artillery in Offensive Operations April 1916*, section 6.
8 CDS 98/4, *Artillery in Offensive Operations April 1916*, sections 6 and 7.
9 *Drill Regulations for the Infantry, German Army, 1906*, p.72.
10 CDS 98, *Artillery Notes. Number 3, Counter-Battery Work*, pp.37–40.

SS 109

Less than a month after the issue of CDS 98/4, in May 1916, SS 109, *Training of Divisions for Offensive Action*, was published. This pamphlet is unusual in that it is signed off by 'L.E. Kiggell, Lieut. General, C.G.S. G.H.Q.' Kiggell had, as the pre-war Director of Staff Duties at the War Office, an encyclopaedic awareness of the content of *FSR*. In January 1913, he had stated, 'We know that the problems of war cannot be solved by rules, but by judgement based on a knowledge of general principles. For that reason, our manuals aim at giving principles but avoiding laying down methods.'[11] It is unsurprising, therefore, that SS 109 emphasises that 'the general principles laid down in our training manuals hold good, and special attention is directed to [those] Chapters [in] Field Service Regulations, Part I', which dealt with protection, reconnaissance, battle, and night operations. SS 109 said that 'it must be remembered that officers and troops generally do not now possess that military knowledge arising from a long and high state of training which enables them to act promptly on sound lines in unexpected situations. They have become accustomed to deliberate action based on precise and detailed orders.'[12] The implication is that this is a training document aimed at raw divisions in the run-up to the Somme. It refers only briefly to the artillery, and there is no suggestion that the divisional artillery might have to accept orders from a higher authority. Divisions are encouraged to plan second-phase bombardments to support their own infantry in major offences, contradicting CDS 98/4.

The Battle of the Somme

The 1st of July 1916 is a day etched on the consciousness of the British Army, but few accounts of it, even at the time, do more than generalise on the role the artillery played on that day, which makes an assessment of all arms combination next to impossible. Drawing conclusions as to whether the artillery combined with the infantry in the attacks, or merely cooperated with them with varying degrees of effectiveness as they had in 1915, is critical to measuring *FSR* compliance. It varied, of course, from corps to corps, and division to division. Each corps and division 'experimented with support and counter-battery fire in pursuit of its own ideas which varied in method and result', says Simon Innes-Robbins, comparing the Somme to battles later in the war.[13] An important factor was the level of competence of the artillery. Wire-cutting, for instance, required an accuracy that not all batteries were sufficiently skilled to achieve.[14]

The 7th Division produced a detailed summary report of their first days on the Somme in July 1916. It goes into considerable detail as to the performance of the various infantry brigades and their battalions, but there is almost no mention of the impact and effectiveness of the artillery support these units received.[15] It is necessary to delve into the artillery records to get details of

11 TNA: WO 279/48: General Staff Officers Conference, 13–16 January 1913, p17.
12 SS 109, *Training of Divisions for Offensive Action, May 1916, issued by GHQ*, sections 9 and 12.
13 Simon Innes-Robbins, 'From Vimy Ridge to Hill 70; General Sir Henry Horne and the Development of British Operational Art During 1917', in Spencer Jones (ed.), *The Darkest Hour: The British Army on the Western Front 1917* (Warwick: Helion, 2022), p.287.
14 See Hutchison, *The Young Gunner*, pp.122–124, for a description of the process in July 1916.
15 WO 95/1631/1: 7 Division, Narrative of Operations from 1st July to 5th July 1916. The report of the 20 Infantry Brigade is similar, but at its conclusion emphasises the importance of its close artillery support.

this. These are supported by a reliable eyewitness account. The 7th Division artillery records are good, and Hutchison kept a detailed journal of his days as a battery commander on the Somme. On the first day of the battle, the 7th Division can be adjudged to be following *FSR* in respect of infantry artillery combination. Quoting from the diary of the 22nd Brigade RFA on 30 June, 'telephone lines for F.O.O.s laid in an artillery trench, and by tunnel to beneath the enemy's front line.' As early as 8:55 a.m. the next day, all the batteries in the brigade were turned onto a German counterattack at Danzig Alley, which was on the far side of Mametz village and nearly 1,000 yards forward, 'by request of the generals commanding the infantry brigades.' Hutchison's 105th battery is referred to repeatedly:

> 9.36 am Fire of 105th on the east end of Mametz proved very effective. 11.07 am Our troops moved north-east into Danzig Alley out of Mametz as a burst of fire was delivered by 105th. 1.25pm Advance consolidated as 105th put on its final barrage. 7.10 pm 105th covering centre of Fritz Trench, supporting 2nd Queen's Surrey and 22nd Manchester's.

Hutchison was not only the battery commander but also a forward observer, directing the fire of his battery while his brigade commander selected the targets, liaising with his infantry counterparts.[16] These mini-barrages were not pre-planned.

Hutchison also showed initiative at battery level. This involved him disregarding orders. *FSR* allowed subordinate officers so to do 'if he is conscientiously satisfied that he is acting as his superior, if present, would order him to.'[17] Hutchison wrote:

> The Manchesters were held up at their first objective, by about 100 German reserves, who took up position on a crest, soon after our artillery barrage, moving strictly to time, had got beyond them. I could see this party opening a heavy fire on our attacking troops. I stopped the fire of the battery and had all guns put onto this target, at the same time informing brigade headquarters. But, before fire could be opened, I was ordered to keep up the barrage fire as per programme. I switched the guns back onto the barrage away beyond, and hurried personally to the colonel. I got permission to fire on the Germans, and the battery did some very pretty shooting. The Col. told us the General was very pleased with the battery's work, but the delay cost us many casualties.

The next day:

> ...we could see very clearly that our men were badly held up attacking Fricourt. I got two guns shooting exactly where they were wanted. Then the colonel arrived, hot and tired, and wanted to know what I was shooting at and told me to stop. I have not been court-martialled, but fancy may have run it close. He did let me proceed when I told him the General had told us to shoot, (but not that this was some time after we had started).[18]

16 TNA: WO 95/1643/1: 22 Brigade, RFA, 1 July 1916.
17 *Field Service Regulations, Part I,* pp.31–32.
18 Hutchison, *The Young Gunner*, p.139.

An enquiry usually followed when a subordinate officer chose to exercise initiative in this way, but Hutchison got away with it, presumably with support from 'the general'. He might not have done so in another division.

There is no doubt that the 7th Division was a very effective regular division, commanded along traditional lines, which meant adhering as much as possible to *FSR*. At the Somme, Major General Sir Herbert Watts commanded, having served under Major General Sir John Capper until his death at the Battle of Loos in 1915. Rotton's 1915 paper on defence, already quoted, suggests that the division endeavoured to act by *FSR* at the time. This was not surprising since Capper served under Rawlinson at the Staff College in 1905.[19] He was then appointed Commandant of the Indian Staff College at Quetta. Paul Harris, in his paper on 'the Staff of the British Army', tells of Capper's authoritative teaching on setting up an *FSR*-compliant operational staff in 1912, after his return to England.[20] Simon Robbins, in his 2001 thesis on 'British Generalship', records that Capper wrote after one 1915 battle that his division 'seems to have been unsupported by any special artillery fire, and to have been isolated' in an attack, quietly pointing out, as many 1915 generals did, that *FSR* was not being followed in this respect. Watts, his successor, did not make the same mistake on the first day of the Somme. Haig called him a 'distinctly stupid man', though he promoted him to corps command, and General Sir Charles Bonham-Carter said that he 'had to rely heavily on his trained General Staff', which is a positive compliment if observance of *FSR* in this respect is a marker of competence.[21] One source asserts that Watts was fond of the *FSR*-compliant aphorism: 'The natural corollary of delegation of authority is intelligent supervision.' The 7th Division was in Henry Horne's XV Corps at the Somme. Horne had been a very competent commander of artillery in 1914 and an equally competent divisional commander of the regular 2nd Division in 1915. Simon Robbins describes his consultative leadership style and says that he, too, 'was heavily reliant on his staff.'[22] It is possible that this phrase was a contemporary euphemism for disdaining a dictatorial approach to command and complying with the *Staff Manual* in the organisation of one's operational staff. Hutchison was in a division whose leadership understood *FSR* despite its appalling casualties at First Ypres in 1914 and Loos in 1915.

However, in a huge offensive, directed as much at corps and army as division level, adherence to *FSR* in terms of infantry-artillery combination was sometimes prevented by firm operational orders. Hutchison's 'barrage, moving strictly to time', is a case in point. That was infantry-artillery cooperation at best, and disassociation at worst. It is not difficult to find examples where artillery fire provided no benefit for the infantry they were, in theory, supporting. The pressure put on infantry divisions to continue to press forward before their supporting artillery had caught up with their most recent advance led to a series of bloodbaths. The attacks on Mametz Wood by the 38th Welsh Division, also of XV Corps, are but two of many examples. The 7th Division infantry had rotated out of the line for a rest, and their artillery, having advanced only a mile or two over the original front-line trenches, remained there despite further infantry advances. Mametz Wood was barely in range. Nevertheless, their artillery was ordered

19 TNA: WO 33/2747: 'Report of a Conference Staff College, January 1905', pp.3–7.

20 Harris, 'The Staff of the British Army', pp.69–70.

21 Simon Robbins, 'British generalship on the Western Front in the First World War, 1914–1918', submitted for the degree of Ph.D. King's College, University of London 2001, pp.80, 161.

22 Simon Robbins, 'Henry Horne as Divisional Commander during 1915', in Jones (ed.), *Courage without Glory*, p.116.

to support the Welsh Division's attacks. For the first assault, on 6 July, both the 7th Division artillery diary and Hutchison's 22nd Artillery Brigade diary record a lack of ability to undertake forward observation, confusion as to the location of the Welsh infantry brigades, and a lack of accuracy in their fire due to the extreme range.[23] A Welsh battalion had to fall back due to being heavily shelled by a 7th Division battery.

But this was just a prelude to a further attack on 10 July by the Welsh on Mametz Wood. The Welsh Division commander had been sent home, and Watts took over temporarily with orders to press home an infantry attack at any cost. He obeyed orders. An artillery barrage was again provided by the 7th Division. All the same difficulties were encountered, and there were huge friendly fire casualties. The Germans had pulled many of their defenders out of the wood in anticipation of the attack. The infantry advanced too fast in some places and got held up in others. The Welsh lost about 4,000 men in the two attacks. At the Somme, as a generalisation, if the supporting artillery was close enough to observe their own fire, if their barrage was intelligently planned, based on detailed reconnaissance, and if the artillery was allowed to engage enemy strongpoints and respond to counter-attacks in real time, infantry attacks achieved limited objectives successfully. This responsiveness was seldom, if ever, achieved when the artillery of one division was supporting the infantry of another.

By 14 July, the 7th Division was back in the line and tasked with a major attack on Bazentin Wood. The attack was successful, though divisional casualties were heavy. The 22nd Brigade's diary states, 'Heavy barrage supplied,' this was preplanned with uplifts every 20 minutes, as shown in the artillery plan (see artillery plan overleaf). The diary continues, 'Counter attack repulsed by artillery fire. Various barrages supplied during the day to assist the infantry in consolidating positions.'[24] These later barrages were not in the artillery plan. They were reactive, based on reports from FOOs, and intelligent liaison – infantry-artillery combination. Success ensued.

The performance of many army and corps commanders on the Somme has been addressed by historians in recent years. Partly thanks to the work of Andy Simpson on 'Corps Command', it is generally recognised that *FSR* required the division to be the main fighting unit, and forbids micromanagement of subordinate units by very senior generals.[25] Not all corps and army commanders complied. David Tattersfield, in his paper on corps commanders, which is partly based on Simpson's work, suggests that 'many of the strengths and weaknesses of the different Corps can be explained by the personalities and abilities of the Corps commanders.' He contrasts Lieutenant General Sir Aylmer Hunter-Weston, of VIII Corps, who 'seems to have given his divisions no room for manoeuvre, his orders for the battle being very detailed', with Lieutenant General Sir Walter Congreve, of XIII Corps, who 'went into less detail.' He contrasts 'the consultative style' of Lieutenant General Earl Cavan, of XIV Corps, with the 'authoritarian approach' of Lieutenant General Edward Fanshawe of V Corps.[26] Although the 'personalities and abilities' of these various commanders are significant, the real contrast is between their degree of adherence to the principles of *FSR*, pertaining to their operation staff, the level at which operations should be planned and determined, and the extent to which artillery was allowed to be used by divisions in meaningful support of front-line infantry. A

23 TNA: WO 95/1643/1: 22 Brigade, RFA, 14 July 1916; WO 95/1639/2/1: 7 Division Artillery, July 1916.
24 TNA: WO 95/1643/1: 22 Brigade, RFA, 14 July 1916.
25 Simpson, 'British Corps Command', Ph.D. thesis, 2001.
26 Tattersfield, 'British Corps Commanders.'

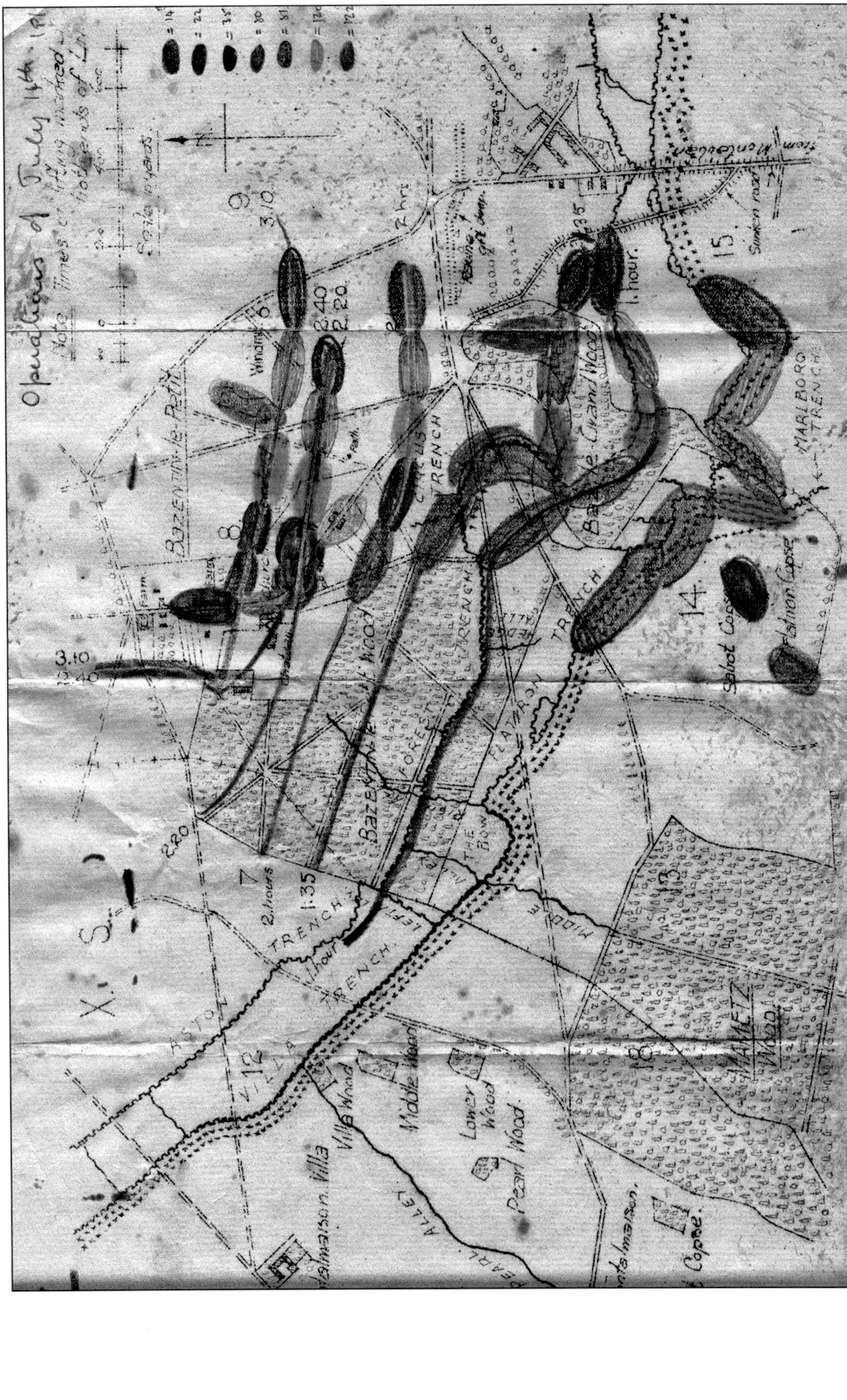

Bazentin barrage plan for 14 July 1916. This hand-drawn map was colour-coded for the individual batteries. (Author's collection)

consultative style correlated with a willingness to allow divisions to use their artillery to support their own attacks. Simpson describes Cavan's approach in planning an attack on Guillemont in August 1916.

> One of the most important points raised was that the GOCRA intended to consult divisional commanders over areas which required special artillery attention, and that although he would indicate the general lines of the barrages, divisions would work out the details. This argues for, if not actual decentralisation of the handling of the artillery, a reasonably high degree of latitude for divisions within the constraints of the GOCRA's plan, which was confirmed in the artillery order for the attack. As in some previous attacks, divisions regained control of their artillery at zero hour, apart from those 18-pounder guns taking part in the barrage and some of the 4.5in howitzers. Corps was exercising a co-ordinating role, not centralising for its own sake.[27]

Tattersfield says, 'The style of command also seems to have been affected by the Army Commander, who would also have had different ideas on how to use the Corps under him.'[28] Some army commanders even micromanaged their divisions.

One such was Hubert Gough, a commander who disdained any pretence of adhering to *FSR* almost from the first week of the war. Gary Sheffield and Helen McCartney, writing in 2006, say that, from 1915, he 'appeared to depart from the principles' of *FSR*, and 'Major General Thesiger [commanding the 9th (Scottish) Division at Loos] was not the only subordinate commander to interpret *Field Service Regulations* in a different manner from Gough.'[29] Sheffield and McCartney are referring here only to the principle of divisional autonomy in *FSR*, but there were many other principles that Gough ignored during his tenures of command. As they subsequently point out, 'Gough's approach differed significantly from other tacticians in the British Army … Rawlinson and Plumer were developing a methodical approach to operations … with the aid of comprehensive artillery support. However, Gough's optimistic breakthrough methods were precisely why Haig' – who they assert had 'largely crafted' *FSR* – 'chose his Fifth Army to later spearhead the main attack around Ypres on 31 July 1917 as it was Gough's views that accorded most closely with those of Haig himself.'[30]

SS 119

The Battle of the Somme started on 1 July 1916, and before the end of the month, a further pamphlet SS 119, *Preliminary Notes on the Tactical Lessons of the Recent Operations*, was published. It is aimed squarely at divisional officers. It begins with the statement 'that the general principles laid down for the Training of Divisions for Offensive Action (SS 109) were correct'. SS 109 is essentially *FSR* compliant, and so is SS 119. But where SS 109 glosses over the role of

27 Simpson, 'British Corps Command', Ph.D. thesis, pp.65–66.
28 Tattersfield 'British Corps Commanders.'
29 Gary Sheffield and Helen McCartney 'Hubert Gough', in Ian Beckett and Steven Corvi (eds), *Haig's Generals*, pp.81–83.
30 Sheffield and McCartney, 'Hubert Gough', pp.81, 86.

the artillery, SS 119 places much more emphasis on the importance of artillery support for infantry during an attack.[31] In three short paragraphs on cooperation between infantry and artillery in attack, it emphasises the critical importance of combination. Although nowhere are the field artillery advised to advance with the infantry to ensure they were in effective range, it implies that they had done so. It discusses the consolidation of captured strongpoints by the Royal Engineers, with outposts being constructed ahead of the main line, and 'with supports and reserves to be echeloned in depth', in compliance with *FSR* principles pertaining to defence in depth. It endorses *FSR* principles on staff work, liaison, and communication of information, too: 'Sufficient time must be given by the higher staffs for lower formations to prepare for' a further attack, implying a methodical approach. Last-minute changes in orders, including artillery timetables, must be avoided. 'Good liaison is of the utmost importance, not only from front to rear but also laterally … In some brigades, battalion headquarters are not allowed to move forward without permission from the brigade. This hampers initiative.'[32] There is nothing in this document which endorses heavy-handed top-down control of front-line activity.

SS 135

SS 135, *Instructions for the Training of Divisions for Offensive Action*, issued in December 1916, is, on the face of it, more of the same.[33] It advises that once the initial attack has been successful, the enemy's prepared positions or 'improvised defences' overcome, and a pre-planned objective line reached, 'some hours' should be taken to allow for consolidation, reconnaissance and to plan a further attack. But the main point of the pamphlet is to revise the instructions to divisions as to their artillery preparations for a major new offensive: 'The following instructions apply specially to methodical attacks against prepared positions. Training for open warfare will be carried out on the principles laid down in Field Service Regulations.'[34] This implies that a conscious decision has been taken at GHQ that some *FSR* principles were not applicable to, and should not be followed, in 'methodical attacks'. All divisional artillery, says SS 135, will accept 'detailed instructions' from the 'G.O.C., R.A. of the Army.' 'The divisional commander, having been allotted his task by corps and informed generally of the artillery plan', is to carry out his own reconnaissance and form his own plan. This revived the proposal in SS 98/4 that corps should direct all the artillery in major attacks, leaving almost no role for the divisional artillery commander – 'The artillery preparations now lie to a certain extent outside the province of the divisional commander.' This meant a potentially reduced role for the divisional commander as well, since he was to be allocated tasks which had already been defined by the artillery plan, which would have sketched out the mode and pace of the attack. There is reference to liaison with artillery, but it was specifically banned at battalion level, and procedural obstacles were placed in the way of it even at infantry brigade level. The brigadier general had to make representations to an 'artillery liaison officer' from corps if he wanted to make any changes. In

31 TNA: WO 95/1631/1: 7 Division, Narrative of Operations from 1st July to 5th July 1916.

32 SS 119, *Preliminary Notes on the Tactical Lessons of the Recent Operations, issued by General Staff, General Headquarters, July 1916*, sections.1, 8–10, 14–15.

33 SS 135, *Instructions for the Training of Divisions for Offensive Action, issued by British General Staff, December 1916* is quite distinct from SS 135, *The Division in Attack*, issued in November 1918.

34 SS 135, *Training of Divisions for Offensive Action, December 1916*, p.8.

contrast to previous guidance, there is no reference to battery commanders being allowed to use their initiative. The principle of top-down control of divisions, denying them local flexibility, is being reasserted.[35]

Reorganisation of the Field Artillery

It was also in December 1916 that a major reorganisation of the field artillery was being planned, with significant tactical implications. During the Battle of the Somme, field artillery and field howitzers were attached to divisions. However, the infantry of a division cycled in and out of the front line on short respite breaks, leaving their artillery in situ, until the division was allowed a prolonged rest break, which included the artillery. This led to difficulties since the artillery of the division whose infantry were rotating out on a respite break had no prior links with the incoming division, and no formal mechanism for establishing them. Communications had to be directed back to corps and then out again to the relieving division. An additional problem was that artillery batteries still moved with more frequency than was desirable. It was calculated that on any one day, 80 batteries were on the move on the Western Front. As Rawlins describes, the loss of firepower, the strain on horses, and the damage done to roads and cables were all significant problems caused by this excessive movement.[36] Even before the publication of SS 135, a solution was being sought.

Following a fundamental review, Birch, at GHQ proposed a new, dual, command structure for the field artillery, which was approved by Haig, his C-in-C. Divisions would drop to an establishment of two enlarged artillery brigades of four six-gun batteries, with all the surplus guns being put under army control. Just under half the available artillery would thus be unlinked from any divisional hierarchy. This cohort would be organised into similarly constituted and newly created Army Field Artillery Brigades. The army would then allocate these new brigades to corps, for attachment to those front-line divisions that would benefit from additional artillery support. 'A new organization can seldom, if ever, have been so quickly and satisfactorily resolved,' Rawlins records.

By 10 November 1916, the scheme for this massive reorganisation of the field artillery had been drafted. On 13 November, the proposal was sent to the War Office, and on 13 December, approval was granted for all but the Dominion Forces, who vigorously protested losing control over some of their own units. There were undoubtedly pros and cons for the men involved. Those allocated to army brigades lost their divisional identity and support, which in turn limited promotion prospects. But poorly performing four-gun batteries were broken up and reallocated to six-gun batteries. There were fewer, but larger, artillery brigades, and both these changes encouraged increased professionalism. There were tactical advantages, too. When divisions cycled out of the line, army brigades remained in position. For the army brigades, this meant short periods of duty under a series of divisional commanders who did not necessarily have identical priorities, but it did ensure that there was continuity of protection in the sector being covered, particularly where corps encouraged the principle of field artillery groups, where the

35 SS 135, *Training of Divisions for Offensive Action, December 1916,* pp.82–84.
36 Rawlins, *British Artillery in France*, p.37.

most experienced brigade commanders were given control of all the field artillery in a sector, be they divisional or army.

While this reorganisation was being put together by GHQ, and just before the plan was presented to the War Office, GHQ consulted army commanders as to their opinion on the proposals. Their responses, during the second half of November, came too late to lead to any modifications in its speedy implementation. Meanwhile, the Dominion's contingents quickly dropped their objections, and the reorganisation proceeded through the first months of 1917.[37]

'Armies' remarks on the proposed scheme were on the whole distinctly favourable,' says Rawlins. 'The Fifth Army [however] stood out for the abolition of Divisional Artillery in favour of Corps Field Artillery on the plea that the Corps had become the fighting unit.' Rawlins continues that, 'This view received no encouragement.' But that is not to say that 'this view' had never been encouraged. Not only CDS 98, of April 1916, and now, SS 135, implied support for this view.

The Fifth Army was commanded by Sir Hubert Gough. His proposal to abolish divisional artillery was not entirely unreasonable. However, it had the very considerable disadvantage that divisions would have to plan a coordinated defence in response to a local attack with corps, an unnecessary complexity, and one that breached an *FSR* principle that a division was responsible for its own defence. Such an emasculation of the divisions had never been formally proposed with such bluntness before, but back in May 1916, GHQ had decided to reorganise ammunition supply to divisions. Brigade ammunition columns were abolished, and divisional ammunition columns were put partially under the control of corps. GHQ explained at the time why this decision was made: 'Our present organization was designed to ensure independence of movement for the divisions; in future the Corps will be the unit for marching and fighting and will probably have to accommodate itself to the frontage formerly occupied by a division.' In response to protests from divisions, GHQ explained that the change had been made as much on pragmatic grounds as doctrinal. The roads to the front line were too small in many places, and there was not enough parking space. But they did repeat that the 'Corps has replaced the division as the unit for marching and fighting', on very thin evidence since it was divisions, not corps, which cycled in and out of the trenches for periods of rest.[38] Nobody below corps level accepted this GHQ assertion, and it was not repeated in any SS pamphlets.

SS 135

Both CDS 98/4 of April 1916, and SS 135 *Instructions for the Training of Divisions for Offensive Action December 1916*, issued by GHQ, authorised, during an offensive, the relegation of divisional artillery commanders to little more than postmen between corps artillery commanders and their brigades – 'The direction of the Artillery operations rests with the Army Commander who may direct the G.O.C., R.A. of the Army formations.'[39] This was an attack on the fundamental *FSR* principle, which designated the division as an autonomous all-arms unit in battle. SS 135 did, however, in its small print, allow considerable latitude to both army and corps

37 Rawlins, *British Artillery in France*, pp.37–40.
38 Rawlins, *British Artillery in France*, pp.33–34.
39 SS 135, *The Training of Divisions for Offensive Action, December 1916*, p.9.

commanders to dilute this basic message. CDS 98/4 had given the same message and was, as has been described, widely ignored on the Somme. As Fox, in *Learning to Fight*, says 'it is important to note that, within [SS] pamphlets, there was built in latitude for interpretation which formations and individuals could take advantage of as their experience and expertise increased.'[40] More important than experience and expertise was belief, or otherwise, by formations and individuals, in the importance of compliance with fundamental *FSR* principles.

Simpson devotes an entire chapter to SS 135 in his study of corps command.[41] He makes the important point that very senior officers could interpret SS 135 as authorising a directive command style with little effective consultation through corps to division. But there are also, in the small print of SS 135, many injunctions for corps command to consult with divisions, particularly in relation to reconnaissance and the planning of infantry assaults. Simpson describes how Lieutenant General Sir Charles Fergusson, in submitting his XVII Corps plan for the battle of Arras in early 1917, 'favoured a consultative management style, and was not prepared to dictate – at [an early] stage of operations – to the man on the spot', and that this approach 'may be taken as typical of those submitted by the corps in Third Army.' Simpson then goes on to say that the evidence suggests that Allenby, the Third Army commander, had 'a prescriptive style, which would accord with the general view of his character.' Crucial as to how an offensive was planned in 1917 was the extent of consultation down to divisional and infantry brigade level. If commanders believed, along the lines of *FSR*, that the division, with supporting artillery, was the fighting unit, this consultation was generally good. If they thought that the corps, backed by an army artillery plan, was the fighting unit, it was generally not. Every army and corps commander had a slightly different approach to planning, and an assumption that any corps plan in 1917 was 'typical' is a rash one.[42]

SS 135 did not ignore *FSR* principles at a sub-divisional level altogether.[43] Simpson says:

> Though corps retained control of the barrage during the attack, divisions [could be] allotted a number of batteries to deal with unforeseen circumstances on their front. Interestingly, the desire to leave this form of reaction to events down to the man on the spot was so strong that the GOC division was permitted to delegate some of this artillery power down to brigade.[44]

SS 135 acknowledges that the *FSR*-compliant principle of infantry-artillery combination at sub-divisional level, and the command structure to support this, might be the preferred approach of some commanders, despite what is said elsewhere in the document.

There is a further ambivalence in the document, again an *FSR* principle under challenge. *FSR* states that the capture of any 'tactical point will constitute a distinct engagement in itself … All important tactical points should, when gained, at once, be put into a state of defence, so that [counter attacks] … may be defeated.'[45] *FSR*, and SS 135, advised that a 'methodical attack' should stop when the last identified tactical objective of the day was achieved. This point should

40 Fox, *Learning to Fight,* p.85.
41 Simpson, 'British Corps Command', Ph.D. thesis, chapter 3, pp.84–113.
42 Simpson, 'British Corps Command', Ph.D. thesis, pp.94–96.
43 SS 135, *Training of Divisions for Offensive Action, December 1916*, pp.13–14.
44 Simpson, 'British Corps Command', Ph.D. thesis, p.89.
45 *Field Service Regulations, Part I,* p.136.

then be consolidated, and the planning necessary to effect it is described in SS 135 in considerable detail. Engineers and pioneers should follow close behind the front-line assault, preparing a track through the devastated landscape suitable for pack animals and artillery if possible. They and the infantry already in situ at the captured tactical point should construct new strongpoints, with outposts in front, and supports behind – defence in depth – to ensure that any gains made are retained. The initial consolidation was projected to take about six hours, after which time, organised, as opposed to small local, enemy counterattacks might be expected. A pre-planned barrage should have been registered on the ground in front of them, to be activated in the event of a counterattack.[46] This is all *FSR* compliant.

But the next section of SS 135 recommends that, in the absence of enemy resistance at the time the last objective was achieved, the forward troops should press on. 'In favourable circumstances, it has been found possible to advance the line 500 yards' beyond the agreed objective. The patrols to effect this further advance will move forward 'about half an hour' after the last planned objective has been reached, at the same time as the covering barrage was tailing off. If these patrols were successful in identifying a defensible line in front of the objective line, the consolidation should then be transferred to this new unplanned line.[47] There are obvious difficulties with this last-minute change in consolidation positions. It would take time to get this information back. Neither artillery nor engineers had the flexibility to respond to last-minute changes of plan. The principle of all arms combination at every stage of an advance was to be abandoned yet again. It also breaches *FSR* in the lack of prior reconnaissance before this advance and the lack of flank protection during it. It is a legacy of the tactics of 1915, with infantry pressing forward, unsupported, and hoping for a breakthrough.

In short, SS 135, *Instructions for the Training of Divisions for Offensive Action December 1916*, reveals evidence of a factional debate in the upper reaches of GHQ, and this debate was whether a fundamental principle of *FSR*, that of all arms combination at a sub-divisional level, at every stage of an advance, should, or should not, be jettisoned in some circumstances. Where an army commander positioned himself in this debate had great implications. It is noteworthy that Horne, at Arras in April 1917, perhaps because he was thoroughly aware of the difficulties caused to the artillery by last-minute changes of plan, did not approve any further advance beyond his stated final objective until his front line had been consolidated. It was 'the universal opinion of Divisional Commanders that if it was desired to press forward, a new objective should be allotted, another attack prepared and carried out, and that the ground so gained should be held.'[48] In other words, it was the 'universal opinion of Divisional Commanders' that *FSR* be followed, and the clause in SS 135, which advocated pressing on in the absence of resistance, be ignored. Required by his orders to continue the offensive, the appalling state of the ground in cold, wet weather prevented Horne's First Army from doing more than consolidating their success of 9 April, and, by 16 April, his army was bogged down.[49] This could perhaps have

46 SS 135, *Training of Divisions for Offensive Action, December 1916,* Section VII, 'Consolidation', pp.34–40, 42–45.
47 SS 135, *Training of Divisions for Offensive Action, December 1916,* Section VIII, 'Exploiting Success', pp.40–42.
48 Simon Innes-Robbins, 'From Vimy Ridge to Hill 70; General Sir Henry Horne and the Development of British Operational Art During 1917', in Spencer Jones (ed), *The Darkest Hour*, p.285, quoting IWM, Horne Papers 43/3, [GHQ], Notes on a visit to Verdun, 5–8 January 1917.
49 Innes-Robbins, 'Horne and British Operational Art During 1917', pp.290–294.

been foreseen if GHQ had prepared a thorough reconnaissance assessment before they issued further offensive orders, as required by *FSR*.

Three armies were involved in attacks at Arras in April 1917, and one in the attack on Messines Ridge of June 1917. All four armies accepted SS 135's proposal that the artillery plan should be under the overall control of the 'G.O.C., R.A. of the Army.' A crucial clause pertained to the divisional commander:

> It is the duty of the divisional commander to make himself thoroughly acquainted with the Artillery plan so far as it affects his task, and to bring to the notice of the corps commander any points that he considers require more preparation, or any modifications in the plan which he may think necessary to insure the successful completion of his task.[50]

Horne's First Army at Vimy Ridge and Plumer's Second Army at Messines both achieved their initial limited objectives in stunning successes, using the British supremacy in artillery to pulverise enemy batteries and defences before the infantry assault was launched. Both believed in a highly consultative approach.

Rawlins, in his history of the artillery, discusses Horne's consultative approach, citing his appointment of Artillery Group Commanders tasked with 'establishing a close liaison between each division and the batteries charged with disruptive trench work to its front.'[51] Geoffrey Powell, in his biography of Plumer, similarly focuses on those qualities which set up conditions for success at Messines Ridge, highlighting effective consultation:

> Harington [Plumer's chief-of-staff] relates how he shaped his own plans in consultation with his Corps Commanders, and how they, in their turn, were encouraged to use the same methods with their Divisional Commanders and so on down the line. Plumer was in the habit of elaborating these consultations during his daily visits to lower headquarters so that all concerned felt that they had been given the chance of stating their case ... He contrasted that with the lack of consultation in other Armies and the unfortunate consequences that followed.[52]

As Simkins notes in an assessment of Plumer, there was a 'recognition within Second Army in 1917 that the secret of tactical success lay in combined all arms attacks.'[53] Simpson, discussing Messines, notes that divisional commanders were at liberty to take four batteries out of the barrage for special tasks, and that divisional infantry schemes 'must be cut and dried, and co-ordinated by the corps before the barrage plan is made.'[54] None of the above papers references *FSR* or the *Staff Manual* in describing Plumer's arrangements, though it would be perfectly easy to do so.

The significance of other doctrinal issues raised by the proposals in of SS 135, *Instructions for the Training of Divisions for Offensive Action*, at a doctrinal level, did not go unnoticed at a

50 SS 135, *Training of Divisions for Offensive Action, December 1916*, pp.82–84.
51 Rawlins, *British Artillery in France*, p.115.
52 Powell, *Plumer, the Soldier's General*, p.171.
53 Peter Simkins, 'Herbert Plumer, Second Army 1915–1917, 1918', in Beckett and Corvi (eds), *Haig's Generals*, p.153.
54 Simpson, 'British Corps Command', Ph.D. thesis, p.110.

sub-divisional level. SS 148, *Forward Inter-communication in Battle*, issued only three months later in March 1917, represents a fundamental turning point in favour of formalising *FSR* compliant infantry-artillery liaison at all stages of battle and especially in the final stages of a divisional advance.

SS 148

Beach has researched the genesis of SS 148, *Forward Inter-communication in Battle March 1917*: 'After the Somme the need to standardize communication procedures had been recognized, and so following a four-day "Staff and Signal Conference" [SS 148] was written up in four days, presumably by some of the participants, and then published within two weeks.' It was written 'to insure the cooperation ... between the infantry and the artillery.'[55] But it also served to let GHQ know the strength of feeling in favour of retaining that cooperation at the sub-divisional level. On this issue, officers active at the divisional level were fundamentally disagreeing with the message emanating from GHQ. The message coming down from GHQ was different from the message coming up. SS 148 did not just restate the necessity for forward liaison between the infantry and artillery. It proposed a formal mechanism to ensure it. An artillery liaison officer, usually the FOO, should be attached to all battalions, and another, more senior, artillery officer should be attached to all infantry brigades if artillery and infantry headquarters were not close enough to enable cooperation.[56] It is perhaps surprising that this is the first time that formal infantry-artillery liaison had been proposed. But it challenged the *FSR* principle of retaining flexibility, at the same time as supporting the *FSR* principle of effective liaison. In contrast, SS 135 proposed abandoning both principles during a 'methodical attack.'

Simpson sees SS 148 as being 'an elaboration of the principles laid down in SS 135', thereby implying that front-line infantry artillery combination during an attack was a new idea, that it was one of the lessons learnt at the Somme.[57] It was only a new idea to those who had never absorbed the principles of *FSR*. But Simpson is right in saying that SS 148 was a significant and long overdue advance. *FSR* expected all front-line officers to liaise with neighbouring units from whatever arm, and make pragmatic arrangements to do so. SS 148 suggested, for the first time, that pragmatic arrangements should be replaced by a formal requirement that liaison officers from the artillery be appointed to all infantry headquarters, in a manner suitable for methodical offence.

Senior army and corps commanders had different views on how to interpret SS 135, and whether to implement SS 148. Hutchison, as the senior battery commander in an army field artillery brigade during 1917, describes serving as an artillery infantry liaison officer when his brigade was attached to Plumer's Second Army during the preparations for the attack on Messines Ridge in June 1917. Front-line liaison was built into Plumer's plans. He then describes a total lack of any infantry artillery liaison arrangements under Gough at Third Ypres from June 1917, and the creation of these posts, again under Plumer, in the battle there, from September

55 Beach, 'Doctrine Writing', p.470.

56 SS 148, *Forward Inter-communication in Battle March 1917* (Washington Reprint 1917), pp.7, 12, 14–16.

57 Simpson, 'British Corps Command', Ph.D. thesis, p.93.

1917.[58] A war diary entry by Colonel Lambarde, who commanded his artillery brigade during the early stages of Third Ypres in August 1917, sums up the infantry artillery cooperation then: 'Brigade did a standing barrage and smoke screen. No indication given to the artillery on this front what the infantry objectives were. Seems a mistake not to give the artillery some idea of what is going on.'[59] Such criticism in a war diary is almost unprecedented.

SS 143

SS 143, *Instructions for the Training of Platoons for Offensive Action, 1917*, published in February 1917, is another pamphlet which seems, in its tone, to have bubbled up from the lower reaches of the army rather than being imposed from above. It was issued by the General Staff as another follow-up to SS 135. The duties and responsibilities of the platoon commander described are completely compliant with *FSR, Part I*, in that he should be personally responsible for the training and protection of his men. The platoon should not form part of a line marching shoulder to shoulder across a battlefield, it says, it should be put in a position where it can plan its own local attack. The platoon commander should reconnoitre, check on the position of neighbouring platoons, maintain communications laterally and back to his company commander, and then press home the assault he has planned. It ticks every box for detailed compliance with the principles of *FSR* as they pertain to junior infantry officers, albeit there is no direct reference to *FSR* in the document.[60] Charles Fair, in his chapter on 'Junior Officer Training' in *The Darkest Year*, describes the training background of this cohort of officers in 1917. They usually had 'combat experience', if only in the ranks, and 'there was a high probability that they would have attended tactical courses in an active sector.'[61] *FSR* was 'used throughout the war, and, where possible, regular army instructors were sought to run training schools', says Fox, in *Learning to Fight*.[62] Even very junior officers in 1917 were not necessarily the naïve and ignorant officers thrown into battle in 1915. Their immediate commanders included regular officers of great experience and surprising youth who had absorbed *FSR* in their pre-war training.

It was not just junior officers who saw advantages in using pre-war, *FSR*-compliant, training exercises, suitably modified. Jeffery Williams writes that Byng, in 1917, before the Battle of Vimy Ridge, 'made a start in improving the training of platoon commanders at the Corps School. But did the minor tactics taught before 1914 apply to the deliberate attack in positional warfare?' In other words, was *FSR, Part I*, still relevant? Was SS 143 applicable? 'He set each of his divisions to study the problem and all concluded that with modifications, they did.'[63]

58 Hutchison, *The Young Gunner*, pp.193, 207–216, 228–229.
59 TNA: WO 95/295/3: 113 brigade RFA, 26 August 1917.
60 SS 143, *Instructions for the Training of Platoons for Offensive Action, 1917, issued by the General Staff, February 1917.*
61 Charles Fair, 'From OTC to OCB: The Professionalisation of the Selection and Training of Junior Temporary Officers During the Great War', in Jones (ed.), *The Darkest Hour*, pp.80–81.
62 Fox, *Learning to Fight*, pp.34, 43, 241.
63 Jeffery Williams, *Byng of Vimy, General and Governor General* (Barnsley: Pen & Sword, 2014 [1983]), p.147.

Summary

Following the unsuccessful battles of 1915, which ignored *FSR* to an extent which greatly perturbed many senior regular officers, there is evidence of a fight-back in the SS and CDS documents produced during 1916. With the exception of CDS 98, *Artillery Notes, Numbers 3 and 4*, the stated policy was to follow *FSR* closely with respect to all arms combination at a sub-divisional level. This in turn, required a consultative style in very senior officers in compliance with *FSR* strictures on the duties of the operational staff of generals. It also required close compliance with *FSR* from sub-divisional officers with respect to their duty to liaise and communicate effectively, taking responsibility for the planning of their own attacks. A substantial proportion of, but not all, corps and army commanders at the Somme agreed with this approach. But there was a persistent faction at GHQ, not discouraged by Haig, which felt that the artillery should be totally controlled at corps or army level, certainly in attack, and that senior generals should impose their tactical plans on their subordinates. This faction stated their case first in SS 98 and then in SS 135, though the small print allowed considerable leeway. Sub-divisional views, as expressed in SS 148 and SS 143, strongly supported the status quo of general compliance with *FSR* principles.

18

Operational Review 1917 to November 1918

The following documents are covered in this review:

SS 161 *Instructions for Battle*, April 1917
SS 198 (draft) *Tactical Instructions for the Offensive of 1918*, November 1917
GHQ Memorandum on Defensive Measures, December 1917
SS 204 *Infantry and Tank Co-operation and Training*, March 1918
SS 210 *The Division in Defence*, May 1918
SS 135 *The Division in* Attack, November 1918

SS 161

After the battles of Vimy Ridge and Arras in April, SS 161 *Instructions for Battle* was issued in May 1917. Generally ignored in most accounts, it is of startling importance in defining Haig's ideas for his 1917 offences. Beach refers to it only briefly, observing that it interrupts the 'genealogical progression' of other pamphlets. It certainly does. Simpson ignores it completely, and many army and corps commanders probably did as well. SS 161 is a statement of 'the principles' to which the 'Field Marshal Commanding in Chief desires to call special attention.' It is an extraordinary document in the context of lessons learnt, or not learnt, by Haig on the Somme. It reads like a newspaper review article based on an in-depth interview, presumably an interview given by Haig in March or April 1917.

As a doctrinal statement, it is the antithesis of *FSR*. It does not emphasise command arrangements or tactical skill at a local level but instead the necessity for a 'a spirit of determination to endure and to conquer at all costs.' It extols the virtue of surprise and says that 'our undoubted superiority in artillery' will enable us to prevail. 'No system of defence, however sound, will suffice to check our advance.' Enemy counterattacks were 'bound to fail against staunch infantry (even without artillery support) who have confidence in their weapons and know how to use them.' This last statement is startling enough, but it was in describing the 'general and normal method of procedure … in a battle on a great scale' that Haig's unrealistic expectations are most clearly articulated. It chronicles a breakthrough on the first day:

> …troops to be held in hand to exploit success beyond the furthest main objective… Small bodies of cavalry (corps mounted troops) working in combination with infantry, tanks and field guns will be best for this duty… It is unlikely during the first day of battle that large masses of cavalry can be got forward sufficiently rapidly … their opportunity will come later… After our furthest objective has been reached, our infantry should be able to hold its own, assisted by such artillery as can be pushed well forward and covered by the light troops thrown out in front.

A note of realism is sounded at the end of the document: 'Unless this can be done, the system proposed cannot be effectively applied.'[1] Haig already knew that it was often impossible for artillery, and even essential supplies, to be advanced quickly to a new front line, particularly if it was wet. In late October 1916, Haig wrote philosophically in his diary of the difficulties of supplying forward troops over ground impassable even to pack animals after a successful local offensive, quoting Lord Cavan's estimate of 'at least four days' before another attack would be possible.'[2]

'The doctrine-writing process is important because it tells us what GHQ wished the reality to be and this is itself revealing', Beach says in his paper on the subject. It is easy to overemphasise the importance of SS pamphlets. They were generally sent to all officers, but whether they were read, even by senior officers, cannot be assumed. They tell us far more about their authors and those who signed them off for publication than they do about the recipients. Beach identifies the main editors from early 1917, when the process became more formalised. Lord Gorell, 32 years old, was a former editor of the *Times Educational Supplement*, who had joined the 7th Battalion, Rifle Brigade, in August 1915 and served with them until he was wounded on the Somme in September 1916. After his recovery, he attended a staff course at Cambridge. Returning to the front in April 1917, he was summoned to GHQ to 'serve under Brigadier General Arthur Solly-Flood in the Training Branch, which had the responsibility of producing CDS pamphlets.' There is nothing in this background to suggest that he was invested in *FSR*. Beach says that, 'From Gorell's papers we can discern three modes for his editorial work … the tidying of other people's work; author or part-author', and finally, acting as 'secretary to the doctrinal committees charged with producing manuals'.[3] Presumably, SS 161 was written by Gorell following an interview with Haig. Its style is compatible with his editorial experience. It is the last significant SS pamphlet written before the onset of the Third Battle of Ypres.

SS 198

SS 198 *Tactical Instructions for the Offensive of 1918* was written in November 1917 but never issued. It is particularly interesting since it encapsulates the doctrinal divide that then dominated debate at GHQ. Beach suggests that it was mainly written by Edward Grigg. Grigg was an ex-colonial editor of *The Times* and was commissioned, aged 35, into the Guards in February 1915. All the evidence of his writing suggests that he was indoctrinated by his career progression into acceptance of *FSR* principles. Within a year, he was on the staff of the elite Guards

1 SS 161 *Instructions for Battle, issued by the General Staff, May 1917*, pp.1, 4, 5, 7.
2 Sheffield and Bourne, (ed.), *Douglas Haig, War Diaries,* p.249.
3 Beach, 'Doctrine Writing', pp.467–473.

Division, being promoted rapidly to serve on corps staff in time for Third Ypres and its preparation in June and July 1917. He therefore endured, albeit at a distance, the horrors of the weeks before and after the opening of the Battle of Third Ypres. He served on a committee of enquiry into the failures of the 30th Division on the first day of the attack. 'Regarding barrages', he wrote at this enquiry, 'the central point was the apparent disconnect between plans made by infantry brigade commanders and the artillery support that they received.' Grigg highlighted the testimony of one brigadier general who said that 'he thought that the barrage was an Army arrangement [as stated in SS 135] and that he could not interfere with it, although he realised that he could make representations about it.' Colonel Lambarde's comments, detailed in the last chapter, testify to the truth of this observation. Grigg moved on to GHQ in September 1917.[4]

If SS 198 was written by Grigg, it is no surprise that he emphasised the requirement for the artillery to liaise during planning down to 'brigade and even battalion' level. This point 'is made quite explicitly', says Beach. 'This evidence not only confirms Grigg's primary authorship of SS.198, but also the clear influence of operational experience upon the doctrinal process.' Operational experience was not the only influence on it. 'Haig's influence upon the conceptual framework laid down in SS.198 can be established from a manuscript note in his handwriting. Gorell's retrospective annotation associates the two documents and indicates that the initial writing process had taken place in September 1917, and that it had involved Gorell himself, Kiggell, and Solly-Flood. Gorell also states that it 'kept on being discussed [and] revised [and] eventually was rewritten' by Grigg.' Beach continues, 'The methodical, bite-and-hold approach suggested by Haig's note and encapsulated within SS.198 would seem to reflect a shift in GHQ's informal doctrinal position during the Third Ypres offensive. This would support the argument advanced by Paul Harris and Sanders Marble that GHQ had undergone an "intellectual conversion … to step-by-step methods" by early August 1917.'[5]

If this was true, SS 198 would have been published. But it is not true. Haig's note does not support a methodical bite-and-hold approach, and it is surprising that anybody should assert that it does. It is a re-statement of SS 161. Beach reproduces Haig's note in full. It is not very coherent, but his core argument is clear.

> 1st Air supremacy. 2. Dominate hostile artillery. 1. When possible the ground The problem. 2 objectives. 1st defeat the hostile advanced troops holding shell holes etc. but this is only a means towards the 2nd objective, viz the subsequent destruction of the enemy's main force which will try & counter attack at favourable a point & moment favourable to the Enemy. These distinct objectives necessitate a division of the attacking troops according to their roles [?rules]. To make suitable dispositions rapidly to meet tactical situations as they occur and to influence effectively the action of our reserves, the commanders position of battalion, brigade & div[isiona]l com[mande]rs is of very great importance. Vide German Instru[ction]s on this. When the strategical situation permits the ground point chosen for attack should be primarily be selected on account of the advantages offered which the ground may be offered by the ground for the advance of our leading detachments by successive steps from defen one defensive position to another. As soon as the advanced troops have gained a suitable defensive position, it is to be fortified etc. without delay steps

4 Beach, 'Doctrine Writing' pp.474–475.
5 Beach, 'Doctrine Writing', pp.474–478.

> are to be taken to move forward the necessary means for exploiting the success thus gained for parrying such counter strikes as the enemy may make. Fresh troops, M[achine]-guns prepare fire positions etc. field co[mpanie]s – a few field guns etc. Barrage plans to be worked beforehand for further advance[6]

This does not endorse a methodical, bite-and-hold approach. He is advocating that second-phase barrage plans and the position of command posts for fresh troops be entirely pre-planned. Once objectives are reached, troops should move on 'without delay.' There is mention of a 'few field guns' advancing to support them, almost as an afterthought – similar mention of the necessary labour battalions and engineers to facilitate this. A methodical, bite-and-hold approach requires that each new advance be planned from scratch, requiring at least three days for reconnaissance, rotation of troops, planning and preparation of supply routes. This note is a précis of SS 161, which Haig had published in April 1917, and which advocates a breakthrough battle. Small wonder that SS 198 'kept on being discussed [and] revised', as Gorell reports, and small wonder that it was never published. SS 135 was reissued with only minor changes in January 1918 in its place. The draft of SS 198 reads far more like an intellectual compromise than a conversion to *FSR*-compliant bite and hold, with robust liaison at the front end of the battle. It is evidence of a fierce doctrinal battle, with both junior and senior officers challenging Haig and Gough's dogmatic views.

Nicholas Ridley's recent book on Gough and Passchendaele highlights this debate. He quotes an *FSR*-compliant memorandum from Brigadier General John Davidson to Kiggell, Haig's chief-of-staff, in June 1917, and compares it with the (non-compliant) principles of battle that Gough intended to follow as expressed in an almost simultaneous circular he sent to his corps commanders. Davidson was the Director of Military Operations at GHQ and an ex-Staff College instructor. Unfortunately, Ridley, like others before him, fails to recognise the doctrinal nature of the debate. The motivation for the Davidson Memorandum is 'most curious', he says. Davidson, in arguing for limited attacks, also emphasised the morale implications. He was of the opinion that there was nothing the troops themselves disliked more than excessive depth in an attack: 'The less the depth … the greater is the confidence of the troops in their ability to reach their objectives, and the fewer will be the casualties. These facts tend to raise morale since they feel confident of succeeding in their task.'[7] Davidson lost the argument, and Gough followed SS 135 in retaining total control of his artillery at corps and army level, and SS 161 in all its incoherence. As Davidson had predicted, little progress was made, and morale plummeted. When Gough was replaced, Plumer paused the battle for some weeks to impose the command philosophy he had used at Messines onto the Fifth Army at Ypres.

SS 210

The next significant pamphlet applicable to the whole army on the Western Front is SS 210 *The Division in Defence*. It was issued in May 1918, too late to provide guidance before the German Spring Offensive, but there was an earlier manifestation of it, which was 'GHQ's *Memorandum*

6 Haig commentary, September 1917, as reproduced in Beach, 'Doctrine Writing', p.478.
7 Nicholas Ridley, *Far from Suitable? Haig, Gough and Passchendaele: A Reappraisal* (Warwick: Helion, 2024), pp.183–185, 277, 283.

on Defensive Measures [which] was sent out as the basis for all the BEF's defences, on 14th December, 1917.'[8] This is the first real evidence of a doctrinal switch to close adherence to *FSR* principles at GHQ since the short-lived revival of them in the early months of 1916. As Simpson explains, this memorandum 'describes the three-zone defensive system to be adopted by the BEF. Defence in depth was the guiding principle. In order to absorb the enemy's assault and render him vulnerable to well-organized counter-attacks, the defences would consist of an outpost (or forward) zone, a battle zone and a rearward zone.' Though he does not say so, this is precisely the plan utilised by Smith-Dorrien at Mons in compliance with *FSR*. 'Each of these would be organized in depth itself. The outpost zone' on the Condé Canal at Mons 'would break up the enemy attack and compel considerable expenditure of his resources. A mile or two behind came the battle zone,' the Harmignies to Dour defence line at Mons, 'would be the main line of resistance,' and so on, and 'lastly, the rearward zone was to be sited four to eight miles behind the battle zone and was a fall-back position in case of difficulty', the line from Maubeuge to Bavai at Mons. Simpson goes on to compare, in detail, the degree to which the different corps and army commanders implemented its recommendations. He describes how Haig appeared to tolerate wide differences in the degree of implementation of these *FSR*-compliant recommendations.[9] Sheffield and McCartney observe 'that Gough did not understand the [*FSR*] principles of defence in depth, [as] is evident in his handling of Fifth Army' in 1918.[10] Beach describes the *Memorandum* as giving 'limited guidance', which meant it could be interpreted freely by the respective corps commanders, in contrast to SS 210, which was more of a directive.

He also records that SS 210 was extensively revised over 10 days by Cuthbert Headlam, who was posted to the Training Branch in April 1918. His background is important. Headlam was a yeomanry officer who had gone to France in 1915, aged 39. Pre-war, he had been a clerk in the House of Lords, and he was brother-in-law to the Earl of Cavan, to whom he became ADC, before transferring to the General Staff as an intelligence officer with Second Army under Plumer and then VIII Corps under Hunter-Weston at the Somme. The main points made in SS 210 differ little from the proposals put forward in the *Memorandum on Defensive Measures*, but it is fuller and more focused on *FSR*. SS 210 has eight direct references to *FSR* in 15 pages, leaving no doubt as to the main source of its inspiration.

A re-statement of an important *FSR* principle that would almost have been a heresy if voiced in 1916 was, 'Ground should not be held just for the sake of its retention.'.[11] SS210 continued: '

> The outpost system … will occupy all the ground in the defender's possession which lies between the main battle position and the enemy … It should form a buffer zone, organized and held in such a way as to absorb the shock of the attack, to deprive it of its momentum, and to break up the enemy's organization as far as possible. The rear positions of defence must be prepared for use in the last resort … sufficiently far in rear of the main battle

8 Brigadier General J.E. Edmonds, *Official History of the Great War, Military Operations France and Belgium, 1918, Volume 1, Appendices* (London: MacMillan, 1935), Appendix 6, 'G.H.Q. Memorandum on Defensive Measures' 14 December 1917,

9 Simpson, 'British Corps Command' (Ph.D. thesis), pp,163,172–177.

10 Sheffield and McCartney 'Hubert Gough' in Beckett and Corvi, (eds), *Haig's Generals*, p.86.

11 SS 210, *The Division in Defence, issued by the General Staff*, May 1918, p.4; See *Field Service Regulations, Part I*, p.145.

> position to make it necessary for the enemy to organize a second and distinct operation in order to attack them.[12]

Surely what was true for the enemy attacking was relevant to offensive planning. A further reference to *FSR*, referring to piquets and other outposts, is:

> In order where possible to give depth to the defence, the infantry in advance of the main battle position should generally be disposed in three lines: a line of observation, a line of supports, and the outpost line of resistance. The line of observation corresponds to the sentry groups of open warfare … There is all the difference in the world between organization in depth and dispersion in depth … No rigid line will stand against the crash of the modern surprise attack, and no scheme of defence is justifiable which packs a narrow area with troops exposed to the first impact of an assault.[13]

After the publication of SS 210 in May 1918, Beach records that Headlam's superior 'assembled the chiefs of staff of the BEF's armies' to discuss it, and despite disagreement on 'one or two matters of nomenclature' they apparently 'agreed thoroughly with the principles.'[14] The use of the word 'principles' in this context is significant. It was not a word used lightly. *FSR* 'principles' had been updated for this publication. Ultimate responsibility for defensive arrangements was held at corps and army level, but 'it is on the main battle position that the divisional commander must be prepared to fight out his battle and to use all his resources in so doing.'[15] The division, not the corps, is the key fighting unit.

SS 210 is noteworthy in the emphasis it places on pre-war *FSR*. Arguably, *FSR*, except in broad principles, was almost irrelevant to the conditions which ruled in 1918. SS 210 addresses air power, gas, the impact of heavier and more accurate guns, and all the evolved complexity of war. But the pamphlet, in repeatedly reminding the reader of the principles of *FSR*, is implicitly endorsing other *FSR* principles such as the front-line infantry artillery liaison described in SS 148, sophisticated reconnaissance, and Plumer's style of leadership, as per *FSR, Part II*, and the *Staff Manual*, in listening to the views of divisional and brigade commanders. There is a remarkable resonance, as the army chiefs-of-staff acknowledged, with the core principles of *FSR*.

As previously noted, SS 210 was issued too late to provide guidance before the onset of the German Spring Offensive, but there is obvious evidence of a disparity between the different British armies in how far they had adopted this approach before it started. Fox records how these ideas of defence in depth were generally known and transferred to the Italian Front by both junior and senior officers of the Italian expeditionary force in early 1918. Major R. Macleod, a battery commander with the 48th (South Midland) Division, deemed the Italian defences 'not altogether sound' and Plumer, who was commanding, soon negotiated with a receptive Italian staff to reorganise the defensive arrangements in line with Western Front best practice.[16] This

12 SS 210, *The Division in Defence*, p.5; See *Field Service Regulations, Part I*, pp.98–105, 170–175.
13 SS 210, *The Division in Defence*, p.11.
14 Beach, 'Doctrine Writing', p.485, referenced to the Dawney Papers, IWM, letters 15 and 16 June 1918.
15 SS 210, *The Division in Defence*, p.13.
16 Fox, *Learning to Fight*, pp.156–159.

was well before the publication of SS 210, and based on the *Memorandum on Defensive Measures* of December 1917.

Cuthbert Headlam's next project, according to Beach, was the preparation of 'SS.214, Tanks and Their Employment in Co-operation with Other Arms, which was published eventually in August 1918.' This was heavily based on SS 204, *Infantry and Tank Co-operation and Training*, issued in March 1918, which starts with a quote from *FSR*: 'The full power of the army can be exerted only when all its parts act in combination.'[17] It is unsurprising, therefore, that Headlam's document complies with *FSR* in concluding, in its introduction, that 'the employment of tanks … does not entail any essential modifications in the … tactics of the infantry.'[18] Training by the principles of the pre-war manuals would be sufficient, albeit the detail would have evolved. The whole subject of the early use of tanks has spawned a vast literature.

Standing back, the arguments at the time can be compared with the pre-war debate on the role of the cavalry in war. *FSR, Part I* requires cavalry to combine with the infantry and support them in their objectives before battle is joined. In 1914, some believed the cavalry should be an independent or semi-independent strike force, opening the way for the other arms. The debate on the role of tanks follows similar lines. Comparable dilemmas were raised on the formation of the Machine Gun Corps. Some argued that they should be treated as a separate force, alongside the artillery, and with a similar role. Some thought that they should be thoroughly integrated into the infantry. These are doctrinal side issues, albeit of great importance. However, the contemporary debates on them cannot be followed without a knowledge of the basic principles of *FSR*, particularly that of all arms combination.

SS 135 (November 1918) The Division in Attack

Although issued too late to have any practical impact during the war, this rewritten version of SS 135 began with a ringing endorsement of *FSR* principles:

> There has been a tendency during the present war to look upon trench warfare and open warfare as two separate things. This has led to a disregard of many of the fundamental principles, laid down in the training manuals issued before this war, as being inapplicable to trench warfare … We have now, however, resumed our allegiance to principles of training employed before the war, and must be careful not to depart from them again.[19]

It follows this introduction by robustly addressing all arms combination, and infantry-artillery liaison, and in doing so tackles the subjects of both tank and machine gun cooperation. This is reflected in the *FSR*-compliant advice that follows.

'Tank Cooperation – The duties of tanks are: (i) to assist the advance of the infantry: (ii) to exploit a success.' So, they are treated in this document as a hybrid arm, halfway between the infantry and the cavalry, when referencing back to *FSR*. In case tank commanders should

17 SS 204, *Infantry and Tank Co-operation and Training*, issued by the General Staff, March 1918, p.5.
18 Beach, 'Doctrine Writing', pp. 486–487.
19 SS 135, *The Division in Attack, issued by General Staff, November 1918*, pp.3–4.

think too much of themselves, tanks 'can also be employed, if necessary, to carry up ammunition, stores, etc. to the infantry.' 'Machine Gun Cooperation … During the initial stages of the assault, a proportion of the machine guns may be employed in close cooperation with the artillery to cover the assault of the infantry.' But their main role in battle was to protect the flanks, cover the advance, and give concentrated fire on strong points. After the battle, they had a major role in contributing to defence in depth as captured positions were consolidated.[20]

It was Headlam who coordinated this remarkable re-write of SS 135 (first published in December 1916), re-titled *The Division in Attack*, which addresses the details of tactical and local command principles that had already been re-adopted by the best units of the British Army. With Headlam as the principal author and given the influence of *FSR* on his previous pamphlet, SS 210, it is no surprise that SS 135 (1918) also re-emphasises *FSR* principles. It is very unlikely that he would have inferred that important tactical principles had been neglected under Haig's watch and warned against further lapses in doctrine without the endorsement of some very senior voices at GHQ. As Beach says, 'it represents a distillation of what GHQ considered to be "best practice" during the victorious "Hundred Days" campaign.' Apart from all arms combination, particularly highlighted is the principle of 'distribution in depth both in attack and defence' by all arms.[21] The title also speaks for itself. The division, not the corps or army, is the fighting unit. To emphasise the point further, the section in this pamphlet on the general principles of an attack is referenced to Section 103 of *FSR, Part I*, and that on reconnaissance to Section 96. This is not to say that SS 135, *The Division in Attack*, reverts in detail to the letter of the pre-war regulations. That would be absurd. War was much more complex. Air power, chemical warfare, and the use of tanks were now significant factors and scientific advances had facilitated the greater efficiency of sound-ranging technology and radio communication.[22]

The narrative of the last few months of the war is complicated in that, on 26 March 1918, Haig was subordinated, in strategic decision-making, to General Foch, Supreme Allied Commander. No longer could he be defined as an independent C-in-C of the British Army, with all the powers and responsibilities laid on him by *FSR*. It was now his responsibility to receive 'brief orders' from Foch, albeit in a spirit of cooperation, and to pass on the intent of Foch's orders to his army commanders. The extent to which Haig was sidelined by this is the subject of much debate. But it seems that Haig, of necessity, was now prepared to accept the principle of limited methodical attacks at the instigation of Foch.

Summary

CDS and SS 'pamphlets were produced and intended to be used in sympathy with the army's pre-war ethos', says Aimée Fox.[23] If *FSR* in 1914 was a doctrine and not merely 'intended to provide officers with precise instructions designed to meet every wartime contingency', as Michael Hunzeker asserts, it would, in his opinion, have standardised army training, educated

20 SS 135, *The Division in Attack, November 1918*, pp.25–27.

21 SS 135, *The Division in Attack, November 1918*, pp.3–4.

22 Keith R. Thrower, 'Army radio communication in the Great War', (Oxford University occasional paper, March 2013) <https://blogs.mhs.ox.ac.uk/innovatingincombat/files/2013/03/Army-radio-communication-in-the-Great-War_V2.pdf>, accessed 13 July 2024.

23 Fox, *Learning to Fight*, p.85.

'junior leaders' to cope with war, created a source of institutional memory, and fostered debate.[24] *FSR, Parts I and II*, did all these things. Just considering debate, there is evidence at almost every stage of the war of debate about the advisability of the various tactics followed and command structures used – and that debate continues to the present day.

Hunzeker's concept of institutional memory is particularly interesting. Some have attributed the development of the tactical use of independent brigades and divisions to provide a continuous rolling advance during the Last Hundred Days to a eureka moment when the army learnt the best way of fighting, the apex of the learning curve, if one will. But almost all these divisions were directed by generals who had scrupulously adhered to *FSR* in 1914, even, in some cases, created it from 1909 or before, and a high proportion of divisions and brigades were commanded by regulars of 1914, who had been indoctrinated with it. The all-arms offensive attack, with limited objectives, followed by a pause for consolidation, fresh reconnaissance, and new planning before a repeat offensive, is pure *FSR*.

It is not the intention of this book to address in detail the impact of *FSR* in the planning of all the campaigns that took place on the Western Front during the First World War. This is particularly complex in 1918 and has been addressed by many historians. The overview suggested by these chapters is that *FSR* principles were recommended and observed as far as possible by the main body of the army right up to 1916, though the generals who planned the battles of 1915 were allowed, by French, to ignore major tactical and command principles. Since these battles were such demonstrable failures, many generals reverted to a stricter observance of *FSR* principles during 1916. But during and just after the Somme, there was a determined attempt to re-impose principles on tactics and command that were at odds with *FSR*, an approach which culminated in the arrangements made for the opening month of Third Ypres under Hubert Gough. There followed a period of pushback, led as much by pressure from the lower echelons of the army as by conservative, or progressive, senior generals, depending on the viewpoint one has. The main principles of *FSR* were largely accepted and re-implemented by early 1918, in that the duties and responsibilities of subordinate officers were broadly compliant: the infantry division, sometimes the infantry brigade, supported by close artillery, was the fighting unit, intent on well-defined, limited aims; combined arms, as a concept, was firmly readopted; and defence in depth was re-accepted as a main principle.

However, as late as July 1918, Major General Charles Harington was writing to Wilson that 'very divergent views are held and entirely different methods exist in the various armies, corps and divisions.'[25] No overview summary of the doctrine followed by the British Army during the First World War can ignore this wide divergence. Haig undoubtedly commanded the British Army as the war was won. But he presided over this divergence and, in many ways, fostered and prolonged that divergence. His final admission, in September 1918, in a letter to Henry Wilson, that to 'a steady adherence to the principles of our Field Service Regulations, Part I, are our successes to be attributed,' is too little, too late to resuscitate his operational reputation.

24 Hunzeker, *Dying to Learn*, p.100.
25 Simon Innes-Robbins, 'General Sir Henry Horne', in Jones (ed.), *The Darkest Hour*, p.282.

19

Administration, Organisation, and Command 1916–1918

Sir Douglas Haig became C-in-C of the British Army in December 1915. Charteris says that Haig's 'self-confidence and his belief in his destiny [never led] ... him to neglect the study of each factor of the problems which confronted him.'[1] It is for this reason that Douglas Haig proved to be such a great war leader. From the day he took office, he set about using all the powers conferred on him as C-in-C to address the many logistical and administrative problems facing the BEF at the end of 1915.

To recap from an earlier chapter, section 8 of *FSR, Part II* states that the C-in-C issues 'orders on all matters connected with the efficiency and maintenance of his forces in the field ... for the success or failure of which he is responsible ... The C-in-C [may] ... modify the organization of any unit', and 'the amended war establishment of the unit [will be] revised in accordance with his wishes.'[2] Section 22 states that he must 'interpose' if administrative deficiencies are adversely affecting the 'efficiency' of his forces, particularly if his senior administrators have asked him to do so. Such questions would only be raised when the senior administrators had insufficient authority to tackle the problems themselves. The section goes on to say that if the C-in-C should fail to act, whether asked to or not, when administrative deficiencies were threatening the efficiency of the force under his command, 'the responsibility is his.'[3] During the tenure of Sir John French, these regulations had not been followed. Even when asked by both his QMG and IGC to intervene, French had refused to engage Joffre on the issues of rationalising port facilities, and the lines of communication from them, which were intersected and impeded by the French lines of communication. Both these problems were limiting the offensive potential of the BEF and leading to inefficiency. He took no action.

Herbert, Earl Kitchener, as Secretary of State for War, was aware that there was a less than perfect understanding between the allies, and Haig's initial instructions addressed the issue: 'The closest cooperation between the French and British as a united army must be the governing policy.' Haig took the words to heart. On 29 December 1915, he attended a meeting at Chantilly with the French President, Prime Minister, and Minister of War, amongst other worthies. 'The meeting went off well,' reports Cooper. Before lunch, 'one of the French Generals complained

1 Charteris, *Field Marshal Earl Haig*, pp.182, 205.
2 *Field Service Regulations, Part II*, pp.26–27.
3 *Field Service Regulations, Part II*, pp.28,44.

of the inefficacy of the French gas masks, and Haig offered to supply them with ten thousand English masks a day while they were developing a new model.'[4]

The goodwill engendered by this relatively trivial administrative cooperation may have surprised Haig. Similar goodwill was hard to garner during hard-headed discussions on tactics and strategy. Charteris says that almost his first act as C-in-C was to 'order his staff to prepare for him forthwith a complete review of the situation', and that 'each day he saw the heads of the chief branches of the staff.'[5] He was determined to address all the responsibilities of a C-in-C, as described in *FSR*.

Part II states that the C-in-C had the 'responsibility of co-ordinating staff work at general headquarters' with all three branches working 'in close cooperation' and, additionally, his chief-of-staff being kept 'informed on a daily basis … in regard to all stocks of ammunition, supplies, stores and material' by the IGC.[6] Christopher Phillips in *Transport Experts and the First World War* says that two factors 'inhibited the British army's development before 1916: a … disinclination to prepare for a static war; and the French army's reluctance to relinquish control over the shared transport infrastructure upon which the coalition's forces depended.' Even in 1914, this reluctance had occasionally eased. For instance, the British Army arranged repairs, under French supervision, of the 'Chemins de Fer du Nord', in October 1914, but any such cooperation was piecemeal and locally negotiated.[7]

From the moment of his appointment, Haig was confronted with administrative problems in many areas and showed a lively awareness of them. Brown lists the principal difficulties he faced – 'shortages of labour, insufficient railroad mileage, poor roads, inefficient docks and ammunition, all of which affected his ability to fight.' He could not plan any offensive operations with any prospect of success while these problems continued. The shell shortage of 1915 was still acute in January 1916, such that 'even the BEF's C-in-C found himself handicapped by the restrictions.' 'The BEFs howitzers had been limited' to 200 rounds per division per week. Rationing was such that even army commanders 'had to get permission from GHQ' if they wanted to mount an operation that exceeded the daily ration.[8] Additionally, Haig identified both a lack of training and a lack of uniformity in training as further problems that had to be addressed. These problems were his responsibility under *FSR*. The principle that all unit commanders, right up to the top of the army, were responsible for ensuring that their subordinates were adequately trained was well established.

Tony Vines, in his thesis on 'Haig as a Military Manager', cites entries in Haig's diary, as early as 19 and 22 December, which document 'meetings with Sir Herbert Plumer (GOC) and his CGS at Second Army HQ, and Allenby (GOC) at Third Army HQ. He pressed both men to adopt the same training system he had laid down at First Army.' Vines goes on to quote from the minutes of his first army commanders' conference on 8 January 1916, saying that 'he instructed his subordinates to establish training schools at army, corps and divisional levels.' In addition, Haig emphasised that uniformity of staff work practices was necessary for all armies. To this end, he ordered that 'the principles laid down in FSR-II must not be departed from.'[9]

4 Cooper, *Haig*, p.285–286.
5 Charteris, *Field Marshal Earl Haig*, pp.182, 205.
6 *Field Service Regulations, Part II*, pp.32–33, 38.
7 Phillips, *Civilian Specialists at War*, pp.96, 102.
8 Brown, *British Logistics*, p.109.
9 Vines, 'Douglas Haig's Role as a Military Manager', pp.203–204.

Taken in 1915 by a subaltern 'to show number of sandbags used'. (Author's collection)

This suggests that Haig did read *FSR, Part II*, to refresh his memory on its contents in the very early days of his tenure.

Phillips reports that:

> Haig's interest in transport issues was [also] apparent from the moment he replaced Sir John French as Commander-in-Chief on 19 December 1915 … On his first day at GHQ, he met with his adjutant general and QMG before touring the various branches of the General Staff, and within his first week he had discussed the railways and roads behind the Third Army with Lieutenant General Edmund Allenby.[10]

Haig followed up his meeting with Allenby by urging 'the value of improved railway facilities' behind the Third Army to the French, and he ordered Lieutenant General Sir Ronald Maxwell (QMG) 'to hasten, and begin at once to build the railway projected into the Third Army area … I also went into the reasons why the narrow-gauge lines in the Second Army area (near Poperinghe) had not been turned to military use.' By 27 December, he could write in his diary with evident satisfaction that: 'QMG recorded that work had begun on the railway in the Third Army area. A B[road] G[auge] line in the direction of Contay … It is just four days since I begged Joffre to help us in this matter.' Phillips says, 'Haig's understanding of the proper place of transportation in the army's activities – and the continued degradation of the BEF's lines of communications as war took its toll, were essential matters for himself as C-in-C to address.'[11]

Despite observing that administrative problems 'concerned him greatly', Brown expresses surprise at the amount of time that Haig devoted to administration in the early months of his tenure, as estimated by an examination of his diaries.[12] But Haig had proved in 1906, into 1908, that he had a remarkable capacity for intensive work on detail. He had been the organising powerhouse behind the establishment of a Territorial Force in well under two years, was unafraid to take expert advice from Ellison and others, and fulfilled Haldane's vision. Within weeks of taking up his post as C-in-C, he was demonstrating the same capacity to absorb his logistical and political briefs. It was a refreshing change after the indecisiveness of French. Charteris, who was both Haig's biographer and on his staff, says that 'he devoted great care and attention to the improvement of the administrative arrangements throughout the whole army', in 1916.[13]

In assessing Haig's role as C-in-C, the different areas of administrative work that he undertook can be distinguished. Reviewing training for the fighting troops was a responsibility conferred on him as operational commander of the army. Addressing the details of supply and transport difficulties was a responsibility conferred on him as supreme commander of the BEF on foreign soil. Negotiating with allies to improve the conditions in which his forces existed was a responsibility with political overtones; it was related to negotiations on strategic planning and was subject to a degree of oversight from London. Haig's 'mission statement' as J.P. Harris, a biographer of Haig, puts it, 'indicated, even more strongly than the one given to Sir John French,

10 Phillips, *Civilian Specialists at War*, p.207.
11 Phillips, *Civilian Specialists at War*, pp.207–208.
12 Brown, *British Logistics*, p.110.
13 Charteris, *Field Marshal Earl Haig*, p.204.

the importance of good relations between the allies.'[14] These areas of responsibility overlapped. As early as 17 January, Haig was negotiating 'with Joffre for the use of training grounds where large scale combined arms exercises with two or three divisions could be practised.' This is merely one of many examples of the rapidity with which Haig involved himself in resolving the problems facing the BEF in 1916, both before and after the opening of the Somme offensive. His workload, well documented by Brown, Phillips, and Vines, was prodigious. 'Haig showed a good grasp of administration's importance', says Brown. He 'appears to have spent a good deal of time ensuring that the lines of communication kept functioning as smoothly as possible; he did so, however, without overstepping the bounds laid out in Field Service Regulations – his concern for the troubles of his administrators never strayed to meddling.'[15] This last statement is not true. When Haig understood the details of a problem and could see a solution, he meddled. Such is the nature of a meticulous organiser.

The chaplain's department was very firmly under the remit of the AG. Vines records that on 13 January 1916, Haig dined with his Deputy Chaplain General, Bishop L.H. Gwynn. He took the opportunity to emphasise 'the importance of sending messages to all [Gwynn's] clergy to preach about the great object of the war viz the freeing of mankind from German tyranny.' Haig also observed that he found many of the clergy too narrow in their views and that he felt they should show more enthusiasm for the cause. Two weeks later, at a second meeting with Gwynne, Haig discussed 'plans for improving the nature of teaching by the chaplains and for putting the best men in the most important positions.'[16]

Gary Sheffield, in his biography of Haig, gives another example of encroachment into the AG's formal brief. Haig was 'influenced by his friendship with Colonel Micky Ryan, his medical officer at the beginning of the war … [and he] persuaded Haig of the value of treating as many men as close to the front as possible.' Consequently, during 1916, 'forward treatment became general across the BEF.' Haig used his authority to make minor changes that had major impacts. Prior to this change, 'if the men are allowed to go to the base, we never see them again.' Those requiring any treatment were transferred back, being, at that point, formally removed from the strength of their units. All officers and men then had to go through a process of reassignment, almost always to a new unit. The importance of such institutional 'top cover' should not be underestimated', Sheffield says.[17] Colin Hutchison explained the procedure to his mother after sustaining a minor wound at Third Ypres in 1917:

> Two German aeroplanes flew low over our trenches dropped two bombs onto us. I was hit on the nose by a very small splinter. I had a rotten passage down … to the wagon line to get myself cleaned up. Expert advice plied much iodine and said leave the splinter where it was. I don't feel any the worse for it and am going up tomorrow morning with the colonel. You'll probably see my name in due course in the wounded list. This is done so that if suppuration should set in, I get the privileges of a wounded soldier, and not those of one with a sore due to carelessness or something of that sort.[18]

14 J.P. Harris, *Douglas Haig, and the First World War* (Cambridge: Cambridge University Press, 2008) p.201.
15 Brown, *British Logistics*, p.110.
16 Vines, 'Haig's Role as a Military Manager', pp.242–243.
17 Gary Sheffield, *The Chief*, p.143.
18 Hutchison, *The Young Gunner*, pp.207–208, paraphrased.

Minorly ill and wounded, from early 1916, were treated, counted, and sent straight back into action.

It cannot be argued that Haig, or any other senior general, was following *FSR, Part II*, in every detail in 1916. Some of its detailed regulations had been found to be unsatisfactory. The revised structure of responsibilities shared by the IGC, QMG and AG, put in place in late 1914, persisted without any radical changes up until the end of 1916. Haig's policy was to work within the existing administrative arrangements, using his authority and his relationship with the French, to oil the wheels of improvement. Vines writes:

> In France, Haig worked tirelessly to promote the BEF's interests within the French military and political establishment. Unlike his predecessor, Haig had a reasonable fluency in the French language. This allowed him to promote empathy and understanding with his allies including Clemenceau, Foch, Joffre and Pétain. Haig attended meetings, made courtesy calls, exchanged visits with his French counterparts, brought senior French liaison officers into his confidence, handed out British military awards to French officers and took the salute at their parades with great aplomb.[19]

In 1916, this cordiality was mainly in the context of agreeing offensive strategy, but it was sufficient for Sir Henry Rawlinson to write to a friend:

> You need have no anxiety as to D.H. getting on well with our allies. He went down to Chantilly the other day and had a most cordial meeting with Père Joffre ... He has since gone down to be present at a meeting of army group commanders and talk over future plans. So I think our cooperation in the future will be much closer than it has been.[20]

Brown describes many initiatives which came to fruition, albeit not always quickly, in this new atmosphere of cooperation. As ammunition supply from Britain increased, its storage and transport was facilitated by improved access to ports and a series of new depots, some even being shared with the French, all negotiated by the IGC under Haig's watchful eye.[21] 'Our business relations with the French, the obtaining of sites and buildings, called for the establishment of a Directorate of Hirings and Requisitions,' Haig recorded in his final despatch in 1919.[22] In April 1916, Haig, on the advice of his QMG, asked 'the Secretary of State for War to arrange for an expansion of the BEF's inland water capability.' The French were delighted that some strain would be taken off their railways. 'By the end of 1916, Inland Water Transport was moving some 100,000 tons per month on 564 vessels of all types, mostly barges', saving perhaps as many as 250 trains a month on the creaking rail network. There was a voracious appetite for timber, and a series of agreements were made with the French to allow access to their main timber markets to ease the pressure on British shipping and transport. By August, 'a battalion of Canadian lumbermen was [even] placed at the disposal of the French. This battalion was to

19 Vines, 'Haig's Role as a Military Manager', pp.73–74.
20 Charteris, *Field-Marshal Earl Haig*, p.191.
21 Brown, *British Logistics*, pp.111–112.
22 J. H. Boraston, *Sir Douglas Haig's despatches (December 1915-April 1919)* (London: J. M. Dent, 1919), p.339.

be allocated an area of pine forest to strip, with the lumber being split equally between the BEF and the French armies.'[23]

Not all problems that Haig had to oversee had an international perspective. Finding manpower was an ever-recurring problem, and through 1916, various committees recommended that some of the administrative directorates should give up men of fighting age, particularly those with military experience, despite their specialist skills being near essential in maintaining the smooth functioning of their directorates. These were decisions that could only be made at the highest level. If overage civilians could be recruited, as in the case of the office of the postmaster general, arrangements were made with the War Office to supply the necessary men, allowing the release of younger men. In May 1916, the commander of the Railway Transport Section protested a request from the War Office to release 975 men. The QMG was quick in his support. The proposal 'would involve the entire dislocation of the maintenance services of the army … They are indispensible [*sic*].' Haig understood the problem, consulted the War Office, and overrode the request. At the same time, in mid-1916, 'Haig proved anxious to get' some companies of the newly raised Noncombatant Labor Corps out to France as soon as they became available.[24]

Brown describes this period as 'Ad Hocism'. He remarks ruefully that 'in no studies [of the Somme] has the administration of the lines of communication come under consideration', this in 1998. 'The transportation system, in spite of the best efforts of the administration to patch it up, could not properly sustain the Somme.' Phillips, in his book, equally ruefully, in 2020, points out that even books that mention logistics seldom devote more than a few 'pages to the logistical complexities and frailties that afflicted the Franco-British coalition before the Battle of the Somme.' Phillips observes that 'Before mid-1916, the British army actively sought out and engaged with the skills and expertise possessed by Britain's transport experts … However, the army's initial attempts to utilize civilians to grapple with the implications of industrialized warfare were relatively small in scale and limited in scope.'[25] The process was further advanced in England and the rest of the United Kingdom. By the end of 1915, spurred on by press criticisms, David Lloyd George, as Minister of Munitions, was actively recruiting senior industrialists to address problems of munitions production and transport. Gradually, that process was extended to reviews of the army's specific arrangements in France. These proved to be of limited value since addressing one problem simply moved difficulties up or down the line.

Phillips continues, 'In 1915 Major General Sir Frederick Clayton [IGC] had proven amenable to the idea of exploiting civilian expertise to improve the BEF's supply operations at the port of Boulogne, but by the summer of 1916 his attitude towards civilian involvement on the lines of communications had become far less welcoming.' Clayton, as IGC, felt particularly threatened 'by the number of investigations into logistical and administrative procedures that took place on the lines of communications' during 1916. His Headquarters was at Abbeville, rather than GHQ, and therefore accessible to 'civilian-led parties', who disrupted the work of his staff. His frustration boiled over on reading 'the findings of a commission into the ongoing congestion at the Channel ports led by the shipping magnate Sir Thomas Royden', under the auspices of a shipping control committee, which was published in July 1916. 'It is impossible for the ordinary business civilian to understand what are the conditions under which we have to work and it is

23 Brown, *British Logistics*, pp.127, 131–133.
24 Brown, *British Logistics*, pp.127–129.
25 Phillips, *Civilian Specialists at War*, p 96.

a mistake to allow them to interfere with an army business that most of us have studied all our lives.'[26] He had a valid point. The relationship between the C-in-C, IGC, QMG and AG, and their sub-directorates, was labyrinthine. Practical recommendations by civilians could not be actioned without concerted reform. The rules of some parts of *FSR, Part II* were impeding such reform, although its principle of elasticity allowed it with respect to other parts. In other words, rigidly defined command responsibilities inhibited the logical transfer of administrative duties from one director to another.

The arrival of Sir Eric Geddes in France on 24 August 1916 is rightly perceived as a major turning point in the history of logistics on the Western Front. Geddes was born in 1875 and brought up in Scotland. Initially, 'a directionless youth' who was sent abroad by his family after attending a succession of schools, he found employment mainly in the railway industry, including spells of work for the Baltimore and Ohio Railroad in America, and the Rohilkund and Kumaon railway in India. On returning home, he was recruited by the North Eastern Railway in 1904, rising rapidly to become, by 1914, their general manager, 'rewarded with the highest salary of any senior executive of a British railway company … A new breed of businessman, [and a graduate of the company's managerial apprenticeship programme,] he favoured statistical analysis as a staple business strategy.' In 1915, Geddes was selected by Lloyd George as his Deputy Director of Munitions Supply. Under his direction, the production of small arms, rifles, and machine guns soared.[27] In June 1916, on the death of Lord Kitchener, Lloyd George became Secretary of State for War.

On 2 August, Haig received a letter from Lloyd George, offering him the expert services of Sir Eric Geddes to investigate the BEF's transport arrangements (railway, road, canal and docks) both at home and in France.[28] Haig responded courteously, and Geddes arrived to interview Haig on 24 August. Haig recorded the visit in his diary: 'He is sent out by Mr Lloyd George to assist over the question of communications. A most pleasant and capable man. He is afraid that the Inspector General of Communications, (General Clayton) resents his visit! I said that I am glad to have practical hints from any one capable of advising.' This is the first mention of Geddes in *War Diaries and Letters*, edited by Gary Sheffield and John Bourne. Sheffield and Bourne opine in a footnote that 'Haig was originally dubious about his appointment.'[29] Presumably they base this comment on the fact that Haig, and his QMG, Maxwell, had had sight of an anonymous confidential report, carried to GHQ by Lord Derby on 7 July 1916, which suggested that all transport to, and within France, should become the responsibility of the War Office and Secretary of State. Maxwell angrily described this proposal as 'quite impractical'. Haig's handwritten comment on it merely speculates on who wrote it.[30] Geddes was not off to a good start with the very senior staff at GHQ.

26 Phillips, *Civilian Specialists at War*, pp.210–211, & 212, referenced to the Granet papers, 'Remarks on the report of the commission sent out by the shipping control committee, 30 July 1916.

27 Christopher Phillips, 'Sir Eric Campbell Geddes', *International Encyclopaedia of the First World War, 1914–1918*, <https://encyclopedia.1914-1918-online.net/article/geddes-eric-campbell-sir/?format=pdf>, accessed 5 August 2024.

28 Vines, 'Haig's Role as a Military Manager', p.86.

29 Gary Sheffield and John Bourne (eds), *Douglas Haig, War Diaries and Letters, 1914–1918* (London: Wiedenfeld and Nicholson, 2005), p.223.

30 Phillips, *Civilian Specialists at War*, p.206.

The narrative of Geddes's wide vision and sweeping reforms is described in many sources, and no more than a summary is offered here. Brown says, 'Geddes began a process that revised the BEF's transport arrangements completely.' He recognised that transport problems were impacted by labour problems, and suggested to Lloyd George, in a letter on 15 September, that one could not be addressed without the other. By this time, the 'QMG and AG had announced the creation of a Directorate of Labor', which suggests that GHQ became closely involved in his personal review from the outset. 'Geddes broke transportation down into five categories: docks, railways, canals, light railways, and roads.'[31] His vision involved reforming the transport arrangements of the BEF, from the ports to the front line, in compliance with modern business practice. This meant creating a Director General of Transport, which would render the IGC redundant. It rapidly became clear to Haig and most at GHQ, including a rueful Clayton (the IGC), that his suggestions made sense, and such was his personality that he convinced Lloyd George of the necessity of the reforms at a very early date. Lloyd George moved fast. 'On 18 September, just three days after the latter had penned his 'preliminary opinion' on matters in France, the Secretary of State for War established the directorate-general of military railways (DGMR) at the War Office', with the right, under the QMG, to attend meetings of the Army Council.[32] On 7 October 1916, Haig asked Geddes to serve as a new Inspector General of Transportation in France.[33]

Geddes, in his reforms, reallocated administrative responsibilities within directorates which had existed since 1914, renaming some, reforming others, and abolishing a few. However, he retained an identical system of descending directorates as described in *FSR, Part II.* Systems were retained, while methods were changed. As *FSR, Part II* states: 'The essence of all efficient organizations lies in due sub-division of labour and decentralisation of responsibility among subordinates, each individual being given duties which he can perform adequately.'[34] Lloyd George made it clear that he wanted the best-qualified people to head important directorates, and if they were civilians, so be it. The Army Council, and some subordinates, notably Brigadier General Richard Montagu Stuart-Wortley, the Director of Movements under the QMG in London, whose responsibilities overlapped with transport, protested, first at being put under the authority of a civilian and secondly at the redefinition of responsibilities which emasculated some existing directorates. Lloyd George immediately appointed Geddes an honorary Major General, which solved the first problem, and required both Haig in France and Sir John Cowans (QMG in London) to smooth over any ruffled feathers.[35]

A recurring and universal theme, articulated by all chief executives taking over a failing enterprise, is to bemoan the lack of investment by his predecessors. Geddes was no exception. On 19 October, Geddes made the startling observation that 'generally speaking the soldier, as opposed to the civilian, asks for less than he really ought to have ... due to the way he has been made to cheesepare, and the fear he has of the Treasury ... throughout, the soldier has almost consistently put forward demands far below the real needs of the situation.'[36] He quite explicitly blamed this on the *Part II* regulations, which urged economy on the administrators of an

31 Brown, *British Logistics*, p.140.
32 Phillips, *Civilian Specialists at War*, p.220.
33 Sheffield and Bourne, (eds), *Haig, War Diaries*, p.239.
34 *Field Service Regulations, Part II*, pp.23–24.
35 Phillips, *Civilian Specialists at War*, p.221.
36 Brown, *British Logistics*, p.143.

expeditionary force. The expeditionary force had a statutory 'financial adviser' whose brief was to control 'expenditure of funds to such extent and in such manner as circumstances may require.'[37] The principle of economy had been impressed on the army since 1909. As Brown says, 'Geddes had no such problem; indeed, he took the opposite approach, to the point that he was accused of extravagance.'[38] Lloyd George authorised the colossal expenditure Geddes demanded, thus ensuring that his proposed new roads, railways and rolling stock would be adequately funded. On seeing this, objections within the army in France melted away.

That such a major upheaval, at a time when the Battle of the Somme was in full swing, was put into practice so smoothly and effectively is a tribute to all concerned. Geddes clearly had an extraordinary ability to convince others of the rationale of his proposals while at the same time making very few real enemies. He understood problems very quickly. He recruited, from army sources where possible, men who had real expertise. He defined logical administrative subdivisions, which could be regarded as redefining, not abolishing, those laid down in *FSR, Part II.* That Geddes' principles of business management and *FSR*'s principles of military organisation were so similar is no surprise. But unsurprisingly, there were problems in the details. Right from the beginning, Geddes worried about Clayton's reaction to his proposals. Clayton, the IGC, had reasons to fear the consequences of a partial imposition of a civilian system on established army arrangements, such as had been proposed in Royden's so recently published report on congestion at the Channel ports. However, on 10 October, 'Clayton [apparently] told Haig that the new system "would work well" and that "he wanted to help in the changes as much as possible"', even though he knew that he would be working himself out of a job.[39]

Clayton was not the only one to express reservations. Maxwell, Haig's QMG, and his principal directors were very aware of the many problems in the systems they were presiding over. They feared, not so much for their jobs as for the army, if their expertise was ignored. Presumably aware of these anxieties, Haig wrote a note, possibly for posterity, which he recorded in his diary in an entry dated 27 October 1916:

> There is a good deal of criticism apparently being made at the appointment of a civilian like Geddes to an important post on the Headquarters of an Army in the Field. These critics seem to fail to realize the size of the Army, and the amount of work which the Army requires of a civilian nature. The working of the railways, the upkeep of the roads, even the baking of bread and 1,000 other industries go on in peace as well as in war. So with the whole nation at war, our object should be to employ men on the same work in war as they are accustomed to do in peace. Acting on this principle, I have got Geddes at the head of all the railways and transportation, with the best practical engineers under him. At the head of road directorate is Mr Maybury, head of the road board in England. The docks, canals etc are being managed in the same way, i.e. by men of practical experience. To put soldiers into such positions, merely because they are generals or colonels, would be to ensure failure.[40]

37 *Field Service Regulations, Part II,* p.43.
38 Brown, *British Logistics*, p.143.
39 Brown, *British Logistics*, p.141, referenced to Haig's Diaries 10 October 1916.
40 Sheffield and Bourne (eds), *Haig, War Diaries*, pp.249–250.

Maxwell met with Haig on 30 October and was sufficiently concerned to offer his resignation. According to Brown, quoting Haig's diaries, Haig was able to reassure Maxwell that 'Geddes had not in fact been sent out by Lloyd George to replace him … Haig had felt Maxwell to be confused about the difference between a staff officer, commander and a director, and that neither Geddes [nor] Maxwell had any real grounds for disagreement.' Haig wrote that 'this seemed to ease his mind! And he said that he would tell his directors to stop criticism.' Maxwell withdrew his threat of resignation.[41] It seems unlikely that Haig lectured Maxwell on the finer details of *FSR, Part II*, pertaining to administrative staff responsibilities, but whatever he said had the desired outcome. Even if he did, Haig was right in suggesting that the business model being followed by Geddes was entirely compatible with the administrative framework described in *FSR, Part II*. The problem, as always, was nomenclature and the redistribution of responsibilities within an expanded system of directorates.

Both Maxwell and Haig knew that the army had to become more ambitious in its transport aims and needed to plan for the forward movement anticipated in the army's ongoing offensives. Even before Geddes arrived, and before the onset of the Somme offensive, Haig had asked Maxwell to arrange plans to feed 'a liberated population in areas likely to be denuded of food by the retiring Germans.' He specified an advance of 60 miles. In June 1916, the committee Maxwell had set up, reported, and issued 'recommendations to armies, corps and divisions, asking that they reserve as much transport as possible for civilian food.'[42] Even if this was largely a show exercise designed to reassure an Anglo-Franco-Belgian committee of their good intentions, both Haig and Maxwell must have been aware that the army hardly had the resources to supply their own men with food and ammunition during an advance, let alone the civilian population.

So, Maxwell worked professionally with Haig's new Director General of Transport, who remained independent as he embarked on a huge expansion of infrastructure supporting the BEF. New railways, broad and narrow gauge, were constructed. Engines and rolling stock were imported to run on them. Old roads were repaired, and new ones built. The routine needs of the army were calculated according to the number and strength of units and arrangements put in place so that extra supplies of ammunition or equipment could be added as required. Brown writes that, 'Efficient operation was the sole objective. Unlike any railway manager before or since, Geddes could ignore costs, profits and even labor unrest, since the laborers were soldiers, P.O.W.'s or Chinese coolies.'[43]

Army commanders were not slow to recognise the importance of the methodical construction of transport infrastructure. When the German forces in front of Sir Henry Rawlinson's army suddenly withdrew to the Hindenburg Line in March 1917:

> …roads, railways and bridges had been systematically destroyed … Rawlinson sent forward only advance guards and cavalry, whose task it would be to cover the construction of roads and railways. He would retain his existing front line as his basic line of resistance and only send his principal body of troops forward when a new strong position had been provided for them.[44]

41 Brown, *British Logistics*, p.141, referenced to Haig's Diaries 30 October 1916.
42 Brown, *British Logistics*, p.125.
43 Brown, *British Logistics*, p.159.
44 Brown, *British Logistics*, p.160–161.

He was enabled to interpret an important principle in *FSR, Part I*, that strong points captured during an advance should be put into a state of defence against counterattack, in a new way.

Honorary Major General Geddes left GHQ in May 1917 to become an honorary vice-admiral with the Royal Navy. His successor was another civilian, Honorary Brigadier General Sir Philip Nash, an example of the 'diaspora of British expertise' recruited by Geddes. In 1911, he had been the equivalent of the assistant general manager of the East Indian Railway, having joined them in 1899. He was recruited to the Ministry of Munitions in 1915 as one of Geddes's assistants, faced with the task of increasing the supply of gun ammunition to the British Army. Under his capable direction in France, the transport system worked efficiently enough that Haig could turn his attention to more pressing matters. In the early months of 1918, Nash was, in turn, replaced as Director General of Transport by Major General Sydney D'Aguilar Crookshank, a Royal Engineer who had served extensively in India and who was specifically recommended by Geddes for the role. Before the onset of the Last Hundred Days, the Transport Directorate was quietly absorbed by the Quartermaster General's Branch in France, back to where it had been placed in 1909 by the regulations of *FSR, Part II*.[45]

Haig did not neglect his other administrative responsibilities through 1917 and 1918. The problem of labour and combing the administrative services for fighting men reared its head again in January 1917. Lieutenant General Lawson's report on the 'Economy of Manpower in France' suggested that 2,900 men of the Army Service Corps could be released. Haig profoundly disagreed. 'In this,' Brown says, 'Haig shows a surprising grasp of the vital importance of his lines of communication – one that had not been entirely evident two years before. By resisting the drastic changes proposed by Lawson, Haig ensured that his lines of communication remained firm in their ability to meet the demands of his troops.'[46]

It is difficult to argue with the assertion made by Brown that 'much of the BEF's success in 1918 can be traced to Haig's decision during the Battle of the Somme to allow Sir Eric Geddes to put the BEF's transportation system in order.'[47] But Haig was enabled to go ahead with the necessary reforms, in this and many other areas, by the duties and responsibilities laid on him by *FSR*. The principle that part of the Commander-in-Chief's job description was that he should identify, and take steps to rectify, any problems that threatened military success was very well established. Haig could act with complete confidence in his legal position. He did not, however, single-handedly enable the necessary changes. He needed the support of Lloyd George in London and that of his senior administrators in France. Writing of 1914, Brown noted that Sir John French had been supported by 'three consummate professionals as his QMG [Robertson], AG [Macready], and IGC [Robb].' Haig had the same help in 1916. All the evidence suggests that Maxwell, QMG, Major General George Fowke, who succeeded Macready as AG in February 1916, and Clayton as IGC, were also 'consummate professionals' in their cooperation with sometimes bruising change under Geddes.

In assessing Haig's administrative achievements, the appointment of Geddes is the most eye-catching, but it was far from the most radical. Every change in GHQ establishment had to be signed off by the C-in-C before being approved by the War Office. As Paul Harris describes in his thesis on the staff at war, the number of staff in post approximately doubled between the end

45 Phillips, *Civilian Specialists at War*, pp.209, 219, 335; Brown, *British Logistics*, pp.194–195.
46 Brown, *British Logistics*, p.167.
47 Brown, *British Logistics*, p.179.

of 1915 and the end of 1918.[48] If Geddes was being profligate in his spending on infrastructure, Haig was not being frugal in his development of a bureaucracy to service his army. Examples have already been given of the improvements that Haig encouraged in expanding training facilities, schools, and the training branch responsible for SS publications. As Fox-Godden describes, by 1917, many at headquarters in France had been actively recruited for having relevant civilian skills to serve in fields such as topography, mapping, observation, and sound-ranging.[49] Haig, by his administrative arrangements and attention to detail, facilitated many other developments, not least the tank. Under *FSR*, only his signature could authorise these many new offshoots of the army command.

Haig did not just maintain an overview of the administrative branches of his army. He kept a firm eye on operational administration, too, both at an organisational and a personnel level. Harris gives some examples: 'The changing nature of the war was illustrated by the introduction of an engineering staff officer at both Corps and Army from the middle of 1916.' Haig also involved himself in removing incompetent operational staff officers and worked to retain efficient officers. In his diary entry of 29 August 1916, he recorded that 'Landon has also been given an indifferent GSO 1, Buzzard by name. I have told Gough to write to the CGS and have the latter changed.' Harris quotes a letter from Kiggell in November 1916, refusing just one of many requests to promote a competent staff officer to command: 'The case of G.S.O.s 1 is a very difficult one and has been carefully considered, not just by me, but by the Commander-in Chief himself ... the needs of the Army and the Empire must take precedence of all personal considerations.'[50] Efficient staff officers were retained in post despite deserving the promotion to command they craved. His final success in integrating the artillery command structure into the fabric of the army by the end of the war was a further major administrative achievement.

Perhaps the best source for obtaining an overview of the extraordinary development of the resources of the British Army between December 1915 and the end of the war is Haig's final despatch, dated 21 March 1919. Its attention to administrative detail is little short of staggering. A section each deals with the development of transport services from docks to the frontline, and with the development of the Signals Service, which expanded from an initial strength of under 2,400 officers and men to a final strength in 1918 of 42,000. In addition, 'the Base Stationery Depot, which went to France in 1914 with a personnel of ten, has expanded into the Directorate of Army Printing and Stationery Services, employing over 60 officers and 850 other ranks.' Nothing, it seems, is too trivial. Carrier pigeons were introduced in 1915, and by the end of the war, 20,000 birds were being kept. 'Through the agency of an Inspectorate of Messing and Economies, regular schools of cookery gave instructions to nearly 25,000 cooks.' He even describes a recycling offshoot. 'The Directorate of Agricultural Production organized farm and garden enterprises for the local supply of vegetables [by harvesting abandoned crops].' A team was appointed, under the supervision of a fire expert, to take responsibility for fire precautions on all army sites. He lists the main civilian welfare agencies that he allowed to be active in France in 1918: 'The Y.M.C.A., the Church Army, the Scottish Churches Huts, the Salvation Army, the Soldiers' Christian Association, the Catholic Women's League and Club Huts, the United Army and Navy Board, the Wesleyan Soldiers' Institute and the British

48 Harris, 'The Staff of the British Army', pp.193–194.
49 Fox-Godden, *Inter-Theatre Learning in the British Army*, p.196.
50 Harris, 'The Staff of the British Army', pp.197, 203, 205.

Soldiers' Institute,' were all personally authorised by him, with consideration of the roles of women in their ranks.[51]

'It may be argued that with the rearward services rests victory or defeat,' Haig says in summing up this section of his final despatch. Haig's administrative genius was indeed the difference between victory and defeat. Douglas Haig was a very great war leader when judged on his administrative achievements. He was enabled to be a great war leader by having a doctrinal handbook to follow, one that not only laid down his duties and responsibilities as Commander-in-Chief with great clarity but also one that was totally accepted by his senior subordinates. As previously described, when, in his first weeks as Commander-in-Chief, he asserted the need for uniform and expanded training, and for improvements in the supply of food and ammunition to the front line, he backed this up with an exhortation for all staff to follow the regulations in *FSR, Part II*. After the doctrinal vacillations of French they were delighted to do so.

51 Boraston, *Sir Douglas Haig's despatches*, pp.334–340.

20

Conclusion

It is easy to lose sight of basic principles in any study of the First World War. Its huge scale, the millions of words written during it, and the even greater complexity of the millions of words written after it, right up to the present day, disguise these principles. But general principles relating to tactics, command and administration were followed by almost all officers in the BEF in 1914, and those same principles, albeit refined by hard experience, were being followed by GHQ and by all the best units of the British Army in 1918. The doctrine that expressed those principles, envisaged by Lord Roberts in 1900, defined by Richard Haldane in 1906, and implemented by William Nicholson and his senior colleagues from 1909, was *FSR*.

It is *FSR*'s influence on operations that will hold the interest of most historians. *FSR* lays down the principle that the Commander-in-Chief is totally responsible for the successes or failures of the force for which he is responsible. Sir John French was thus completely responsible for the conduct of the army's campaigns in 1914 and 1915. His decision to give Haig free rein, particularly at Loos, after the failure of earlier battles, was his and his alone. If Haig is to be judged on operational grounds, the verdict of history must be that his contribution in 1914 and 1915 was unimpressive at best. However, he was a subordinate. It is not he who was responsible. If blame is to be allocated pertaining to these battles, it is French who must shoulder it. All the evidence suggests that French embraced *FSR* in the pre-war years. As Inspector General of the Forces, he was diligent in enforcing compliance with it on the wider army, but, nevertheless, he did not follow it himself as Commander-in-Chief with respect to his duties and responsibilities. He failed to react when Haig fundamentally challenged *FSR*'s command and operational principles in 1914. Worse, by tolerating Haig's challenge to his authority under *FSR*, he allowed a doctrinal rift to open at the top of the army that would cause problems until 1918. Haig's increasingly influential rejection of *FSR's* operational principles, as his power in the army increased, set the scene for the disastrous battles of 1915, despite the passive resistance offered by most of the senior hierarchy of the BEF. By early 1916, *FSR*'s operational principles were being reasserted, both in CDS publications and in army best practice. But with Haig as Commander-in-Chief, this renaissance was short-lived. Haig continued to reject the principle of all-arms combination at the divisional level, believing that the corps, not the division, was the basic fighting unit. He believed that British infantry, as a single arm, had the necessary qualities to prevail against an all-arms enemy force. It was not until he had presided over the disaster that was the first month of Third Ypres in 1917 that his views were institutionally rejected, and adherence to *FSR* principles was explicitly readopted by GHQ and most senior generals, with the full support of their junior subordinates.

Some may regard this book as mounting a sustained attack on Haig and his contribution to victory. Nothing is further from the truth. It merely avoids Haig-centrism. Credit is given to Haig for his prescient handling of artillery in the battles of 1914. *FSR* was not always applicable, and adherence to it was not always the right course. Because he rejected the *FSR* principle that the division was the unit that fought battles, believing it was the corps, his handling of the artillery at Mons and at the Aisne in 1914 was superior to that of Smith-Dorrien. There were other principles he rejected. Maybe attrition, for instance, a concept foreign to *FSR*, was necessary. Haig was Commander-in-Chief when the war was won, and, by that time, his army was fighting broadly in compliance with the operational principles of *FSR*. The fact that it was administered and supplied sufficiently well to maintain the pressure through the Last Hundred Days is a tribute both to his supreme competence and to his close and prolonged adherence to the administrative principles of *FSR*.

The narrative given in this book is not universally accepted. On the first page of his book *How the War was Won*, written in 1992, Tim Travers muses on the factors that led to victory in 1918:

> Did new ideas make a difference? Did new tactics and strategy affect the outcome? Did new weapons and technology make the difference? Or was success the result of using old technology, but much more of it? Was 1918 really a victory of attrition for the BEF, so that manpower was the key? Perhaps a revitalised leadership was the key, with Douglas Haig now coming into his own? Maybe the whole BEF had simply become more efficient.

This book argues that there were no 'new ideas', no 'new tactics.' Travers is asking the wrong questions. But it is not till the last paragraph of the book that he sets out, with crystal clarity, the flawed premise that led him to do so: 'The older generation of officers had conducted the war according to their inherited traditions and experience of small-scale nineteenth-century wars.'[1]

This book relates in detail why this statement is not true. But there is one important source that supports this assertion. Haig's operational analysis of the war in his final despatch suggests that he had indeed relied on 'inherited traditions'. In his section, a 'Single Great Battle', he interprets the war in Clausewitzian terms: 'If the operations of the past 4 years are regarded as a single continuous campaign, there can be recognised in them the same general features and the same necessary stages which between forces of approximately equal strength have marked all the conclusive battles of history.' He acknowledges that the successive stages of battle happened quicker at Waterloo in 1815 than they did in the First World War. He spends no time analysing his battles of 1915, but the point is made.[2] Echoes of this narrow definition of the debate on the operational evolution of the BEF from 1914 to 1918 persist to the present day in studies of the war. Travers and his followers cling to the hypothesis that the British High Command fumbled through a nebulous Clausewitzian ethos that was embedded in their collective consciousness until they discovered, and implemented, effective combined arms tactics. This view has arisen because analysis of the war has depended on analysis of Haig. Haig-centrism is the enemy of scholarship.

1 Travers, *How the War Was Won*, pp.1, 182.
2 Boraston, *Sir Douglas Haig's despatches*, pp.319–321.

It was the intelligent application of a pre-war army doctrine, focused on a small number of key principles as defined by *FSR*, that guided the British Army to ultimate victory. Haig's operational summary of the Western Front campaign is incorrect. He states that 'the operations of the last four years' constitute a strategic continuum, when, in fact, they can be divided neatly into four specific campaigns, separated by pauses for reflection and taking stock. In terms of size, state of training, state of organisation and administration, and state of morale, the British Army was completely different on the first of January in every year of the war.

Haig, unsurprisingly, does not cite the impact of operational *FSR* on the British Army's performance. He was, under *FSR*, personally responsible for the success or failure of the campaigns of 1916, 1917 and 1918. He defined their intent and selected the commanders he thought most suitable to carry out that intent. After he was subordinated to General Foch, Supreme Allied Commander, on 26 March 1918, his duty to define intent for British offensives was at least diluted, if not surrendered. But a valedictory last despatch was not the time to analyse individual battles. To 'a steady adherence to the principles of our Field Service Regulations Part I, are our successes to be attributed', he had written, in September 1918, to Sir Henry Wilson, a principal pre-war author of them. This private acknowledgement that perhaps he had not always been entirely correct in his perceptions of the route to victory is the best that we can expect from a stubborn traditionalist in tactical and strategic thought.

However, at least as important as operational competence are logistics and administration. Sometimes, during the war, *FSR* principles were so smoothly applied that they are barely noticeable. The almost effortless expansion of the establishment of both staff and fighting units between 1914 and 1918 is a case in point. It was the Commander-in-Chief, first French, and then Haig, who, under *FSR*, presided over and orchestrated this expansion of the army in France and Belgium. No work has assessed Sir John French with reference to *FSR*. He diligently implemented it in the pre-war period, yet he did not fully assume the duties and responsibilities mandated on him as Commander-in-Chief in August 1914. He was required to strictly define operational intent for his subordinates, and all the evidence suggests that he abrogated this responsibility with respect to I Corps and later his First Army. He was required to identify and address 'inefficiencies' in the administrative branches supporting his army, and he failed to do so. Sir William Robertson and his colleagues stepped up, and it is well that they did. French also failed to address problems of artillery command.

French's poor leadership in all areas is brought into sharp focus when Haig became Commander-in-Chief at the end of 1915. Haig embarked on a visionary and decisive reorganisation of the administration of the army, as he was both entitled and mandated to do by *FSR*. On taking up his post, Haig immediately recognised that he was responsible for identifying and addressing inefficiencies. Within weeks, he had implemented changes that improved the training, transport, logistics and general welfare of his army. It was a pleasant surprise to Sir Henry Rawlinson when he heard how Haig had gone out of his way to be affable with the French High Command at Chantilly on 29 December 1915, and it may well have been a surprise to Sir Ronald Maxwell (QMG) and Sir Nevil Macready (AG) when Haig summoned them to daily meetings from the very early days of his command.[3] In this, he was adhering completely to the spirit of the *Staff Manual 1912*. His subsequent actions and the acceptance of his responsibilities comply closely with the principles articulated in *FSR, Part II*. That Haig

3 Charteris, *Field Marshal Earl Haig*, pp.191, 205.

recognised this is confirmed by his reference to *Part II* in his final despatch, under the heading 'Training and Organization':

> It may be accepted as a general rule that previous organization should be upset as little as possible in war. As each war has certain special conditions, so some modification of existing ideas and practices will be necessary, but if our principles are sound these will be few and unimportant. In the present war, new organizations and establishments for dealing with the demands of both the fighting and the rearward services have been brought into being continually, and added to or absorbed by our existing organization and establishment.[4]

He is recognising that the framework laid down by the *Part II* regulations as they related to an expeditionary force in 1914, and the flexibility they provided in allowing him to upgrade both operational units and staff duties, facilitated the smooth and relatively painless expansion of the army. He recognises no blips or break points. *Part II* was relevant from August 1914 to November 1918. Even his reorganisation of transport followed a continuum of logical improvements to the *Part II* framework. He says that 'the principles of command, Staff work, and organization elaborated before the war have stood the test imposed upon them and are sound. The militarily [Staff College] educated officer has counted for much, and the good work done by our Staff Colleges during the past 30 years has had an important influence upon the successful issue of the war.'[5] Douglas Haig understood and accepted the duties and responsibilities of a Commander-in-Chief, as defined by *FSR*, with respect to administration and organisation.

This book suggests that *FSR* defined a doctrine for the British Army in 1914. It suggests that this doctrine had evolved from practical lessons learnt in the small wars of the Empire and the cathartic experience of the South African War at the turn of the century. The men charged with developing *Combined Training 1902* into *FSR 1909* also digested reports from the Russo-Japanese War in Manchuria in 1904. They doubted the relevance of principles that had evolved from Napoleonic and subsequent campaigns. The impact of so many new technologies – railways, telephones, motor cars, machine guns, smokeless rifle cartridges, quick-firing artillery, aeroplanes, and balloons – looked to have changed the face of warfare forever. They accepted the necessity of adopting modern business management techniques to coordinate the administration of what would become a huge continental army. The doctrine of *FSR* was new and a step change from the military ideas of the nineteenth century. Of course, echoes of its philosophy can be cherry-picked from the plethora of contradictory military advice offered in guidance handbooks for the different arms before the South African War. Echoes can also be found in the writings of Jomini and Clausewitz, as refined by G.F.R. Henderson. But neither the Edwardian army nor Edwardian society relied on legacies from the past. *FSR* was a product of its time, absorbing so many new ideas that, to repeat a quote from the first chapter, 'many retired officers found they could not adapt to the changes wrought by the introduction of the new Field Service Regulations.'[6]

Embedded in the consciousness of the army by 1914, it remained demonstrably relevant at every stage of the long war that followed. Because this is so, it is impossible to address, let

4 Boraston, *Sir Douglas Haig's despatches*, p.343.
5 Boraston, *Sir Douglas Haig's despatches*, p.343.
6 Simkins, *Kitchener's Army*, p.217.

alone make any authoritative judgement on, the tactical, command or administrative conduct of the First World War without a knowledge and appreciation of it. It is necessary to know who developed the doctrine and why they did so. It requires an understanding of the concept of the professionalisation of the fighting arms, allied to a simultaneous civilianisation of the administrative arms between 1909 and 1914. Only once the extent to which *FSR* dominated the thinking of the British army of 1914 has been appreciated can the serious historian move forward and tackle the developments in tactics, command and administration that occurred after August 1914. There is no issue on which *FSR* does not have a bearing.

Major Ferrers-Guy, a junior staff officer during the war, considered non-compliance with *FSR* a very major issue. He wrote to James Edmonds as late as 1937 to say that the staff 'cannot say that their orders were always framed on sound tactics based on Field Service Regulations (FSR) Part I.' They expected 'gallant and brave men to do what was impossible [giving] them no sporting chance of a fight' wasting good officers and men in offensives which were ill-prepared and showed a 'total disregard of the opinion of Officers, NCO's and men who had to do it.'[7] My own grandfather voiced much the same sentiments in his letters to his mother as he manned his guns during the battles of Festubert in 1915 and Passchendaele in 1917. This book is my tribute to him.

7 Robbins, *British Generalship*, p.21; M.C. Ferrers-Guy to Edmonds, 29 July 1937.

Bibliography

War Office and United States War Department Publications

Amendments to Combined Training, Field Service Regulations Part I, 1905 (London: War Office, 1907)

Cavalry Training 1907 (London: War Office, 1907)

Combined Training, (Provisional) 1902 (London: War Office, 1902)

Combined Training, Field Service Regulations, Part I, 1905 (London: General Staff, War Office, 1905)

Drill Regulations for the Infantry, German Army, 1906, translated for the United States War Department by Francis Behr (Washington: Government Printing Office, 1907)

Field Artillery Training (London: General Staff, War Office, 1914)

Field Service Pocket Book, (Provisional), 1907 (London: War Office, 1907)

Field Service Regulations, Part I, Operations, 1909 (London: War Office, 1909)

Field Service Regulations, Part I, Operations, 1909, Reprinted with Amendments 1912 (London: General Staff, War Office, 1912)

Field Service Regulations, Part II, Organization and Administration, 1909, Reprinted with Amendments 1913 (London: General Staff, War Office, 1913)

Infantry Drill 1896 (London: War Office, 1896)

Infantry Training, (provisional), 1902 (London: War Office, 1902)

King's Regulations and Orders for the Army, 1908 (London: War Office, 1908)

King's Regulations and Orders for the Army, 1912, reprinted with amendments up to 1st August 1914 (London: War Office, 1914)

Regulations for Mobilization 1914 (London: War Office, 1914)

Staff Manual (Provisional) 1911 (London: War Office 1912)

The War Office List and Administrative Directory for the British Army, 1905 (London: H.M.S.O., 1905)

The War Office List and Administrative Directory for the British Army 1908 (London: War Office, 1908)

The War Office List and Administrative Directory for the British Army 1903 (London: War Office, 1903)

Central Distribution Section (CDS) and Stationery Service (SS), War Office and GHQ

CDS 2 *Notes from the Front, Part I*, collated by the General Staff, December 1914
CDS 3 *Notes from the Front, Part II*, collated by the General Staff, May 1915
CDS 4 *Notes from the Front, Part III, and Further Notes on Field Defences*, collated by the General Staff, February 1915
CDS 5 *Trench Warfare, Notes on Attack and Defence*, collated by the General Staff, February 1915
CDS 24 *Object and Conditions of Combined Offensive Action, issued by the General Staff*, GHQ, June 1915
CDS 50 *Tactical Notes, issued by the General Staff*, GHQ, 31 July 1915
CDS 98/1 *Artillery Notes, Close Shooting in the Field*, January 1916, as reprinted in *Field Artillery Notes*, issued by the Army War College, Washington DC, May 1917
CDS 98/3 *Artillery Notes, Counter-Battery Work*, 1916, as reprinted in *Field Artillery Notes*, issued by the Army War College, Washington DC, 1917
CDS 98/4 *Artillery in Offensive Operations April 1916*, France, GHQ, 1916
SS 101 *Notes for Infantry Officers on Trench Warfare March 1916*, War Office, 1916
SS 109 *Training of Divisions for Offensive Action, May 1916*, GHQ, 1916
SS 119 *Preliminary Notes on the Tactical Lessons of the Recent Operations*, GHQ, July 1916
SS 135 *Instructions for the Training of Divisions for Offensive Action*, GHQ, December 1916
SS 143 *Instructions for the Training of Platoons for Offensive Action, 1917*, GHQ, February 1917
SS 148 *Forward Inter-communication in Battle March 1917*, Washington Reprint 1917
SS 161 *Instructions for Battle*, GHQ, *May 1917*
SS 204 *Infantry and Tank Co-operation and Training*, GHQ, March 1918
SS 210 *The Division in Defence*, GHQ, May 1918
SS 135, re-issue *The Division in Attack*, GHQ, November 1918

Archives

Military and Regional Archives

Bodleian Library, Oxford
OT 5/1/1: Officer Training Corps, Oxford University Contingent Part I Orders Oct 1912 – June 1913

Imperial War Museum (IWM)
Document 92168: Letters, Captain Ralph Blewitt, RFA, 1915
IWM 73/1/2: Diaries of Field Marshal Sir Henry Wilson

National Army Museum (NAM)
NAM 7101/23: Roberts papers
NAM 8704/35/33-38: Ellison correspondence and papers

National Library of Scotland (NLS)
Acc.3155/98: Douglas Haig Papers

Royal Artillery Museum (RAM)
RAM MD/425: Journal, Lt E. Schreiber, XXV brigade RFA, 1914
RAM MD/931: Journal, Captain, later Major, J L Mowbray, 1914
RAM MD/1150: Journal, Lieutenant (later Colonel) Roderick McLeod, RFA, Journal, from 1913

Sandhurst Collection Archives (SCA)
Box 90, and loose papers
Box 142, pre-war exam papers, Royal Military Academy/Royal Military College, 1907–1912

Private Collections
Letters, and journals of Colin Hutchison, RFA 1913–1919
Letters, and journals of Duke Marshall, RFA 1915–1917

The National Archives (TNA)
Pre-1914 records
CAB 37/85: Confidential Memorandum embodying a General Statement on the subject of the Organization and Training of the Territorial Army, 23 November 1906
CAB 38/16/21: Co-ordination of Departmental Action on the Outbreak of War, Committee of Imperial Defence, November 1910
WO 27/508: *Annual Reports of the Inspector General of the Forces, 1909-1913* (London: War Office)
WO 32/4730: Committee on Staff Duties in the Field, War Office, 1911
WO 32/4731: Staff Manual, and correspondence, 1912-1914
WO 32/4735: Army Organization, Draft Field Service regulations, 1907–1908
WO 32/4736: Army Organization, Draft Field Service regulations, 1908–1909
WO 32/6776: Royal Field Artillery Mobilisation Arrangements at home, 1909
WO 32/6785: Report of Committee on Cavalry Peace Organization and Mobilization Arrangements 1909
WO 33/2747: Report of a Conference and Staff Ride as carried out at the Staff College by Senior Officers of the General Staff, January 1905
WO 33/2982: Naval and Military Tour, carried out in April–May, 1907, Joint Report of the Commandant, Staff College, Camberley, and the Captain, Royal Naval War College, Portsmouth
WO 33/3369: Richard Haldane, A preliminary memorandum on the present situation, being a rough note for consideration by the Members of the Army Council, 1 January 1906
WO 33/3373: Richard Haldane, Notes on the Organization and Administration of the Military Forces of the United Kingdom, 14 June 1906
WO 33/3379: Richard Haldane, Further Note on the Military System, Administrative System in War, December 1906.
WO 33/3386: 1907 War System-Peace System Notes
WO 106/1453: Report of Aldershot Command Staff Tour 1912, Aldershot 1912
WO 231: Directorate of Military Training, Administrative/Biographical Background
WO 231/403: Memorandum on Army Training, 1908
WO 231/404: Memorandum on Army Training, 1909
WO 237/13: Recommendations of Committees on Army Matters, 1900–1920
WO 242/2: Directors' Meetings 1907, Minutes of meetings 42-71

WO 260: Directorate of Staff Duties, Administrative/Biographical Background
WO 279/7: Report on Combined Manoeuvres 1903
WO 279/8: Report on Army Manoeuvres 1904
WO 279/9: Report of a Conference and Staff Ride as carried out at the Staff College by Senior Officers of the General Staff, January 1906
WO 279/14: Report of a Staff Ride held by Director of Staff Duties under Instructions from the Chief of the General Staff, 27th to 31st May 1907
WO 279/17: Report of a Staff Ride held by the Chief of the General Staff October 1907
WO 279/18: Conference of General Staff Officers at the Staff College, 7th to 10th January 1908
WO 279/22: Report on a Staff Tour held by the Chief of the General Staff, 26-30 October 1908
WO 279/25: Report of a Conference of General Staff Officers at the Staff College, 18th to 21st January 1909, held under the direction of The Chief of the General Staff
WO 279/27: Cavalry Staff Ride of Director of Staff Studies, March 1909
WO 279/29: Cavalry Staff Ride of Director of Staff Studies, June 1909
WO 279/31: Report on Army Manoeuvres 1909
WO 279/39: Army Manoeuvres 1910
WO 279/42: Report of a Conference of General Staff Officers at the Staff College, 9th to 12th January 1911, held under the Direction of the Chief of the Imperial General Staff
WO 279/45: Report of a Conference of General Staff Officers at the Staff College, 15th to 18th January 1912, held under the Orders of the Chief of the Imperial General Staff
WO 279/47: Army Manoeuvres 1912
WO 279/48: Report of a Conference of General Staff Officers at the Royal Military College, 13th to 16th January 1913, under the Direction of the Chief of the Imperial General Staff
WO 279/52: Army Exercise, 1913
WO 279/495: Report of a Conference of General Staff Officers at the Royal Military College, 12th to 15th January 1914, held under the Orders and Direction of the Chief of the Imperial General Staff
WO 279/496: Report of a Conference of General Staff Officers at the Staff College, 17th to 20th January 1910, held under the Direction of the Chief of the Imperial General Staff
WO 279/512: Report on a Staff Ride held in Scotland under the direction of the Director of Staff Duties in May 1906
WO 279/516: Report of the Preliminary Training for the IInd Army-Corps and its Implementation in the Army Manoeuvres 1903
WO 279/526: Report on Staff Tour, held by the Chief of the General Staff, India, 1910
WO 279/532: Report on Staff Tour, held by the Chief of the General Staff, India, 1911
WO 279/552: Army Training Memorandum, War Office, 19 December 1912
WO 279/553: Army Training Memorandum during the Individual Training Period 1912-13
WO 279/554: Army Training Memorandum during the Collective Training Period, 1913

Unit War Diaries

WO 95/1/2: General Staff War Diary, August 1914
WO 95/1/8: General Staff, Commander-in-Chief BEF, Diary August 1914
WO 95/1096: Cavalry Division War Diary, August 1914

WO 95/1138/1: 5 Cavalry Brigade War Diary, August 1914
WO 95/1227: 1 Division War Diary, August 1914
WO 95/1274: 3 Infantry Brigade War Diary, August 1914
WO 95/1274: 3 Infantry Brigade War Diary,, 21 August 1914
WO 95/1283; 2 Division War Diary, August 1914
WO 95/1326: XLI Brigade RFA War Diary, August 1914
WO 95/1342: 1 Irish Guards War Diary, August 1914
WO 95/1342: 3 Coldstream Guards War Diary, August 1914
WO 95/1343: 5 Infantry Brigade War Diary, August 1914
WO 95/1375: 3 Division War Diary, August 1914
WO 95/1400: 8 Infantry Brigade War Diary, August 1914
WO 95/1401: XLII Brigade RFA War Diary, August 1914
WO 95/1425: 9 Infantry Brigade, War Diary, August 1914
WO 95/1521: 5 Division Artillery War Diary, August 1914
WO 95/1572/2: 1 Dorsetshire Regiment War Diary, August 1914
WO 95/1581/1/2: 6 Division Artillery, War Diary, August 1915
WO 95/1631/1: 7 Division, War Diary, July 1916
WO 95/1638/4: 7 Division Artillery War Diary, August 1915
WO 95/1639/2/1: 7 Division Artillery War Diary, July 1916
WO 95/1643/1: 22 Brigade RFA, War Diary, July 1916
WO 95/2471/1: 35 Division Artillery War Diary, June 1916
WO 95/295/3: 113 Brigade RFA War Diary, August 1917
WO 95/3744: 118 Brigade, RFA, War Diary, April 1915
WO 95/3949/1: Staff Diary of Inspector General of Communications, August 1914
WO 95/588/1: I Corps Staff War Diary and Reports, August 1914
WO 95/588/4: I Corps Staff War Diary, August 1914
WO 95/629/4: II Corps Staff Intelligence Diary,1914
WO 95/630/1: II Corps Staff War Diary, August 1914
WO 95/668/1: III Corps Staff War Diary, September 1914
WO 95/707/1: IV Corps General Staff War Diary, January 1915

Official Histories and Reports

Akers-Douglas, the Right Honourable A. (Chairman), *The Report of the Committee approved to consider the Education and Training of the Officers of the Army* (London: HMSO, 1902)
Annual Register for 1903 (London: Longmans, Green, and Co. 1904)
Army Orders 1905 (London: Harrison & Sons, 1906)
Army Orders 1906 (London: Harrison & Sons, 1907)
Army Orders 1909 (London: Harrison & Sons, 1910)
Edmonds, Brigadier General J.E., *History of the Great War, Military Operations, France and Belgium 1914: Volume 1, Mons, the Retreat to the Seine, the Marne and the Aisne, August-October 1914* (London: MacMillan, 1933)
Edmonds, Brigadier General J.E., *History of the Great War, Military Operations, France and Belgium 1915 Battles of Aubers Ridge, Festubert, and Loos* (London: MacMillan, 1928)

Edmonds, Brigadier General J.E., *Official History of the Great War, Military Operations France & Belgium, 1916, Volume 1, Appendices* (London: MacMillan, 1932)

Edmonds, Brigadier General J.E., *Official History of the Great War, Military Operations France and Belgium, 1918, Volume 1, Appendices* (London: MacMillan, 1935)

Esher, Viscount, J.A. Fisher, G.S. Clarke, *Report of the War Office (Reconstitution Committee) 1904, Presented to both Houses of Parliament by command of His Majesty* (London: HMSO, 1904)

Hart, Lieutenant General H.G., *Hart's Annual Army List, Militia List, And Yeomanry Cavalry List,* (London: John Murray, 1902–1915)

Roberts, Field Marshal Lord, *South Africa 1900, Proclamations, Army Orders and Circular Memoranda,* (London: Harrison & Sons, 1900)

Royal Commission on the War in South Africa; Minutes of Evidence Volume II (London: War Office, 1903)

Statistics of the Military Effort of the British Empire During the Great War 1914–1920 (London: War Office, 1922)

Memoires and Collected Letters/Journals

Boraston, J.H. (ed.), *Sir Douglas Haig's despatches (December 1915-April 1919)* (London: J.M. Dent, 1919)

Callwell, Major General Sir C.E., *Field-Marshal Sir Henry Wilson Bart., GCB, DSO, His Life and Diaries, Volume 1* (Kindle reprint Ontario, Legacy Books, 2021[Cassel & Company, London, 1927])

French, Sir John, *1914* (London: Constable and Co. Ltd., 1919)

Gough, Sir Hubert, *The Fifth Army* (London: Hodder & Stoughton, 1931)

Macready, General the Rt. Hon. Sir Nevil, *Annals of an Active Life, Volume 1* (New York: George Doran, 1925)

Robertson, William, D.R. Woodward (ed.), *The Military Correspondence of Field Marshal Sir William Robertson, Chief of the Imperial General Staff, December 1915–February 1918* (London: Bodley Head for the Army Records Society, 1989)

Scott, Douglas, *The Preparatory Prologue, Douglas Haig Diaries and Letters, 1861 to 1914* (Barnsley: Pen & Sword, 2006)

Sheffield, Gary, and John Bourne (eds), *Douglas Haig, War Diaries and Letters, 1914-1918* (London: Wiedenfeld and Nicholson, 2005)

Smith-Dorrien, General Sir Horace Lockwood, *Memories of Forty-Eight Years' Service* (New York: E.P. Dutton and Company, 1925)

Biographical Sources

Beckett, Ian, and Steven Corvi (eds), *Haig's Generals* (Barnsley: Pen & Sword Military, 2020 [2006])

Bond, Brian and Nigel Cave (eds), *Haig, a Re-Appraisal 80 Years On* (Barnsley: Pen & Sword, 2017 [1999])

Charteris, Brigadier General John, *Field-Marshal Earl Haig* (London: Cassel & Co Ltd, 1929)
Cooper, Duff, *Haig* (London: Faber and Faber, 1935)
De Groot, G.J., *The Pre-War Life and Military Career of Douglas Haig* (PhD, University of Edinburgh, 1983)
DeGroot, Gerard, *Douglas Haig, 1861–1928* (London: Unwin Hyman, 1988)
Dictionary of Irish Biography, <www.dib.ie>, accessed 25 February 2024
Encyclopædia Britannica (Cambridge: Cambridge University Press, 1910)
Farr, Don, *The Silent General, Horne of the First Army* (Solihull: Helion & Company, 2007)
Harris, J.P., *Douglas Haig and the First World* War (Cambridge: Cambridge University Press, 2008)
Jeffery, Keith, *Field Marshal Sir Henry Wilson, a Political Soldier* (Oxford: Oxford University Press, 2006)
MacDiarmid, D.S., *The Life of Lieut. General Sir James Moncrieff Grierson* (London: Constable, 1923)
Mead, Gary, *The Good Soldier, the Biography of Douglas Haig* (London: Atlantic Books, 2014)
Phillips, Christopher, 'Sir Eric Campbell Geddes', *International Encyclopaedia of the First World War, 1914–1918*, <https://encyclopedia.1914-1918-online.net/article/geddes-eric-campbell-sir/?format=pdf>, accessed 5 August 2024
Powel, Geoffrey, *Plumer, the Soldier's General* (London: Leo Cooper, 1990)
Prior, Robin, and Trevor Wilson, *Command on the Western Front: The Military Career of Sir Henry Rawlinson 1914 – 1918* (Barnsley: Pen & Sword, 2004 [1992])
Ridley, Nicholas, *Far from Suitable? Haig, Gough and Passchendaele: A Reappraisal* (Warwick: Helion, 2024)
Shand, Alexander, *The Life of Sir Edward Bruce Hamley* (London: Blackwood & Sons, 1895)
Sheffield, Gary, *The Chief, Douglas Haig and the British Army* (London: Aurum Press, 2011)
Simpson, Robert, *Major General Sir Gerald Francis Ellison KCB KCMG MiD*, <https//:www.anzac-biographies.com/2017/05/29/ellison-major-general-sir-gerald-francis-kcb-kcmg-mid/>, accessed February 2020
Spiers, Edward, *Haldane; An Army Reformer* (Edinburgh: Edinburgh University Press, 1980)
Terraine, John, *Douglas Haig, the Educated Soldier* (London: Leo Cooper, 1990 [1963])
Von Kluck, Alexander, *The March on Paris, the Memoirs of Alexander Von Kluck, 1914* (Barnsley: Frontline, 2012 [1923])
Williams, Jeffery, *Byng of Vimy, General and Governor General* (Barnsley: Pen & Sword, 2014 [1983])

General Works

Anglesey, Marquess of, *A History of the British Cavalry 1816-1919, Volume 4, 1899-1913* (London: Leo Cooper, 1986)
Beach, Jim, *Haig's Intelligence: GHQ and the German Army, 1916-1918* (Cambridge: Cambridge University Press, 2015 [2013])
Becke, Archibald Frank, *The Royal Regiment of Artillery at Le Cateau, Wednesday, 26th August, 1914* (London: Woolwich, 1919)
Beckett, Ian, Timothy Bowman and Mark Connelly, *The British Army and the First World War* (Cambridge: Cambridge University Press, 2017)

Bidwell, Shelford, *Gunners at War, a Tactical Study of the Royal Artillery in the Twentieth Century* (London: Arrow Press, 1972)
Boff, Jonathan, *Winning and Losing on the Western Front: The British Third Army and the Defeat of Germany in 1918* (Cambridge: Cambridge University Press, 2012)
Bond, Brian, *The Victorian Army and the Staff College, 1854-1914* (London: Eyre Methuen, 1972)
Bowman, Timothy and Mark Connelly, *The Edwardian Army, Recruiting, Training and Deploying the British Army, 1902-1914* (Oxford: University Press, 2012)
Brown, Ian Malcolm, *British Logistics on the Western Front 1914-1919* (Westport: Praeger, 1998)
Dunlop, Colonel John, *The Development of the British Army 1899-1914* (London: Methuen, 1938)
Fox, Aimée, *Learning to Fight, Military Innovation and Change in the British Army, 1914 – 1918* (Cambridge: Cambridge University Press, 2018)
French, David, *British Economic and Strategic Planning:1905-1915* (Abingdon: Routledge, 2006 [1982])
Fuller, Captain J.F.C., *Training Soldiers for War* (London: Hugh Rees Ltd., 1914)
Gardner, Nikolas, *Trial by Fire, Command and the British Expeditionary Force in 1914* (Westport: Praeger, 2003)
Gilbert, Adrian, *Challenge of Battle, the Real Story of the British Army in 1914* (Oxford: Osprey, 2014)
Gooch, John, *The Plans of War, the General Staff and British Military Strategy c. 1900-1916* (London: Routledge & Kegan Paul, 1974)
Green, Andrew, *Writing the Great War: Sir James Edmonds and the Official History 1915-1948* (London: Frank Cass, 2003)
Griffith, Paddy, *Battle Tactics of the Western Front* (New Haven, Yale University Press 1994)
Haig, Major General Douglas, *Cavalry Studies, Strategical and Tactical* (London: Hugh Rees Ltd, 1907)
Hamilton, Richard, and Holger Herwig (eds), *War Planning 1914* (Cambridge: Cambridge University Press, 2010 [2009])
Hamley, Sir Edward Bruce, *The Operations of War, Explained and Illustrated* (Oxford: Blackwood and Sons, 1886)
Hay, Ian, *The First Hundred Thousand* (Edinburgh: Blackwood, 1915)
Henderson, G.F.R., N. Malcolm (ed.), *The Science of War: A Collection of Essays and Lectures 1891-1903* (Alpha Editions, 2019 [London: Longmans, Green, 1912])
Hunzeker, Michael A., *Dying to Learn, Wartime Lessons from the Western Front* (Ithaca: Cornell University Press, 2021)
Hutchinson, Colonel H.D., *The Campaign in Tirah, 1897-1898* (London: Macmillan & Co., 1898)
Hutchison, David, *Mons, an Artillery Battle* (Warwick: Helion, 2018)
Hutchison, David (David Keable-Elliott), *The Young Gunner: The Royal Field Artillery in the Great War* (Kibworth Beauchamp: Matador Press, 2016)
Hutchison, Lieutenant Colonel G.S., *Machine Guns: Their History and Tactical Employment (Being also a History of the Machine Gun Corps, 1916-1922)* (London: Macmillan, 1938)
Iarocci, Andrew, *Shoestring Soldiers, The 1st Canadian Division at War, 1914-1915* (Toronto: University of Toronto Press, 2008)
Jones, Spencer (ed.), *Stemming the Tide, Officers and Leadership in the British Expeditionary Force 1914* (Solihull: Helion, 2013)

Jones. Spencer (ed.), *Courage without Glory, the British Army on the Western Front 1915* (Warwick: Helion, 2019)

Jones. Spencer (ed.), *The Darkest Hour: The British Army on the Western Front 1917* (Warwick: Helion, 2022)

Kearsey, Alexander, *1915 Campaign in France, The Battles of Aubers Ridge, Festubert and Loos, considered in relation to the Field Service Regulations* (Aldershot: Gale and Pollard Ltd, second edition, 1929)

Layland Needham, Lieutenant Colonel J., *The Solution of Tactical Problems, Fourth Edition Revised* (London: Hugh Rees, 1909)

Legge, R.F., *The Officers' Training Corps Examiner for Certificate 'A'* (London: Gale and Polden, 1909)

Luvaas, Jay, *The Military Legacy of the Civil War, The European Inheritance* (Lawrence: University Press of Kansas, 1988 [1959])

Marden, Thomas Owen (ed.), *A Short History of the 6th Division* (London: Hugh Rees 1920)

Messenger, Charles, *Call to Arms, The British Army 1914-18* (London: Cassell, 2006)

Mitchinson, K., *The Territorial Force at War 1914 – 1916* (Palgrave Macmillan, Kindle edition [2014])

Olsen, John Andreas, and Martin van Creveld (eds), *The Evolution of Operational Art: From Napoleon to the Present* (Oxford: Oxford University Press, 2010)

Palazzo, Albert, *Seeking Victory on the Western Front, The British Army and Chemical Warfare in World War 1* (Lincoln: University of Nebraska Press, 2000)

Phillips, Christopher, *Civilian Specialists at War: Transport Experts and the First World War* (London: University of London Press, 2020)

Rawlins, Major S.W.H., *History of the Development of the British Artillery in France 1914-1918, from records in the Office of the Major General Royal Artillery at General Headquarters* (privately published, 1918)

Robbins, Simon, *British Generalship on the Western Front, 1914-18: Defeat into Victory* (Taylor and Francis e-library, 2005)

Sheffield, Gary and Dan Todman (eds), *Command and Control on the Western Front, The British Army's Experience 1914-18* (Staplehurst: Spellmount, 2004)

Simkins, Peter, *Kitchener's Army: The Raising of the New Armies, 1914-1916* (Barnsley: Pen & Sword, 2007 [1998])

Simmonds A., *Britain and World War One* (Abingdon: Routledge, 2013 [2011])

Terraine, John, *Mons, the Retreat to Victory* (London: Batsford, 1960)

Travers, Tim, *How the War Was Won, Factors that led to Victory in World War One* (Barnsley: Pen & Sword, 2005 [1992])

Travers, Tim, *The Killing Ground, The British Army, the Western Front & Emergence of Modern War, 1900-1918* (Barnsley: Pen & Sword, 2009 [1987])

Whittingham, Daniel, *Charles E Callwell and the British Way in Warfare* (Cambridge: Cambridge University Press, 2020)

Winter, Denis, *Haig's Command, A Reassessment* (Barnsley: Pen & Sword, 2005 [1991])

Articles, Chapters, and Theses

Bailey, Brigadier Jonathan, 'Deep Battle 1914-1941: The Birth of the Modern Style of Warfare' *Field Artillery Journal*, July-August 1998, pp.23–35

Barr, Niall, 'Command in the Transition from Mobile to Static Warfare, August 1914 to March 1915', in Sheffield and Todman (eds), *Command and Control*, pp.13–38

Batten, Simon, '"A School for the Leaders": What did the British Army learn from the 1912 Army Manoeuvres?', *Journal of the Society for Army Historical Research*, vol.93, no.373 (Spring 2015), pp.25–47

Beach, Jim, '"Issued by the General Staff": Doctrine Writing at British GHQ, 1917–1918', *War in History*, 19 (4), 2012, pp.464–491

Boff, Jonathan, 'Combined Arms during the Hundred Days Campaign, August–November 1918', *War in History*, 17 (4) 2010, pp.459–478

Bourne, John, 'Haig and the Historians', in Bond and Cave (eds), *Haig, a Re-Appraisal, eighty years on*, pp.1–11

Connelly, Mark, 'Lieutenant General Sir James Grierson', in Jones (ed.), *Stemming the Tide*, pp.133–150

DeGroot, Gerard, 'Ambition, Duty and Doctrine: Douglas Haig's rise to High Command', in Bond and Cave (eds), *Haig, a Re-Appraisal*, pp.37–50

Dighton, Adam, 'Jomini versus Clausewitz: Hamley's Operations of War and Military Thought in the British Army, 1866–1933', *War in History*, 27 (2), 2020, pp.179–201

Duncan, Andrew George, *The Military Education of Junior Officers in the Edwardian Era*, PhD thesis, University of Birmingham, 2016

Evans, Nick, *From drill to doctrine: forging the British Army's tactics 1897-1909*, PhD thesis, Kings College London, 2008

Fair, Charles, 'From OTC to OCB: The Professionalisation of the Selection and Training of Junior Temporary Officers During the Great War', in Jones (ed.), *The Darkest Hour*, pp.78–109

Fox-Godden, Aimée, 'Beyond the Western Front: The Practice of Inter-Theatre Learning in the British Army during the First World War', *War in History*, 2016, 23 (2), pp.190–209

Gardner, Nikolas, 'Command and Control in the "Great Retreat" of 1914: The Disintegration of the British Cavalry Division', *The Journal of Military History*, vol.63, no. 1 (January 1999), pp.29–54

Harris, J.P., 'The British Army and its Approach to Continental Warfare, 1905-1914', in Dennis and Gray (eds), *1911, Preliminary Moves, 2011 Army Historical Conference* (Australia: Big Sky Publishing, 2011), pp.283–300

Harris, Paul, 'The men who planned the war: A study of the Staff of the British Army on the Western Front 1914-1918', PhD Thesis, King's College London, 2013

Harris, Paul, and Sanders Marble, 'The "Step-by-Step" Approach: British Military Thought and Operational Method on the Western Front, 1915–1917', *War in History*, 15 (1) 2008, pp.17–42

Hazlehurst, Cameron, 'Asquith as Prime Minister, 1908-1916', *The English Historical Review*, vol.85, no.336 (July 1970), pp.502–531

Hodgkinson, Peter, 'The Infantry Battalion Commanding Officers of the BEF', in Jones (ed.), *Stemming the Tide*, pp.293-331

Howard, Michael, 'Haig Bashing', *London Review of Books*, vol.13, no.8, 25 April 1991, <https://www.lrb.co.uk/the-paper/v13/n08/michael-howard/haig-bashing>, accessed 21 April 2022

Hutchison, David, 'The Effectiveness of German Field Artillery at Mons and during the Retreat in August 1914', *Journal for the Society of Army Historical Research*, vol.95, no.384 (Winter 2017) pp.331–337

Hughes, Jackson, 'The Monstrous Anger of the Guns, the Development of British Artillery Tactics, 1914 – 1918', PhD thesis, Adelaide University,1992

Innes-Robbins, Simon, 'From Vimy Ridge to Hill 70; General Sir Henry Horne and the Development of British Operational Art During 1917', Jones (ed.), *The Darkest Hour*, pp.279–305

Jackman, Steven, 'Shoulder to Shoulder: Close Control and "Old Prussian Drill" in German Offensive Infantry Tactics 1871-1914', *The Journal of Military History*, vol.68, no.1 (January 2004), pp.73–104

Jones, Spencer, 'Scouting for Soldiers: Reconnaissance and the British Cavalry, 1899–1914', *War in History*, vol.18, no.4 (November 2011), pp.495–513

Jones, Spencer, 'The Influence of the Boer War (1899–1902) on the Tactical Development of the Regular British Army, 1902–1914', PhD thesis, University of Wolverhampton, 2009

Jones, Spencer, and Steven Corvi, '"A Commander of Rare and unusual Coolness": General Sir Horace Lockwood Smith-Dorrien', in Jones (ed.), *Stemming the Tide*, pp.151–170

Lloyd, Nick, '"With Faith and without Fear": Sir Douglas Haig's Command of First Army during 1915', *The Journal of Military History*, vol.71, no.4 (October 2007), pp.1051–1076

LoCicero, Michael, 'A Coda to the Second Battle of Ypres: International Trench 6–10 July 1915', in Jones, (ed.), *Courage without Glory*, pp.312–360

Marble, Sanders, 'Command of Artillery: the case of Herbert Uniacke', in Sheffield and Todman (eds), *Command and Control*, pp.195–212

Marble, William Sanders, 'The infantry cannot do with a gun less: the place of the artillery in the BEF, 1914-1918', PhD thesis, King's College, London, 1998

Maurice, Major General Sir Frederick, 'Haig's principles', *British Legion Memorial Number*, March 1928, pp.244–245

Melvin, Major General (Retd) Mungo, 'Field Service Regulations 1909, Douglas Haig and the "Man on the Spot"', *Records, the Douglas Haig Fellowship's Journal*, no.27, December 2024, pp.1–31

Mitchell, Stuart, 'An Inter-Disciplinary Study of Learning in the 32nd Division on the Western Front, 1916-1918', PhD thesis, University of Birmingham, 2013

McDermott, J., 'The revolution in British military thinking from the Boer War to the Moroccan crisis', in Paul Kennedy (ed.), *The War Plans of the Great Powers 1880-1914* (Abingdon: Routledge, 2014 [1978])

Olsen, Richard, 'Major General Sir Thompson Capper', in Jones (ed.), *Stemming the Tide*, pp.189–208

Philpott, William, 'Beyond the "Learning Curve": The British Army's Military Transformation in the First World War', *RUSI Analysis*, 10 November 2009, <https://www.rusi.org/explore-our-research/publications/commentary/beyond-learning-curve-british-armys-military-transformation-first-world-war>, accessed 4 June 2020

Philpott, William, and Jonathan Boff, 'Introduction: Transforming War, 1914–1918', *British Journal for Military History*, Vol.5, Issue 2, October 2019, pp.1–18

Pope-Hennessy, L.H.R. (published anonymously), 'The British Army and Modern Conceptions of War', *Edinburgh Review*, vol.213, no.436 (April 1911), pp.321–346

Pugsley, Christopher, 'We have been here before: the Evolution of the Doctrine of Decentralised Command in the British Army 1905-1989', *Sandhurst Occasional Paper*, no.9, 2011

Puncher, Sebastian, 'The Victorian Army and the Cadet Colleges, Woolwich and Sandhurst, c.1840-1902', PhD thesis, University of Kent, 2019

Robbins, Simon, 'Henry Horne as Divisional Commander during 1915', in Jones, (ed.) *Courage without Glory*, pp.103–124

Roberts, Lord, of Kandahar, 'Memoir', in Henderson, Malcolm, (ed.) *The Science of War: A Collection of Essays and Lectures 1891-1903*, pp.xiii–xxxviii

Sheffield, Gary, 'The makings of a Corps Commander: Lieutenant General Sir Douglas Haig', in Jones (ed.), *Stemming the Tide*, pp.111–132

Sheffield, Gary, and Helen McCartney, 'Hubert Gough', in Beckett and Corvi, (eds), *Haig's Generals*, pp.75–96

Simkins, Peter, 'Herbert Plumer, Second Army 1915-1917, 1918', in Beckett and Corvi (eds), *Haig's Generals*, pp.141–163

Simpson, Andrew, 'The Operational Role of British Corps Command on the Western Front, 1914-18', PhD thesis, University College, London, 2001

Simpson, Andy, 'British Corps Command on the Western Front, 1914-1918', in Sheffield and Todman (eds), *Command and Control*, pp.97–118

Sloan, G., 'Haldane's Mackindergarten: a radical experiment in British military education', *War in History*, 19 (3) 2012, pp.322–352

Sneddon, John Mason, 'The Company Commander', Jones (ed.), *Stemming the Tide*, pp.314–331

Spencer, John, 'The Big Brain in the Army: Sir William Robertson as Quartermaster General', in Jones (ed.), *Stemming the Tide*, pp.89–107

Spiers, Edward, 'The British Cavalry, 1902 – 1914', *Journal of the Society for Army Historical Research*, vol.57, no.230 (Summer, 1979) pp.71–79

Spiers, Edward M., 'University Officers' Training Corps and the First World War', *Council of Military Education Committees of the United Kingdom*, Occasional Paper No 4, 2014

Strachan, Hew, 'Operational Art and Britain, 1909–2009', in Olsen and van Creveld (eds), *The Evolution of Operational Art: From Napoleon to the Present*, pp.96–136

Strachan, Hew, 'The British Army, its General Staff and the Continental Commitment', in French and Holden Reid (eds), *The British General Staff, Reform and Innovation, 1890-1939*, pp.75–94

Sweetman, John, 'Towards a Ministry of Defence: First Faltering Steps, 1890-1923', in French and Holden Reid (eds), *The British General Staff, Reform and Innovation, 1890-1939*, pp.26–40

Tattersfield, David, 'British Corps Commanders in the Great War,' *Western Front Association*, <https://www.westernfrontassociation.com/world-war-i-articles/british-corps-commanders-in-the-great-war/>, accessed 17 March 2022

Thrower, Keith R., 'Army Radio Communication in the Great War', (Oxford University occasional paper, March 2013), <https://blogs.mhs.ox.ac.uk/innovatingincombat/files/2013/03/Army-radio-communication-in-the-Great-War_V2.pdf>, accessed 13 July 2024

Todman, Dan, 'The Grand Lamasery revisited; General Headquarters on the Western Front, 1914-1918', in Sheffield and Todman (eds) *Command and Control*, pp.39–70

Travers, Tim, 'Learning and Decision-Making on the Western Front, 1915-1916: The British Example', *Canadian Journal of History*, vol.18, Issue 1 (Spring, 2016) pp.87–97
Travers, Tim, 'The Hidden Army: Structural Problems in the British Officer Corps, 1900-1918', *Journal of Contemporary History*, vol.17, no.3 (July 1982) pp.522–534
Travers, Tim, 'The Offensive and the Problem of Innovation in British Military Thought 1870-1915', *Journal of Contemporary History*, vol.13 (1978) pp.531-553
Trythall, Major General A J, 'J.F.C. Fuller: Staff Officer Extraordinary', in French and Holden Reid, (eds), *British General Staff*, pp.143–158
Venter, Louis, Dr Marietjie Oelofse and Dr Johan Van Zÿl, 'The Composition of the Imperial British Forces in the Anglo-Boer War, 1899–1902: A Military and Socio-Historical Overview', *Scientia Militaria, 2024*, vol.52, No. 2, pp.53–69
Vines, Anthony John, 'The Heroic Manager: An Assessment of Sir Douglas Haig's role as Military Manager on the Western Front', PhD thesis, Kings College London, 2015
Watts, Patrick, 'Douglas Haig and the Planning of the Battle of Neuve Chapelle', in Jones (ed.), *Courage without Glory*, pp.183–203

Index